Praise for

What There Is to Say We Have Said

———

"An invitation to draw up a chair and enjoy two good friends as interested in their rose gardens as their writing."

— *Richmond Times-Dispatch*

"These loving and revealing letters guide us back to the fiction of both authors."

—*Wall Street Journal*

"A valuable portrait of a unique and lasting friendship, and a celebration of a certain kind of joy that is rapidly disappearing — the joy of writing and sending, receiving and reading personal letters." — *Tulsa World*

"[A] deeply rewarding collection." — *Entertainment Weekly*

"This collection of letters takes us into the world of Eudora and William. We get to see how their friendship deepened over time and became something special." — *San Francisco Book Review*

"To read *What There Is to Say We Have Said* is to feel the noise and speed of the present era fall away, to sense the natural world reasserting itself. Time slows, and you arrive in a more pastoral moment."

— The Progressive Reader

"For 50 years, Welty and Maxwell communicated in full detail, with deep and genuine affection, serving up revelations about themselves that give these literary figures a greatly wonderful human dimension . . . This is one of the richest and most riveting collections of famous-people letters to emerge in some time." — *Booklist*

"Inspiring . . . A vivid snapshot of 20th-century intellectual life and an informative glimpse of the author-editor relationship, as well a tender portrait of devoted friendship." — *Kirkus Reviews*

"A literary revelation. Suzanne Marrs's editing of this rich collection is superlative." — Roger Mudd, journalist and broadcaster

"What a glorious collection! These letters make a map into the very heart of friendship and creativity. They are bursting with intelligence, tenderness, and insight. Every page is a privilege to read."

— Ann Patchett

Praise for

Eudora Welty

"An admirable, engrossing and gently gripping biography fully worthy of its remarkable subject." — *Los Angeles Times Book Review*

"Eudora Welty was probably the best loved writer in America. To read this biography is to understand why." — *Cleveland Plain Dealer*

"It's a relief to see this daring and imaginative writer finally set free from traditional perceptions of her as an 'ugly duckling' who just happened to write great stories. We get the 3-D view." — *San Diego Union-Tribune*

"Captures the humorous and unconventional spirit of one of the South's greatest writers." — *Dallas Morning News*

"Marrs has written that biography of *Eudora Welty* — a book that debunks the myths and quotes enough of the writing to make you hunger for the novels and stories. Marrs takes pains to refute the image of Eudora as a perfect 'Southern Lady' . . . the rest of us get to love her as a writer, and with this biography — the whole of her extraordinary world."

— Dorothy Allison, *Publishers Weekly*, starred review

What There Is to Say
We Have Said

BOOKS BY SUZANNE MARRS

Eudora Welty: A Biography

One Writer's Imagination: The Fiction of Eudora Welty

The Welty Collection: A Guide to the
Eudora Welty Manuscripts and Documents at
the Mississippi Department of Archives and History

What There Is to Say We Have Said

THE CORRESPONDENCE OF

Eudora Welty and William Maxwell

EDITED BY

Suzanne Marrs

MARINER BOOKS
HOUGHTON MIFFLIN HARCOURT
BOSTON NEW YORK

First Mariner Books edition 2012

www.hmhbooks.com

Library of Congress Cataloging-in-Publication Data
Welty, Eudora, 1909–2001.
What there is to say we have said : the correspondence of
Eudora Welty and William Maxwell / edited by Suzanne Marrs.
p. cm.
Includes bibliographical references.
ISBN 978-0-547-37649-3
ISBN 978-0-547-75032-3 (pbk.)
1. Welty, Eudora, 1909–2001—Correspondence.
2. Maxwell, William, 1908–2000—Correspondence.
3. Authors, American—20th century—Correspondence.
I. Marrs, Suzanne. II. Title.
PS3545.E6Z48 2011
813'.52—dc22
[B]
2010042105

Book design by Greta D. Sibley

Printed in the United States of America
DOC 1 2 3 4 5 6 7 8 9 10

Permissions credits appear on page 478.

To Timothy Seldes

CONTENTS

What There Is to Say
We Have Said

Introduction

LETTERS, reading them and writing them, claimed the rapt attention of Eudora Welty and William Maxwell throughout their adult lives, and books of letters by fellow authors—Lord Byron, Anton Chekhov, Roger Fry, William Faulkner, Robert Louis Stevenson, and H. L. Mencken, for instance—they found particularly engaging. In 1983, Maxwell collected and edited a book of his friend Sylvia Townsend Warner's letters, and eight years later Welty included many letters when she coedited *The Norton Book of Friendship*. In the introduction to that book, she noted:

> *All* letters, old and new, are the still-existing parts of a life. To read them now is to be present when some discovery of truth—or perhaps untruth, some flash of light—is just occurring. It is clamorous with the moment's happiness or pain. To come upon a personal truth of a human being however little known, and now gone forever, is in some way to admit him to our friendship. What we've been told need not be momentous, but it can be as good as receiving the darting glance from some very bright eye, still mischievous and mischief-making, arriving from fifty or a hundred years ago.[1]

For both Welty and Maxwell, letters provided a way of expanding the range of their friendships. Letters provided a more comprehensive sense of the person who, whether or not that person was someone they had actually known, stood behind the stories, poems, and essays they valued or found interesting. Although Welty and Maxwell awarded letters a modest place in the hierarchy of literary genres, it was a place of importance to them. So it is not surprising that in 1976, when a second volume of Virginia Woolf's letters came into print, both Welty and Maxwell, two longtime admirers of Woolf and two of America's most distinguished fiction writers, separately reviewed the book.

These reviews (by two old friends whose literary opinions rarely diverged) struck dissonant tones but had a common focus. Welty opened her review by quoting from Woolf's novel *Jacob's Room:* "Life would split asunder without letters." That statement, Welty went on to suggest, described the role correspondence played not only for Woolf's characters but also for the writer herself. "A need for intimacy," Welty asserted, "lies at the very core of Virginia Woolf's life. Besides the physical, there are other orders of intimacy, other ways to keep life from splitting asunder. Lightly as it may touch on the moment, almost any letter she writes is to some degree an expression of this passion, of which the eventual work of art was *The Waves.*"[2] To Welty, even letters filled with lacerating wit were a way of reaching for connection.

Maxwell did not fully agree with this assessment. Instead of discussing a desire for intimacy in Woolf's letters, he described a lack of self-assurance: "Even though Virginia Woolf was, I think, a writer of the first rank, she could not rest secure in the knowledge of her talent; the prevailing tone of the letters written in her maturity is disparagement." Particularly distasteful to Maxwell was Woolf's habit of ridiculing others, and he felt that "strangers get off lightly compared to what happens when she is writing about friends." Though he sought to avoid moral judgments based on material not intended for publication and though he recognized that no friendship is without its prickly moments, Maxwell felt that Woolf could take "pleasure in being cruel." Still, there were letters of a different sort, and Maxwell particularly lauded one that Welty also admired. In that 1922 letter, Woolf

acknowledged her own vulnerability to doubt and sent encouragement to a young, then unpublished Gerald Brenan.[3]

The Virginia Woolfs who emerged from the Welty and Maxwell reviews were strikingly different people, but undergirding both reviews was a belief that letters should be a way of embracing, supporting, and uniting with friends and that letters communicate most profoundly when they do not mask vulnerabilities. This shared belief is everywhere evident in the letters Eudora Welty and William Maxwell themselves wrote. "Orders of intimacy" other than the physical are often tragically missing from the lives of characters in their stories and novels. There the powerful need for friendship is typically defined by its lack. Not so in their correspondence.

Welty shared intimate and voluminous exchanges of letters with many friends, including her agent Diarmuid Russell; fiction editor Mary Louise Aswell; childhood friend Frank Lyell; and the two men she loved over the course of her life, John Robinson and Ross Macdonald. Welty and these friends saved the letters they exchanged, and as her friends faced death, they stipulated that the letters Welty had written be returned to her. Although Welty at one point considered destroying these two-sided correspondences she came to possess, she ultimately willed them to the Mississippi Department of Archives and History.

Maxwell's correspondence with friends was as extensive and generous as Welty's. He corresponded with fellow writers such as Frank O'Connor, Sylvia Townsend Warner, John Updike, John Cheever, and Larry Woiwode. He allowed his correspondence with Warner and O'Connor to be published. In the late 1990s, he gave his alma mater, the University of Illinois, a huge collection of his papers, including many letters from Eudora Welty. His estate has made his remaining letters from Welty available for this book, and Maxwell's letters to her are preserved as digital scans at the Eudora Welty House, a museum in Jackson, Mississippi.[4]

For more than fifty years, Welty and Maxwell wrote to each other, sharing their worries about work and family, their likes and dislikes, their griefs and joys, their moments of despair and hilarity. Reading their letters admits us into the friendship of these two intellectual, imaginative, and erudite individuals. We learn that they were great in-takers—at times fascinated, at

times appalled by the world about them, but always describing it vividly with deft turns of phrase. Their letters often sparkle with humor, but their humor can also take on an ironic dimension. A generosity of spirit pervades the correspondence but is never saccharine. Although literary friendships are famous for going bad, Welty and Maxwell weathered inevitable moments of discontent. Issues of jealousy, resentment, cruelty, or condescension never threatened their relationship, which began in 1942, deepened over time, and found eloquent expression in their letters. In those letters, neither engaged in posturing or affectation. Instead, they both achieved the "triumphant vulnerability" that can result from daring to trust, empathize, and communicate.[5]

Near the end of her introduction to *The Norton Book of Friendship*, Welty asked, "Did friendship between human beings come about in the first place along with—or through—the inspiration of language?" And then she attempted to answer her own question:

> It can be safe to say that when we learned to speak to, and listen to, rather than to strike or be struck by, our fellow human beings, we found something worth keeping alive, worth the possessing, for the rest of time. Might it possibly have been the other way round—that the promptings of friendship guided us into learning to express ourselves, teaching ourselves, between us, a language to keep it by? Friendship might have been the first, as well as the best, teacher of communication.[6]

Friendship and life as a writer, Welty implicitly suggested, can be closely related, and the writer need not make (as distinguished psychologist Howard Gardner believes creative individuals typically do) a Faustian bargain, opting for an ascetic existence, isolating herself, or exploiting others in the quest for artistic fulfillment. Instead, Welty asserted, friendship and the word can "rise from the same prompting."[7]

For Eudora Welty and William Maxwell, the pleasures of friendship and the love of language certainly rose "from the same prompting." They met in 1942 in New York when both attended a party given by *Harper's Bazaar* fiction editor Mary Louise Aswell. For Mr. Maxwell, Miss Welty immediately proved as compelling a storyteller in person as she was in the fiction he wanted to acquire for *The New Yorker*, where for three days a week he

worked as an editor. Immediately after their meeting, he wrote to ask her for submissions, but Welty, who had just published a novella and completed a collection of stories, had no unpromised pieces to offer as 1942 drew to a close. She instead suggested that Maxwell contact her agent, Diarmuid Russell, about future work. Russell, however, had reason to be skeptical of *The New Yorker*. From 1940 to 1941, the magazine had rejected three Welty stories and an essay, and Russell chose not to send its editorial staff the two Welty stories he circulated in 1943 and 1944. Neither did he send them her novel *Delta Wedding*, which the *Atlantic Monthly* published in four installments in 1946.

In September of that year, Welty told her agent that Maxwell had again written to ask for a story, and on October 31 Russell offered "The Whole World Knows" to *The New Yorker*. Maxwell lobbied long and hard to have the story accepted but was defeated by the magazine's founder and editor, Harold Ross, who found the story too "arty."[8] Maxwell did not object in 1947 when first Welty's "Hello and Good-Bye" ("one of her lighter efforts") and then "Music from Spain" (one of her longer efforts) failed to gain acceptance at the magazine.[9] But he had nevertheless won Welty's regard. Because they lived half a continent apart and were able to meet only once or twice a year, when Eudora made pilgrimages to New York, the bonds of friendship between them would be nourished, as they would subsequently be maintained and strengthened, by correspondence. Although there was no sustained correspondence between Welty and Maxwell from January 1943 to August 1949, the two clearly grew closer during these years and occasionally wrote to each other. By summer's end in 1949, Maxwell was comfortably addressing Welty as "Eudora," telling her of his household chores, signing himself "Bill," and sending his love along with that of his wife, Emmy.

Eventually, the trust built by their ongoing friendship enriched their relationship as editor and author. In 1951, Bill and his colleague Gus Lobrano finally convinced *The New Yorker* to accept a Welty story. "The Bride of the Innisfallen" was the first of seven pieces Eudora published there, and Bill was her editor for all of them. From the start, Eudora had confidence in Bill's judgment and he in hers, always editing her work with a light hand. He paid careful attention to details of punctuation or verb tense but left

final decisions about such matters to Eudora. If any substantive revisions seemed advisable, he suggested rather than attempting to impose a change. For instance, in editing "The Ponder Heart" for the December 5, 1953, issue of *The New Yorker*, he offered this suggestion about a somewhat confusing time sequence: "This is the only serious query that I have to make to you. It would [...] be an enormous help to the reader if you could suggest somehow [...] that the whole business about Miss Teacake took place before Uncle Daniel was consigned to the asylum. I have suggested an insert which you may find clumsy, but which might give you a clue to how to do it."[10] Similarly, in editing the periodical version of "The Optimist's Daughter," which occupied almost an entire *New Yorker* issue in March 1969, Bill wrote:

> You have until the week before the story appears to decide on the title, and whatever you decide is all right with us. Meanwhile, I will continue to tell you what I think, but not, you understand, trying to persuade you. I am still partial to "The Optimist's Daughter", because, by its ironic tone, it suggests a certain distance between the writer and the woman in the story, and because it also, again by its irony, suggests, matches somehow, the full horror of the subject matter. The Flickering Light of Vision is, by comparison, abstract, and to me less inviting. Also, I like titles that don't state the idea of the thing but are more oblique.[11]

Eudora clearly valued Bill's advice, and in these instances as in many others, she followed his suggestions, although at times she was, to use Bill's words, "firm about the unhelpful suggestions."[12] Bill found that his role as Eudora's *New Yorker* editor brought him great joy, and he happily answered requests for advice even when *New Yorker* publication was not involved. For example, in 1961, when he read a partial draft of *Losing Battles*, a long novel not completed until 1970, he could not contain his enthusiasm:

> Well I find it very hard not knowing how they got the car down in time for the funeral. Or what part Miss Footsie Kilgore played in the operation. Don't worry about the form. It has it. And don't whatever you do cut any of the physical descriptions of the place, the night, the moon, etc. The whole going to bed passage is so beautiful that it is like reading an opera. The mind supplies the music. Harold Brodkey has a theory

that most novels run out of gas, that is to say the original inspiration, after the first seventy or a hundred pages. And then the novelist gets his second wind, with a different inspiration. This doesn't run out of gas, but it takes on a certain musical solidity when they are at the table and begin to talk about Miss Florence Hand. Partly from the fact that they talk so long about her, and up until that point have refused to stick to any one subject for longer than three sentences. Anyway, it builds, all the way to the end of part III. There are a hundred remarks that delighted me they were so much like the people I remember. And made me laugh out loud. The only book I ever read that it reminds me of is Delta Wedding, it is so completely just like you and nobody else. It also has the richness of being the only thing you have been working on all these years. One feels that, more and more. Now what else can I tell you?[13]

Bill's delight in the novel was like his response to a visit from Eudora — friend and editor were one. Eudora herself adopted a sort of editorial stance in their friendship as she encouraged Bill's work on *The Château* (1961), work that like hers on *Losing Battles* took place in fits and starts over many years. And at times Bill turned to Eudora for editorial advice. Before he settled on *So Long, See You Tomorrow* as the title for his last novel (1980), he wrote to her, "I wanted originally to call it 'The Palace at 4 AM' but unfortunately Howard Moss had used that title for a play. Does this title seem all right?"[14]

Clearly, Eudora and Bill produced both titles and books that were more than all right. Eudora's five collections of stories, three novellas, and two novels were matched by Bill's six novels and five story collections. Both wrote books for children. Both published collections of their essays. Both wrote books dealing with family history. And both proved impatient with the conventions of genre. The stories in Eudora's *The Golden Apples* (1949), for instance, are tightly interwoven, with protagonists in one story becoming minor characters in others, but she chose "not to bother with plot-threads and all that, but just to take up these people whenever and wherever in their lives that might interest me."[15] She preferred the irresolution of experience to the tying of bows. Bill was similarly experimental in *So Long, See You Tomorrow*, shifting between memoir and fiction and for a time pre-

senting the story from the viewpoint of a dog. Even using the dog proved a wise choice.

Bill's and Eudora's willingness to take literary risks led not only to a sense of artistic fulfillment but also to a tandem set of awards. Over the course of his career, Bill received a National Book Award and the William Dean Howells Medal for fiction (both for *So Long, See You Tomorrow*), the PEN/ Malamud Award, the Gold Medal for Fiction from the American Academy of Arts and Letters, and the Ivan Sandrof Award for Lifetime Achievement in Publishing from the National Book Critics Circle. For her part, Eudora received the Howells Medal for fiction (for *The Ponder Heart*), the Pulitzer Prize for Fiction (for *The Optimist's Daughter*), the Gold Medal for Fiction from the American Academy, the National Book Foundation's Medal for Distinguished Contribution to American Letters, the Presidential Medal of Freedom, the National Medal of the Arts, and the French Legion of Honor. Ultimately, the Library of America included two volumes of her work and two volumes of Bill's in its series of books designed to keep "America's best and most significant writing" always in print.[16]

Of course, Eudora and Bill's relationship was sustained by more than their professional association and accomplishments. Their common love of writing sprang from an uncommon passion for reading. In their letters, Bill and Eudora discussed works by authors ranging from Jane Austen to Virginia Woolf, from William Faulkner to Frank O'Connor, from Willa Cather to Langston Hughes, from Agatha Christie to M. R. James, from Lady Charlotte Guest to Lady Ottoline Morrell, from Frédéric Mistral to Larry Woiwode. And they discussed encounters with fellow writers. In January 1959, for instance, Bill and Emmy attended a dinner for Isak Dinesen. After dinner, Dinesen read from her story "The Deluge at Norderney" for a film series on outstanding contemporary writers. Of his dinner conversation with Dinesen, Bill wrote:

> She didn't do more than consider and reply to my remarks, until the dessert, and then something, I forget what, the fact that I had just fin-ished making a doll house, perhaps, for my daughter, made her melt, and she talked to me—but still not personally, not as if she liked me or ever wanted to see me again. But in such a way as to make me love her forever. Her voice is so beautiful, the accent isn't either British or Amer-

ican. It has notes that are like cello music. It's like listening to Hayden. And those burning black eyes. It is several years too late to be her friend, but it is not too late to remember what she is like, as long as I live.

Of the filming and refilming of her reading, he noted:

> For nearly four hours we listened to that story, and looked at that extraordinary face, without for one second tiring of either one. And you could look because she never looked back. She looked at the camera as if it loved to hear stories more than anything in this world, and I certainly hope it did. She was able to repeat and recapture phrasing, cadences, pitch of voice, even fleeting expressions, time after time, as if she were an actress. She did not even look tired, until it was all, at last, over, and then suddenly when I turned around, she was sitting, in that black fur coat, but rather longhaired, not caracul or Persian lamb or anything ordinary, with a black chiffon scarf over her head, leaving a white wedge of face, with two burning black eyes in it, and the whole body in the posture of exhaustion.[17]

Eudora demonstrated a similar reverence for the creative individual when she described hearing octogenarian Padraic Colum read at the 1964 Suffield (Connecticut) Writer-Reader Conference, where she was also on the program:

> If I had had to walk all the way from Jackson and work free all the week through, I would have gladly because of Padraic Colum. Imagine having him in the same place as you and telling stories, reciting poems of anyone anywhere any time in the whole history, and just remarking [...] To think of his still being with us and the liveliest one for miles around— the last link with all that. Last night came his lecture in the barn, which is the Suffield Academy Theatre, and of course it was so much more than a lecture—about growing up in his grandmother's house, with the peat fire which you look <u>down</u> on, and so is so much better than other fires, and the greyhounds sleeping "in a loop" on the hearth, and the story-teller coming, taking a seat (in his grandmother's house there was always a pile of clean grass and leaves kept ready near the hearth for any wanderer) and beginning "Now by the power that has seized me, I will tell you:" (better than that, can't remember right now).[18]

The enthusiasm with which Bill and Eudora listened to and read the works of fellow writers was but one of many enthusiasms they shared. A love of gardening at times seemed to rival their love of literature. Their letters include references to almost sixty different roses that one or the other grew, to nurseries where plants could be obtained, to books on the art of cultivating roses or on the history of gardening. But neither Bill nor Eudora was content merely to tend a garden and to read and write stories. They both supported liberal Democratic candidates for public office, with two-time presidential candidate Adlai Stevenson at the top of the list. Both loved the theater and reported on plays they had seen. And both loved the rewards of travel. As Eudora told Diarmuid Russell, "I would agree to try almost anything for a trip."[19] Bill might not have made so expansive a declaration, but encounters with different cultures, the sight of architectural wonders, and the opportunity to see great works of art delighted them both. Eudora recounted her pleasure in seeing the Barnes collection in Philadelphia:

> Today I got taken to see the Barnes—you know how hard it is to see, and now, as I felt nearly every step I took to stand before another picture, I wish for you to see it. Have you ever? I can't even send you a card with a reproduction of a single one, because no reproductions have ever been made. The Cezannes—50? 60? of absolutely radiant staggering beauty And drawings!—the Monets—Picassos (Blues & Pink—Saltambiques (sp?))—a dozen wild Rousseaus—a Van Gogh Postman with a green beard and a sty, not my favorite painter, but just to show you. I felt drenched by the whole color of blue—and Matisse! Dozens, dozens of prime Odalesques & girls & goldfishes, lights & airs & chaises & [readers] & <u>you</u> know—It was a great feeling of being in the Presence.[20]

Bill told Eudora of a glorious visit to London and especially to the Tate Gallery: "We have had such a happy time in London [...] The weather like Rupert Brooke's poem. And all the squares full of flowering trees and daffodils. There were five huge rooms full of Turners at the Tate, a big Constable show, and the original drawings for <u>The Tailor of Gloucester</u>—which drove me half out of my mind with pleasure—" Eudora offered this description of Wales: "After changing trains madly all day I came into Harlech about 6:30 of an afternoon and it was like coming into the center of a big jewel—

all of it glows, mountains, sea, dunes, castle, clouds, hedges and stones."[21] And both Bill and Eudora shared stories of their travels to Ireland, England, France, and Italy.

In 1983, after more than forty years of friendship, Bill read a draft of Eudora's autobiographical work, *One Writer's Beginnings*, and realized that the groundwork of their friendship had been laid long before they met. "There were enough similarities in our two childhoods," he wrote, "to make me feel [...] that we grew up on a tandem bicycle."[22] Born in 1908 and 1909, respectively, Bill and Eudora spent their youths in small towns that were much alike, despite the fact that Lincoln, Illinois, was in the North and Jackson, Mississippi, in the South. The clothes children wore, the books they read, the wind-up Victrola they played, the atmosphere of the schoolroom and the Sunday school, the movies they saw, the family car rides shared with neighbors, and the sewing women who came to the house—all had produced shared memories. So, too, had their encounters with the evils of racism and with the social conventions of white middle-class life. And there were other similarities—their fathers' common employment in the insurance business, their mothers' elaborate precautions against the spreading of illness, the very ways the two future writers managed to read long past bedtime. The death of Bill's mother when he was only ten and of Eudora's father when she was but twenty-two shaped their respective writing careers, though these losses were treated differently in their fiction. Bill's writing was clearly autobiographical, Eudora's less frequently and more indirectly so. As she told Bill about the use of a deeply troubling real-life event, "I'm glad you think the disguises are deep enough."[23]

Both Bill and Eudora spent their undergraduate years at midwestern universities—he at the University of Illinois and she at the University of Wisconsin—and both spent a year of graduate study on the East Coast, Bill at Harvard and Eudora at Columbia. Neither felt suited for a life as a teacher, and the dreams of both centered on New York City. Having already published *Bright Center of Heaven*, Bill settled in New York in 1936, working at *The New Yorker* and publishing *They Came Like Swallows* the next year. Eudora had a one-woman photographic show in New York in 1936, found a literary agent there in 1940, published her first book (*A Curtain of Green*) in 1941, and began a pattern of regular visits to the city.

The tandem nature of their lives, established before they met and continuing afterward, was a strong bond between them, but a difference in their lives created a bond that was equally strong. Although neither of the two significant romantic relationships in Eudora's life led to marriage, her recollection of her own parents' mutual devotion had established for her the enriching, if complicating, nature of family life. Surely, this is a key reason Eudora embraced the entire Maxwell family. She responded to Bill's love of his wife, Emmy, and their daughters, a love that is expressed more vividly in his letters to Eudora than in any previously published work about him. "Did you ever hear Emmy really laugh?" Bill asks in one of his letters, and then adds, "It's like the fountains of Rome." When Emmy had to be away from home, Bill suffered. Of one such time, he wrote to Eudora, "The silence in the house is deafening, but Em left me one of her best soups, and some short ribs of beef to heat up in the oven when the potatoes are nearly baked, and I will get through the evening somehow, but I must say it is no way to live." His love of Emmy was matched by his love of their two daughters, Kate and Brookie. Shortly after Kate's birth, he wrote to Eudora about the joys of her first days at home: "I got to carry [Kate] from her bed in the back room, to the chair and ottoman in the living room where Emmy nurses her in the day time. And carrying her back again, I would feel that little head collapse on my shoulder, and turn against the side of my neck. In my youth I was continually susceptible to ecstatic pleasure of one kind or another, and sometimes I have thought I must have overdone it, because it seldom came any more. But here it is again." Two years later, he sent Eudora this description of Brookie:

> Well actually she's as shy as a robin, when it comes to perching on anybody's lap for any length of time. She did this morning, so she could get at the lid of the sugar bowl, which has a china rose on it (Japanese onion pattern), and she lights on me in the evening while I am mixing drinks because from my left arm she can see quite well into the liquor cupboard, the ice box, and the kitchen cupboard, and eventually get her hands on a piece of ice. Do you gather that she has Emmy's big eyes and is adorable?[24]

The desperation that had descended on Bill when his mother died in 1919 and that had prompted a suicide attempt during his college years was

long since gone; he and Emmy had established their own deeply cherished family.

 This sort of family life was not Eudora's own, and the lack of it, Bill felt, was the source of a melancholy that troubled Eudora later in life. "There is also the matter of living alone," he wrote to her. "If you live with somebody you are saved (often by petty irritation)," he noted wryly, "from having to confront despair." But although she lived alone after her mother's death in 1966, Eudora was not without family. She had loved her parents and two brothers deeply and enjoyed spending time with her two nieces. When the girls were young, she took them on trips, like the one in 1956 when they met "Mr. Maxwell" in New York. After this vacation, Eudora assured Bill, "For your future reference—except that you don't need me to say it—two girls are more fun than one on a far excursion—they do so much for each other to have a good time." Later, after having lost both her parents and her brothers, Eudora rejoiced when her nieces themselves became parents. Of Elizabeth Welty Thompson's first child, she told Bill, "Do you know what happened? Gruss an Aachen opened its first flower on the morning that my niece Elizabeth had her first baby—I took her the flower, and she told me she pressed it and put it in a book. I thought you'd like to know it was a real and wonderful as well as lovely Gruss." The rose lover Bill, who had received a Gruss an Aachen rooted by Eudora's mother just before the birth of his daughter Kate and who had himself recently sent Eudora a new Gruss, knew how lovely both baby and rose must be. Ultimately, Bill felt that Eudora was part of his own family. In 1986, when she sent him a copy of a limited edition book inaugurating the Eudora Welty Chair of Southern Studies at Millsaps College, Bill responded, "Such a beautifully made little book. And that fact that you wanted us to have it reinforced an idea that occurred to me recently, which is that we have become your family. I hope this is correct."[25]

In *The Outermost Dream*, a collection of his essays and reviews, Bill began by saying, "I can never get enough of knowing about other people's lives." And letters are perhaps our best source of information about other people's lives—they are of the moment. But letters also exist, as James G. Watson has asserted, "midway between art and life."[26] Despite the spontaneity with

which Eudora and Bill composed their letters, and despite the vulnerabilities they revealed, these two friends were inevitably selecting which of the myriad details of their lives to report—which topics to avoid and which to focus on. Eudora's interest in politics, for instance, was intense, but her letters to Bill seldom broach political issues. For Bill's part, nowhere in his letters to Eudora does he reveal the occasional tension his daughter Kate recalls in her relationship with her father.[27]

Of course, all writers of letters construct as well as unveil images of themselves, but few letter writers can create the sort of prose Eudora and Bill did. Their letters are filled with vibrant, beautifully crafted descriptions, some of which I have already cited, and with distinctive expressions that beg to be quoted: Eudora anticipates that a journey will be "a hard day's Greyhound into night," invoking both the Beatles and Eugene O'Neill; Bill calls innocence "the crowning accomplishment of maturity." Eudora reports that Jane Austen's house "looks big, but is really small. The opposite of her novels." Bill asserts that in the last line of E. M. Forster's *The Hill of Devi*, "Forster's mind had taken its stand confidently, and then been interrupted by a cry from his heart."[28] The letters containing lines like these often possess their own storylike architecture and thematic motifs. They have circular and associative structures, moving between past and present as they develop and then return to the starting point. Such letters deserve to be read as literature, for they satisfy the two demands that Bill asserted we should make of an author: "that his characters have the breath of life in them and that behind the interplay of action and ideas, perhaps at times even intruding on it, there is a presence we feel, often in the very first sentence." For Bill, "the greater the literary artist, the clearer our recognition is of the presence, the voice, the invisible signature of the mind in which the whole fancy took place originally."[29]

William Maxwell and Eudora Welty both brought the "breath of life" to their letters—letters that close with visible signatures but are pervaded by "the invisible signature of the mind." The keen intellect, the sense of humor, the lack of self-absorption, the embracing of experience in all its complexity, the capacity for love, the generosity of spirit, and the ability to face loss and death—these constitute the invisible signatures of Welty and Maxwell, signatures that are as powerfully present in their letters as in their fiction.

In an effort to reveal the artistry that characterizes the correspondence between Eudora and Bill, I have rejected the use of excerpts and have included complete letters, except for eight that exist only as fragments, eight that have a very few lines excluded at the reasonable request of the Maxwell estate, and eight in which, for the sake of their privacy, I have deleted the names of individuals mentioned. Deciding to use complete letters does, however, create one negative consequence. Not all of the almost five hundred extant letters, many of them quite long, are collected here. The Maxwell estate asked that two, which focus on individuals other than Bill, Emmy, and Eudora, not be used. In selecting which of the other letters to include, I wanted to keep in balance the number by each writer, but numbers alone could not guarantee balance. After 1981, Eudora's letters tend to be shorter in length than Bill's, and without doubt, as Eudora notes in her letters, the writer's block that affected her fiction ultimately affected her correspondence. In any case, there are a total of 197 extant letters from Bill to Eudora and 109 from Emmy to Eudora. Eudora's extant letters include 88 to Bill, 9 to Emmy, and 87 to Bill and Emmy. From these, I have chosen to include in this volume 156 letters written by Bill, 170 by Eudora, and 19 by Emmy. The focus here lies on the exchange between the two writers, although Emmy was an integral part of the Welty–Maxwell correspondence: Eudora's fondness for Emmy matched her regard for Bill and was returned. I have excluded brief thank-you notes, cover letters for enclosures, or letters I was unable to date with any confidence. I have also excluded letters that reiterate information, concerns, or patterns of language that have been fully established elsewhere in the correspondence.

The selected letters appear chronologically so that they may provide the autobiography of a friendship. I have also included a brief introduction to each chronological period and occasionally have inserted connecting commentary between letters in an effort to ensure narrative continuity. The heading for each letter identifies the author, recipient, and date. For the most part, Eudora wrote and received letters in Jackson, Mississippi; Bill in New York City or in nearby Yorktown Heights, New York, where the Maxwells had a "country" house. I have not included these default locations in the headings. However, when letters were written at or mailed to other locations, I have included that information whenever possible. I have provided

explanatory notes that identify books, persons, or events being discussed or establish the biographical or historical context of the letters. Following the example Bill Maxwell set in his edition of Sylvia Townsend Warner's letters, I apologize in advance for any notes "that may strike the reader as egregious."[30]

Throughout this volume, the letters stand as written except for silent corrections of obvious and unintentional typographical errors—spelling "treasure" as "toreasure," for instance. Even clearly unintended typos stand when Bill and Eudora have commented on them. Eccentricities of punctuation and spelling are unaltered: commas and periods frequently lie outside quotation marks, dashes abound, parentheses appear within parentheses, and names such as Dylan and Haydn may be spelled "Dillon" and "Hayden." (Bill was a confessed misspeller.) When errors seem likely to result in confusion for the reader, I have made corrections in square brackets. In addition, I have placed square brackets around ellipses, clarifying information, or dates that I supplied. The original letters are peppered with marginal notes, which I have silently incorporated according to Bill's and Eudora's indications. Neither Bill nor Eudora ever used a computer, with its ease of formatting. Two-thirds of their letters were typed, and to underline titles, as they often neglected to do, would have slowed the typing process. Such lack of formatting is retained here. I hope that these editorial practices will help readers to experience the spontaneity with which the letters were composed and the ease that Bill and Eudora felt in writing to each other.

Working with these letters—transcribing, annotating, and introducing them—has been a joy and an honor for me. Eudora was my close friend, and in her letters I had the opportunity to hear again the conversational voice that had for almost twenty years enriched my life. I did not know Bill Maxwell personally, but it is my great good fortune to have met him in these letters. Like Eudora, he possessed a genius for friendship that equaled his genius as a writer. Having their correspondence in print will allow a host of readers to participate in their friendship, to relish the language that conveys it, and to return to their magnificent fiction with heightened understanding and insight.

1

"Never Lose Letters from an Editor"

IN 1942, when Eudora Welty and William Maxwell first corresponded, they were young writers who had already claimed national attention. Welty was thirty-three, Maxwell thirty-four. Maxwell had two novels to his credit— *Bright Center of Heaven* (1934) and *They Came Like Swallows* (1937). Both had been well reviewed, and the second had become a Book-of-the-Month Club selection. For her part, Welty had, in rapid succession, published a story collection called *A Curtain of Green* (1941) and a novella titled *The Robber Bridegroom* (1942). In these two works, Marianne Hauser of the *New York Times Book Review* believed, Welty established and then reiterated "the wealth of her talent."[1] Although Welty had by this time completed the stories for a third volume, she was finding it hard to write. Her two brothers, a number of her friends, and the man she loved had all entered the military shortly after World War II began, and worry was the order of the day. During these years, Maxwell was experiencing his own difficulty writing, struggling with material for the novel eventually to be titled *The Folded Leaf* and spending much of his time in editorial work for *The New Yorker*.

Although *The New Yorker* had rejected three of Welty's stories and an essay, Maxwell admired her work. After he met Welty, he wrote to solicit a

new story from her, but none was forthcoming. Maxwell's letter has been lost,[2] but Welty's witty reply has not, nor has Maxwell's equally witty answer to her reply. A common sense of humor would be a strong bond between the two during the close friendship that developed over the ensuing fifty-eight years.

Eudora Welty to William Maxwell, December 22, 1942

Dear Mr. Maxwell:

I will tell you the truth, your letter somehow got in my unabridged dictionary—do your letters often do that?—and was out of sight, out of mind, till just now when after a long arid period I again went to look up a word. My apologies for not answering, though all I can answer is that I haven't any material at all right now. Fresh out, as you will remember the Mississippi expression. But it may be that one day I will have something that you might like to read over, and I will tell Russell & Volkening to watch out for this, and if you ever have a desire to see something at any particular time, call them.[3] They never lose letters from an editor, I know. It was nice to see you in New York and I hope you have a nice Christmas and a good New Year. I have just bought the new Geo. Price[4] book ("You're the first white man to scale this peak. I'm part Indian.") for a present to myself and am wrapping it up and a little dog is going to carry it to me in my bed on Christmas morning and I am going to have something for <u>him</u>. All in honor of the funniest man in the world. I'm glad you've got him.

Sincerely,
Eudora Welty

William Maxwell to Eudora Welty, January 7, 1943

Dear Miss Welty:

Some of my letters get into my checkbook, and some into my overcoat pocket (which has a hole in it, so that I don't know what happens to them after that) and some into The Milwaukee Settlement Cook Book, and some in the top dresser drawer, which is theoretically sacred to socks. So I am in a perfect position to understand and condone your leisurely reply.

The thing that troubles me, however, is that sentence about calling Russell and Volkening if we ever have a desire to see something at any particular time. Because our desire is neither particular nor temporal. However, some arrangement will have to be arbitrarily arrived at. A telephone call, say, every six weeks, until they get thoroughly annoyed and go out of business. Unless you help out, from your end.

I had a happy Christmas and a merry New Year, which is confusing but not unpleasant. I'm sending your letter along to Mr. Price, who will, I know, value it highly.

Yours,
William Maxwell

Maxwell, who went to work at The New Yorker *in 1936, was the most ardent of the magazine's editors who championed work by Welty. Eudora herself had earlier sought a position at the magazine. Had she been successful, she and Maxwell would have been colleagues. Instead, their working relationship became one of author and editor. Here is Welty's 1933 letter of application to* The New Yorker, *one that makes her December 22, 1942, letter to William Maxwell seem remarkably restrained.*

Eudora Welty, New York City, to the Editors, The New Yorker,
March 15, 1933

Gentlemen,

I suppose you'd be more interested in even a sleight-o'-hand trick than you'd be in an application for a position with your magazine, but as usual you can't have the thing you want most.

I am 23 years old, six weeks on the loose in N.Y. However, I was a New Yorker for a whole year in 1930–31 while attending advertising classes in Columbia's School of Business. Actually I am a southerner, from Mississippi, the nation's most backward state. Ramifications include Walter H. Page, who, unluckily for me, is no longer connected with Doubleday-Page, which is no longer Doubleday-Page, even. I have a B.A. ('29) from the University of Wisconsin, where I majored in English without a care in the

world. For the last eighteen months I was languishing in my own office in a radio station in Jackson, Miss., writing continuities, dramas, mule feed advertisements, santa claus talks, and life insurance playlets; now I have given that up.

As to what I might do for you—I have seen an untoward amount of picture galleries and 15¢ movies lately, and could review them with my old prosperous detachment, I think; in fact, I recently coined a general word for Matisse's pictures after seeing his latest at the Marie Harriman: concubineapple. That shows you how my mind works—quick, and away from the point. I read simply voraciously, and can drum up an opinion afterwards.

Since I have bought an India print, and a large number of phonograph records from a Mr. Nussbaum who picks them up, and a Cezanne Bathers one inch long (that shows you I read e. e. cummings I hope), I am anxious to have an apartment, not to mention a small portable phonograph. How I would like to work for you! A little paragraph each morning—a little paragraph each night, if you can't hire me from daylight to dark, although I would work like a slave. I can also draw like Mr. Thurber,[5] in case he goes off the deep end. I have studied flower painting.

There is no telling where I may apply, if you turn me down; I realize this will not phase you, but consider my other alternative: the U of N.C. offers for $12.00 to let me dance in Vachel Lindsay's <u>Congo</u>.[6] I congo on. I rest my case, repeating that I am a hard worker.

Truly yours,
Eudora Welty

2

"Wonderful to Be a Writer.
Wonderful to Grow Roses. Wonderful to Care."

EUDORA WELTY and William Maxwell seem to have exchanged few letters between 1943 and 1951. In fact, there is no extant correspondence between January 1943 and August 1946, none between September 1946 and August 1949, and none between September 1949 and June 1951. Their correspondence began in earnest only after Maxwell became Welty's editor in 1951. Had they written more often before that, their letters might have told of important developments in the lives and careers of both. In 1943, Welty published a story collection called *The Wide Net and Other Stories*, stories she had completed by the fall of 1942, before wartime worries seriously hindered her fiction writing. During the war, she was able to write essays and reviews, spend several months working at the *New York Times Book Review*, and publish one short story. But not until the war had ended was she able to complete a new book, this time a novel, titled *Delta Wedding*. During the war, she had sent chapters of the novel overseas to John Robinson, a fellow Mississippian with whom she had been romantically involved since 1937, and after the war she resumed her romance with him. In the summer of 1946, she asked "Mr. Maxwell" if *The New Yorker* might like a story

by Robinson, and he accepted the story on behalf of the magazine. Then in late 1946 and early 1947, Welty made an extended visit to San Francisco in order to be near Robinson, who had moved there, and she did so again in the fall of 1947. In the fall of 1949, after publishing a story cycle called *The Golden Apples*, Welty used a Guggenheim Fellowship to finance an eight-month visit to Europe. Robinson followed her there, but the romance was doomed.

During these years, Maxwell received a deferment from military service; bought a "country" house on Baptist Church Road in Yorktown Heights, New York; wrote *The Folded Leaf* (1945); and met and married Emily Noyes (1945). Emmy, a graduate of Smith College and thirteen years his junior, was a woman of tremendous talent and generosity. She quickly became his most trusted reader. After the war, Maxwell published *Time Will Darken It* (1948) and took an almost four-month trip to Europe with his wife. Late in 1948, the Maxwells rented a New York City apartment on East Thirty-sixth Street for weekday residence, keeping the Yorktown Heights house for weekends.

Maxwell left *The New Yorker* in May 1947 to write full-time, but he returned to editorial duties there in the fall of 1948, discouraged by the sales figures for *Time Will Darken It* and apprehensive about his publishing future. Welty's stature was by then well established, and her work had become the subject of literary criticism, including an essay by Robert Penn Warren. By 1949, "Miss Welty" and "Mr. Maxwell" were on a first-name basis, and Emmy had joined the friendship and the correspondence. Both Bill and Eudora had now turned forty but had yet to join forces at *The New Yorker*. It would be two more years before Bill helped convince the magazine to publish one of Eudora's stories and before he and Eudora began the regular exchange of letters that would give a compelling and complex account of their lives during the next five decades.

Eudora Welty, New York City, to William Maxwell, August 9, [1946]

Dear Mr. Maxwell,

　　Sorry I missed you—you'd just gone swimming—Do you remember

me? I wanted to speak to you about the enclosed MS but after all, you can read it without an introduction—It's a little sketch a friend of mine enclosed in a letter—badly typed on some ranch out west—& he didn't think of my presenting it to any editor, but to me it looked so good I thought of the New Yorker[1]—Thanks if you'll read it—I enclose an envelope addressed to me in Jackson, as I'm leaving shortly. I don't usually do this kind of meddling—but hope you like the story—Thanks, and good wishes to you—

Eudora Welty

William Maxwell to Eudora Welty, August 19, 1946

Dear Miss Welty:

Will you tell John Robinson that the editors all like "Landlady in Algiers" very much and that the check for it will come along to him in a week or so. I feel sure that this is only the first of many pieces we shall be taking from him, and that we are indebted to you for discovering a natural New Yorker writer.

After we left you, last Wednesday, we went to look at the pewter lamp and, like the baby bear's bed, it was just right. It was so nice seeing you again, and we both hope, for our sakes, that you come back in October.

Sincerely,

Eudora Welty to William Maxwell, August 21, 1946

Dear Mr. Maxwell:

The news that you're taking John Robinson's story is a pleasure to get, and thank you for sending it so soon and quick. He will be glad to see your letter, which I'm mailing him. His address for the time being is John F. Robinson, General Delivery, San Francisco, California, which you can use instead of c/o me. I hope he will be convinced he might do others for you and this should do it.

A relief the little lamp was still there—and that it was just right. I'm glad you didn't miss it—I would have been sorry for otherwise our nice time on my last afternoon was just right too. It was fine to meet Mrs. Maxwell—I

hope some time again we all meet, New York or Mississippi—let me know about Mississippi.

<div align="right">Yours sincerely,
Eudora Welty</div>

P.S. I meant to ask you—the day I came by the office I saw a young man with a large portfolio going into your building—laughing heartily—all by himself. Which cartoonist? I started to say "Let me see".

William Maxwell to Eudora Welty, August 30, 1946

Dear Miss Welty:

Thank you for sending John Robinson's address. I have sent his story along to the printer and the check should reach him soon. I wish I knew, for my own sake, who the laughing young artist was. Mostly they are glum. It's a difficult profession.

Would it be too much to ask of you, the next time you send Diarmuid Russell a story under, say, twenty-five pages, to let us know, so that we can beard him in his den?

<div align="right">Cordially,</div>

Welty visited New York in November 1946, but she declined Maxwell's invitation to lunch—she feared the appearance of currying favor while he considered two of her stories for The New Yorker. *She didn't return to the city in 1947 but spent the summer of 1948 there and in nearby Bedford Hills. It seems likely that she saw the Maxwells during those months. Then in May 1949, she reported visiting "Bill and Emmy" at their Yorktown Heights home and afterward told John Robinson how much she liked them both.*

William Maxwell to Eudora Welty, August 24, 1949

Dear Eudora:

I had finished reading (while the lawn mower stood idle on the lawn)

the first section of The Golden Apples, and was three pages along in June Recital, when Emmy came out on the porch to get away from the cereal worms she had been pursuing through the kitchen cupboard, and I went back and read her the three pages and she smiled and said "It couldn't be nicer." She is dreadfully critical and so I was as pleased for you as I would be for myself that she was pleased. She went back into the house and I went on reading, stopping once to take the folding chair out into the yard, lay a fire, and get the stepladder and take some things to the attic, at her polite request, and then, having done all these things without my mind, rushed back to your book. At one point I was aware that I was holding my breath, a thing I don't ever remember doing before, while reading, and what I was holding my breath for is lest I might disturb something in nature, a leaf that was about to move, a bird, a wasp, a blade of grass caught between other blades of grass and about to set itself free. And then farther on I said to myself, this writing is corrective, meaning of course for myself and all other writers, and almost at the end I said reverently This is how one feels in the presence of a work of art, and finally, in the last paragraph, when the face came through, there was nothing to say. You had gone as far as there is to go and then taken one step farther.

We are driving up to the Cape for the weekend, and I will pick up the book there, when what I have just taken from it has sifted down through my mind, and made it ready for more. But I wanted to write you now, because when a book first comes out, it is really like a party, and when I am invited to a party I like to come early. A childish fear, perhaps, that, if I were to come later, the hostess, distracted, might not notice I have come.

<div align="right">We both send love,
Bill</div>

In 1951 Bill was delighted finally to convince The New Yorker *to accept a Welty story for publication. He won acceptance for two more stories in 1952 and for a novella in 1954. The friendship between Eudora and Bill had taken on the added dimension of author and editor.*

William Maxwell to Eudora Welty, London, June 6, 1951[2]

Dear Eudora:

I love your train story ["The Bride of the Innisfallen"] beyond all possibility of telling you. I loved it so much, while I was reading it, that I could hardly bear to pass it on to the next reader.

Emmy is in Dedham with her Auntie Betty [...] I am trying to keep house with Floribunda and her two kittens, Little Black and Little Grey, born about seven weeks ago in our kitchen cubbyhole. For two weeks before she left she put up and let down hems in a frenzy. I have learned to deal with these not very often absences by getting myself asked out to dinner every night. It's very simple. You just explain you are alone and look exactly the way you feel and up pops the invitation that will stand between you and a morbid evening.

We were sorry to miss Elizabeth Bowen. I wrote her a note but no word came back and so it must have been the wrong address. Everyone I know who knows her loves her. The reason I wanted to see you before you left for Europe that time is that I had it in mind to tell you about Beaulieu, where, for ten days, I was not only wildly happy but young, in a way that I never was when I really was young. We stayed at the Hotel Frisia, which I caught a glimpse of as we were taking the bus from San Remo to Nice. I pulled the cord, and off we got, the driver remarking Monsieur vous avez une bonne idée. There was one waiter for thirty people, and he climbed over the chairs without spilling a drop of soup. Emmy wandered all day by the sea collecting and discarding and refining her collection of tiny pieces of broken steamship china, rounded and polished on the floor of the Mediterranean. There was, during our stay, a carnival—a three day affair given under the auspices of the jeunesse de Beaulieu—and every night the fathers danced tirelessly, until one o'clock, with their two and three year old daughters. Do they still dance that ta-ra-ra-boom-dy-ey, in which girls throw their strapping partners up in the air? And the tea-house in the late afternoon, and—but perhaps I'd better stop. A little remembering is all right but too much is a disease I am terribly prone to. When are you coming home? And will you, when you do, come and have dinner on our porch again?

Affectionately,

Bill

William Maxwell to Eudora Welty, [May or June 1952]

To: Eudora
From: Bill

Yours of the 13th received and contents noted. It's been hotter than Illinois in August, and Emmy got very red in the face yesterday noon and took to the bed in the back room, but was better toward evening—enough better to steal a slip of a <u>white</u> wild rose. Do you have such things in Mississippi? This was the first either of us had ever seen, and it was single and like an Austrian briar.

I read KIN right straight through, looking for large sections that could be cut, and I couldn't find any.[3] Here it is. See if you don't think it is the very best story that anybody ever wrote.

<div align="right">Love,

B</div>

Eudora Welty to William Maxwell, June 19, 1952

Dear Bill,

Thanks for sending down the note and the proof—they came yesterday, but it was so hot I waited till very early this morning to read the story with no vapors over the brain if possible. It does hearten me that you don't see where cuts can go—I too feel that all belongs in it, and I think that after we packed in the first part more tightly, and successfully, I believe on reading it in coolness, that it stands all right now as it is, and I wouldn't know how to do any more to it myself. What I hope is that Mr. Shawn[4] feels he can agree with you and me—and Diarmuid feels the same—and I'll just hope steadily he can. I'm pleased and grateful to you of course about it all. Here's the proof back—I did suggest deleted lines on a few sheets, if agreeable, and wondered if "professional" needed to be defined on galley 41, and still feel I like in it the trunk & costumes image in the parlor, though not violently— all for whenever you look it over next. Yes I <u>am</u> fond of this story! and feel glad you like it too. That white rose sounds lovely & I hope Emmy's feeling cooler—isn't it really ferocious. We have a white wild rose called the Cherokee, which also comes in pink, and if Emmy would like a cutting of it I'll

send up along with Gruss an Aachen, but my mother tells me to wait till the fall to send it. I'll remember. The gardenias are blooming now, but all is dry as can be and we water all day.

Some good names nobody would believe: in the paper a wreck happened, with Mr. Dill Pickle, white, colliding with Hercules Small, 8, colored. (But it turned out sadly.)

<div style="text-align: right">Love to Emmy and you and thanks again for all,
Eudora</div>

William Maxwell to Eudora Welty, August 7, 1952

Dear Eudora:

"No Place for You, My Love," just came back to my desk this morning with sheets and sheets of praise attached to it. Actually, it's beyond praise, and of course The New Yorker wants it. As always, there are some questions, some matters of clarity, and so forth. I'll be sending you an annotated proof in a few days. The story is scheduled tentatively for the issue of September 13th, and that means no grass is going to have a chance to grow under anybody's feet.[5]

As you probably know, Diarmuid is away, but I've told Mr. Volkening[6] that we are taking the story.

Wonderful time in Oregon, visiting all the places Emmy knew as a child. What with camping on the beach and in the mountains and horseback riding and rushing from rose garden to rose garden, I had the loveliest kind of vacation.

<div style="text-align: right">Emmy sends her love with mine.
Bill</div>

Eudora Welty to William Maxwell, August 11, 1952

Dear Bill,

I'm so glad you like that story. It was nice of you to write me direct about it, yes, Diarmuid is on vacation. What lovely luck this is, I think, though my mother said, "Won't you wear out your welcome?" Of course I'll be glad to study over all comments and will do the best I can here. Thanks too for that

other letter, written as you were going off, saying all looked fair ahead for the "Kin" story—all very cheering to me.

The vacation sounded beautiful, and all those roses too. It must have put mad ideas in the head. A place I just ordered some lilies from is out there too somewhere—Boring, Ore. (Named by some strange, non-lily-loving people perhaps—or could there <u>be</u> some Borings, naming towns after themselves?) Walter Marx's Gardens. The cool must have been a blessing too, and I hope the fall weather follows soon. We are just getting ready to go out and watch for those Perseids.[7]

It's fine the new story's coming out soon, and I'll be here in Jackson, for proofs or anything, till at least the first week in September, but then I hope to come up to New York that month, later on.

Thanks for such good news, and I'm so pleased.

<div style="text-align:right">

Love,—I forgot to say, how much I enjoyed that grand
Pritchett story lately—how I adore his things,[8]
Eudora

</div>

Eudora Welty to William Maxwell, August 23, [1952]

Dear Bill,

Here this is, and my hope is we got it ["No Place for You, My Love"] better. You were helpful as could be. The worst places I typed off in revision on yellow paper and pinned on, as you'll see—and I answered most questions right on your pages, not wanting to clutter up the proof any more. There's a little floor plan in there somewhere too. I do feel the story's more <u>out</u>, clearer, but the main thing (and the trouble) was I felt it essential to keep the mystery in it, as you understood. In Galley 25, please use your judgment (this is the last day and I have to mail it, and shall be satisfied either way) about leaving in or taking out the parenthetical sentence on my typed sheet. And whether, if in, it should be in a parenthesis. (I remember Mark Twain said somewhere that anybody that would wantonly use a parenthesis would steal.) I don't see a thing I can do about the end, the last paragraph—if it isn't understandable I truly can't help it, as I see no other way, at present, to say it. Yes, your idea was right about it.

One thing I'm stupidly ignorant of, and can't find out in Jackson at all,

it seems, is how many l's in Galatoire's—Mr. Lobrano surely knows—I put two in and he didn't change it, but I'd like it checked.

It was so nice to talk to you, though, as you found out, I'm not at all bright on the telephone, ever, even not talking about a story and even not using up a fortune while I look for it. (It was because we're painting the house spending the money <u>from</u> the story that I couldn't find it.) Henry [Volkening] sent that beautiful check and thanks to all for that too.

I hope all's well about the story now, and thanks once more for the help, and your carefulness. To get the story right is the idea in all our minds, but I expect it worked out better in your office because I took three times as long by myself. Must dash to the P.O.

<div align="right">Love,
Eudora</div>

Eudora Welty to William Maxwell, August 30, [1952]

Dear Bill,

Here this is back, and I hope all's well now. I missed any more typos, if any, so let's hope they're just not there. All the punctuation changes I'm sure are right, but in one or two places where the rhythm got thrown out, for me, and where the choice between comma and dash didn't seem too weighty, I put back the original—if that's all right. Thanks again for all the help.

Brandywine does sound beautiful—don't you love yellow roses! It's a new name to me—I just read about it in the Rose Annual. By the way I'll be mailing you the little cuttings airmail, since that's speedier than by hand— by my hand, as I come up on the train. I hope they take root and "never look back." It looks now as if I could, by putting my mind to it and nothing happening, come up to New York by the second week in September, which is when Rosa Wells says I can stay in her apartment two weeks while she's away.[9] Maybe you and Emmy could get down as far as Twelfth Street some time to see me—is that too far? But I'll call you.

<div align="right">Love,
Eudora</div>

William Maxwell to Eudora Welty, September 2, 1952

Dear Eudora:

I haven't followed your instructions in two places because to have done so would have been to do just what you (from your notes) didn't want. If you don't put a comma after alligator in the sentence "The cars and trucks, then the foot passengers and the alligator waddling like a child to school, all disembarked and wound up the weed-sprung levee", waddling modifies everybody. I have this on the highest grammatical authority. "... waddling like a child to school" surrounded by commas is a phrase that can be lifted from the sentence, and has to modify the word immediately preceding the first comma, which is alligator. Something tells me this will amuse your mother.

And by inserting that "had" in the sentence "When she (had) looked clear around, thinking they had a fire burning somewhere now, out of the heat had risen the full moon" you have destroyed the sequence of tenses—in some states a hanging offense—without, I'm afraid, really establishing that the moon is rising in front of them in the East. It was perfectly clear, and perfect, the way you originally had it.

If you even so want me to make these two changes I will, naturally. There is still time. I almost called you about it, for the pleasure of talking to you, and then decided that you would take more kindly to an airmail letter. Emmy also counts the telephone among her inanimate enemies. "by the second week of September" is almost as good as instantly, and 12th Street is not a bit far.

If you haven't already mailed the cuttings, I believe the office would be quicker than the country. How I long to have this connection, this kinship, between your garden and ours established. Emmy is very clever about cuttings. I'm sure they will grow for her. At this moment there is a bouquet, in a thin glass tumbler, that is intended to duplicate the roses in your story ["Kin"], as nearly as we can with our resources: two crimson glories, a brandywine, Christopher Stone, Donald Prior, and two Edith Nellie Perkinses. As searchlights go, it's not bad, and each time I bend over it I say to myself with surprise, oh <u>that's</u> what roses smell like!

Love,

B

Eudora Welty, [New York City], to William Maxwell, October 22, 1952

Dear Bill,

I don't know how foolish & shaky & unreliable you'll think I am, but when it came right down to it, I just couldn't sign this thing [a first-reading agreement with *The New Yorker*].[10] It's for no reason except something inside me, that just doesn't fit in with contracts—as I told you—. But I don't think you'll cherish it against me—will you?—when you know how much I value all the good things about it. I've called you but you're at a long lunch & now I have to go but wanted to get it said.

It was lovely seeing you & Emmy the rainy night—smelling the heliotrope & eating those darling tomatoes & all. (I didn't see the shell curtains—may I still?) Love to both—I'm going out now to see about an apartment I can move into next week & if it's nice I hope we can all meet again at it—

Call me if you have time so I'll know if you're annoyed or not—at Oregon-4-5640—will you?

Love,
Eudora

Emily Maxwell to Eudora Welty, January 7, 1953

Dear Eudora,

There are little edges of snow on the buildings outside the window and what I think is jambalaya in the oven, waiting for Bill to come home for lunch. The lovely star of Bethlehem's are still fresh. The stars have a greenish tint, a reflection from the green centers I guess, but it makes them seem unbelievably white and crisp. They are with some lemon leaves, and the combination looks a little like lilac, but nobler.

We have been reading A Curtain of Green aloud, a story at a time.[11] When your darling letter arrived it was like hearing the same tone of voice that's in the stories, and you were very much here. What a marvelous book it is.

I hope you have seen the news that 500 people saw saucers last night, some from airplane towers, etc. . . . We heard it over the radio quite late because Stevenson was supposed to speak at Sandburg's 75th birthday party. But Sandburg himself droned on and on, and in his pauses Stevenson could

have delivered a major address on the Tidelands. I begin to feel that we invented Stevenson.[12]

Bill is home and wants to write you a note. I hope this reaches you before you come back to New York, and that we shall see you very soon.

Much love from us both, and our thanks for the beautiful flowers.

Emmy

In mid-January 1953, Eudora arrived in New York and spent the next six weeks there. During that time, she worked on a novella to be called The Ponder Heart, *and one day she read the entire novella to Bill and Emmy Maxwell. In 1988, Bill recalled that day: "I see Eudora standing by the window with the manuscript in her hands. It went on all morning and all afternoon, as I remember, with time out for lunch. As a reader Eudora is better than a whole company of actors and when I am moved to laughter, it is often accompanied by tears of amusement. I shed them all through the first half of the book but was dry-eyed during the second half, not because it wasn't funny, but because the tear glands gave up."[13]*

Emily Maxwell to Eudora Welty, April 10, 1953

Dear Eudora,

We loved hearing from you, and here are the pictures to remind us all of that lovely day of reading. Bill is very amused by the one where you and he are worrying the ending.

I thought your review of Jerry's stories was penetrating and beautiful — Like the best reviews it was within rather than outside the stories themselves.[14]

It's 11:00 o'clock, and we are boarding the boat at 1:00, with sandwiches, chocolate cake, and champagne. It is raining hard, but I love to see rain coming down on the water.[15]

Thank you for sending the letters from the high school student — weren't they lovely!

I must close as we are really leaving now —

With love from both of us —

Emmy

William Maxwell to Eudora Welty, July 17, 1953, Telegram

THE NEW YORKER HAS TAKEN THE PONDER HEART. SHAWN
AND LOBRANO BOTH FEEL IT IS A CLASSIC OF AMERICAN
WRITING. YOU KNOW HOW HAPPY I AM=
 BILL

Eudora Welty to William Maxwell, July 17, 1953

Dear Bill,

Thank you for that wire. It was the nicest way to tell me. What marvel-
ous news, it keeps on astonishing my head. How far from our heads that
day we read the story was the thought we'd meet over it again some day for
the New Yorker. Later when Diarmuid mentioned you'd been visited by
a dream like that, I thought it was Paris in front of you making you light-
headed. But since the impossible has happened—that any magazine at all
would consider that long a thing—I couldn't have stood for it <u>not</u> to be the
New Yorker. I realized that.

So you'll be editing it—I'm glad, and you've seen I rearranged the last
page as it came to us that day. The scene in the parlor's a little changed,
but maybe not shortened enough—I added one witness—Well, all can be
talked over later—can't it! I'm pleased Mr. Shawn and Mr. Lobrano speak
so well of the story. How can I thank you enough. But for it to please you
that this has happened to it makes me feel proud besides grateful, which I
already did because you liked it. Love to Emmy and you—I long to hear
your news, Europe, the novel—there must be so much, I hope all of it is
happy. Thank you again, Emmy, for the pictures of that happy day, sent the
day you were sailing, for I looked at them again just now. It was lovely to get
the Dufy postcard about the Illuminations.[16] Was Floribunda all right? This
is a speechless letter but brings thanks and love. Luck like this to you is what
I wish.

<div align="right">

Yours,

Eudora

</div>

William Maxwell to Eudora Welty, July 20, 1953

Dear Eudora:

Howard[17] is away so I am wading in poetry, but I must answer those questions. I cannot bear for you not to know that Floribunda was not only all right but sitting in the catbird seat, when we got back. She had, unfortunately, learned to catch birds from the other cats, but I think she has mostly forgotten how by this time. I brought back, among the souvenirs, a good idea for my book, but you know it slips and slides, comes and goes. But anyway, I finished a story I had been working on for over a year, mostly because Emmy went through all the various fragments of it and the nineteen versions, until she had found it all, and then called me up to tell me she liked it. So I went home and finished it.[18] Europe was simply wonderful. The sun shone on us the whole two weeks we were in England; we had three simultaneous visits going on in England, so it was really six weeks we spent there, and what with the flowers, and following in your footsteps to Elizabeth Taylor's,[19] and being taken by the T's to Oxford, and seeing Churchill lose his temper in the House of Commons, and being simply wild about the English anyway, it couldn't have been nicer. Then eleven days in that darling little car. To Sens, to Vezelay, then right up over the Massif Central, through rain, through fog, past snow, and down into the valley of your most exquisite dreaming. China, the moon. Houses perched over space, bridges, sheep, all time, and too beautiful. And then eleven or twelve very queer days in Paris, that culminated in our discovering the footbridge over the Seine, between the Institute and the Louvre, at Midnight. Do you know that bridge at midnight. If not, you must spend some of the New Yorker money getting there. And then we came home by way of Scotland and Iceland. Making five trips in all—no seven. Three in England, two in France, two coming home—eight; the voyage over, on the Liberte, was like a second delayed Honeymoon. We danced till three in the morning, at the ship's party, and got terribly behind on sleep, and all that. Eight voyages to Europe for the price of one.

I am so glad you are pleased about the New Yorker taking the story. In this weather one needs astonishment in the head to keep the heat out. Your

mother's Cherokee sent a fine new shoot into the air, through two inches of buckwheat hulls, and within six hours it was crisp as bacon.

Love from us both
B

Eudora Welty to William Maxwell, [July 24, 1953]

Dear Bill,

Those were the things I wanted to know—what seat Floribunda was sitting in—the catbird!—and all the news of summer, the boat, the book, that you sent. So happy to hear about the story and wishing for the day when it can be read—how soon? I will start immediately looking for it in the magazine which ought to be a safe way. And any book idea that sprang from <u>that</u> trip must have sprung full-fledged, so the novel must be going forward with all energy and pleasure these days. Eight voyages plus the ninth of a novel.

I think I'm in a state of shock,—from the New Yorker taking that story, but you know from what. Haven't worked a lick—and can't seem to either take anything in or put anything down, though all kinds of tasks surround me. Made some watermelon rind preserves but it didn't help. This may take a long time.

Keeping a promise, I'm bringing my niece for a week of sightseeing to New York because she's 9, and though it's her trip and I don't expect to have much of a chance to see anybody, I'll hope for some kind of getting in touch with Emmy and you. I'll phone you. It'll be from Aug. 23. This visit may re-charge the batteries a little and my senses start to come back—maybe in the zoo.

Love to you both,
Eudora

William Maxwell to Eudora Welty, July 29, 1953

Dear Eudora:

I am sending Henry Volkening (in Diarmuid's absence) this afternoon a check for your account for $6150. In a way it is a shame that you don't really care about money. And in another way, it's a damn good thing.

Love,
Bill

William Maxwell to Eudora Welty, August 3, 1953

Dear Eudora:

Joy! I'll try to have the preliminary galleys ready for you to take back with you—I won't impinge on [your niece] Elizabeth's trip to the extent of going over with them. The editing so far is virtually nothing, and I don't look for any problems. Lunch with Mary Lou today, who looks very pretty with a new haircut.[20] I expect your ears were burning. Tell your mother her Cherokee is putting out shoots, to my immense satisfaction. I guess it intends to stay. I don't know if Elizabeth would enjoy the Baptist Church Road, but Emmy has a new recipe for poppyseed cake which is partly her own invention, which I long for you to sample. And if only I can produce a Fred Edmunds while you are here. It's a wonderful rose, that goes on and on like a sunset, sometimes five or six days in a glass of water. The apricot glow. Did that dahlia live? Something tells me it didn't.

Love from us both,

B

William Maxwell to Eudora Welty, August 12, 1953

Dear Eudora:

I thought it might be easier if you got these preliminary galleys before you left home, and then we could talk about anything that bothered you when you are here. All the editing is tentative, as always, and where a story is told through a narrator, of course, there is virtually complete leeway, anyway. Miss Edna Earle's conversation is a landscape in itself, and where I have questioned anything it is only to ask if she is in focus. You who made her are the only one who can know this.

Love,

William Maxwell

Eudora Welty to William Maxwell, [August 1953]

Dear Bill,

Thanks for the letter, and the galleys and questions came safely too—I can tell they're going to be no trouble at all to us, and it was nice of you to

send them ahead. The questions were so reassuring. It will be fine to go over the story in New York—easy too, because we're staying across the street, at the Algonquin—and my little niece won't mind, she's got to sit down <u>some</u> time.

It's lovely to think of seeing Baptist Church Road—as Templeton the Rat says, "What you say tempts me,"[21] and if Elizabeth could imagine it she'd be tempted too—but she's so little, I think you should think twice about it, truly. To think of missing the poppyseed cake and the Fred Edmunds and most of all a talk and visit—all Europe to ask about—is an ache, but my feeling or my conscience tells me that most of my company this trip will be non-human—animals and planets and the transportation system etc. It's nice as can be to be invited though—and thank you. But the galley guarantees a meeting so that's to look forward to. Love to Emmy and you, and I'll telephone you next Monday morning and see what day we'd better go over the story. Will you have a story I can read?

<div align="right">Yours,
Eudora</div>

One reason I said reassuring—your questions—is a copy just came of the story that the publishers set up in a mimeograph book and on the title page it's called "a novel."[22] Somebody just drew a line through what <u>I</u> called it. And I'll tell you about the dahlia too. Our cleaning woman put it out with the trash. I've felt dahlia-less all summer—(kin to shame, only worse)

Eudora Welty to William Maxwell, [Early September 1953], Incomplete letter

Dear Bill,

It was so fine to see you—and to talk to Emmy that evening—and the roses and fortunes and Nicely-Nicely remain with Elizabeth and me both all surrounded with pleasure and thanks to you. I never expected to see much of human company at all, and so all these pleasures were unexpected as well as lovely.[23]

It was terribly nice of the New Yorker to let Harcourt use a set of their proofs [of "The Ponder Heart"], and they were here when I got home, so I went to work promptly on the two of them, saving much time and work. Here they are—your set—and I hope the lenience in time I took advan-

tage of won't make anybody rush at that end. All help appreciated. As you said, most of the questions were minor and easy to answer or deal with. In the case of idiom—like "carry him home" for "drive him home," I think the meaning's clear enough, and the use of "carry" is so general in the country here that I left it, hoping you agree. The same goes for repetitions like "busy, busy, busy"—I doubt if Edna Earle ever said she or anybody else was just busy. But if it grates, you can cut a few of those. "To the good of the heathen" would be a legitimate idiom, and I suppose it's clear enough. I changed positions of the words in "lighting out front," because the "out" was supposed to go with "front," and lighting simply means alighting there. Etc.

Thanks for getting me steady on the times and ages, again. For seasons, there <u>is</u> a little early June peach—though mostly they ripen in July, and so do the good watermelons. As for the trial coming up so promptly, you can lay that to Ponder influence—I think it would work. I made Grandpa getting "plenty old" instead of just old. Etc.

William Maxwell to Eudora Welty, [Early September 1953]

Dear Eudora:

You left just in time. It got worse and worse, until finally people began to look both sick and despairing. What in the end finished me was the continual alternation between air-conditioning and heat, which I do not particularly in itself mind. On Friday morning I left the office and went to see Louis Forster[24] off on the United States, off for Europe, that is, and there were some other people there and some champagne, so I just drank as much as I felt like drinking, which is always with champagne generous, and happy feeling, and ate caviar, and then came back to the office for a while, and during the noon hour went to see The Beggar's Opera, which I was afraid wouldn't be in town by the time we moved in, and I should have known this was merely on the way to bed (because it was all fairly unlike me, champagne in the morning). Because I arrived home with the grippe, spent the next three days coughing and complaining, and rushing out of the house in my bathrobe to spray the roses, and reading the new life of George Sand that Francis Steegmuller had left with me, and Monday it

turned cool.[25] Of course nothing happened to the roses, they got the best of care, and are now glowing like the windows of Chartres. And on Tuesday I got into town where there was some codein terpenhydrate, and that fixed my cough, and I am practically though not quite as good as when you and Elizabeth, whom I now count among my friends, last saw me.

I thought it was extraordinary how you kept your wits about you, as Elizabeth would say, with the galleys. The fixes were always funnier, so that I know it has not yet gone stale on you. And you were firm about the unhelpful suggestions, which is something I always have it on my conscience to worry about. The next set of galleys will be the final ones, with, I should imagine, not very many things to worry you. You didn't delay things at all. L [Gus Lobrano] gets back from his vacation next week and couldn't have looked at the galleys before he left. The transposing of 109 and 110 I thought a good one. The effect on 110 is better because of it, and so is 109. And I loved the picture of Justice not saying anything but just eating. There may be a few errors, because of marking the proof for the printers, but nowhere have I overridden anything that you wanted, so if you see something that is different it is a mistake, and don't hesitate to point it out.

Now that the galleys are out of the way, here is the story [Maxwell's "What Every Boy Should Know"]. It's the only copy I have with me—the other having gone off, but I thought it would amuse you anyway to read the paste-up version.

The carpenter has fixed the three gables of our house, so that the siding goes all the way up instead of turning vertical above the windows, and it looks much prettier. Emmy is also turning the chicken-house into something rainproof, with an eye to future almost anything. And moving peonies. And cleaning up after carpenters. And reading Proust. She read volume 2 before volume 1 of Swann's Way, accidentally getting started on the wrong one, with terribly interesting results. She didn't know all through the first volume (not even when she came to the wonderful sentence about loving somebody he didn't even like, who wasn't even in his style) without knowing that Swann had married Odette. The first Emmy knew about it was when the "I" met Odette and little Berthe (?) in the park. She was bowled over, of course. Who wouldn't be?

I hope the coolness has come your way, and don't feel that politeness—because I sometimes think you are the politest friend I have—requires that you don't send any more stories here until The Ponder Heart is published.[26] You won't, no matter what your Mother says, wear out your welcome. I have let only Howard Moss see the galleys before the revision, because he, as a poet, I thought deserved to see any version that there is, and he was beside himself with pleasure over the story. And remember me to Elizabeth and your Mother, and come back soon, and you won't forget—on purpose, I mean; out of politeness, I mean, and delicacy—that you are going to let us have one of the recordings? It would be one of our treasured things, like Eliot reading the Quartets and Joyce reading the Anna Livia Plurabelle.[27]

Love,

Bill

Eudora Welty to William Maxwell, [September 10, 1953]

Dear Bill,

It's a lovely story ["What Every Boy Should Know"], and I don't know when I've seen interior and exterior marching so beautifully together. From the title on, it works its powers on those places in the heart and mind that most stories never reach, and don't know how. The short paragraph about age and patience, patience and age, knowledge, disappointment, and unspokenness, is the finest to me, but I loved all of it. Thanks so much for letting me have the chance to read it—I'd be glad to know when to look for it in print.

I do see from this how elegant rubber cement is. I'm so used to writing with a pincushion that I don't know if I can learn other ways or not, but I did go right down and buy a bottle of Carter's. The smell stimulates the mind and brings up dreams of efficiency. Long ago when my stories were short (I wish they were back) I used to use ordinary paste and put the story together in one long strip, that could be seen as a whole and at a glance—helpful and realistic. When the stories got too long for the room I took them up on the bed or table & pinned and that's when my worst stories were like patch-

work quilts, you could almost read them in any direction. No man would be bemused like that, but Emmy will understand—and on the whole I like pins. The Ponder Heart was in straight pins, hat pins, corsage pins, and needles, and when I got through typing it out I had more pins than I started with. (So it's economical.)

That was simply awful, that heat—and then to have the grippe on top of that. I hope they've gone off together, by now. It was cool here when we reached home, but today it's 98—this is our hottest month. Our roses look nice too and are plentiful and glowing in color. It's too hot here to safely take the cutting up, but we have it for you, and won't send it too late for it to be set out. We haven't had rain yet—have you?—and water almost all day long.

I'm glad to know the fixes seemed all right—the main thing is to have all accurate, clear, and in the right place and time, which your questions were bent toward all of them, so I was exactly with you only maybe a little more lax on the idiom, which I may be too fond of? So pleased Howard did read the story and like it. Tell him hello from me.

The house sounds filled with exciting new things, and sounds so pretty. Think of our picnic, Bill and Emmy, at the fall of the year. By the way, I was looking in a copy of an old herb book and found the enclosed recipes, which I thought you and Emmy with your herbs ought to see, if just to make you think. (Isn't it just like that Lady Colchester to call for something hard, like Biathaganthis Frigidi?)[28]

Yes, I've written the record people to ask that they send my allotment down—I thought they'd sent them to Diarmuid's office, but there was only one for me and one for the office—D. took the office one home and played it and he and I neither one think it's good. So don't expect it to be anything but a souvenir—but I wanted you and Emmy to have it. If they'd let me hear a proof of it, I believe I could have made it better, but maybe I couldn't have.

Elizabeth still likes her trip, and sends you hello and wishes. So does my mother, and so do I, with love to both, and thanks again for letting me read the story. A good story cheers me up more than anything, and this one does more than cheer. But I mean cheers me as a writer.

I loved the Pritchett—all that man writes—by the way.[29] If you see him,

for I heard somewhere he was in America, Princeton or somewhere, can't you pull more out of him?

Did you hear Stevenson Tuesday night? Oh, I know you did.

Love,
Eudora

Eudora Welty to William Maxwell, October 7, [1953]

Dear Bill,

The records showed up and I sent up one to you and Emmy, let me know if it comes folded, melted, or dog-eared and I'll wrap one up another way. Wish it were better.

Are you both well and are things going nicely,—nicely? We still pine for a drop of rain, but the first Camellia Sassanquas are in bloom, like little apple blossoms, anyway. How are the leaves?

I got that vast additional installment of cash from the New Yorker and it's like How the Salt Came to Be in the Sea, do you remember that mill that nobody knew how to stop working?[30] It's lovely at this end—and thanks once more to you, very much.

Also, I appreciate the kindness of somebody at the New Yorker who agreed with Harcourt to help out a bookstore lady in Jackson who wanted to sell copies of the book before it came out—for Christmas presents. Then or never, she felt, and I agree, she's pretty-near right about Jackson. All my friends are going to have to give the book to each other, after having read the story in the New Yorker.

Do you remember we were speaking of bread? And you said Emmy had the address of people who had the right flour. I wonder if sometime you could ask her to send it to me; as you guessed, my mother would love to have it. She's making bread just now as I write, which I smell in the oven, so I was reminded.

How much writing are you getting done? I hope a great deal. I'm working now to finish my book of short stories, and for a while my spirit got low because of not being able to fit the time in to get something finished as I wanted, a story—just things that had to be done and the time of year—but things have eased up a little now and I feel I can make it.

No, I don't feel I'm wearing out my welcome, I only feel aglow with pleasure to come in the house, at the New Yorker, and I'll probably knock any time. Is the story you let me read coming out in it and soon, I hope so.

Love to Emmy and you,

Eudora

William Maxwell to Eudora Welty, October 12, 1953

Dear Eudora:

I've been so down, physically, since the heat wave, that I think I haven't thanked you or even answered, I'm afraid, your angelic letter about my story; but it was a comfort, it sustained me. I'm better now, though I seem to wobble a little, so far as energy is concerned. The record was on my desk when I came in this morning, and I am going to leave it safely sealed in its case until we get home tonight. Emmy is driving Sally Fitzgerald and three of the children and Sally's brother and 3 big suitcases, 1 dufflebag, and I don't know how many small suitcases to Idlewild, and I am meeting Robert and the two older children at the Italian airlines at 3 o'clock, and going with them to the airport.[31] They are migrating to Tuscany for a year, to save their sanity, all the children being under six, and the Jugoslav maid having departed in a fit of paranoia, if that's how you spell it. It was Gus Lobrano who saw no reason why Harcourt shouldn't help out the bookstore lady in Jackson. I tell you, not that any one else here resisted the idea, but so I can also add that he is and has always been your staunchest admirer and friend. Strictly speaking, he is the friend of your work, which is the best kind of friend of all, I say.

The story I sent you is coming out in Perspectives, I think next spring.[32] The sexual life of adolescent boys is out-of-bounds to The New Yorker. Any deviation from simple adultery, I guess, is. A question partly of the mails and partly because Mr. Ross was fortunately a rather prudish man and he thought we ought to have a care for what we put on the parlor table. A book, he said, you more or less knew about when you bought it but a magazine there was no way of telling about, and ours was (and I guess is) a family magazine, so it had better be reasonably pure. This theory has only one fallacy, that I can see: it supposes that the young are reasonably pure, too,

and I'm not sure that innocence isn't the crowning accomplishment of maturity, but anyway.

The chicken house has been plugged up, made rainproof and all that, and the outside painted a beautiful peacock blue, in the expectation that if the Cradle should suddenly come and get that infant we were speaking of, a playhouse will be ready for it to use when it grows up.[33] The house is having a second coat of pink paint, last fall it had the first; the carpenter is coming to floor the attic, the contents of which are awash in my study, where they don't do any harm, because I am outside digging holes for Crimson King, Nelly Moser, and the Duchess of Edinburgh. Now that the clematis is all in, I have to put my mind to the rose holes: How does this sound to you? 2 climbing Mme. Edouard Herriot by the front wall, with the Eglantine moved to the far corner. Lady Hillingdon between Christopher Stone and the Grand Duchess Charlotte, May Wettern next to the Condesa de Sastago, and Donald Prior behind Frau Karl Drus[c]hki? Then Dr. Huey by the driveway, where the ramblers and honeysuckle are now joined in battle, and Nevada out in the open, with Mme. Gregoire Staechlin above it decorating the pole that holds up the clothes line. And then at the backdoor, two Fashions, Nigger Boy, Gruss an Aachen, Isobel, and Dagmar Spath. The musk has to be moved too, out of the garden, and where to put Dainty Bess. Well, all that is bad enough, but we have no water, and are moving into town tomorrow until it decides to rain. So if I wire you, will you drop everything, and come and help us <u>dig</u>?

<div align="right">

Love from us both,
Bill

</div>

And I can't thank you enough for sending the record!

The leaves are marvelous, and so is the weather, but I wince as one fine day succeeds another, and no rain, and our water table disappearing down the drains of New York City, as it does when they lower the reservoirs. I'm so glad things have eased up and you can write. I feel that New York will do that for me. There is nothing but the living room, the bedroom, the bathroom and kitchen and hall. No OUTDOORS.

<u>Bread</u>: The address is The Great Valley Mills, RFD Ivyland, Pa. and Emmy gets as a rule 6 lbs of hardest white flour and 3 lbs of fine ground whole wheat flour, and the organic is finest for pastry, and wheat germ she

adds to her bread. But the best thing is to just write and ask them to send you the catalogue. Your Ma will have ideas about what she wants, no doubt. I'm sure it will please her and ultimately your sense of smell.

William Maxwell to Eudora Welty, October 19, 1953

Dear Eudora:

We played Why I Live at the P.O. the night we got to the country, and the next morning while I was frying the bacon by way of luring Emmy out of bed, I turned on A Worn Path. It made me cry. It always does, but leaning over the skillet it hurt more. So silly, because nothing can happen to that little boy and that old woman. Thanks to you, they are quite immortal. So I don't know exactly who I was crying about. The narrow margin, I guess. The story makes me feel instead of just think how narrow the margin of safety is, for every one.

The third story ["A Memory"] we are saving for this week end. The first is inexhaustible in its humorous beauty, and I laughed at many things for the first time, though it is as familiar to me as Old Doc Yak. The recording carried me right straight back to the YMHA.[34] They are wonderful to have, and we both can't thank you enough.

The two May Wettern roses that were to have arrived from Ireland in the diplomatic pouch can't because Dickson's won't dig them up before November 1st. But the holes are dug, anyway. And maybe some other way will be found to import them. You know about the May Wettern rose? Emmy saw it in the Portland rose garden, and told me to write down the name, which I did, and then I lost the paper I wrote it down in, and a year later Emmy's mother found it and mailed it to us, and then I wrote the American Rose Society, who went through 98 catalogues before they felt safe in telling me that it wasn't offered for sale in this country. It is not uncommon in England and Ireland, and is either white with a pink edge or pink with a white—pink with a white, I think. Anyway, it doesn't look like Peace.

I started to get some writing done, but there was an interruption. Blessed are the interrupted, for they shall etcetera.

Love to you,

B

William Maxwell to Eudora Welty, October 27, 1953

Dear Eudora:

Here are the final proofs on "The Ponder Heart," and I can only be thankful that it isn't, I assume, any longer hot weather in Mississippi. My own work on it ended with the preliminary galleys and what you are faced with here is Mr. Lobrano's queries, the proofreaders', and such changes as the copy desk made, all unbeknownst to me. I usually tell them to keep their hands off your stories entirely, and this time I forgot, so there have been changes in punctuation, spelling, and occasionally capitals have been changed to lower case to conform with the usual style of the magazine. I have been through it fairly carefully, and in places pointed out changes that I thought you would particularly want to consider, but in any event any change in type that doesn't seem felicitous to you you are free as always to put back the way it was before. Mr. Lobrano's queries are marked with an "L" or with numbers. All the rest are the proofreaders', which are meant to be suggestions only.

One thing more before the numbered queries: We are trying to get this issue of the New Yorker out of the way ahead of schedule since it will be mostly taken up by your story, and would therefore appreciate having the galleys back as soon as you can easily manage it. We would not appreciate your killing yourself to get them back a day or two earlier.

At (1) on galley one, Lobrano was stopped by "lighting from the country," which you remember was a change because I was stopped originally by "lighting out front, from the country." One of the things that bothers us both is that the Studebaker doesn't "alight," people alight from it, but that is fairly pedantic, and a more serious objection is that the phrase "lighting from the country" really isn't necessary at all and stands out as a piece of conspicuous vernacular, whereas universally one is not aware of this at all in the story. Would you consider cutting it?

Mr. Lobrano found the sentence marked (2) on galley one a little hard to follow, and says, "If he gave you something today, how <u>could</u> he give it to you again tomorrow? A white-faced heifer calf, for instance?" I have suggested an insert that would answer his objection. But here and in other places where he has raised points of this kind, the obscurity is no more than momen-

tary, and the question in his mind is whether, in a story of this complexity and brilliance, it is a good thing to have such "stoppers"—especially when no serious purpose is served by them. We leave it up to you, as always.

He was stopped again at (3) on galley three, because in the previous sentence you have said when the children saw Uncle Daniel coming, etc., but you have not said that Grandpa was with him, and therefore Mr. Lobrano was momentarily stopped by "Grandpa used to make short work of them," and didn't understand what it meant. It seems clear enough to me that Grandpa was habitually with Uncle Daniel and that making short work of the children consisted of driving them off with his cane, but you might consider the point anyway.

At (4) on galley three, Mr. Lobrano wonders whether Miss Cora Ewbanks was running the hotel when Uncle Daniel gave it to Edna Earle, and did Edna Earle take it over immediately and send Miss Cora away?

At (5) on galley seven, there is an uncertainty about the time sequence which lasts for the next two and a half galleys, until just before the white space when you explain that Grandpa carried Uncle Daniel to the asylum after the failure of his marriage to Miss Teacake. This is the only serious query that I have to make to you. It would, we both think, be an enormous help to the reader if you could suggest somehow, on galley seven as well as at the end of this piece, that the whole business about Miss Teacake took place before Uncle Daniel was consigned to the asylum. I have suggested an insert which you may find clumsy, but which might give you a clue to how to do it.

At (6) on galley eight, Mr. Lobrano wonders whether nine times around on the Ferris wheel is not too many times for one ride. I can't remember.

At (7) on galley eleven, Mr. Lobrano says in his notes, "OK if author thinks so," about the double use of "knew."

At (8) on galley thirteen, a careful examination of the context makes it clear that Sam can only be Grandpa, but the reader does have to stop and figure this out, whereas if there were any natural way somewhere in the first twelve galleys that you could refer to Grandpa as Mr. Sam Ponder, this would be avoided.

At (9) on galley thirteen, are you sure that it's all right to have a throttle on that car? The throttle used to be on the steering wheel, and I think for

a brief period was transferred to the dashboard, along with the choke. But modern cars, of course, don't have any throttle and so it sounds like a locomotive. I think you could check easily enough there in Jackson, and it's the kind of thing that, if wrong, you would be bound to get letters about from devoted New Yorker readers.

At (10) on galley fifteen, Lobrano says in his notes, "<u>What</u> was Bonnie Dee Peacock?" You'll have to read back extremely carefully to answer this question. I take it to mean that it was the surprise De Yancey had for Miss Edna Earle, and that the surprise was that Bonnie Dee Peacock had married Uncle Daniel on trial. It would read a lot easier if you changed it to something like "But you haven't heard yet what I have to tell you about Bonnie Dee Peacock!" or some such thing as this.

At (11) on galley nineteen, Lobrano says, "This seems to mean that Uncle Daniel was served before anybody else was even called to the table. That right?"

At (12) on galley nineteen, he would appreciate your considering seriously this sentence that Uncle Daniel had outgrown the habit of giving presents. It seems, from the previous galley, that he still empties his pockets to the children, and of course at the end of the story he has given away his entire bank account. Perhaps it is a question of phrasing here.

At (13) on galley twenty-three, Mr. Lobrano says, "Why 'evening'? It's nine-forty-five in the morning."

At (14) on galley twenty-eight, he says, "I wonder why on the running board?" You haven't said what kind of car Miss Edna Earle drives. If a coupe or a roadster there wouldn't be, of course, any other place for Narciss to sit since Uncle Daniel was usually along, but do you want to explain this matter in any case?

The note on galley thirty-eight is not to you, but to all those—proofreaders, printers, etc.—who will leap upon Dr. Lubanks and say, "My, what a fine boy am I!" Let us both pray that it will get into the magazine correctly.

<div style="text-align: right">Love,</div>

<div style="text-align: right">Bill</div>

P.S. You don't have to justify any disagreement with any suggestion or correction on the galleys. Just cross it out or say "no" or something simple like that that will save you work.

Eudora Welty to William Maxwell, November 2, [1953]

Dear Bill,

This came along all right and I hope it's back as soon as you need it. Thanks for the notes, and also for all the carefulness everywhere. I yield to The New Yorker in punctuation for knowing better than I do, except in a few cases where I restored the dash for reasons of Edna Earle's speech or character. She's essentially a lady of dashes, I think, with lots of afterthoughts and sudden additions to what she's saying, and not a lady of the considered semicolon, and where it was a question of the little mark or the character, I chose E.E. I don't <u>know</u> how many times you get to go around on the Ferris wheel, and nobody I ask does either. Nine sounds like a nice number. In little county fairs I'd guess it was optional with the operator of the wheel. About "<u>Good</u> evening!", it prevails in this section as a comment meaning "You're a little late coming up with that, aren't you?" or "Fancy seeing you here," or the like. "Pulled out the throttle" is just an expression to me, and I believe I've heard it used just that way, meaning to take off in a hurry; but if it's worrisome, you could right now change it to "stepped on the gas," and it would be all right with me. I'm grateful for the observations on the number of tables in the dining room (I had seen it as one big one in the middle, which was always used, and others, 2 or 3, around, never used, which was meaningless, so I deleted the others and left the one.); (how's this punctuation?*%) and DeYancey's meaningless remark over the telephone, which I fixed; and on the reference to Grandpa's name since the day he died, which is cleared up now. Yes, Uncle Daniel started things off by being served first. Narciss <u>liked</u> to ride in to town on the running board— a sport, but I also think there was no room in E.E.'s Ford for her. Oh yes, I tried to make it plainer about the time sequence on galley 7. Fixed Grandpa's name early. I don't see any easy way, or too much use in looking, to explain anything about "Grandpa used to make short work of them," because it's plain enough immediately—the next paragraph goes on to say they're always together. Oh yes, I cut the troublesome "lighting from the country," which didn't matter that much, and inserted the "tried to" in Uncle D.'s giving something away over again.

Once more the New Yorker's helped me on book proofs, and I'm ask-

ing them if there's time to fix the two or three little places in the story where words are changed, but it's in page proofs, so there may not be time. But anyway, I'm grateful.

Must dash down to mail this—again thanks for the work on this, I hope nobody has headaches, Mr. Lobrano or you, or even the man who would have wanted to change "Mr. Lubanks" and got stopped. Love,

Eudora

Before The New Yorker *or* Harcourt, Brace and Company *had brought "The Ponder Heart" into print, Eudora asked Bill, Emmy, and Mary Lou Aswell if she might dedicate the book to them. All were honored by this request and were delighted to accept.*

William Maxwell to Eudora Welty, November 4, [1953]

Dear Eudora:

We are both so happy to be identified in your mind with that story, and the story with that afternoon, and so touched, and if you think it really would be Uncle Daniel's wish—but who would know better than you what his wish would be, and on Tuesday we are going to Mary Lou's for supper in honor of everything. Make no other engagements, so you can be with us in spirit, and if that is too far, where would half-way be—Cincinnati, Memphis, Pittsburgh? Shall we meet and congregate in Marietta, Ohio?

The galleys arrived this AM, and are now on their way to the printers. You were wonderfully patient, and "play like" shouldn't, I have it on the highest authority, be hyphenated, and everything is I think as you want it, and your "fixes" were excellent, and there is no question but that Miss Edna Earle is a lady of dashes, and the entire makeup department wants to thank you for getting the galleys back so promptly. And don't, if you can help it, remember the distinction between restrictive and non-restrictive clauses.

Gruss an Aachen had better wait, I think. It would need watching over. I have tried not watching over rose cuttings and it doesn't work. The Cherokee is now about four feet long, and if it survives the winter (because this

time I can't protect it all under a mason jar) should reach the wall in time to start blooming with Silver Moon. The house has been painted a better pink, and I hope you will be here in June, to see the grandest effect of our summer. This weekend we are covering the roses and next weekend closing the house for good, I think. So that is what I mean by not watching over Gruss an Aachen. I would try it in a pot in the city, but hardly anything lives there, because of the gases, and a rootless cutting probably wouldn't have a chance.

Did I write you that we had a dinner party, in town, for Kenneth Younger and Mrs. Y, and the Shawns (first time entertained ever) and the Urquharts. Brian Urquhart is in the UN, in the Secretariat, and when we went to London last April he wrote Mr. Younger, who is an MP and was in the Labor government, to ask us to lunch in the House of Commons, and he did, and so we heard Mr. Churchill misunderstanding something and Mr. Atlee putting him straight.[35] So they all came to dinner, and we had eggs en gelee and a baked ham and spinach and your watermelon pickle and Bavarian cream pumpkin pie (ask Emmy for recipe) and they all wanted to know who made the watermelon pickle. Floribunda spent the evening with the Dodsons on the first floor, and Albertha served. We ate in the bedroom (first time) and after coffee went up on the roof. I'm not sure how the Shawns enjoyed it. Where to draw the line between not having the boss to dinner. The wine was Pouilly Fumé. I could live on Pouilly Fumé and your watermelon pickle. The roses did not come with the ambassador, so are now to come with sailors and sea captains. The time is coming when I will have to do something about that novel. This winter or never. It has gone on too long and could go on forever.[36] It has rained and rained twice, and the well was up four feet so I took a bath and we flushed the toilet and the first thing we knew there wasn't any water in the well. Now, being more judicious, we space it out through the day without having to haul from Mrs. Magee's faucet in milk cans. But should we do anything about a well is the question. The attic floor has exhausted my imagination. If there were a dowser, I would start to do something, but I feel there should be a dowser. When you come again we will take you to the Baptist Church Road Baptist Church. In many ways it is inferior to the China Grove Baptist Church but the graveyard is nice and there are chandeliers. The part time minis-

ter dragged the Christmas carols and so I never went back. I hate a dragged Christmas carol. Before my voice changed, I could sing. Soprano. In high school, Freshman year, we sang the soldiers' chorus from Faust and when we came to the highest note of all they let me do it, and I wouldn't be at all surprised if that isn't why I can't sing now. Not even Go Tell Aunt Rosy, Her Old Gray Goose is Dead.

Love,
Bill

William Maxwell to Eudora Welty, [Late November 1953]

Dear Eudora:

How kind of your mother to root a Gruss an Aachen for me! Now if it can travel up to me in the spring with you as escort! I know those Thomasville tea roses, by catalogue only, but have ordered Lady Hillingdon for the spring (from there!). It is sometimes hardy, I've read, and in Paris I saw a climbing Lady Hillingdon which was so beautiful. S de la Malmaison you must tell me about, because I keep hesitating about it. It reads so temptingly, and I think it is hardy. Joseph Mitchell[37] said one of the things he liked best about The Ponder Heart was the fact that in telling the story Miss Edna Earle always named the roses people were wearing. "That kind of woman would," he said, nodding very seriously. And then burst out laughing because it was so many years since he had heard "looked like the last of pea-time," and he never expected to read it in the New Yorker. The Irish roses haven't arrived yet. They were—as I guess I told you—supposed to come in the diplomatic pouch, but weren't dormant when the diplomat took off, and are now presumably coming by sailor or sea-captain, to be smuggled in. If they do get here, they will surely be the most romantic roses. The ground isn't frozen yet. Also—did I tell you—I am thinking of growing some delicate roses like Gloire de Dijon in tubs. The ground is getting crowded, and it might be an interesting experiment.

The French novel I have put aside—suspecting that it is a kind of trap—because I always enjoy taking it up again so, and enjoy working on the detail, whereas the truth is that it is only partially there, and if you are patient in time the missing part comes to you. Instead I'm trying to enlarge an un-

successful story. The missing part of that came eventually, and maybe it will round itself off. If it does, I'll send it to you.[38]

All we have seen in the way of theater is a dreadful amateur performance of [George Bernard Shaw's] The Simpleton of the Unexpected Isles. The cast was excruciating, and there was one good person in it—making a very queer effect. Tell Elizabeth to tell her little sister for me that I will send my regards to her just as <u>soon</u> as I know her name. She wouldn't want me to do it not knowing, would she?[39] And I am hoping that someone will think that I am just the person to give The Hill of Devi to, for Christmas. If they don't, it will be all right, because I can trade in the Joyce Cary that Harpers is sure to send me, because I have told them I can't read Joyce Cary and they don't believe that such a person exists, for it.[40] I read sections of it [The Hill of Devi] in manuscript, but not the whole, because somebody here had tried an intricate selecting job, telling the story of the Maharajah, which didn't work out. You can't, of course, monkey with Forster. I wish he had bestirred himself, though, and made a novel of it, as he would have done, no doubt, if Elizabeth had been at his chair.[41]

You know, I had several times tried to see what The Ponder Heart looks like, in the magazine, and each time I fall into a trap; I find myself reading it instead of looking at it. You will have to tell me, I guess.

Emmy says she thinks Valley Mill Flour is nice just to touch, too. I'm glad it turned out to be what your mother wanted. Will you ask her to dictate—the next time you have occasion to write us—<u>her</u> method of making rose cuttings root. The Cherokee is my one success. It was about four feet long when I covered it with straw and dirt, for the winter. How easily the mind slips back to roses.

Floribunda is expecting a visit from the vet, this afternoon. She has ear mites, and has been treated three times, and is better, but gets into such a state in the taxi that we are trying having the vet come here. To the house, I mean. I'm at the office, waiting for Mr. Truax to come upstairs from a conference with Mr. Fleischman.[42] Mr. Truax is a dear and very funny man, but he is also full of reiteration and it stretches conferences out interminably. . . . Well he came. That summoned him.

Before the waters of Christmas close over me, let me say one more thing.

Do come in the spring if you can. Your place is in the inmost petals of our affection and we miss you.

Bill

Eudora Welty to William Maxwell, [Late November 1953]

Dear Bill,

It was wonderful of you to send me that copy so fast—how surprised I was, and not least to know that the New Yorker ever exists as a "Rough Copy"—I thought it came out like Athena. The story was in there when I got it, and it was when you sent it, so Q.E.D.—Ponder Heart exists. I don't read it, but I pick it up and feel the weight of it, and so I know we're safely over the moment of publication. I hope you're not all worn out with it for Christmas. Thanks for the nice long letter—so glad to get it, and I will answer it rightly, this is just a note to say thanks. Or is it? for we have been planting roses all morning—here they came, just as usual, an hour before a storm. Trust Thomasville doesn't ignore your shipping date as it did mine, they sent their roses by return mail, last week, and then in came some from Armstrong today along with Mr. Hennessey's Gloire Dijon etc. (though we asked for them for "after Dec. 1")[43] What is the official Oregon opinion of Mr. H? And Maxwell opinion? Anyway, I too had been looking for a Gloire Dijon and he has it. Put it on the garage wall along with "Beauty of Glazenwood," which is described as yellow flaked with red and the rose always seen on old barns and walls—also named "Fortune's Double Yellow." It's the one you see from train windows, I feel—do you know it?—Also the Thomasville roses arrived pruned away back, and shipped dry in an old box, no wrapping around the roots. I fear for yours from them.

Yes, I will send the local method for rooting of cuttings, but I think it's just the general one—anyway it takes well but then we are able to do it in the fall of the year, and you couldn't get that good start on them where it's cold.

I hope the Irish roses come in safety. Mary Lou and I know a lady who came back from there hung over with plants like a Christmas tree, she had on a rainy day outfit to get off the boat—many deep rubberized pockets and

boots on. But a lady might do that for herself, but would she for a friend—just any lady? It would have to be a trusted friend you asked, especially if the boat comes in on a bright day in June. For a boat present as she sailed off you could give her an Aquascutum, with hood. Then she could have flowers in her hair.

Oh, I hope for a trip there some day, like in spring. It's hard to know. My mother's sight is bad, and she doesn't drive or anything, and her amusements are getting so limited—reading's hard—that I hate to be gone long now, though in order to assert her independence, which has always been strong, she keeps bringing it up that I do take a trip. Will see by spring. I long to come, for I miss seeing you and Emmy, Mary Lou, and Diarmuid, or the prospect of it, practically every day. Give my love to Emmy, and love to you,

<div style="text-align: right">Eudora</div>

William Maxwell to Eudora Welty, January 6, 1954

Dear Eudora:

A sheaf of letters. The three page one, from Beloit Wisconsin, is from the darling girl who as a side line to being Mrs. White's secretary types my letters. She has only been at that job three months and I knew nothing about her except her office behaviour, but acting on a hunch, I walked over to Liberty Music shop and picked up your record. When she saw what it was, she made a curious abrupt movement that I have made myself under circumstances that mean only one thing: The heart has been hit. I thought you ought to see it, that it would hearten you.

We are both enchanted with the pecans from Mississippi, which bear the same relation to pecans in stores that oranges direct from Florida do. Emmy has certain recipes that she has been longing to put into practice clearly marked out in her mind, and I slip in and undermine them by a nibble each day. It was so sweet of you to send them, and we all, including Floribunda, were gratified to have you suddenly rise from the pile of gifts under our tree on Christmas morning. Because of course it brought you to us, lighted with Christmas lights.

Mary Lou is coming over this afternoon, after lunch with Nancy Hale.

Possibly they are both coming. Mary Lou has written a story about her Grandmother that might possibly work out.[44] If I can undo a little the work of her Grandmother—it is very well written but constantly preserves a decent reticence, a proper economy of detail, and what is reticence in our line of work but the only fatal mistake?

I ended up buying myself The Hill of Devi—books showered down upon us, marvelous and beautiful books but not that one—Emmy the Virginia Woolf diaries to read on the train going to Newtonville Massachusetts to Sandy Lobrano's wedding, and it was a nice wedding—that is, the bride was more interested in the groom than in how she looked, and she looked sufficiently like a bride, and the groom was patient and endured the attendant publicity, and they both skipped off into the night under a rain of pink and white (tell Elizabeth) paper hearts. Not rice. And we drove home in Jerry Salinger's jeep, arriving in 36th Street at 4 AM after eating wanton soup and egg roll and tea in a Chinese restaurant a little below Hartford. Emmy has been sick in bed since, with a sore throat brought on by talking about Hindu mysticism above the roar of the engine. I am more accustomed to jeeps, from riding to the station with Kirk Wilkinson,[45] and confined myself to remarks now and then, to spare my vocal cords. I am proud of us for having done it, at our age, and don't suppose we will or would again.

And before that (Jan 2) we gave a small New Year's Eve party: Emmy's brother, and a friend of his and mine, and friend's girl, and Margot Morrow;[46] and some French people dropped in, and left; but we sat down at the table at 8:30 and got up (except to leave the room during parlor games) at four, and it was the nicest party I ever went to, but that is partly because I'm so small town I don't really enjoy myself unless everybody present knows me.

The roses that I had all but given up for lost were still in Dublin, doing nicely, and they are due to arrive on the Irish Elm, some time in January. If the captain of the Irish Elm gets them past the customs and if the ground isn't frozen, you may yet get a slip, tell your Mother. Fortune's Double Yellow I have lusted for, but it wouldn't do in this climate. I ended up ordering such a queer lot: Mrs. Arthur Curtiss James, Nevada, Mermaid, Mme. Edouard Herriot, Fashion, Innocence, Dainty Bess, R. Moyesii, another R. Hugonis (ours only has one blossom every 2 years), another Donald Prior, Gloire de Dijon, Lady Hillingdon, Gloire de Mousseau, Mme. Gregoire

Staechlin, and I forget what else. (Paul's Lemon Pillar) More than there are holes for, I know that.

And Mary Lou says there is a prospect of dramatizing The Ponder Heart. If it does come about, don't let somebody else do it. At least, not without collaboration with you. In the first place, it would be fun, and in the second place somebody once started to do a dramatizing of They Came Like Swallows, and the first act was full of pregnancy jokes so I pulled down the curtain. But if you make a play of it (and I'm sure there is a wonderful play in it, all ready to step forth) that means you will have to come in the spring. See that you don't, like Krishna, neglect to come. Oh yes, we also discussed acting in the play. Mary Lou hasn't decided what part she would prefer, and I said why not Eva Sistrunk and she said you had already spoken for Eva Sistrunk. I would like to be Mr. Truax Bodkin, if nobody minds or has a better claim to that part.

I thought the Hill of Devi was a work of art pretending to be the material from which a work of art had once upon a time been made. Simply marvelous, from beginning to (and especially the) end. The injury done to Forster by Col. Wilson is so serious as to make him uncertain forever of the Rajah's affection; what more serious injury is there? And before he had been so sure he was loved! All, every protestation, every taking his part, makes the doubt a little deeper. Because the Rajah also loved Col. Wilson, and now look. It is so sad. "Not yet can they understand each other." And then that last sentence, after so many disowning and disclaiming the religious experience. As if Forster's mind had taken its stand confidently, and then been interrupted by a cry from his heart.

Well it's wonderful to be alive. Wonderful to be a writer. Wonderful to grow roses. Wonderful to care. Isn't it?

Love,
Bill

William Maxwell to Eudora Welty, January 11, 1954

Dear Eudora:

The reviews, the ones I have seen, are so excruciatingly stupid that I cannot bring myself to send them along to you. Especially Pritchett's.

Though all are praising, nobody happened to have any talent for that kind of writing. So few reviewers do know how to do it intelligently. You and Francis [Steegmuller] and Brendan Gill and Miss [Katherine Anne] Porter, about exhausts the list. Anyway, I winced my way through them, and wished somebody would have had the sense—somebody with his head on his shoulders—to say that The Ponder Heart is a comic masterpiece and let it go at that.

The copy of the book arrived on Friday, and guess what I did? Sat down and commenced to read it. I read quite a lot of it, in fact, before Emmy called me to supper. And again last night. Apparently it is like Huckleberry Finn—the more times you have read it the better it is. The pictures are very good as pictures—beautiful, in fact—but only partly right, don't you think? Uncle Daniel escaped him, and I thought of Bonnie Dee as being more stick-like, as to her arms and legs. After all, one does not expect a fairy to have curves. I didn't think the pictures injured the book. Only rarely have they helped.

That Emmy's and my name should be forever—because I feel sure it is going to be read that long—associated with it—that it should have been Uncle Daniel's wish—is a pleasure and satisfaction that I will never—<u>that I do not intend ever to get over</u>.

<div style="text-align: right">

Love,

Bill

</div>

Emily Maxwell to Eudora Welty, January 12, 1954

Dear Eudora,

I am so happy and proud to see my name on <u>The Ponder Heart</u>. We have both reread it in its latest incarnation, and it remains as fresh and surprising as when you first read it aloud. I like Mr. Krush's drawings very much in themselves, & they certainly don't bother the book, though illustrations always remind me how immaterial literature is. It's always a shock to the imagination to be forced into a mold, even a handsome one. The jacket and the title page are less explicit and very beautifully drawn, and Bonnie Dee behind the bead curtains is irresistible.

The pecans have been such a pleasure to us to nibble on with our

drinks before dinner. I cut something out of Sunday's paper called "The All Around Pecan", telling how to make pecan loaf, etc... but I think we'll just go on <u>eating</u> them, and put northern-bought pecans into loaves.

We are having a lovely January, reading our Christmas books (V. Woolf's <u>Journals</u>, Berenson's <u>Renaissance Art</u>), having our ice skates sharpened, enjoying 10 inches of snow & collecting concert & theatre tickets in our bureau drawer against February torpor. This afternoon we are going to see the new wing at the Metropolitan.

Pause... We have just finished a lunch of Welsh Rarebit, leek tops braised in tonight's stew, & beer. I feel like the Snowy Owl.

<div style="text-align: right">With much love & thanks for your delightful letter
Emmy</div>

Eudora Welty to William Maxwell, [Early 1954]

Dear Bill—this is just to say thank you for the letter you wrote, and the feeling you had about the reviews, & the letters you let me read, & at last the review by Granville Hicks—All sustained me & are sustaining me & I will write you soon, but I felt I oughtn't to have your mail down here any longer—how kind it all was, and she sounds like exactly the right secretary —you do honor me about the record—I'm so glad she did like it. I look for a free moment to write in, that's all—& I'm holding out not to write when it's a day like today. Just the patter of little nuisances—ridiculous! How are you? Is it still terribly cold? What happened to the garden, when will you know? I hope you & Emmy are eating the most delicious warm things—she told me about the leek tops. Love to her & I'll write soon, when I see how a little onion tart turns out with a new touch. Tonight.

Here the thermometer jumps up & down like an ibis—?—I mean from 77 to 28, is that like an ibis—& back up now. Doves sing, a lizard came out in the wall at noon, & the tea roses are still in green leaf—& they say down again tonight—

I love <u>The Hill of Devi</u> so, too—with that special feeling Forster gives of "at last!"—in its aching sense as well as all its other meanings. (That doesn't say it—) you feel he would never write anything at all until this way of being able to write it at last seemed the possible one. It's like a bridge over wild

chasms & overpowering beauty—a very good & calm bridge now, & you can come this way. Though he didn't—

I'm reading Virginia Woolf's diaries too but they're painful—to me—It doesn't seem quite right that they were printed—like this, anyway—But it's the feeling most diaries give—

I have to be going on errands, & sending much love will say goodbye—& thanks for these again & forgive my keeping them. Are you seeing any plays you like? Heaven knows what <u>Ponder</u> will be but I'm told we can trust Mr. Herman Levin. Just now I dream of coming up in the summer & looking over the shoulder of whoever's putting words in Edna Earle's mouth— You be on the other side, & we'll take fountain-pens into his ribs when he makes a mistake. How is your story? Love to both, Eudora

William Maxwell to Eudora Welty, February 25, 1954

Dear Eudora:

To answer your letter paragraph by paragraph—I haven't respected Pritchett since he reviewed Francis Steegmuller's life of Maupassant and while he was at it pretended that <u>he</u> was supplying the interesting new facts, not Francis, that made the book important. People who would do that would also suck eggs.[47]

The Irish rose is still in Ireland. Mrs. Brennan, who is I have come to think a force of nature, decided (quite sensibly) that an ocean voyage might be hard on a rose bush, and so she didn't give it to the captain of the Irish Elm, after all. She is sending it by plane, but how you smuggle that large an object off a plane I wouldn't know. Meanwhile, the two—for there are two—bushes are in her back yard in Dublin doing fine. I sometimes wonder if possibly—but now No, I don't suppose she is merely waiting to see what May Wettern looks like, do you?

Coriolanus is seen, and was excellent—a very gripping play. Ondine is to come.[48] The Nutcracker was overpraised. I have been writing, but it has been slowing down. And of course we are living in such a drama, from day to day. Today was the blackest. I do not expect anything so bad for some time to come. There is a receding from the bloody act, until the consequences take architectural shape, on which a worse deed will be constructed. The

watchword is November. We have this time to get them out of office, while there are still elections.[49]

Last Saturday we went to the country, to see a well man, and the tips of the daffodils only were showing. The rose bushes were still dormant (I hope just that) and the air was like a Shakespearean song.

I'm sure Rubinstein was eating a lot. Josef Lhevinne always ate a lot.[50]

About our coming. Your asking us to come with Elizabeth Bowen was such a compliment![51] This is how things stand. I have three weeks in the summer, and we expect to go to Oregon, to visit Emmy's mother and father. But sometime during the year another week is coming too, by a new policy of the magazine, and it has to be taken in the winter spring or fall. If we should get a baby from the Cradle, I will stay home and help Emmy get squared around. If we don't, we think of coming down to see you. It would be in the fall, after the hot weather is over. Would that be sensible?

I said to Emmy that your letters had a sad overtone ever since the publication of The Ponder Heart, and she said, with her much greater perspicacity, that they have had a sad sound ever since you went home, having just discovered that you could be happy living in New York.[52] Perhaps we are both imagining.

The talk all day long has run on the subject of assassinations. So gloomy.

<div align="right">Love,

B</div>

Eudora Welty to William Maxwell, March 31, [1954]

Dear Bill,

Just a little line to wonder if you'll be there in May? I hope to come up for a week or two in the summer, as you know, and it turns out there's a ticket for Ondine for me on May 11, secured by my kind unknown friend the producer, Mr. Levin, that took Ponder Heart. So I guess that sets the day. What I hope is that that doesn't happen to coincide with the vacation to Oregon.

How are you both? Is it spring yet? It's bright and full of green here—a Climbing Charlotte Armstrong this morning, just beautiful. Dutch iris are

over and the bearded coming. Smells fine everywhere. I'm trying to get my book of stories all typed up and put together. How is the novel?

Love to Emmy and you, happy spring, and luck. I hope everything's going well and to please you. If I leave here Eight-o-May (Emancipation Day) I'll see you soon, provided you haven't emancipated to Oregon. So tell me the news.

With love,
Eudora

William Maxwell to Eudora Welty, April 5, 1954

Dear Eudora:

We will be here in May, and be prepared to shout above the sound of the well-driller. In my mind's eye I see you coming with that little Gruss an Aachen that there is a place all ready for—in my gluttonous mind's eye. And we have tickets for Ondine on May 10th, so we can compare notes. I thought of you coming, just suddenly. I said, in the middle of the night, it is almost time for Eudora, if she is coming, and she must be, on account of the play. We go to Oregon in July. Spring was here, until the end of last week. I had barely got eighteen roses in the ground, and turned around three times when the thermometer dropped to twenty-five and stayed that way all Saturday, filling me with alarm for the old roses, which were partly uncovered, and in bud or leaf. So I covered them up as high as I could, and that night it went down to 10. I don't think any of them were killed, but it can't have been very encouraging for them. Fortunately, I hadn't uncovered the Cherokee, which has spent the winter in straw under dirt, looking like a child's grave; as if we had buried a child at the foot of Silver Moon. It should bloom this year, if it is all right. So in the midst of everything, Mr. Hansen came and said he couldn't shingle (for somebody else) so he might as well dig the asparagus trench he had refused to dig before, when I beguiled him with cups of coffee and admiration for all he was doing under the back bedroom. Well in the end, it turned out that Mr. Hansen had bit off more than he could chew, and together we dug and planted asparagus, seventy feet of it. There is news of sorts—The Cradle is sending someone in May— maybe you will coincide with them—but they hint at giving us a preschool

child, rather than an infant, and a preschool child we wouldn't have had to go through nine months of this and that to get in the first place, and what Emmy wants, naturally, is something in the smaller size. Well, something will happen or nothing will happen. I am working, happily, and think another five years will probably see my novel completed. Meanwhile, the real pleasure is working on it, not having it published. That's the state I'm in.

<div align="right">With love,
B</div>

Eudora Welty to William Maxwell, [Late April 1954]

Dear Bill,

Just a little note to say that rose in hand, I'll be there Eight o'May (Emancipation Day) and also that it turns out my date for Ondine is May 10 too, and I bet the seats are all next to each other. Your letter had good news all through it—I hope the Cradle is coming through with triumph of the right age and size, and the novel goes on & on in happiness. It's hot here now, everything is deepest green, and the following smells are in the air: rose, jasmine, honeysuckle, iris, daylily, and chinaberry flower. Finished up my little collection of short stories at last and sent it in—the name of which, as I see it now, is The Bride of the Innisfallen. And if people buy the book thinking it is by somebody across the water, that is their hard luck, say I. Love to you and Emmy, and see you soon. I'm going to be in Hotel 33, have you ever noticed it, at 33 West 51? Trying it. Luck and love,

<div align="right">Eudora</div>

William Maxwell to Eudora Welty, May 3, 1954

Dear Eudora:

Now isn't that wonderful that we should all be at Ondine together. When we left Yorktown Heights yesterday afternoon the lawn was apple blossom petals and dandelions. The lilies of the valley didn't make it (the first of May) but the bleeding heart did. I think the title of the collection couldn't be better, and did you know I own, and keep always within reach in my office desk, the longer version of that story. I never could decide which was

better, because I love both.[53] When you get here we will have news for you. We have it now, but I think it is nicer for you to be crossing the country toward news.

Love from us both,

B

That the rose, the rose is coming—that news, too. I hope it doesn't weigh you down, but I can't find it in my heart to suggest that, if it is too heavy, you leave it home.

The Maxwells' news was worth traveling cross-country to receive: Emmy was pregnant, and the Maxwells' ardent desire to become parents would come to pass without the need of an adoption.

Following her May visit to New York, Eudora returned home to prepare for her role as a faculty member at the 1954 Cambridge University Conference on American Studies, and she also briefly ventured to Madison, Wisconsin, to receive an honorary degree from her alma mater, the University of Wisconsin. Then it was back to New York to board a ship for England. In Cambridge, she delivered three lectures, including the now well-known "Place in Fiction," and afterward she traveled to Wales.

Eudora Welty, Harlech, Wales, UK, to William Maxwell, August 17, 1954

Dear Bill,

I hope all goes beautifully. I've thought of you and Emmy as being mercifully in the country and out of the city heat. The opposite has prevailed in England—the five weeks I was in Cambridge were cold & rainy every single day but the last day. That is, I would call them cold and rainy, but the English distinguish them, they're heavy, close, thundery, damp, or hot, in addition to being cold and rainy. I had a strange time—did the work all right, I guess, and met some darling people, but it's not an experience I'd choose to repeat—lecturing. The outside things that came my way were all fun—I'll hope for a chance to tell you about it, in October when I get home. I sail on Sept. 24, the equinox, by way of Bermuda, on the Britannic.

I came to North Wales on a journey of respect—in Cambridge a young

man (teacher) named Alun Jones, now at Oxford, brought me some Welsh stories to read—he had great trouble finding a copy of an old Penguin collection at Foyle's, as the Welsh don't get published much in England. "We show our stories around to each other, and the Welsh magazines print them, but we aren't much occupied in getting them published elsewhere." Anyway there's a writer named Gwyn Jones that's simply a marvel. Some of the others are too, but this man is an experience. I asked Alun Jones if he'd think of making a collection of these stories by the best Welsh writers, that I could show publishers in America, and the light that came in his face I can't forget—he is passionately fond and proud of them, and he says in England there's not even anybody he can talk to about them. I think they are as good as, or better than, Frank O'Connor, for instance—enormously vital and beautiful. You can see that Dylan Thomas was just one of a whole country of that. Jack Fischer was in Cambridge for a lecture and I asked him if he thought Harper & Bros would be at all interested, just to sound out somebody, and he read the little Penguin collection (it had been a Shelter Library book) and asked if he could take it back to America—he wants to print the one by Gwyn Jones in the magazine.[54] Well, that's fine, and the thing is Gwyn Jones has written dozens that good or better, and is still a relatively young man, I gather—lives down further south, not sure exactly where. He does something or other for a living—teaches school maybe and edits "The Welsh Review," I see. I thought of how you would enjoy reading him and think I'll send on ahead a little second-hand book that I've just found and begun on. And I wanted to ask what you thought, about this boy doing all that work. Jack Fischer is not specially a fiction expert, you know, more non-fiction, and I thought I would ask you and Diarmuid for insight. I couldn't stand it if he went ahead and did all that work and wrote a preface and all, with maybe nobody to see it and enjoy it, and nothing back from it. He's very poor, and I think has a wife and child. He says he would love to do it no matter if nothing ever happened—of course!—but I wanted to get the facts to tell him now. After you see some samples in the book I'm sending, I'd be glad if you'd tell me what you think. Heavens! but they can write. I thought those stories were worth coming to England for.

After changing trains madly all day I came into Harlech about 6:30 of an afternoon and it was like coming into the center of a big jewel—all of

it glows, mountains, sea, dunes, castle, clouds, hedges and stones. This is where Branwen, of the Mabinogion, happened—by the way Gwyn Jones has just made a new translation of that and it's not like the Lady Charlotte Guest's—where if you come traveling you stay feasting for seven years, with the birds of Rhiannon singing unto you.[55] I'm intending to stay 5 days—I'm at a hotel, of course, full of English come for the golf course that lies along the sea with Snowdon over it, but it's lovely to just walk and read and eat and sleep, after 5 weeks of what felt like a kind of exposure. I'm going to Edinburgh for a short stay too, rather mad traveling—then to Bowen's Court to see Elizabeth for 2 weeks, then back to London, then home. If you have time, send me a little line c/o Elizabeth—Mrs. Cameron, Bowen's Court, Kildorrery, County Cork—I'll be there the first two weeks in September. Much love to you and Emmy. I wish you could have seen the roses. They thrive in all that thunder. Is there any way I could bring you a cutting and if so, of what? I am always wearing a raincoat with deep pockets.

Love and wishes,
Eudora

Eudora Welty to Emily and William Maxwell, December 8, [1954]

Dear Emmy and Bill,

How are you, is everything lovely? I think of you—practically every day I expect to write you—oh, this typewriter is worn out on the lowest form of drudgery. Why not have a little fire in here, and draw up? Have things all gone according to wish and plan, in the house and toward town for Christmas and the baby? I hope everything's beautiful.

It was good to get to talk to you both and to see you, Bill—I wish I could have seen Emmy too and come to the country and seen everything that's changed—and all that's the lovely way it was too. Tell me. The well? The roses? The house? I made it up in my head on Hallowe'en by the previous pattern, and enjoyed that. Have you been listening to a lot of music and reading the cool days and nights, it being a little far along for picnicking? How is Floribunda? She <u>knows</u>, of course—did that day I came to hear the news for myself.

We've had a long, slow, warm, late fall, the leaves have stayed on the

trees and turned gold, the fields are colored too, and the sky in late evening puts a light like firelight across everything—I go the long way round to the p.o. I've been catching up on the house (kitchen painted, etc.), typing, reading proof on new collection of stories ("Kin" is the one seems to stand up the strongest to me now—I really love that story) and every day, taking my morning look at the avalanche of odds & ends, I say Today's just like yesterday—not a line till tomorrow. When I think of you, Bill, writing in the summertime with all that happening & going on, I'm ashamed. I've been reading your books again, to deepest pleasure. I wish you had more— it cheers the heart that will be so, soon. (I use "soon" in writing for everything I can count on ever.)

Our Thomasville roses had done well too—and had grown so well we had to move three of them not long ago. They were blooming up until just about a week ago, when a cold snap snapped. The camellia year isn't going to be worth a thing this time, owing to that too—after a dreadfully dry summer, the sudden cold whacked the buds—as doesn't ordinarily happen unless it gets much colder. However, those on the north of the house, oddly enough, are fine and full of buds—camellias are so temperamental. I have about 20 seedlings big enough to bloom a year from now—who knows? Chances are small for a good one, but it's possible.

"Oh, I dread Christmas!" my niece of 7 says. "After Christmas I've got to learn to write." She still believes in Santa Claus. I ordered her a fairy costume out of our magazine—crown, wand with star, and buckram wings with elastic harness. By the way I'm going to make you a little cake, fruitcake that is, and started to send you a wire saying which do you like best, white or dark? But realized that might involve a long answer. I'm making the light, for some reason because Emmy doesn't like gold in her slip covers. But this is to say it will come to the New Yorker because I've a feeling you may be in town by then.

I have the greatest wish to come up and see the baby! I don't know when it will be, but I balance the idea on my head to walk straight through a lot of stuff.

England couldn't stand the Ponder Heart, did you know? "Too mysteriously transatlantic" they said, then the rest was worse. Jamie Hamilton [publisher Hamish Hamilton] was depressed—a little like the prophecy—and

I do feel sorry for him because he had made a hurrah about it though he now says sorrowfully he wishes they could have brought me out with another, longer book, and I'm just cold to that. Of course I mind the bad notices but strangely enough they're just like the good ones, and don't seem to pertain to the work of the story. It's still just that and what a handful of people think that can matter.

Have you seen any plays? I wonder if The Boy Friend is as delicious as it was—to me—in London. Absolutely a dear thing. We saw a TV performance of Judith Anderson and M. Evans in Macbeth, but she looked like spinach. I doubt if you looked at it. It was filmed in color they said, but it came out in Jackson as black and white. They left out the wonderful recipe scene (should I have called it that—double double) and some other scenes as well. It gave no feeling of any stage—any frame, form, company—no figure size, no proportion came through. TV is so non-heroic, isn't it, besides all the other things it is—anti-heroic. It homogenized Macbeth all right—and with Hallmark greeting cards, too. This summer I'd got to see Macbeth in Edinburgh—in that stark, dark old Assembly Hall, with the family tartans and the pipes, and the horses moving outside on the cobbles, and real, smoky torches, and probably real Birnam branches—anyway, savage, austere, marvelously layered back & back. The distances that characters walk and that voices have to travel on a stage, and exits and entrances, all that to be lost because of TV! And when Lady M. carried out the candle, in her nightgown—you had to have that hall. She had to.

By the way, a baby I know, aged 1, witnessed that TV show from his bed and has been washing his hands ever since, trying to get out that damned spot, with a good deal of relish.

Let's write soon—I'm fine and looking forward to Christmas—and good news from you—and send much love and many wishes to you.

Yours,
Eudora

3

"Similar Discoveries"

FOR BOTH BILL AND EUDORA, family life was the source of meaning and joy, and at times torment. It was also a subject of their work. From late 1954 to early 1959, however, the demands of family limited their production as writers. After the births of two daughters, the ecstatic pleasures and nagging worries of parenthood were at the center of Bill's life; the pleasures of travel with her nieces, the need to help her mother through eye surgeries and recuperations, and efforts to support her brother Walter as he faced a devastating illness preoccupied Eudora. Then in January 1959, both Eudora and Bill faced the deaths of family members: Walter Welty and William Maxwell Sr. Eudora's relationship with her brother had been a loving and devoted one; his death was pure loss. Bill's relationship with his father had been more distant and complex. For Bill, grief would prompt the reconsideration of old antagonisms.

During these years, there was little sustained time for writing. Eudora's collection of stories *The Bride of the Innisfallen* was published in 1955, but she published no subsequent fiction in the fifties. Although she struggled with two long stories, she completed neither. Bill published a story and ten fairy

tales, but his work on a novel proved frustrating. Still, Bill felt that he and Eudora were making "similar discoveries" during this time, and those discoveries—about gardening and writing, friendship and family bonds, love and mortality—would eventually enrich both their lives and their fiction.

William Maxwell to Eudora Welty, December 19, 1954, Telegram

BEAUTIFUL LITTLE GIRL BORN THIS MORNING EMMY IS FINE=
 BILL=

Eudora Welty to Emily and William Maxwell, January 1, 1955

Dear Emmy and Bill,

First letter—it's that baby that makes me think of the New Year. I wish it a happy one—also you both—it's surely that now and that only piles up the wishes.

It was wonderful of you to send me Colette—also psychic. I'd ordered it to send a friend that was homesick for France, for Christmas, and it had to be sent before I could read it—I was feeling nobly disappointed—then here it came upon the waters from you. You know I love her. I still have not had the chance to read it, refusing to do so in the confusion. So it's still to come— what could be a more delicious state and I thank you right out of it.

Oh, if only I could have been coming to New York—but that will be in the spring, I think now. What a beautiful age the baby will be.

We had a nice Christmas—fine day, narcissus open in the yard, a few camellias—bright and warm. Too warm—you know what the roses are doing, putting out. This was my niece Mary Alice, Elizabeth's sister, on Christmas Day in her angel costume, in which she gave out the presents in great heat. That looks like a Carmen Miranda hat but is really the magnolia leaves hanging on the door. She is a snaggle-toothed 7 and must look enormous to you. Anyway, to say Happy New Year with the right equipment.

<div align="right">

Much love to all of you

Eudora

</div>

William Maxwell to Eudora Welty, January 8, 1955

Dear Eudora:

I am in exile; in the study or behind a gauze mask by day, and on the living room couch by night. The New York Central switched on some cars without any heat in them, last Wednesday morning. It isn't serious, in that I'm not miserable with it; am dressed, in fact. But it presents a constant danger to Emmy and the baby. And today is Saturday, and Monday morning Albertha leaves, and theoretically I take over. Fortunately it is not nose, but only throat and chest. So maybe all will be well by Monday.

It was an inspiration on your part to decide in favor of the white cake. Emmy doesn't like the dark ones, and neither of us has ever tasted anything to compare with this one. Will you sometime send the recipe, as reading matter and to treasure.[1] Emmy says it is of the same incomparable order as your watermelon preserve. It was a pleasure—still is, because we are stretching it out—to all of us. I don't know how you managed a work of such monumental proportions before Christmas.

Christmas was a footnote—on page after page—to the baby's birth. After the third day, Emmy had the baby in her room until evening, which meant that nobody could come and see her during the day time but me. But I couldn't come until the middle of the afternoon because I had to go to the New Yorker in the morning, and I tried, at odd times, to do a little with her mother and father, so that, on the whole fortunately, I think, she was able to be quiet and sleep and nurse the baby in peace (except for a monstrous nurse, about which we will tell you when you come) and in the evenings, all three or four, including [Emmy's brother] Humphrey, were there sometimes, and I had to go to a piano recital of a protégé of Humphrey's—a Negro named Eugene Haynes, who has first rate talent—at Town Hall, so that all that week I felt bobbing up and down contrapuntally like a Bach Fugue. I got them both, and Albertha (coloured, from New Orleans, who cleans for us in town?), home a week ago last Sunday. The baby—Katharine—will be three weeks old tomorrow morning at 10:24. She is still beautiful, and hungry, in an erratic way—anywhere from three to five hours and sometimes six is <u>her</u> schedule—and good (She cries only in the early evening, beginning about six-thirty as a rule, which as anybody knows is a very melancholy time

of day; Emmy regards her crying as a reproach, which I'm sure it isn't, be-
cause the baby is gaining weight, and says it is like a knife through her head.
To me it sounds more like Ravel. And like a loon that used to inhabit Gust
Witt's pond, about two miles down the creek from Bonnie Oaks, where I
did part of my growing up, in Wisconsin.) and clever: she has, and in fact
did at an early date, full use of her thumb for sucking. Some babies never
do, I gather, and those babies get bad marks in manual training and sewing.
But perhaps there is some mistake here, because the earliest picture of me
in existence shows me with my thumb in my mouth, and my marks in man-
ual training were frightful, mostly because of a hexagonal lamp stand that I
had to do over and over. The footstool was smooth sailing.

Albertha has been extraordinary. She has no children, though married
about as long as we have, and to see her and hear her with the baby is some-
times heartbreaking. This morning she was lying on her bed holding the
baby over her face, like all the mothers in the world, talking and laughing,
in that New Orleans accent. But it has been wonderful for Emmy, who has
had a chance to rest during these crucial two weeks, when the milk gets
established, because Albertha keeps the baby in her room at night. And,
somehow, cooks and cleans and does the washing and reads and fails to
solve the Tribune scrambled towns puzzle owing largely to an insufficiency
of reference books. At first it made me feel I was living in the past—not
only because we had a servant then but because we loved the servant and
the servant loved us. There is a catch in it, of course—the classic catch:
she is spoiling the baby, so that when she goes, on Monday, we are going
to be in for trouble. But not at all the kind of trouble we would have been
in if we'd had a baby nurse. And who knows whether it isn't more impor-
tant that the baby be picked up and see the world face down from Alber-
tha's knee. If love is what makes them sprout, she's had it. One night Emmy
sat up out of a sound sleep and reached for the baby, who was two rooms
away. And two hours later, Albertha started wandering around the room
in her sleep, searching for the baby, who had been put back in her bassi-
net after nursing by Emmy, instead of by Albertha, as usually happened,
so Albertha could sleep. All I do, of course, is drop delight on her, which
she fortunately doesn't seem to mind. Until this miserable seclusion, I got
to carry her from her bed in the back room, to the chair and ottoman in

the living room where Emmy nurses her in the day time. And carrying her back again, I would feel that little head collapse on my shoulder, and turn against the side of my neck. In my youth I was continually susceptible to ecstatic pleasure of one kind or another, and sometimes I have thought I must have overdone it, because it seldom came any more. But here it is again. So I don't know what to think. Or about love, either, since it is possible to be so dippy about a little thing that doesn't know you exist. She knows Emmy exists—because her little hands, which are marvelous, come to rest on Emmy's face or thumb or breast—and Albertha, because Albertha can make her stop crying. And my time is coming, of course. But I will be glad when she is big enough so I can squeeze her. Mary Alice seems quite squeezable, if you can catch her, I mean.

If you are coming in the spring, come in May, so you can see the baby <u>and</u> the Austrian Copper Briar.

<div align="right">So much love from us both,
B</div>

P.S. Her eyes are now hazel, which means they will turn brown, doesn't it? She gives all the appearances of being blond, but I don't see how that could be, and probably it won't. We haven't got around to the middle name yet.

Emily Maxwell to Eudora Welty, January 31, 1955

Dear Eudora,

Yesterday, at three days short of a venerable six weeks, Kate alighted on a happy plateau, where she enjoys her baths and our jokes, and sleeps after dinner which she rarely did before. Her smile is so lovely and funny, and gives us such excessive pleasure, that she smiles again at our reaction, and we react again to her smile, and so our life goes. It will be such fun when you come to see her. I hope she won't be too big—she already is getting chipmunk cheeks, which she inherits from me—or from my baby pictures. Now she's belying what I've just said, because it's after dinner and her eyes are bright and she's talking to herself.

Your fruitcake was as unlike any other as your watermelon pickle was— it was more like an idea of what a fruitcake should be—all fruit but only the

rarest & best of fruits—And it was good to have something from your hands. I only like the parts of Christmas that people make.

Bill is hurrying me to take a nap, because Kate still eats once or twice in the middle of the night, and also lately we've been catching mice on the kitchen stove, and that noise and the necessity to dispose of them (let them free to go back in the basement & from thence straight to the stove again) takes care of the interstices between feedings—

With much love and everything happy for your coming year—

Emmy

Eudora Welty to William Maxwell, April 4, [1955]

Dear Bill,

She thinks and feels, that's what she does—the minute I saw the picture I was glad on the side of Emmy's sheltering arm coming down. You know how happy I was to see Kate, both times—three weeks, 2 months, both lovely, and the difference! She looks (I have her out before me (have never put her back in the envelope)) so ready to be seen in the flesh by absent friends! I'm so pleased she's wearing my cap on her visiting day. Thank you and Emmy for both these pictures. But the last one! That beautiful regard in her eyes for what's around her. (I believe she's going to have judgment.)

This is just a little note, I'll write later. The news here is Mother got along fine in her eye operation, and the doctor is now able to say that he thinks she'll have "pretty good vision" (instead of "pretty good vision," as his early prediction was), so that makes things much finer around here. This was an eye she hadn't seen out of for 30 years, and nobody knew what lay back of that cataract. Seems miraculous—a little more vision each day. It's the eye she'll use when the other is operated on, also for cataract—and until then.

Are your roses safe? Ours had a desperate blow—they'd been standing up like little pipe organs, all in full bud and the blooms beginning, when the temp. dropped from 82 to 28 overnight, and they were all of course frozen through. We had sort of timed Mother's operation on when those roses would bloom, so she could open the eyes on all that. I don't suppose the

bushes are killed to the ground, but to tell you the truth I haven't looked yet. Fortune's Double Yellow though had already come into its earliest flower and I think it's the loveliest little rose I ever saw in my life. You know it, I think—I never saw it until this bloomed. The colors of the summer rising moon, that flaky pink on the soft buff yellow that stops your heart. And the fragrance. I think I will name my novel after it—had sort of thought I might. (Not written—just bloomed.)

How is your work coming? I long to hear all the news. I hope it's good. Maybe the roses hadn't even started, owing to late freezes and wisdom.

I may get up after all in May and see Kate, if my mother gets fitted with glasses by the end of April, as expected, and can see well enough to be by herself a while. I won't know till the glasses are tried. I'd like to do some work. I started to say "while I'm on the trip" but that may be a state I'm getting into—lately I've been saying to myself, Now while you're disposed of getting the wash done and these errands over, I'll have a free afternoon for writing some letters. Probably Kate will cure me. Mrs. Josephson wrote me from the Am. Academy she was asking you for the Ponder ms., and so reported they're giving me a medal for it—I think that's lovely and in the spirit of Ponder.[2] The playwrights came down here in the middle of the hospital, practically—and left a version of a draft of their play that I only had time to read last Saturday night and it confused me a good deal.[3] I know I was a seismograph, though. I'll tell you about it when I see you. They didn't make it dirty, or anything, the [way] those did "They Came Like Swallows." They made Uncle Daniel a self-conscious innocent, diminished Edna Earle to nobody and gave all her lines to Uncle D., changing the person. Bonnie Dee is made to think up her own financial arrangements and legal status. There's no feeling of the town for Uncle Daniel except "Everybody likes to see a good man cut down to size," which is the opposite of the right feeling. Oh well, it's just a draft. It's written for "parts" and they speak of Tom Ewell for Uncle Daniel—I've never seen him, have you? The men were nice—especially Mr. Joe Fields—and they did come all the way down here, which must be extraordinary for Broadway writers. The version came before the trip, so maybe something changed. I wrote them that I thought the texture was thin and would have to be thick, and that everybody had to love Uncle Daniel, and that he couldn't stand up there naked explaining himself, and that

when I said Bonnie Dee could make change, that was the extent. Of course it's <u>their</u> play!

> Much love to Emmy and you—thank you
> for the pictures. That little face!
> Eudora

William Maxwell to Eudora Welty, April 4, 1955

On the train[4]
Dear Eudora,

When I came to "a patchwork quilt going like a camel through the yard next door" I burst out laughing, and everybody for seats around turned and said "What's <u>that</u>?" Such a <u>pleasure</u> this book is![5] Also Kate's first book anybody ever sent her. It makes me hungry for a manuscript of a new story by you (though there are several in the book that are new to me) that I can see turning into galleys and page proofs. Speaking of which, a lady told me in strictest confidence (I went home and told Emmy) about the Howells medal, and wants to exhibit the galleys, ms. (carbon, actually, is what we have—nobody, it seems, knows where the original is) page proofs et. al. It's all right with The New Yorker if it's all right with you.[6] They do themselves honor by giving you that medal is what I say. I am terribly pleased, and part of my pleasure is knowing that if I took a gold leaf off the ground and pinned it on you by the stem it would make you just as happy as giving you a gold medal. It would <u>be</u> a gold medal, of course. While I was reading just now I thought how beautifully alive your sentences are—like Kate, when you hang over her, and she begins by smiling and then her shoulders start moving, and then there is the tremendous explosion that is her legs and you think she's getting ready to fly. Your sentences are reluctantly on the page, as she is reluctantly on the bed. You must come soon and help us love her.

I have succumbed to the diaries of Will Hennessey.[7] I even bought <u>Hennessey on Roses</u> (defective copy—just when you get to what to do with peat moss) and ordered Angels Mateu, Dainty Bess, and Irish Fireflame, just to show my feelings. He sent 2 Dainty Bess (I never got a <u>good</u> gift rose before) but held back the other two till Fall, because he didn't have bushes he was

willing to send to our climate. Will you be here in June, do you think? For the grand opening?

The roses put in this spring are Agnes, Golden Wings, 2 Dainty Bess, & Duchess of Wellington. Still to come: Gloire de Dijon (for a time: it won't stand the climate), Mermaid, Black Prince, White Wings, and Rose à Parfum de l'Hay. As usual I bit off more than I can chew, what with three clematis holes and a peach hole still to be dug. This practically the last (except for an occasional replacement)—The collection is as complete as I have the strength for. Yesterday it rained all day, and I worked on a story, which isn't right yet, but has possibilities.[8] Emmy's life with Kate has to be seen. Come see it.

<div style="text-align: right">

Love from us both, and our delighted thanks for the book.

You know how much it means to have it <u>from</u> you,

B.

</div>

Eudora Welty to William Maxwell, April 27, 1955

Dear Bill,

Thank you for your train letter, and the little one after when our letters had crossed—I meant to write right back. I was so pleased to hear from you about stories (how did the one turn out you were writing?), all the growing that was going on, indoors and out, everything. Thank you about the medal, and let's all pin leaves on each other in June, to celebrate lots of things— I think I'll be there to take part. Can I possibly come and see Kate one day in the first week of June? The doctor yesterday said all was going quite well enough for me to be away a while then, and a plan sprang whole from my brow to do it. I think I'll be in NY from May 23–28, then go to Ohio for a weekend to a college that asked me some time back (Western Coll. for Women), but after that—and even if the previous part falls through—I am as sure as I can now be that I'll be in NY for a week in June, maybe longer. I know that life with Kate has to be seen. Also I'd love to see the grand opening in the garden. How are the new ones? I bought that book by Hennessey too, out of succumbing to him, but I was disappointed because I think his wife corrected it. It's not what his catalogues are by a long shot, is it? His roses are beauties that he's sent here, and have all done beautifully, and he's

sent us 2 Helen Traubels the way he sent you Dainty Besses—and he has so many of the roses you <u>want</u>—the question is just is he going to let you have them. Your new ones sound so lovely, each by each and together and I wish I were smelling now Rose à Parfum de l'Hay.

Just today the little teas burst up into bud again—that is, Malmaison, Pink M. Cochet, D. de Brabant, and Safrano, but G. de Dijon and Fortune's Double Yellow think once was enough—they'd been covered with buds before the bad freeze. Today Rosa Mundi is blooming. Also Silver Moon.—Not a burst, just a few thoughtful blooms.

Thank you about letting the lady at the Acad. have the galleys or whatever she wants. She thought I was crazy probably, because I told her you had the original, then when she said not, I told her to ask Giroux at Harcourt, and she called up and he didn't work there any more. I hope we wrote over those galleys enough to please her. You'd like a transcript I have that somebody lent me of a real trial. Such as

Q. What was the man's demeanor when you saw him?

A. You mean where was he headed?

And the nicest was the defendant's mother who said sure, she signed that account of things. "I stuck my name on it. But I don't say it's so."

If there's anybody that already knew (speaking of witnesses etc) how I wrote "No Place for You" etc. it's you so I didn't figure it was worthwhile to notify you I'd tried to put it down for Robert Penn Warren, who asked me to write about a story for a new edition of "Understanding Fiction." I stuck my name on it—but had the worst time getting it said. (No use saying any <u>more</u>.) I long to be writing a story. The new one of yours worked out all right, I hope—will that be something I can look at too, when I get there?

Much love to Emmy and Kate and you and I hope in a month from now and a little over I can see all of you in a row—I'll feel like some obstruction's been removed from <u>my</u> eye then, it will be such a bright sight.

Eudora

William Maxwell to Eudora Welty, May 11, 1955

Dear Eudora:

It didn't. The thing is, I never can get far enough away from the people I

am trying to write a story about. The next one I attempt I am going to imagine I am describing everything and everybody through the wrong end of a pair of pearlhandled opera glasses. I'll let you know how it works.

The first week in June will probably find me in an insufferable state of ownership of roses. You are the only person I have ever met to whom one can show roses not in bloom. Roses in bloom may bring on a rush of blood to the head. To both our heads. But if you can, call me in May, before you leave for Ohio. In the end, the lady from the academy didn't want anything. She had the galleys from Harcourt, and I wanted to tell her that what went on on The New Yorker galleys was the real thing, and pride stopped me. And last fall I had lunch with two old friends from Urbana, one of whom (Charles Shattuck) published a piece—not a story, I gathered—of yours called Ida M'Toy, and he said he had sent you some copies of the magazine—Accent, this is—and I wondered if you have any left. For our collection of you. He turns pale when he speaks of you. "Miss Welty," he says, white as a sheet, and all adoration. So good for writers, I always think, to be appreciated. Bea Steegmuller says that all Francis needs is for somebody to tell him every morning that he is a good writer, but it has to be a different person each morning; she isn't enough, and so she has given it up, except that she understands how he feels when somebody does. And other writers.

I've tried twice to reach Mary Lou, to tell her your plans, but by this time you undoubtedly have written her yourself, and Pearl said she would tell her.[9] The weather is such that Kate can wear her best pink batiste (I suppose; anyway it's very light and transparent) dress with white embroidery, slightly pulled down to earth by wool bootees, on all formal occasions. She loves people with low voices, and would prefer that strangers spoke in whispers. Perhaps we all would. But did you ever notice how often people roar and scream at babies, without any encouragement from the baby? I think it is so peculiar. There are buds on climbing Mme. Edouard Herriot, Harrison's yellow, the Duchess of Wellington, and the Austrian copper briar, but one half of one Fashion turned yellow, day before yesterday; waterlogged.* Making me anxious about all the others, which I had watered on the strength of some remarks of Will Hennessey, after eight days of no rain. Do you think I should persist in ordering Black Prince? Did you ever see it? I am beginning to wonder if maybe I couldn't make a fountain of Thor, in-

stead. So far, I have no bush or vine that makes a bushel of dark red roses, which I think we ought to have. And I have been putting plastic bags on all slow starting things, with remarkable success. All the notches burst into bud, on lilacs, peach trees, rose of sharon. But there is going to be a frost tonight, in Westchester, and I just got the peppers and tomatoes in. Paper will save them, I guess. So happy about your mother. Come soon. Love from us three,

B

P.S. I read the Virginia Quarterly piece again for the third time this morning, on the train.[10] It gives itself gradually, as a story does, or a piece of serious music. Because it is so condensed and witty, for one thing. And because you seriously are trying to say everything there is to say, with each sentence. You do realize how good it is, don't you?

*I now think maybe a magnesium deficiency.

**Kate has been mildly valetudinarian (heavens, the thing slipped out), but fortunately she didn't know it: a dry racking cough, which amused her, and a degree of temperature, which brought on a lovely color and lots of smiles. Temperature is down, and steam kettle made her room smell like a nice ferny cave, and Emmy said every time she sat down and nursed Kate she felt as if she were giving her medicine, which of course, she was.

Eudora Welty to William and Emily Maxwell, June 29, [1955]

Dear Bill and Emmy,

That day was so perfect, and as they say about the right roses, it has keeping powers—I held it coming down in the train, and have still got it. Kate I think of every morning and when I wake up expect she's already been enjoying life for two hours—and will have a height to every day, like her walk raised on shoulders through the leaves, and of course she's had time to change more and more and still has more Kate-like pleasures and feelings attached to the day. I'm so glad I got to see her that very day and those very moments of it—I don't need to tell you she's beautiful, but I enjoy it so— she is beautiful. That Berenson word just fits her, like her little sunsuit— she's "life enhancing." I wonder how we got so many delicious things into one day—I think because time stretched out—I for one never once thought

of train time or felt the slightest responsibility for it—not while we had Kate, roses, strawberries, Colette, conversation, beet greens—but I won't let a list even appear to be forming over the surface of that pleasure—so think of my thanks like a little spring. I hope all is still going as beautifully as ever—with a tent now.

How is the printing of the speech coming? I long to read it.[11] And hope all the writing these days goes to please you both.

My mother (who is most gratified to hear of the Gruss an Aachen) went back to the hospital to have a little minor follow-up operation on her eye, only to have it become for some unaccountable reason infected, so she's had a week of antibiotics, drops, doctor visits, etc. It seems to be under control now and the doctor—a good one—thinks all will slowly come right with the sight. But I felt that was trying her too far.

We've had bright hot mornings, cloudy, thundery, sometimes rainy afternoons, cool nights. The H.T.s [hybrid tea roses] are mostly spent for the time being, but the little bush of the Duchess is full of pearl pink globes every morning. On account of the rain is mostly all threat, have a good deal of watering to do, and am behind. Just now the west is navy-blue but the sun's still out, and the shadows are lime-green. Mother knew Spanish Beauty under the other name of Mme. Gregoire Staechelin, and late last night I was pleased to read what you doubtless know, that [Spanish rose breeder] Mr. Dot crossed it from Frau Karl Druschki and Chateau de Clos Vougeot. We've got the mama but not the Chateau, though Hennessey has it ("Chateu de Clos Vought")—"Put in a small greenhouse and be greatly pleased." Pernet–Ducher—"the progeny of unnamed seedlings" (Mod. Roses)—I'm sure you've read every word, "dbl., very fragrant, deep velvety red overlaid garnet," but helplessly go on, "sprawling"—though Roy says "such a slow grower," though I suppose it could be both—"a slow sprawler" then. (This sentence was a rambler.) By the way in case you <u>haven't</u> got the 54–55 spring catalogue from Hennessey, you ought to read it because that's his real style, not corrected by his wife, as he brags his book is. I enclose sample. Incidentally he must be wrong about calling that rose Cl. Daily Mail—that and your Madame Edouard Herriot are two different subscriptions entirely.

The two holidays must be near by now. I hope you have the finest time all three, happy journeys and good weather. Good luck and love to you and a beautiful summer.

<div style="text-align: right">

Yours,
Eudora

</div>

June 29
P.S. Coming down through Tennessee the train track was one long lane through wild pink roses — Must have been Pink Cherokee.

William Maxwell to Eudora Welty, November 3, 1955

Dear Eudora:

Emmy says every four or five days "Have you written to Eudora?" and I have, of course, in my mind. And three times I have started to call you long distance, in spite of knowing what the telephone does to you, but decided that it didn't make sense. And probably I know how things are with you, but we both so hope that they are better, and that your mother's eyes are responding to the treatment and that there haven't been any more of those frightening infections.

Kate went to the doctor for her smallpox shot yesterday, and the nurse tore her out of Emmy's arms, undressed her (screaming) weighed her, took her height, and returned her half an hour [later] to Emmy saying, "She doesn't like people, does she!" Emmy could hardly tell me, she was still so angry. Who Kate doesn't like, of course, is that nurse. Emmy is weaning her. The cup at noon, the breast morning and night. So far so good. It is interesting to watch. I think E is the one who is being weaned; she is docilely giving up the marvelous isolation and delight. I don't think Kate intends to for one minute. She may put up with the cup at night. But when that cup shows up at breakfast there is going to be hell to pay. She is a very passionate child with an incorruptible sense of what she has to have, because she wants to have it. Though she cannot walk, to my astonishment this morning, I saw her get down off the bed safely this morning, feet first. Emmy had taught her how to do it. She crawls, she stands, she moves from chair to sofa. I turn my back for half a second and she is drinking my whiskey sour.

She is especially fond of bones. Chicken bones, lambchop bones, marrow bones, steak bones. After she had chewed on one so long she turns to me with a fond expression and rubs the bone in my hair, or offers to go havers. Her hands still look like starfish, and her laughter is as beautiful as Emmy's. Did you ever hear Emmy really laugh? It's like the fountains of Rome. There are only two or three people who can produce it, and I'm not one of them. No, that's not right. I have produced it, but unintentionally. She was laughing at me. It's also like the cups on the pantry shelf.

I used—borrowed is more accurate—the china night light to describe your stories for the New Yorker Christmas book ad. <u>Does</u> it exist or <u>did</u> it? The one with the Fire of London in it, I mean.[12]

I am expecting Cl. Crimson Glory, Angels Mateu, Irish Fireflame, and something else from Roy Hennessey. I ordered Cl. Mme. Henri Guillot, and he begged me not to ask him to send it but to trust him, and so I had to, this once. You won't believe how high Gruss an Aachen is after all the rain this summer, and still blooming.

Did I write you since we came home from Oregon? On a letter I never mailed I know I told you that the roses there are as big as peonies, but that nobody I met loved them the way we do. And did I write you that Jerry Salinger is expecting a baby—Mrs. S, too, naturally—shortly before Christmas?

I can't finish. I have to run. But I can tell E that I wrote you, and you will know that we are thinking of you. Love,

B

Eudora Welty to William Maxwell, November 4, [1955]

Dear Bill,

Thanks keep flowing your way—even if invisible. It's excellence that <u>really</u> buoys up the heart—and when it appears to you in such spontaneous, quick, beautiful and signifying dress, it brings true joy. And of course when it's fulfilling an expectation too—What a gratified reader you had in me in that speech, as well a moved and a joyous one. I think it's far too valuable a document not to spread wide. Not that I don't love it in this little booklet all its own—but I'd like to think of more people getting to see it than may know how to get hold of this. Hol[l]iday [bookshop in New York City],

I noticed, will let you have it, which is good—but do you know whether publication in some commoner form is likely?[13] I treasure my copy, and it brought back the lovely day with you and Emmy and Kate and Mary Lou when I got promised it, and the memory is attached to my copy, like a piece of binding, to touch when opening.

How are things with all of you? I was worried about the floods and storms that plagued Westchester, and comforted my mind, perhaps falsely, that you were too far west and too high up to get your house and your garden full of water. And how Floribunda would have hated it, about her feet. I started to call. I distrust myself even to ask an urgent question over the phone, from the morbid certainty that's just when I can't hear the answer. How were your journeys—what kind of traveler does Kate turn out to be? Delighted, I bet.—Oh, and I did wonder about that little brook we crossed and followed on walks—it didn't act up—or did it? And that wonderful brown house that stood over the water. I hope everything is well, all snug, all safe returned and home. Were the roses brilliant and the leaves just the same as they were that Hallowe'en I was out—just before that snow?

I've been so slow about writing, you might have wondered if my senses were working. Nothing is really wrong that won't be all right in the end, but Mother still has some infection in her eye, that got in some inexplicable way during the second operation in June—and we still treat it daily, hopefully, and still it flares up. It doesn't hurt—but she can't see out of it at such times. The worry is to get it clear before the other eye, which also has a cataract, fails too much to see by. Our doctor is fine, and is doing all he can. She is wonderfully patient, but it's a maddening way to live for an active person like herself—can't cut her roses, or read, or weed, or do much. I'm assured it will at last clear up—but the eye, having almost no circulation is slow to throw off any infection. How are your eyes and Emmy's and Kate's (bright!)—I have the habit of looking everybody in the eye and want to give most people drops. It turns out I needn't have felt such a specialist, as I needed glasses myself—noticing the new moon looked like a bunch of bananas two months straight is what sent me. This letter is my first effort combining the spectacles and the typewriter.

How is your work going? When you have time—I know how little there must be—let me know about yourself, Emmy, Kate, roses, novel, floods, news

—I send love to all but the floods—and miss you, but I don't imagine I'll be coming up yet awhile to see you, and Kate must be changing, changing—it won't be long till that girl is <u>one</u>.

The news on that play about Ponder Heart is all ridiculous & dismaying. I can't tell you how far the script has traveled from the story, but you can guess—or can you, I was surprised at first—the direction. Dialogue, which is interchangeable among the characters, is about being in bed, and has gags. The director, a man named Robert Douglas, was here five days, took, my car and went around the little towns, showed me the script his last day (how I marked it up! TAKE THIS OUT, all the way—but they'll just put in, I know), and went off taking the town buffoon to try out for Mr. Springer, a man whose specialty is putting on ladies' bosoms and singing with a record for (men's) luncheon clubs. [erased insertion] I can only say that this fits in perfectly with the script and he could play any part in it as it stands, especially Narciss, in blackface. It's supposed to open in New Haven on Dec. 28, I'm told—but I can't believe it can keep on to New York, can you? I was reminded of what you told me they did to "They Came Like Swallows,"[14] and though there wasn't anything in this story delicate enough to do that to, they've done what they could—both times to innocence, it's true. It's their choosing these stories that's so mysterious. My last hope is in David Wayne—do you know him? Is it true that he's a fine and intelligent actor? If so he might take a stand on Uncle Daniel, if he cares for his part. Well, I don't really worry too much, for it's all fate, as I knew from the start—it's been fascinating in a sort of hair-raising way to get a little education about the theatre world.

I'm about to try out Colette on Mother—It's not Colette who won't qualify, but the reader—I'm one who has to rely on conversation to keep listener and reader awake both—we're neither one talented for our parts—we have to keep to Jane Austen, Shakespeare, and detective stories (so confining!), and all the while Mother's despising to be read aloud to, she wants to see it. I'm the same way. It's really comic—"Mother, do you mean to say you slept right through that murder?" "Oh, well, I had foreseen it for a long time. Go on." We laugh our way through. You & Emmy, such experts (Proust!), would shudder but if you can suggest something I could try on her, tell me.

Did you see wonderful roses in Oregon, besides visiting and showing around Miss Kate? Did you happen to go to Scappoose? Mr. Hennessey wrote me about Cl. Ruth, which I yielded to his blandishments and ordered—blandishments? Threats—a little post card: "If you give Cl. Ruth a lot of shade and do not Forget that shade does not mean drying up by trees you will be very happy with it even tho it does need protection from frost or else it will freeze down yet I feel it is worth the effort with its huge orange blooms."

I also yielded to my sight of Spanish Beauty in your garden and ordered that from Hennessey under the name of "Mme. Gregoire Staechlin," which I hope is right.

Our roses are about to come out in their main fall bloom now, and look pretty well—and our camellias have buds as big as bobbins, some of them—so that will be nice. We've had the opposite weather from yours—had to water since June—and now there's a beautiful, though dry, fall—the streets are bright and the sky lovely above the trees.

Much love to all. Thank you for "The Writer as Illusionist"—the title, all by itself, is a stroke of magic.

Yours,

Eudora

William Maxwell to Eudora Welty, November 7, 1955

Dear Eudora:

When I got home one day last week, the day I wrote you, I found that Emmy had got tired of asking if I had written you and had written you herself. So all three letters were in the mail at once. It reminds me of the way Kate leans with love. If I hold her, she leans toward Emmy, and if Emmy is holding her she leans in my direction, thus keeping things going. She is a very loving child, and—I'm not sure there isn't some connection—not a bit interested in moral development. Perhaps it is too soon. Spock is silent on the subject—just says no pillows in the crib under a year, and no salted nuts. Artichoke leaves though are what she really loves. And bones.

Our new basement had eight or nine inches of water in it, because the gutters couldn't [carry] it off fast enough and I improvidently told Mr. Han-

sen to dig the cellar stairs right where they'd catch it. But an overhang is projected. The garden tools and fertilizers all got rusty and soggy, but no serious harm. The ground has been spongy for a couple of months. Croton Dam was vibrating, and that was exciting. But it hasn't gone yet. What you write about the dramatization of the Ponder Heart is worse than I expected, and I thought I expected the worst. It is no good this way. Next time anybody wants a play made out of anything of yours, tell [them] you'll do it, if you want to do it, and if you don't, tell them to go dramatize something by Herman Wouk.[15]

The thing about being read to and falling asleep is that the person being read to mustn't be lying down. I am, always, because there seems no reason not to be comfortable and besides if I were physically able to sit up I'd be reading to myself. Sometimes I not only fall asleep but answer remarks that people make in the story. Emmy like your mother has a tendency to sleep through climaxes, but only if she is lying down.

I am waiting for Hennessey's roses, and moving roses, and winter-covering, all at once. This year I am trying burlap windbreaks to see if they maybe won't die back less. And of course cones of dirt, all backbreaking. Esp. since the tender ones like Paul's lemon pillar need a couple of wheelbarrows to get them completely under.

Our eyes are all good, though Emmy has a tendency to styes if she sews at night. Kate's are by far the brightest, and the whites of her eyes are blue white, inherited from her mother. Thank God your doctor is good.

Novel comes to life, dies on me, comes to life, and dies. I wish it would do one or the other permanently. I hope the Colette you are trying on your mother is My Mother's House.

Mme. G. Staechelin is Spanish Beauty, as I'm sure you are only politely pretending not to know. But I have grave doubts about my Duchess of Wellington. It came from that unreliable Bobbink and Atkins. Why the most unreliable firm in business should advertise the roses nobody (not even it, as it often turns out) else has, I wish I knew. Do you know Clarice Goodacre? Miss [Sylvia Townsend] Warner is devoted to it. A. Dickson, but I don't know whether it is sold in America. I will envy you Ruth.

Nothing being done about the little pamphlet. It is in the Northampton and Holliday bookshops, and I figure if people want it they can always write

for it. I'm happy you enjoyed it. Terribly happy that it seemed alive to you. What I think of when I think of it is sitting at Newton Arvin's typewriter in his office across from the Smith auditorium and watching the people go in while I was still typing inserts in the notes.[16] It was, somehow, processional, like Meistersinger. And such a lovely, still, responsive audience. It wasn't that they listened sympathetically as much as that we gave it together. They were just as intent on it as I was. We had the experience. Then, afterward, when we had to separate, it was like a party, they were so nice.

So are you, to carve time out for a letter, just because we wanted so much to hear from you.

Keep everything as a memento is what I seem to have dredged up from my unconscious as a pressing parting message. Love,

B

Eudora Welty to Emily and William Maxwell, [December 21, 1955]

Dear Emmy and Bill,

Sitting out in the backyard—afternoon, a white half-moon—and your fruit cake inside—me, not the moon, though that speaks for where it could aim at, in its excellence. It's so beautiful and <u>cakey</u>—fine texture not lost for the maraschino cherry—and what <u>was</u> that—<u>marrons glacés</u>? It was all so delicate a combination of tastes—As you see, I opened it like a letter. It came like a letter, & besides it had a center of gravity, that means something to eat. When I got permission (going through Kate on the cover (She was willing for anything)) from your note, I waited no longer, and called Mother to have some. Those earliest home for Christmas have been fortunate—but I've been fortunate the most steadily—Really it is the nicest and lightest I ever tasted. How sweet you were to think of making it—I was, & am, so delighted—I didn't know whether its name was First Class Cake or Manna Cake—but Mother calls it Emmy's Cake which is more inclusive. Our weekly cleaning woman said "Have you the recipe for that nut-cake (sic) on the sideboard? I didn't take any, just thought it <u>looked</u> so good!" I of course let her have some—officially—in good time, she asked away before dinner—The recipe I have a feeling is your own original one—Our next recipe-swapping on Bill's typewriter, maybe I can copy it down? I'll try

to get mine into recipe form—it's not original, just a sort of anthology, from ladies—but it's a kind of child's play cake after that subtle one, and its virtue comes of living where the nuts come from—

Darling Kate! Brimming—Eyes—fingertips—look, over the table—herself every inch—I love the drawing. It's up on the mantle with a good view of the Christmas tree—

Everything must be wonderful this year! I'll be thinking of you on Christmas and imagining it with a border of snow, & with a hearth of fire (did I mean heart or hearth?)—It's our usual March-like Christmas weather here, after a spell of cold—mild, & fresh winds, & soft skies—Things are idiotically budding (spirea) & flowering (a small Etoile) & narcissus open down in the corners. Birds singing, & those awful fire-crackers we light in the South at Christmas are going off (why you can't read some of this). Bernice Bodey, a camellia, opened.

One day I did make something for Christmas tasting, & one day you'll get the little jar—Do you like Kumquat jelly? (supposed to be marmalade, but it all rose to the top). I packed it like the Crown Jewels, gave it a pilot's test simulating P.O. handling, looked, & it _was_ spilling. I left it out of that little box at the last minute, on the warming promise to myself I could bring it. It was the spirit of the thing—

I love Christmas this year! Things seem better here, & we get along fine—Friends are beginning to get home—In Jackson I belong to a bunch of old friends, half of us are old maids & old bachelors off teaching school or something, that have been spending Christmas together since early childhood, & all still get back for it—We have eggnog Christmas morning here—It's always warm, usually raining by nightfall, & we're still talking—

I sent some copies of The Writer as Illusionist away for Christmas, and all of a sudden I thought, like an inspiration, Bill Maxwell would love this! I'd just gone out by one door & come back another.

It gets dark so soon! (Forgot this was the shortest day of the year though)

It was lovely to get the letters. I like thinking of them all in the air at once, in an arc, like some Sassetta birds—¹⁷

Don't think I am sending [this photograph of] Virginia Woolf's house out as my Christmas card—this is just for you and one other & me. It is not when she was alive—it shows I think. But nobody was home, & so I thought

it would be all right if I took a picture—I didn't know whether it was better with the step showing in the gate, or what—Emmy will know.

I have to dash out & see my niece Elizabeth dressed up for a <u>dance</u>—Hold on, Kate!

<div align="right">Much love to all,
Eudora</div>

Thank you Bill for that paragraph from you about The Bride.—(It's a real night light but just one I saw.)

William Maxwell to Eudora Welty, [Late December 1955]

Dear Eudora:

I am minding Kate for Emmy (they both have colds) and so don't be surprised if a certain distraction creeps into this letter. Your presents gave us both the most extraordinary pleasure. The photograph of Virginia Woolf's house [in Rodmell] is so beautiful, so full of unanswered questions, and the fact that you took it makes it like a twosided gold coin. Of the two, I think the one showing the step is a little the better. But the other shows something that isn't in the first. Both are the best.

Distraction indeed, it's three days later. E's cold got worse, and I had to go to town, in an ice storm, leaving Kate to take care of her, which she did, bringing her books and kleenex, when requested to, and keeping her company. Both are better, and I can go on now to that marvelous Mrs. Cameron.[18] For some reason it is plate 49, Ellen Terry as a girl, who breaks, which breaks, my heart. She doesn't look like Emmy really, but the way her hair grows is like. And to think that such a public figure was once young and beautiful like that. And those bearded poets, each more inspired than the last, with such tarnished reputations. Darwin, on the other hand, you can see at a glance, is going to last. Can it be that regularity of feature is the key to the whole thing. Offhand I cannot think of anybody with regular features and real talent. Can you? And don't you feel that God neglected to bring father safely home? I am quite convinced that if I had been born in the reign of Queen Victoria, I would have had "aged 7 months" on my tombstone. My little tombstone. Having taken one good look around and decided that it was not for me. But there isn't a one of these people, regular featured and

otherwise, that I would have wanted to miss knowing. (one too many negatives) It will be a continuing joy to know them through their photographs. I do not feel, remembering V. Woolf's essay on Mrs. C, that she was as sad as that first plate makes her out to be. Though perhaps she would have liked to be. But a woman who accompanies her guests in a tea gown, stirring a cup of tea, to the suburban railway station shouldn't, by all the laws of human character, be sad.

I am—we both are—so glad to know that things are better "seem" must "be", or would you be coming up for the opening of the play, I tell myself. Mary Lou said, a few minutes ago, over the telephone, that she would be writing you this evening, so I won't go into anything but our satisfaction (lest confusions ensue) at the prospect of seeing you <u>and</u> the little jar of kumquat jelly very soon. (This is the way the gentlemen ride, tuddledy, tuddledy, tuddley... This is the way ladies ride, trup, trup, trup, trup....) From the next room. And fancy, Elizabeth dressed for a dance. She will surely end up in a novel by Jane Austen, don't you think?

I don't know how to tell you how much the photograph of Rodmell means to me. I live so much by these magical properties—how much my life as a writer depends on them, on the voice of artifacts. We will be living with it the rest of our lives. Now you must come and see Miss Kate. She is so precious, so affectionate, so <u>intelligent</u>. Emmy says I am not to go into your present to her, or the matter of recipes, so I won't. Except I must tell you that Kate is a great reader.

Love, from us three,

B

Eudora had not been in New York City for many months, but her mother's health had improved by the end of 1955. As a result, she was able to attend the February 1956 Broadway opening of The Ponder Heart. *Bill and Emmy, along with other friends, joined her for the opening-night festivities. Eudora, who had been apprehensive, found that she liked the production, and she fell in love with the cast. As a result, she returned to New York at the end of April, this time bringing her mother to see the show and to visit the Maxwells and their garden. During this visit, Bill was delighted to announce that he and*

Emmy were going to have another child. Eudora was again in New York in August, this time with her nieces. The Ponder Heart *had closed, but Eudora took the girls around Manhattan, to the theater, and to see William Maxwell.*

Eudora Welty to Emily and William Maxwell, [March 4, 1956]

Dear Emmy and Bill, I've missed you from the time I got on the train with the carrots. Circumstance seems to have grabbed hold of us. I read in the paper (late) about poor Gus Lobrano and think of all sorts of extra & troubled work coming from the office—all aside from feelings.[19]—We have company in the house—upstairs & down—first we were looking for them for 10 days, then we were looking at them—our own relatives from West Virginia—nice as they can be though—But I have a catch in the back from something & can't type even if they go out.—It's been so long I am ashamed. Every time I think of Kate it turns on a light, & such pleasure as I had seeing her, and you, is shameless—not writing to tell you just doesn't dim it. It was a lovely day—The weather always does something special outside to match inside, on my chances to see you. Remember that bright snow flying in the sun. And Kate walking, & laughing—in that blue. Ant and bee, and strawberries & wine, & music and coming. How are the rosebushes? I wanted to send you the crop of Gloire de Dijon—they aren't any prettier than they should be, but they are earlier than should be. Lady Banksia is also in bloom—Dutch iris below—Safrano blooming too—We ate the carrots, with tarragon & chives, and they were relished. I wish the rest of the lunch had suddenly appeared! When I was on the train back to New York, a lady from Buffalo riding beside me openly disbelieved me when I told her we didn't arrive in Penn Station—and she looked pointedly at my baggage—a can of carrots on my knee.—Oh, thank you for everything!—The play is still with me in a way. I saw it in circumstances blessed to me but hard on my friends—I couldn't have gone without you! The lines still don't connect with the story, to me, but the acting was something else—David Wayne put in so much out of himself that the boys [dramatists Jerome Chodorov and Joseph Fields] didn't even know belonged there. He is a terribly nice man, I think, and I wish he had a better play. The Lord only knew what he went

through on the road to keep out the Broadway gags that he <u>did</u> keep out. I
owe him the greatest debt. He has to play down & cancel out so much, all
the time he's making you think it's something else—I realized it when I saw
the show again just before leaving town—when the performance seemed
much more relaxed and the curious parts effaced in comparison, and quite
warm & nice—which was David Wayne—

When will you be going into town?

My summer plan has a date attached to it now by your college [Smith
College], Emmy—they're going to give me an hon. degree, and in June—
I feel terribly honored. The other thing I have to come up for, at Vassar, is
May 1—What I <u>wish</u> is that I could simply stay between the two dates in
N.Y. & quietly settle in. I hope to bring my mother at one end or the other
for as long as she'll stay—a week, 10 days, I should judge. She is getting
along all right but I don't like her to be by herself—and if she won't come to
N.Y. I won't consider staying there that month. It will be up to her wishes &
feelings, & she doesn't know yet. One thing I feel is that a little solid piece
of time away from here, like that, is getting to be almost necessary to me, if
I'm to get back to work. But it will work out somehow—

I didn't realize Gus Lobrano was so ill.

Friday. Cold blowy March morning, fire in the room, company gone, and
your letter came. Yes, too much has happened. How are things now? Kate
is saying apple. What a beautiful word! I have to agree with her. And I've
been sent Marianne Thornton to review, and I wish you were reviewing it
instead, Bill, you are the one. Forster is so marvelous with her.[20] I wanted to
tell you that Marianne—such a person—preferred in her reading of French
memoirs while laid up in France with a cold, "Mademoiselle, La Grande
Mademoiselle…she is perfectly exquisite, I hope you know her, if not let
me have the honour of introducing you—she is a most royal Boswell, but
the worst or perhaps the best is that she is Johnson to herself. During all
the last half I was afraid that I was taken in, for it seemed impossible that
a <u>woman</u> could have written it of herself."[21] There is nothing in the world
poetic about Marianne, and there is everything else—I'm halfway through.
This was on her first trip to France when she was 19, in 1816—Napoleon
ever so real.

I wanted to copy this mail for you—pencil-written from an RFD address in Miss. [There follows a letter from a Mrs. Roberts, telling Eudora that the "mythical" town of Clay in *The Ponder Heart* is not mythical but real, the place where her husband was born.] I thanked her and said I wished she could see the Ponder Heart and wished I could see Clay which I hadn't known existed. [Mrs. Roberts, despite a broken arm, then wrote back to give many more details about Clay.] This is such pure Mississippi—especially writing with the broken arm to a stranger—so touching, and so expected, to me—

Also I love people's punctuation. (Those parentheses are sort of flourishes.)

So many thanks and much love, and I hope things are working out all right everywhere. Thank you for the review that I found in my purse (so welcome to start in reading when that lady didn't believe me about Penn Station), and thank you for the clippings. I can never bear reading reviews of my books either, but this is reading things from the point of view of allegiance to a company of 34. I'd missed these items, but I'm keeping everything—again unlike reviews of books. In the library I look in everything up to the Rosicrucian Digest and the Illinois Central Trade Journal to see what they think of David Wayne, and enjoyed getting freshly mad at Eric Bentley in the New Republic—he's always so gloriously off-beam, so pretentiously off the subject.—Of course I realize now what was wrong with the whole project of the play, having somebody else writing it for me (not particularly that one, any play). That's nothing for a middleman to do, and no wonder it stood all our hair on end. All things that matter in this life are first-hand and direct and person-to-person. Our mistakes had better belong to us.

I'll write again soon. Much love to all of you,

Eudora

Eudora Welty to Emily and William Maxwell, [July 1956]

Dear Emmy and Bill,

How are you? How are Kate and the garden and the house—all well with much new added? My heart is with you, so's whatever of the mind operates, and you see I <u>have</u> a typewriter, no need for rescue again—but my expectation each day that I'll write to you is just like a rose in our garden,

comes out a lovely bud in the early morning, holds all day, then by evening when there's time to enjoy it, it didn't get gathered while I may and the heat's got it. I _can_ write an occasional stupid business note is the crazy part, it's you I can't write to, the ones I think of. Too much to say is the trouble always. I long to hear your news—I wish there were lovely things to swap with you. It's my visit up there that was the loveliest, and you know all about that. Mother glows to think about it too—it's a tie, who mentions it most, or first, in our house, but your names are being said so many times here, and we have the pictures. Besides being such joy it was triumph for me, the dearest ones meeting. Mother took the greatest pleasure in her trip I believe, and she liked all the friends of mine she met, but the day we were at your house is the most unfaded, I can tell. Thank you, all over again, for making it so perfect, it was perfect truly, and I guess we can all of us turn some thanks over to Kate, that little shuttle of happiness so busy back and forth. What are now her favorite books? Did she like the peonies when they bloomed— I remember she liked them when they were cushions. Did the new start of tomatoes come up all right and safely? And oh, what of the roses—Never a break in the Daily Mail I trust, but what of the others?

Is the novel all right?

The secretary and the new office are working out fine, I hope.

There isn't much news from here. Mother's eye that she uses is about the same, and the one she doesn't is about the same too, though it has fluctuations. On trial now is an air-conditioned room, one of those window contraptions like in the New Yorker office, to see if filtered air helps. It is boring to be a hermit and I don't think the experiment will be carried on much longer—it's just our own idea. The doctor of course is still prescribing too, and we're to see him again tomorrow. Ordinarily I get up early and do a half hour or hour's bit in the garden before the heat strikes, and it's best to keep all the sprinklers going all day, but today looks promising of rain. I have an air-conditioner in a room upstairs too, and expect I'll get some work done in it one of these days. It's been 95 and 96 the last couple of weeks, regular courtroom weather, Edna Earle would say. Figs look hopeful this year, after none for the last two, and just the thought of a bowl of cold ripe ones with cream on them for breakfast is worth all the rest of July to the undersigned. I

wish I could send you some. In the garden there's not much blooming these days but gardenias and a few lilies, the last daylilies, and the small summer roses in between the real bloomings. Not much goes on among human beings either—now and then a few of us go up to a little country hotel and sit on the upstairs porch and rock awhile quietly, having drinks in the shade and country stillness, or we sit in the dark in somebody's Jackson porch to talk & play records. There's something hypnotic about the steady heat and with the Cool Room, as the children call it, to run to and cool off, the way you run to a stove in winter, that's nice too.

Which of Elizabeth Taylor's books was it you hadn't read, Bill? A View of the Harbour or At Mrs. Lippincote's? The brain didn't work as to which, so I sent the two the other day, don't feel you must read them right away, until a good time comes. The pipes [a recording of bagpipe music] I've had ever since Edinburgh so you must have them now. I wonder what expression will cross Kate's face at such strange, calling sounds? I hope she won't cry. Of course she might do a fling. She might simply raise an eyebrow. She might go pull all those kitchen pots down again, the Lord forbid, for a noise of her own. And of course she might smile.

Do you know what E. M. Forster did? He wrote me a letter, to say he had seen the review I did of Marianne and liked it—it was so extra kind and darling of him because he must have known I wrote it with all the extra feeling of having been there at Kings when he was working on it, with Marianne all around the room, and known how hard it would make it to say anything at all—on top of one other little fact, that the book is a wonderful book.[22] An extraordinarily kind thing to do, and how much it is like him. He had got back from Greece—as I suppose Elizabeth Taylor has too?

A nice letter came from Newton Arvin, who said he had seen you. Mary Lou wrote a note the other day that she was well and working, getting along all right in Santa Fe. The fact of Fritz's being there, and the chance of the meetings always present, worries me some—just the fact, no matter what feelings have been put in certain compartments.[23] She is planning to come by Jackson on her way East in the winter, I think and hope.

I heard the most beautiful name—it belongs to a colored girl, Evergraze. Evergraze Hicks.

It didn't rain at all, just stayed very dark and still, birds quiet, nothing moving. I was sad to read about the death of Walter de la Mare, and knew you were.[24]

It's time to go—I hope everything is going beautifully for all Maxwells. It won't be too long before things are even finer than they are now.[25] Much love to you. Many thoughts, and some day I'll write you better. Thank you for everything. Here's love from Mother too.

<div align="right">Eudora</div>

William Maxwell to Eudora Welty, [July 1956]

Dear Eudora:

I know you didn't think you had some money coming to you from The New Yorker but you have, you did, and here it is. That clipping that you gave Sid Perelman he wrote a piece about, and here it is.[26] Not to be shown anybody but your mother, of course, and very funny, and he and I both hope fervently that the next time you come across a clipping that looks as if he might do something about it, you send it along.

The record [of bagpipe music] arrived unsat on, and has been played and played. Softly, loudly, with us outdoors standing under the study window, and for company. It is much better than any I have ever heard, and I so like the idea of sharing records, as you would a book.

Nothing very much has happened with the house. The foundation got done yesterday, six or seven weeks after it was promised, and we didn't nag or even complain about it, with the result that we are happy instead of bitter. The carpenters probably started today, and from now until the middle of September, there will be hammering and the electric saw. Kate wakes if you open the drawer where the rose pruning shears are, but slept through the cement mixer. It didn't interest her, being a girl, and the pruning shears do.

She is talking a blue streak. Sentences of ours handed right back to us, slightly bent out of shape but recognizable, and sentences of hers that you have to be her mother to understand. Emmy came back from White Plains with a rubber swimming pool—wading pool, really, and the back yard is full of children and parents and the general relaxed atmosphere, what with the mess of building materials all over the front yard, of somewhere south of the

Mason and Dixon Line, which I guess is where Kate is. So fond of people. And the roses didn't start blooming till the end of June, and are now—usually the blank month—simply splendid, the bushes enormous this year, because of the burlap, and covered with blooms and the blooms being eaten by Japanese beetles because I haven't enough of those little nylon bags to cover them all. But enough so that the house is full and running over with roses. Sometimes, of course, when I come on the shreds of one that was exquisite in the morning and raddled by noon, I have murder in my heart, but it was probably there already, and the beetles are a convenient drawing off of it. The Austrian copper briar is now about two feet high, and going to pull out of the disaster. Only one of the other delicate ones lived, but that gives me a chance to meditate and choose again. Crimson Glory is particularly fine, and the Daily Mail, as you surmised, came in.

I'm so glad you have two air conditioners. They had to change them at the office, and I got one to take home, and we're putting it in Kate's room, for blistering hot August days. At Mrs. Lippincote's is the one I hadn't read, and it should arrive in time to take on my vacation, and ideal for it. We are going back to the beach, near Black Point, where we were for two weeks in June, but the next beach down, for the first two weeks in August. Emmy and Kate were both benefited by the sea air, and this is Kate's summer of learning to love the water, as next December will be her year of learning to love Christmas. I finished the Forster book at Black Point, with an extra special delight in his own reminiscences, especially that page about his friendship with the childish maid. It seemed to me that, with his usual characteristicness he had set about rectifying a residuum of injustice—There was more to be said in favor of those terrible people in Howard's End than it suited the purposes of that novel to say. But having taken a whole book to see that justice was paid them, he inserted a single devastatingly honest sentence: It was his mother's people that he loved, and belonged with. I was left, as I have so often been left by him before, with my mouth open and my hands in my lap, deeply deeply amazed.

Your mother's dear letter made us both very happy. Now that she knows the way to our house, she must not wait too long before she comes again. Just long enough for the carpenters to pick up their clutter would be ideal. The novel?—Oh, I don't know. I haven't seen hide nor hair of it for weeks.

But I finished, did I tell you, a story which the New Yorker took, for next October.[27] And remind me to give you the Century Club recipe for stewed peaches. Love, and to you both, from all of us, B

Eudora Welty to William Maxwell, [September 30, 1956]

Dear Bill,

It was lovely to see you. The girls [Eudora's nieces, Mary Alice and Elizabeth] have their postcards in treasured places, and I still carry mine in my purse—giving myself the illusion it couldn't have been longer ago than yesterday we had such a nice breakfast and visit. It was wonderful of you. And practically on moving day at your office. How is it? It's nice to think of space, and help, and such comforts around you at the New Yorker. I'm hoping all goes beautifully at home. Not that I feel much trust in that carpenter, but maybe after Labor Day he threw a fit of work for you—You'll have to start moving things around in the new house, too—Kate's new house. Is Emmy feeling fine? I am so happy to have those pictures! The one of Kate on the wing is one of the most beautiful of her.

I got the girls home safely and in time for the school bell—all the promises fulfilled and then the unlooked for joys & surprises to boot, like our Algonquin meeting and morning—I felt we took your whole morning. For your future reference—except that you don't need me to say it—two girls are more fun than one on a far excursion—they do so much for each other to have a good time. The 8-year-old one still has that eye for the minute— Uncle Hubert, the children and I all had a meeting with Lehman in Sardi's, as you can imagine, our only sortie into there—Lehman got them a split of gingerale in an ice bucket, to pour into a cocktail glass with some fruit in it, and a filet of sole, and all Sardi's could do to accommodate itself to the young, and afterwards Mary Alice said "Lehman was right, there weren't any bones in the fish—but there were two seeds in my lemon."[28] She added that her favorite part of the lunch was the cottontail. Straight out of Peter Rabbit. Did I tell you she was refused admittance to the U.N. lunch room—she had to be 10. After mastering cottontails, chopsticks, a Marchi dinner (of which she just remembers the police dog outside) and all the

other national spots I took them around to, Elizabeth remembers as fresh as the day it happened going with you to eat Chinese, and how "Mr. Maxwell gave me his fortune." She loved being an old hand.

Mother was pleased to hear news of you and Emmy and sends love — she was so happy to see the picture too. We're having a terrible droughth (I cannot ever spell that word) and much watering must be done, but the days are so lovely, cool nights, hot days, fall winds full of falling pinestraw, and the moonlight and Marslight. I've let the roses get too much little twiggy growth and they are having chewer trouble, but after one experience with that Isotox that you know too well too — when you have to wear goggles and burn your gloves and shed your clothes after using it, I decided to let them do the best they could on arsenate of lead. Are yours still blooming away? Is your hand well?

You've probably heard that Diarmuid is in a hospital in Concord, Mass., after a heart attack on his way home from taking [his son] Will to school — he was in the house of friends, mercifully. He seems to be doing fine, feeling all right, out of pain, but recovery will be slow — I got this from Henry in a letter. I guess [his wife] Rosie has come back home now, Henry thinks so, to her job, so all must be going extra-well, wouldn't you think? I imagine Diarmuid must be the worst patient in the world — so dashed about it all — and I wonder if they even let him read. Awful to have happened far from home too.

When will your story appear, I mean real exactly?

I started working a little, in a fit of determination like the one I wished on your carpenter and plumber, but there's only a little order coming out of it so far. I hit myself in the ribs coming home in the train, tearing something but not breaking a bone, and though I've started breathing again I've only just typed a little, but all is mending too fast now to have an exam. Anyway, as you and Mrs. White know, it takes a typewriter, and even then I am a poor risk.[29] But for better or worse I'm going to get the story on paper. I hope your work goes with great energy and even haste, because it will soon be October. (Tomorrow.) Let me know when you can get time how things go and how they are looking. I hope all fortunately and blessedly and beautifully. Tell me what Kate is saying. (Have you ever made a little record of

her voice?) Tell me how Emmy is, and give her my love. Next time I see you, just think.

Mother sends wishes too, and love.

<div style="text-align: right">

Along with mine,

Eudora

</div>

Emily Maxwell to Eudora Welty, October 21, 1956, Note card with image of Animal Caravan, *paper and wood, 1882*

Dear Eudora,

We have a new little girl, born October 15th, two weeks early, thereby depriving Kate of a long look at the Central Park Zoo animals—but she's really still too young for New York & it would have been very difficult for Bill to have her all by himself.

We're taking the baby home tomorrow still without a name. She is small, even for a baby, black-haired, and dark-skinned, & so far very peaceful.

With much love to you and our warmest greetings to your mother—

<div style="text-align: right">

Emmy

</div>

William Maxwell to Eudora Welty, December 3, 1956

Dear Eudora:

In a fit of changing my life and becoming orderly, I put things into folders where they are out of sight, and, therefore, out of mind until the next fit of becoming orderly overtakes me. One did this morning. I opened a folder marked correspondence and in a sealed envelope addressed to you there was this absolutely mysterious communication. Do you understand it?[30]

The weekend was demoralized but cheerful. Beginning today, the play group—Kate's—is meeting every Monday, Wednesday, and Friday morning in our bedroom. So strange to wake up and see all those little chairs. And farm animals and trucks. The weekend was devoted to the making of the school room, and in the midst of it along came May DeLuca's father, who is a great big man who chews tobacco, with a truck full of laurel, rhododendron, and little pine trees, white pines, to make the front of the addition more homelike. Emmy was nursing the baby and I couldn't think what

to do with them, and Mr. DeLuca seemed to know what he was doing, so I let him—always a mistake in Yorktown Heights. He put them in a straight line—pine, laurel, rhododendron, pine laurel rhododendron, across the front, where they looked like the wrath of God. When he'd gone off to get some more, Emmy came out of the house and, since she can't bear classic balance, even on the mantelpiece, moved them around in her mind some, and what could be moved I pulled up out of the mud and moved, but the ground was frozen five or six inches deep and when I swung the pick nothing happened worth mentioning. So I waited for him to come back, and he did, and was very sullen about those wasted holes, night coming on, and this and that, but gradually he grew more cheerful, because E was right, and they now look lovely. A little snow fell on them in the night. They were given a lick and a promise, so far as planting and soil are concerned, and will need all the loving care from the sky that they can get.

The new baby is at last named: Emily Brooke, and called Brookie. It seems to suit her. If it doesn't or styles in names change and she doesn't like being called Brooke, she can revert to her first name, which God knows is pretty enough.

Kate is in her nocturnal period, which means that she wakes shortly after midnight and wants to be read to, wants all her books in the crib, but is persuaded, with a little rocking and singing, to go back to sleep until five thirty or six, when she does have all her books in the bed with her. Adorable, but how Emmy has had her hands full. How the washing machine and the dryer have been at it. And the procession of impermanent part time help. The kidnappers have gone, thank God.[31] They made me so nervous.

Mrs. White wants to know if you are writing.

Love,

B

In December 1956, Farrar, Straus & Cudahy published Stories, *a book containing three of Bill's stories, along with stories by John Cheever, Jean Stafford, and Daniel Fuchs.* Stories, *according to Christopher Carduff, was "the literary equivalent of a group exhibition of recent work."[32] Bill sent a copy of the book to Eudora, and in the new year she wrote back, commenting on his stories.*

Eudora Welty to William Maxwell, [February 1957]

Dear Bill,

I've meant to write, steadily with the days. Just now I saw Gruss an Aachen with buds. I loved so reading the stories more and more times each, and together. "The Trojan Women" was new to me as of this book, and gave its new pleasure. I still think "What Every Boy Should Know" is the most beautiful and moving of any of yours—and as soon as I pick out one, I want to say, wait. Not on "The French Scarecrow," because I'm not acquainted with part of its vocabulary, and (probably for that reason, ignorance) details bother me, like the elaborate eye of the scarecrow, that would fall into place and design if I knew how to read them in other ways still than I do. I don't know one thing about psychoanalysis and with the (I'm sure) proverbial ignorance of those who don't, I still think the writer's instincts—provided the writer is somebody like yourself[—]are a lot more trustworthy and com-municative. I'm not sure they do coincide, do they? or combine, always? I feel they must be parallel lines at least <u>part</u> of the way. (I remember the axiom, but I'm speaking of feeling.) I'll never forget the sight of the scare-crow sprawled by the furnace at the foot of the basement stairs—<u>that</u> haunts me, but through my understanding all right. There was a piece of paper in the typewriter all last week to write you, from the day I read your piece on the Woolf–Strachey Letters. It was like having a conversation with you about the book, for each thing we would have mentioned about it, I felt, was taken up, and I was joining in with you—like a girl I know here who talks <u>with</u> you, you both end up on the same word, which she is uttering right behind you, nodding as you try to rush on and beat her. I hope we still have the conversation. I've since read Clive Bell's book and he's even more maddening about not telling—have you seen it?[33] Only he withholds as much from laziness as from social prudence, I think—more. He says things like (this isn't a quote, just an impression) (à la himself) "The letter itself is, I daresay, at the bottom of one of four or five tin boxes resting this moment in the library at Charleston"—wouldn't it be fun, he laughs with you, if we had it here! But then this isn't a real book, is it, he laughs, because either I've written about Virginia before or given all my ideas to someone else, and was glad to, of course—or because this isn't the right time, is it, to be tell-

ing. Or he's forgotten exactly, or wonders what on earth became of that? Or, unfortunately, he didn't go. The English really are a remarkable race, aren't they—the oddest anywhere, I have a feeling, really complete strangers in some surprising ways. Such extraverts about sex for one thing, in conversation, behavior and all—for instance, the printing that letter from Lytton to Virginia. They would hold back on who was tipsy at a party, but publish that. I'm not sure I go as far as you in thinking it was let damage Virginia. Their protective mechanisms are absolutely unlike ours I feel at times. But I don't mean to sound like the people who wrote the other reviews, besides yours, of the Letters, who all made me so impatient—"such was Bloomsbury" indeed! Such were they, Lytton and Virginia.

How are the girls? I hope Brookie is perfectly well these days, and nights. Kate must have a lot to say. Will you thank Emmy for me for her sweet letter, which I am going to answer soon? I think of all of you so much. Just now I was wondering why I'm such a terrible letter writer and decided it was probably because of a feeling, more of a wish, that a letter should be written to a friend only on the kind of day the friend would be happy in, bring news of interest appropriate only to the reader of the letter, and arrive only at a moment when he was ready for it. In which case when could I write to you that I'm real tired, think I've pruned the roses too soon (but can't cut off those buds, either), have warts on my typing fingers probably inviting psychoanalysis, the very thing I was having something to say about. Oh what nonsense, but the truth is I write letters out of homesickness to see my friends and often it's too strong to get down to brass tacks—which is probably just what my warts are. If this sounds like a bad case of spring fever, it is—our spring is two weeks ahead of time, with redbud out, spirea, quince—the camellias suddenly over—all the rose bushes in at least red leaf, the pink hyacinths coming up over the blue—wild yellow jasmine. It's sometimes like Beaulieu in the backyard, in the morning, warm sun under the wall of the house and climbing roses, delicious cool fragrant air—not the same fragrance, but equal—and clouds in the sky that give the impression of coming in from the sea.

Did Hubert Creekmore happen to come in to see you? I must guiltily report that he wrote to me a month ago saying he had been talking to someone at The New Yorker about possible work of some kind there, and

would I write and remind you that you had once met, should the thing come to your attention. I don't know when, possibly once with me, as he is an old Jackson friend and my niece's uncle Hubert. I am ashamed if I mention it too late. He is the author of several books of verse and three novels, has done editing for New Directions, free-lanced, brought out some good poetry anthologies including the Scribner one of World Poetry which has some of his own translations. He is a nice man and perfectly able to speak for himself, yet I should have written as he asked, and then.

Are you having time to work? Soon it's going to be time for those roses to go in those holes. Excuse me for sending you this Bibb lettuce seed, but I just had to. I ordered it from Max Schl[ing] for our garden but it's arrived far too late to be planted here, and I promise never to ask if it froze. I'm sure if anyone could coax it to do well in Westchester, it would be between you and Emmy who could do it best. Just big enough bites for Kate to pop in her mouth—maybe.

I'm still writing a too-long story, at intervals, not clear and no title, so not really mentionable. Mary Alice wants it to have a title, you know, (my niece) so asked, what's it about? I said about a family reunion. "Well, call it 'The Family Reunion.'" I said I couldn't. "Then—if you don't mind a title that's a little long—The Reunion of the Family on the Hill." Sounds to me like a story about rabbits, and she's just about right, a cast of thousands.[34]

I must go and let you go. Mother sends love to all of you. Her poor eye is still allergic and sensitive to everything and only one of her strong constitution could keep on being sane and good. I'm down on the YMHA program for April, end of month, but whether or not I come depends of course on how things go. We are trying a new drug, results yet to be seen.

Do you know of a young girl writer in England called Bridget Brophy? Knopf sent me a paperback, did they perchance send you, of a new novel by her, and while I thought the novel lacked some desirable things for novels, the writing seemed so fresh and young and immediate and sensitive and especially adaptable to short stories.[35] But I don't know if she's written any. Mrs. K is the one that sent it and I wrote and asked her, but of course she didn't answer the question. (I gave a quote & she said thanks, we will make full use.) I've never met this formidable lady but was sorry somehow she was

the one publishing Miss Brophy. I thought for another Irish lady down from Oxford she outshone Iris Murdoch and she's younger and not pretentious.

Did you know Howard is printing my Christmas card to him in the magazine? It's about some guineas, and I liked putting it down but had no idea it was publishable and am nervous at the idea of its exposure as a poem.[36] Has this happened to you?

Write me when time and all lets you. I remember reading in Edward Lear's biography that he often wrote 36 letters before breakfast! And drew on them.

Thank you again and often for sending the Stories. Yours are of a different order from the others and as different as flying is from a birdnest to me but I've liked reading them too, and cherish the book.

Love to all,
Eudora

William Maxwell to Eudora Welty, March 3, 1957

Dear Eudora:

It's Sunday morning, and I'm about halfway through my second Hayden [Haydn] quartet. At my back, in the study window, are Souvenir de Malmaison and Lady Hillingdon. I dug them up last fall and put them in gasoline cans and stored them in the basement, because they are so tender that they always die back to the level of the ground, and it takes them all summer to recover. So of course the first warm day I couldn't stand it any longer and brought them upstairs. They are now in full leaf, and even have some buds on them. This is probably a mistake, but think if it should turn out not to be!

I like "What Every Boy Should Know" much the best of those three stories. The psychoanalysis in The French Scarecrow is kind of an elaborate joke—not that I think it is, but neither do I think it is the means—a means—for writers of prose fiction to convey meaning. In short I agree with you. I meant it in this story as an equivalent to going to the dentist or the beauty parlor, and of course everything that that exceedingly childish man says on the couch is wrong—says about the other characters, I mean. He gets everything wrong, and it doesn't matter, so far as the Germanic ac-

cent is concerned, because in that room during that hour nothing is right, nothing is wrong, it is only a chain of thinking. What I wanted to do with the story is to write about the periphery of vision. You know that second of looking at a Marin and thinking those black lines that frame the picture are your own eyelids looking at it, just barely beyond the edge of seeing? I wanted to do the various kinds of fear that exist in the world of the periphery. The eye, the elaborate eye of the scarecrow, is just that the actual scarecrow Emmy made had only one eye, because my old hat was pulled down over the other, and the artist in Emmy couldn't put something in for convention's sake, lilies though they were unseen on the tops of the pillars of Solomon's temple. But they weren't for convention's sake either. Anyway, I didn't mean it to mean anything.

I've read Clive Bell's book, too. And kept it for that marvelous letter of Mrs. Woolf's he quotes. But I don't suppose you'd be persuaded to do a parody of that kind of British memoir? You did one, actually, in the letter, but it is something The New Yorker could use, I would think. I didn't know how the poem got into galleys but absolutely loved it, more than tongue can tell. It is the quintessence of you, and made possible I think by all these months of not being writing. Really good, and really your voice. And real guineas crossing a real road. It is what Louise Bogan calls breaking through.[37] I hope your mother's eyes will find the strength to throw off this acute sensitivity to infection, first and foremost for her sake, and second and hindmost so we can see you in April. By that time maybe you will be able to admire my pruning. You will certainly have no difficulty in admiring Kate and Brookie. Brookie is a splendid brownhaired unblinking baby. A great talker, like Kate. A great talker to her Mother, mostly. Three nursings a day, beginning Monday, and solids. She's the one that's solid. Kate is very unadventurous physically, and has not even learned how to escape from her crib, but boldness itself when it comes to talking. Since this is the age of pure feeling, it is possible to have amazing conversations with her. The age of making up has not yet set in, so it is all gospel truth. I guess. And so tender and touching.

I came on Hubert Creekmore (whom I met at Mary Lou's party for you, before the opening [of *The Ponder Heart*]) in the supplement to Twentieth Century Authors the other day, but I have not seen him nor heard him men-

tioned in the flesh. I will put my ear to the ground, but probably not hear anything till Mrs. W[hite] gets back from Florida at the end of the month. We have just bought a new long story of Jerry Salinger's.[38] Now if that long story you are working on and that I promise not to mention again and that Mary Alice named (or did you?) should turn out also to be something that I would have the exquisite pleasure of seeing into print! I have been working at night on the snapshot album, and did a number of pages about the life in the apartment on 36th Street, and took a special delight in mounting those of you and me talking about the manuscript of The Ponder Heart. The tears that flowed that day.

We are delighted to have the Bibb lettuce, as a talisman, a token of spring in Mississippi. I imagine it and you coming to Yorktown Heights, and playing the record of the Scottish bagpipers, and then a series of Hayden Quartets with the windows open. At this moment the wind is howling like Wuthering Heights.

Beautiful picture of Mary Alice. I hope you can get your hands on a print of it without screen. It has much more richness than one expects of newspaper or indeed most any photography but yours and maybe one or two other people that are better at thinking up excuses for taking pictures than they should be.[39]

And it is of course more likely than not that Mrs. Woolf was not damaged by the proposal. There aren't enough words in the language to convey tentativeness, and anyway, it has become a kind of rhetorical device and people don't believe you, but I did mean it most tentatively and hesitantly. How do I know, how does anybody know except the person herself. And I agree wholly with you about the British. Chilling though the French are, one can see what they are thinking and feeling. They are almost indecent about their indifference to having you see. And warm though the British are, one needs to have them explained to one, and everything is through the looking glass.

Oh do come and bring picnic weather. Emmy sends love. She made pigsfeet jelly that turned out a little queer. Margaret McBride is a treasure.[40] I send love to you both,

B

Eudora Welty to William Maxwell, [Spring 1957]

Dear Bill,

Thank you for your letter, in its whole and its parts, for it was a true an-swer, and an answering letter is something people only get in books, most of the time. No wonder Lady Hillingdon blooms to reward you for such things. I hope Souvenir de Malmaison is not far behind. What an achieve-ment! (to change you from being rewarded to bringing it about yourself). I think it beats the winter-protection achievement—well, just in the time el-ement, maybe, but that was the idea. Thank you for telling me about the periphery of vision and those Marin lines—I'm sure I was a fool to need to be told, and I would have felt a fool for asking you except that I had to know, and you could tell me—I made an exception of myself in my rule that nobody has any darn business asking a writer any more about a story than is therein provided. It's all beautifully plain now—I had been just on the edge of the periphery, I guess—now OK. I still like "What Every Boy Should Know" better than almost anything of yours I've read. I'm glad the eye didn't mean anything—probably it's just because I've got eyes on my mind all the time that <u>that</u> one smote so vividly.

I can just imagine the house full of talk, any time at all, or just continu-ous? with those little girls. It will be ever so nice to meet Brookie, and re-meet Kate, who will be so changed in size at least. I still hope to come, but can't quite commit myself to myself, though I have done it to business peo-ple—so that means that unless some emergency comes up I'm bound to make it, by end of April.

Thanks for the word on Hubert—and of course I remembered at once after I'd written that the one meeting was bound to be the one at Mary Lou's. It's so lovely about Mary Lou's stories you're printing. (I think she must surely produce a book! Do you agree? I think the material has a book's focus, somehow—I don't know if she agrees.) Wonderful about the new Jerry Salinger. Soon? Knowing about a good story you haven't read is like watching for a comet.

Tentative! Don't I know and believe! And Virginia Woolf of all people in the world simply inspires it, of herself, word and act—the inspirer of ten-tativeness—also of inspiration. She was so bold, but she was walking on a

thread—I think she might have wanted the imagination and the generosity of guesses made about her, to help maintain the only thing that really mattered. I can see that sentence doesn't make sense. Wasn't her letter to Barbara marvelous?[41] Now you know he [Clive Bell] could have produced so much like that, and it was upstairs. Yes, I think a parody should be done of all this Bloomsbury non-reminiscing, why not by you, though? By the way I note that E. M. Forster comes in just for his tea and goes, in these memoirs. Being still alive he's being kept pretty quiet, isn't he? All I want anyway is for him to last them all out.

Thanks for liking the guineas—that pleases me a great deal. Yes I would love you to read this story I'm working on if I ever get it all finished, but it couldn't be for The New Yorker I'm as sure as sure, it's so leisurely and crazy at the same time. Your remarks on it would be of great worth and especially if I were present, and I may bring up as much as I have, anyway.

Much love to Emmy and the girls. My mother sends hers too. It is a lovely spring day, Climbing Thor time, and oak trees in little yellow stars and epaulettes. A thrush is sitting on her nest in the spirea bush within hand's reach of a cat who has not the manners of Floribunda (I don't dare make that a question). When will the orchard be in flower?

<div align="right">

Love,
Eudora

</div>

Eudora Welty to Emily and William Maxwell, [June 1957],
Incomplete letter

Dear Emmy and Bill,

I think of you every day, but it's taking my letter almost 80 Days to come & say so. This time it was so specially nice, with a town visit & a country visit—meeting Brookie for the first time—seeing Kate in a good deal of glory—seeing all the changes, human and household, having chicken for dinner, (& cornbread), forgetting about time out under the apple trees— And if it was beautiful in the country, wasn't it fine in town? Had I been a fortune-reader & known just what would unroll in "Around the World in 80 Days" I'd have thought, I want to see this from beginning to end with the Maxwells. So how fortunate! I did have the loveliest times with you, and

Eudora Welty to Emily Maxwell, [Summer 1957]

Dear Emmy,

I dearly love the picture—It shows how Brookie participates in the moment, just the way she was doing at the table when she came to Sunday lunch, the day I came. And wearing the same little dress, doing it a lot of honor, I think, having her picture taken in it. I'm so pleased you sent it to me! She looks even more like Bill in a picture than in person, maybe—do you think? My mother admires her a great deal too—I put her up on the mantle shelf when she came (next to E. M. Forster's picture that came on his Christmas card—<u>they</u>'re congenial) and what fun to look up & see her. It's a beautiful (looking), sensitive photograph isn't it—Still I give the subject the credit every time—I love having Kate's drawing too—It's got rhythm— gaiety—tasteful color combinations—& it's not too much. In fact I can see her letting fall the purple crayon at the <u>moment</u> interest departed—! It really is charged with fun. I like it, Kate, thank you. (It's on my typewriter.)

I've just been taking my two nieces to New Orleans to see "Around the World in 80 Days" and had been thinking of you and Bill all along. The screen was not <u>quite</u> up to scratch—so the balloon ride wasn't total— some of the panoramas had tips & toes clipped. The S. S. Grant didn't show every inch of sail—but the feel of it all was there—It was lovely to see again & I'm sure will still be, & still be there on Broadway, when Kate and Brookie are big enough. The two I took were completely absorbed and it was a good excursion—We spent two nights, just to round it out (the world)—

All goes well these days, and I hope it does with you—You'll have a spell of cool at the shore now soon—isn't that your plan?—for as long as you can, I hope! Isn't it hot! We're having a cool breeze this morning from somewhere—I won't ask—Much love to all of you, and thank you again for the picture of Brookie—and the picture by Kate—Eudora

Emily Maxwell, near Old Lyme, Connecticut, to Eudora Welty,
[Summer 1957]

Dear Eudora,

I have just taken a gingerbread out of the oven, and there are two dozen

baby ears of corn waiting in a big pot of water, & Margaret & Brookie & Kate and Bill have gone off to Old Lyme to look for a book and buy some steaming clams, and it occurs to me that all of that (except the book) is a very odd combination, and if it weren't for our sea-appetites an impossible one.

I envied you seeing "Around the World in Eighty Days" again, and in such good company. I long to see it again soon. As I look out at the bay from Mrs. K[...]'s little table in the living room window, it looks like a giant curved Cinevision screen—the water's down about forty or fifty feet and the curve of the horizon (a raised railroad track on one side & Block Island far far away on the other) just exceeds the curve of my vision. The trains roar by every half hour, some of them the longest freight trains in the world surely, which Brookie loves. I wish this place could be one of the pleasures we've shared together. The house is bare, underfurnished no more recently than 1900. When we pull down a shade it makes a dry little sound and all the tacks let go. The floor wet-mop is made of old Mr. K[...]'s black wool bathing suit of 1920 vintage. And there are two quite beautiful antique egg beaters, only one of which revolves. We have been enjoying the thriftiness and New England conservatism of the house since we came, but it's more fun since we learned this morning that when Old Mr. K[...] died last winter he left over a million dollars, and apparently his wife is sitting on it, unwilling to share it even with her son & daughter.

Kate loved her rows of dancing dolls so, and I thought the papers you used were charming. I have saved one row to paste in her photograph album.

...This is the next afternoon. Fortunately Bill wasn't able to find steaming clams yesterday, so we were able to have cold chicken. We have all just returned from a visit to the Thomas Lee House—half of it was built in 1641 [actually, around 1664] by the forbears of Robert E. Lee, whose branch, a brother of Thomas, apparently left almost immediately for Jamestown. A lovely house, peaceful and plain and not too reconstructed, with a marvellous dedicated 82 year old woman showing it (for the past 40 years) with such love (10 to 5 with no intermission for lunch & no pay) and intelligence it was a pleasure to hear her. The house has that mysterious perfection—of scale is it?—that makes you happy for a long time after being in it.[42]

I'm knitting a sample of some multi-colored yarn that may turn out to be a cap for Brooke or a doll's blanket or God forbid a potholder, or a scarf for Floribunda on whom it really does look well—but otherwise it looked much better in the ball of yarn than knitted. It's the first time I've ever succumbed to the practicality of beginning with a swatch, and it all goes to show one never should.

<div align="right">With love,
Emmy</div>

Love to your mother.

Eudora Welty to William Maxwell, October 14, [1957]

Dear Bill,

By now she [Brookie] is probably running from Emmy to you and back again like a bobbin. What lovely news. Now I can look at her picture and say...YOU WALK!

I was so glad to get your letter, and Emmy's that she wrote from Mrs. K[...]'s table—I could see it all, down to the wet-mop made of old Mr. K[...]'s black wool bathing suit, and I aim to write her soon—to find out for one thing what the rainbow-colored yarn turned into. A fascinator for Floribunda? I would give much to see all of you, and to be taken on a tour—who would go in front, Kate? To see the new summerhouse—everything. In fact, there was a letter I started to Emmy when I was thinking of all those little tomatoes that must be gathered green just before the frost hits, wondering if she had the old recipe we have of green tomato mincemeat—and the letter is lost and the recipe is lost with it. If you get it (somehow) do give me the recipe back in your next! But I think it all vanished together with something else I was going to send, a piece of a Chicago Herald for July 1911 that a friend had (I do not know why) with a column by Lillian Russell, answers to questions. Most of the questions were how to develop the bust, and the answer was "Breathe deeply." There was an ad for Fourth of July Fireworks for Your Celebration and the $1.25 pack had dozens, scores of items, and Oh I wish I had that list! There was an ad for Mellorose Cosmetics with a testimonial from Julian Eltinge.[43] He was never going to be without. The travel etiquette column told you to leave your furs at home and travel on

board your ship in your Tam O'Shanter, and not to forget your black tights. It's true my desk is in a shape—but I don't see how all that could have vanished, yet I have looked and looked—a distinctive color, all the items—ecru.

Your summer did sound lovely, and I hope when you came back you found it had rained some. Your drouth was a match for our wet—wettest Sept. in 44 years—we had mushrooms all over the yard, but they didn't look at all divine. Did you get any writing done at Mrs. K[...]'s, or were you forever steaming clams and eating Emmy's cooking and sleeping and harking to Kate?

The sparrows—as soon as I got home, set off by your reading the story & liking it, and by Diarmuid's word too, I did some work on it—tightening—but I've never put it through the typewriter for the last go. It's true it got interfered with by a new story, and the new story has to have its last go through the typewriter too.[44] This summer was not good as a time to write in, but that's past now and I feel so ashamed to have nothing to show—and determined to make up for it. I still keep intact my feeling about the story and the glow of knowing you like it.

My best to Mrs. White—it was kind of her to ask about me. The letter Mr. White wrote about the radioactive waste in the ocean was so marvelous, wasn't it?[45] I've read it out loud to so many people.

Mother sends you her love. She is all right, but her vision in her good eye gets less with its cataract, and the other eye doesn't seem to improve much, though it doesn't get worse, and though it's pretty certain the trouble's allergic and takes shots for that. She feels sad too for her two old aunts, both 90, who died this summer, leaving her the oldest. I think she feels misused there.

The lady who told me to paint my ailing roses with Garden Volck, and I did, almost immediately had to go into the hospital for shock treatment, but though I'm sure the shock treatment is what the roses got from Volck they didn't die. Neither did they get well. They just took it, and now there are some nice enough flowers on the bushes, though some of the flowers seem like reproaches—misused too. Are yours doing well? This is a sweet smelling time of year here—sweet olive, and the pine straw falling in the sun. Write when you can. I've been a terrible correspondent all summer I

know. More later—and meantime much love to you and Emmy and Kate and Brookie, which comes without my ever mailing it and regardless of this desk.

E.

William Maxwell to Eudora Welty, November 11, 1957

Dear Eudora:

Well actually she's as shy as a robin, when it comes to perching on anybody's lap for any length of time. She [Brookie] did this morning, so she could get at the lid of the sugar bowl, which has a china rose on it (Japanese onion pattern), and she lights on me in the evening while I am mixing drinks because from my left arm she can see quite well into the liquor cupboard, the ice box, and the kitchen cupboard, and eventually get her hands on a piece of ice. Do you gather that she has Emmy's big eyes and is adorable?

Would green tomato mincemeat be what we called picklelilly in Illinois, or is it really a form of mincemeat? The letter alas never came, but if it does, by way of Persia or China, you will be the first to get a copy of the recipe. Receipt, my mother would have said.

Emmy worries about you, maternally, so far as I can see—that is to say, knowing nothing that is wrong or could cause worry, she nevertheless keeps asking me if I think you are all right. I say that there is nothing wrong that won't be all right as soon as you have given those two stories a last go through your typewriter.

Kate is now so intelligent she puts me to shame. Where it will end I don't know. I explained to her that animals could not come into the house when she was sound asleep at night and therefore there was no need for her to wake up in the middle of same and cry for her mother, who needed her rest, because (if you follow the conversation and I'm sure you do) every night before Daddy went to bed he locked the doors. All the doors.

"And why do you lock the doors, Daddy?" she asked, smiling at me in triumph and her face shining with supernatural intelligence. Emmy burst out laughing, quietly. I never locked a door in my life until we remodeled

the house and Kate was around the corner and down a hall from us instead of a mere hop skip and jump in the dark, and the answer to her question would only have precipitated more questions because it is this: I lock the house every night because of the little Lindbergh baby.[46] It is my private madness and horror.

The roses are all (all but Mrs.—not Mrs. Whiteman Cross, the other one, the yellow climber, I can't think of it) in their cones of dirt, (Mrs. Arthur Curtiss James) she got left uncovered because the yardboy began to look peaked, from all that shovelling. And Paul's Lemon Pillar and Spanish Beauty moved to the basement, for the winter, with Lady Hillingdon and Souv. de Malmaison—all showed a tendency to die back to the ground every winter, so I am letting them come in with us.

Emmy has done the children's book lead for The New Yorker, and quite nicely.[47] It all took place during the month of October, when the children both had colds, and I did too, and she was up every night with one or the other of them, and Kate was often in tears because she couldn't understand why they weren't her books right then and there (instead of after the checking department gets through with them) to do as she pleased with.

You would have anyway, but you must read the Agee book.[48] And just sit right down and get those two stories out of your system, because there is more waiting, and how can you get on to that if you don't? Also, <u>I am waiting</u>.

<div align="right">Love,
Bill</div>

William Maxwell to Eudora Welty, [December 1957]

Dear Eudora:

When I should have been getting on with it I was enjoying your piece in the Christmas <u>Mademoiselle</u>, which, happily, came to me last, so I can take it home to Emmy.[49] You couldn't have done it better.

Also, it seems you have been much in our thoughts. We had to put together some cardboard furniture, a cupboard and a stove, for Kate's Christmas or birthday, I don't know which. All this on the living room floor after

she was in bed. And I said "How Eudora would love reading these directions." So here they are.

Love,

Bill

Eudora Welty to Emily and William Maxwell, December 24, [1957]

Dear Emmy and Bill,

I was thinking of you and it was a lovely time to write, early morning, a mild springlike day. I can see from my window a single shell-pink camellia with one petal to go to be wide open. (name: Bernice Bodey.)

Your tray all spread came safely—and how to imagine a tray from your house not spread—so ready, like the table that appears on a wish in a fairy tale. I sat to myself with one good friend who had the luck to be in the house—and only stopped her a minute because I saw what had become of the vari-colored yarn. It seems to me that whatever Emmy Maxwell picks up can't leave her hand without the touch of imagination. How luscious & Mediterranean the whole feast looked, and tasted—the green & red of the pistachios, the shining dates (so huge! & so good), the yellow-pink almonds (toasted & salted of course!) & the bright little Peruginas, it was like an Impressionist still life, wicker & glass division walls & all, but with permission to eat it, which made it different from a Matisse. It was a perfectly lovely idea & I loved it for being early—when do you long for a magic tray more than when you ought to be out running those errands for others, à la the Christmas spirit? Pure creature comfort! Thank you—and there is still a bite or two left for late tonight, after everything's ready—a reward after all.

The mantle shelf has Kate's Doll Party sitting up between some Wise Man and Mr. Forster's King's Chapel Angel, and is so adorable—and gives me a very clear idea of what Christmas will be like in the morning on Baptist Church Road. That assembly—I hope Kate keeps it up. That getting together of a little variety at the table—I wish I could overhear the conversation, well-supplied I'm sure.

Did you get those x-flaps folded in to complete bottom, when they did not have small tab as in step 23? Surely you remember step 27 of the Range

Kit. Of course I made the whole thing in my mind as I read, rather quickly. I think, since you made me the coin box, I don't have any worries about these 2 items, which look slightly less complicated. I'm enclosing the one I wish life were like, or at least story writing.

I'm so dubious about my Christmas present to you getting there. Naturally, for it means trusting the U.S. mail, a Doubleday Bookshop, & Caedmon Records, none of which I do. A few weeks ago I asked the Doubleday on 52nd St. to mail you Caedmon's recording of Walter de la Mare reading, and (just to make myself dubious) enclosed a self-addressed postcard for them to mail me saying, "We sent it." No sign at all, & this is the last day. If nothing happens, tell me. And of course—which is why I had the store up the street from you send it—change it if you have the record already. Whenever it comes, it's with love from me.

Thank you for your kind words about that Mademoiselle piece— They've asked me to try an assignment every year & I've not done it, & this year, because I was so mad at the way I couldn't get my stories done, I punished myself with that deadline. They changed my title & my last sentence—to make it Christmassy—I never could somehow stand a Christmas Carol. So I'm glad if it came out all right in the main, it was fun to write after all. You were

Dec. 26—You were and are, but Christmas came into the middle of that sentence. Did you all have a wonderful day? I was hoping so & imagining so. Here, the day was so soft & mild it began to rain like early spring, & kept it up off & on, then a low, gold sunset—Today bright again & cooler. We had a good Christmas and many old friends were home, as usual.

A small white Roman hyacinth out this morning, also iris stylosa—a delicious smell in the air, which may be partly people burning their Christmas wrapping paper—Emmy, by the way, speaking of hyacinths, I mailed you the other day a book by a friend of mine in North Carolina about small bulbs, because I could so often imagine you entering the conversation.[50]

Much love to all of you. Is Kate turning through a Christmas book this morning, I wonder? I liked the Children's Book piece so much, especially the way you took hold of it, Emmy, saying what would be & what would

not be considered—sweeping clear all but those choice ones. Did you see
& like the photograph book of "The Red Balloon?" I think it's for children
with nostalgia for Paris—that means us, in a way.

Happy New Year to you all & love & happiness—from Eudora
The last nougat was gobbled up last night at 12 o'clock by a glad friend for
whom it was saved.

Eudora Welty to Emily and William Maxwell, [March 25, 1958]

Dear Emmy and Bill,

Are all of you down there, under the snow, like 4 bulbs? Come up soon,
for I want to look at you—I hope to snatch a trip to New York getting in
Monday, even for just a little while. I'll call you up. The March 21 one
sounded the worst of all—I hope you had a warm house.

It will be lovely to get your news. Bill, the two tales were highly satisfy-
ing. There's such a pleasure in having the writer be omniscient again—in
a tale, that's where the writer can say "For every deprivation there is a gift"
and the felicity of it keeps us nodding yes all the way. And in a tale, things
have consequences. So beautifully done, and the second one when it says
among other things that the real thing is going to have a hard time ousting
its substitute, is marvelous. Of course I liked that gipsy wagon, in the first
one. Did you write those in the summer, by the sea?[51]

I'll be leaving spring to come up, having waited so long for it—though
it's not high spring yet, being late. Roses all in leaf, though, and one Dutch
iris is blooming. Redbud and the first pale green in the trees. The winter's
seemed long too because my brother's been sick, but he is better now.[52] I
hope all is well with all of you. I'm going to stay at the Algonquin again and
will telephone. How lovely to look forward to.

<div style="text-align: right">Love,
Eudora</div>

Eudora Welty to William and Emily Maxwell, May 21, [1958]

Dear Bill and Emmy,

It's nice to know exactly what you're doing: it's May 21 at 3 o'clock and

you're at West 156 Street getting $1000 from the Nat'l Inst. of A&L.[53] I think that's a safe sound thing for them to do—which I believe is sometimes their touchstone—and it's gratifying from our end too. Three cheers for Art from Jackson—for a little, when I first opened & read my invitation, I thought I might be on hand to clap, but couldn't, and after all, I'd had my visit.[54] Long ago as it's been now, and as long since I've written. I'm sorry for my long wait, due solely to "daily life", yet it shows you how long I can go feeling in touch before I just have to write. It was lovely to see you each cherished time. All of your welcomes and one spell are with me still. (I told my niece Elizabeth about the goose spell that had to come out, though its order was immediately countermanded, but Elizabeth gave me a niece's look and said "How do you know it isn't going to work yet?" I've noticed things myself.) I felt that Kate's radiance is multiplying like a star's, and her magnitude's all love, and there's so much pleasure in just watching her. And Brookie in her kingdom cavorting in a way just as bright, and wondrously different. Are they both well? By now all must be green outdoors, and the strawberries probably making. I hope the roses kept their fine growth and put still more on, and that all will burst out soon. What has appeared by the brook in the woods? Are the azaleas in flower?

Oh, that day was so bright and warm and Kate and Brookie swung so well, the lunch on the ground so delicious, the little grass basket so sweet here with me, now, because it was my birthday too. I liked our theatre together so well, Emmy—I've wondered if you saw it, Bill, and if you liked it in the same way or degree? (I enjoyed Mary McCarthy's piece up to a point, but she makes me impatient when she gives out that aura that it's all right to like this, and to have reasons provided you—or do I sound as catty as I must feel?)[55] It was lovely to have dinner twice at Cyrano's which I think is really twice as good as once there for the food, and many more times as good as once for holding meeting. It was lovely to meet Mrs. Green too, and Dr. Huber—who by the way left a message at the hotel he'd called, but I only got it as I was racing for the train near midnight. It must have reassured all concerned to read the fine notice of our concert in the Times next morning.[56]—I felt so plain lucky to get to see you so many times, and it was so very fine and happy for me that you made them possible, each one.

Here it's summer, the roses have finished the first flourish, the last of

the climbers (Mary Wallace) just now over—I came home to Lady Banksia. No, the Mermaid will keep it up for a little while yet. Spanish Beauty, that I planted after seeing yours, was marvelous, it's got a nice start now. The Confederate jasmine (whatever its real name is) is so heavy in fragrance these days that we have to close down against it—it's all over one side of the wall outside the dining room and up in a big tree. Lightning-bug time, and soft, cool nights. We've had heavy rains just as you have, but now that they've let up the heat rushed in. Which I like.

Our family health has grown better, rather slowly, and not letting go our apprehensions wholly, but it's so much better than it was. My brother, who was in the hospital in New Orleans while I was in New York, came home a few weeks after I got home and is doing pretty well. The little girls are going to camp the second half of the summer, which will get them away from the sort of worrying atmosphere they don't so much understand as feel. Both of them are fine. My mother was delighted with every word I could tell her of you all. She is well. She sends love.

Tell me of what's happening about the Fables and about Knopf, if you can and feel like it, Bill. Are <u>all</u> the Fables to be in the New Yorker. Then will they all be in their own book? I should like a sight of <u>that</u>, soon as may be![57]

Later.—In the last week or so I've been putting in some hours of work, and have hopes now. How wonderful it will be to tear up all these other versions, and have only one, for better or worse. Such a plot in my country story you have never seen, I like to think even P. G. Wodehouse would find himself with the brows raised, in some brief alarm & bafflement. It is bafflement on a much higher scale than simply not knowing how many children a character has, or who a great-grandmother was. It's about machinery more than some of the time (if you remember). Can't imagine how I got into it, but I'm enjoying the conversations, as I type up.[58]

I must tell you of a grand thing that happened to me, a Bryn Mawr fellowship, the Lucy Donnelly award, was given to me for next school year. Do you know about it? It gives all and asks nothing, as far as I can see—for all you are asked to do is come some time during the school year at your convenience and be available to let students who like writing come and

talk to you. It is cash and since the fellowship supposedly starts in the Fall, I welcome it as practically the certificate for a trip in October or the like, and on up to New York, if all goes well. It is (at this moment I looked out my window and saw two rabbits leaping and chasing each other on our front lawn—which, since we live just on a paved street no longer near the woods, always seems like a vision of some friends of Kate's and Brookie's. They often feed out there, singly, but these are having a good time in some clover that ought not to be there. They have a little one, who comes by himself—don't know where they've left him or with whom.) As I was saying, the fellowship is wonderful, and brought me a good deal of cheer.

Kate by the way will get a book of verse from William Jay Smith, who offered to sign it for her and mail it down from Vermont. But hold it until I send some reasonably exact facsimile in size, weight and color for Brookie. I know how this is. I'm very fond of Bill Smith, and know his little boy for whom he wrote the verses when he was perhaps a little older than Kate is now. But of course Kate may not laugh. Just because it's named "Laughing Time" is no sign! How do we know?

Across the street at the girls' school, it's practice time in the music room, and you should see those rabbits prancing about to Beethoven. It's like follow the bouncing ball. It's the Appassionata!

I'll go mail this. I wish I could tell you the right thank-yous for all our good times. I loved them and remember them with love now. I hope all goes well with all of you. Write when you can. I'll do better here. Love and wishes to you,

　　　　　　　　　　　　　　　　　　　　　　　　　Eudora

Maybe Mary Lou is there about now. How happy she'll be to see you.

William Maxwell to Eudora Welty, [June 1958]

Dear Eudora:

Here is Kate's first story, which I ran through the photostating machine, not being able to part with it wholly. I think you will like it, and I must say you are the ideal reader for her. Beautiful, simply beautiful—that little book they made of your lectures. It is enough to make Mr. Knopf restless.[59] I dare say they knew it. And Bill Smith's charmingly autographed book for

Kate made me want to know him better. I don't know how this is to be ac-
complished unless you raise a finger at just the right moment. And I have
something else being copied for you—an essay of Mr. Forster's, with a be-
ginning that undid me with its sweep and—er—ah—<u>talent</u>. You know how
slyly hegoesabout makingeverybody else in the entire writing world look
like a monkey. (a pencil under my typewriter did that running together) We
are going to Mr. Knopf's country place for lunch on Saturday, and I hope
they don't have too many forks and spoons and that nobody says Grace af-
ter I have started to eat or that sort of thing, but at my first meeting I liked
him. A pasha is what he seemed like. Pleasure loving. So am I. So are you.
So should everybody be, <u>I</u> think.

The roses, for the second time in succession, are two weeks late, but this
year it is the rain, and not killing sprays and frosts, and so they are show-
ing every sign of being about to be magnificent, except for five casualties,
which aren't there at all, but may not be dead. I'm giving them time to
make up their minds. The Daily Mail is in bud, and about ten feet high,
by the front wall. Harrison's Yellow, Agnes, and Nevada are actually bloom-
ing, and so is the Austrian Copper Briar. In a few days the house will be
clogged with roses in vases, but at the moment it is a matter of one at a time,
with everything still to come, including the Japanese beetles, which you
can thank your lucky stars you know nothing about. Brookie is an insatiable
smeller and her favorite is a yellow tree peony that Mary Lou sent us and
that bloomed this year for the first time. It is so beautiful that if I had my life
to live over I would raise peonies, if you know what I mean, which is, I'm
afraid, that I would raise peonies <u>and</u> roses.

I heard a funny story yesterday at lunch from Russell Lynes,[60] about
Katherine Anne Porter. It seems he had asked her, as a result of something
in a letter to him, to write a piece about the Twenties, and she wrote him
and said she had forty thousand words and was stuck. So he went to see her
and found, on a big eight foot or so table, piles and piles of manuscript,
each pile about something different, and he read through every last pile and
then started in. "Put this here, and that there…and then this…and then
this…and then you can use these two piles, in this order, and then…and
then…and then you have it."

"Wonderful," she said. "Simply wonderful. I don't know how you do it."

And very pleased with himself he went home and that was the last he ever heard of it. I was pleased to know that she also works from piles of this and that. I don't suppose she pins. Nobody in the world pins but you, so far as I know. If you are having any troubles, I would be happy to send you a package of them—the unfolding kind—compliments of the Management.[61]

I thought of you when they were giving out the gold medals. It was [a] very agreeable occasion, actually (I have a delightful step-uncle, the kindest man in the world, who used to love to say "You can't make a man mad by giving him money.") and I didn't even worry about the fact that I forgot to shave. I started to, and then Brookie or Kate called me, and I just forgot. Anyway, it is the sort of thing that makes people say if he is that absentminded he must be a serious writer, but the truth of the matter is that they were so excited about Marilyn Monroe's being there, with her husband who was being inducted, (which reminds me, are you?) that I could have forgotten to wear my eyebrows and nobody would have noticed.[62]

I am delighted about the Bryn Mawr elevation, which sounds as if it would be bound to bring you to us, which is ideal. Our elevation.

My love to you both,

B

Eudora Welty to Emily and William Maxwell, September 16, 1958

Dear Emmy and Bill,

There's an unfinished letter to each of you in this box—unfinished but all thanks, for everything from the angry young robins on.[63] Has Kate written any more stories—I say written, but that's because it was full callibre. (What does this mean, & how do you spell it?) It was a masterpiece of taking down. I loved the story. I'm going to put it in the bottom of my trunk, as Ida M'Toy used to tell me when I took down what <u>she</u> said.[64] The piece by E. M. Forster was good too. The wobbly tripod. That darling man, I wonder how he is right now.

The summer must have been a full one for you. I've loved the Fables— that started off one letter. It will be wonderful to see them all at one blow, between hard, beautiful Knopf covers. When? How does the novel go?

This summer I seem to have been too stupid to get through the word

barrier, but nothing is really any different or worse here than at the start of the summer—it was just me, and I'm ashamed of it. Yaddo wrote they would pay my way up and back to a meeting next weekend, and though it at first seemed wildly impossible, I believe if things look all right here to-morrow and Thursday (it's my mother's worries, of each day as it passes, that make me wonder what's the right thing to do) I'll jump on the Panama Limited. Anyway, if I go to Yaddo, I could stop a week in NY, and speak to you, for goodness sake. I'll postcard you from on the way if I go, and only hope you'll have hours to come have dinner with me or something. It would be such pure joy.[65] Things must be in a confusion again at the of-fice, with the death of Mr. Gibbs. (I must say I got a strange feeling when I read in the paper that the magazine had invited Kenneth Tynan to be guest critic—remembering you and me sitting in the Biltmore, Bill, saying what a nice guest that would be.) The Times sent me Mr. Perelman's new book to review. That is, it hasn't come yet, but I already love it from afar.[66]

So much to talk about, and if I don't get there I'll write a decent letter soon. This is just a note in the middle of making a birthday cake for a niece, it's cooking.

Emmy, out of the box of letter paper I took this recipe I'd copied down for you—I found the original—but it gave such uncertain measure-ments. You are probably the only one who'd know whether that gallon of ground tomatoes is measured before or after grinding. The other day this other recipe appeared in the local paper. I attach both, if you want to look them over.

Another bad thing I did this summer was make you some fig preserves wrong. Sealed the jars wrong, rather and the preserves just proceeded to "turn"—utterly stupid, and nothing to do about it because that was the last of the figs, the rains came. (I don't know what you can say to that! Just growl at me, would be a good thing.) The cake!

All is well—but I'll mail this on tonight and it's such a lovely idea that soon I might get to see you. I hope everything's going beautifully at home with Kate and Brookie—the garden—all. Is it?

<div style="text-align: right">

Much love to you.

Eudora

</div>

Eudora Welty to Emily and William Maxwell, [September 17, 1958]

Dear Emmy and Bill,

It was a false alarm, this time I won't get there, but it can be planned better for later on in October and I can come then, I hope. I'll write. Everything's just the same as usual and if it keeps on this way, I can feel freer with safer arrangements. Is everything all right there?

The Perelman book came. Do you remember the upstairs housemaid that entered the scene, named Pandemomium? And "my escort, a Miss Chicken-Licken?" How could you forget?

Much love and I will still be seeing you, I cross all my fingers, and still do the touch system [of typing].

Eudora

William Maxwell to Eudora Welty, September 22, 1958

Dear Eudora:

Ah, well…is what I said as I went past the rose bed in the dark last night. Because of the long rainy summer, everything is at least a foot and a half higher than ever before, and just coming into its September bloom. You wouldn't have believed it. And in another way, I am grateful, because if someone you long to see says I am coming, then for days you think about their coming, and them, and in effect have a visit from them that not even their not coming can take away.

I loved the Woolf review in yesterdays Times.[67] Exquisite, really, and such a comfort to have you cry out, with me, and to cry out with you, "That beautiful mind!" I love the book. I particularly loved "Marie Corelli was sure a poppy" and didn't you feel you heard the sound of her voice when you read "those two glorious geese, somebody-or-other and Ella Wheeler Wilcox…" I could not believe I had never heard it. What wouldn't you give for a recording of her reading "To the Lighthouse," on one side and "The Waves" on the other. It's enough to unsettle my reason, just having imagined it. I'll try not to think about it any more.

Since you aren't coming this minute, and are making arrangements, I want you to make these two, for me. (1) arrange to finish that story about

those sparrows [*Losing Battles*] before you come, or (2) arrange for some arrangement after you get here where you can hole in, where nobody knows where you are, and finish it while you are here. I am not a presser, really I'm not. I just wait and when I feel the time has come I say "The time has come." It's come. Don't you yourself feel that it has? I want to read it now, not next Spring.

Everybody at home is adorable. Their faces, their minds, their clothes, their hearts. And they think of themselves as full of problems. Brookie's is that there is a doggie bokking. Doggie won't get me because I'm in a house and the door is closed. Doggie won't get my porridge.... Kate's [is] that Brookie is going to destroy her house, the house where her current (as of the last five minutes) family is living, talking, carrying on out loud. No, you can't come IN (Brookie goes in, the nail to the magnet...)...and Emmy's is that Kate is third in the waiting list for the Croton nursery school, and stutters slightly when she gets excited (like her father) and should we move to New York, to Katonah, to somewhere, or stay where we are, where the schools are....

I have put myself on one half of one half time, in the hopes of finishing Opus Y before Christmas. I get to the office at two, three days a week, unless there is some reason to come in earlier, in which case I work at home till ten, and arrive at noon. This is paying off, though I've only been at it two weeks. Don't mention it to me. I am superstitious. Just hold the thought, will you? And give my love to your mother. And come when you can. I long to look at you and hear your voice and what you have to say.

Love,
Bill

Eudora Welty, Bryn Mawr, Pennsylvania, to William Maxwell,
[November 1958]

Dear Bill,

I was so glad to get your letter. I meant to answer straight back, and here I'm at Bryn Mawr already. And that's nearly there. I long to see you and Emmy. Are you well, and the children well? Margaret? You've had snow — are the roses all right? As winter closes in will the novel grow?

I came in a rush but with a secure feeling, because we'd got a young man student from the college across the street to come and sleep and study in the house for the month of November, and the maid to come every day. If all goes all right with the health at home, I'll be in New York Nov. 18–30, and have my reservation at the Algonquin—and, as you thought of, the typewriter. Isn't this all full of promise?

Of course the time isn't really all that long, and the busy time too with you there. I thought I would pluck a date and ask you if it would be easy, or not too hard to think this far ahead, for you and Emmy to come in & have dinner with me and talk or do anything we liked on the 19th (the quickest)—or the 25th?—or the 28th? If there's a play Emmy has been dreaming of, or you, we could try for that. But anyway let's don't be tight-knit, only let's meet, that's all, anyway at all you and Emmy would like to do it.

Have either of you ever been upstairs in the Deanery at Bryn Mawr? Miss Thomas and Miss Garrett, friends, president and friend, occupied the rooms at this end of the 2nd floor hall. You probably know all about them. I didn't, just walked in on this bed, of Constantinople origin, metal from apex to toe, filigree birds, passion flowers, lotuses, some panels burnished bright, some dark. When it lightnings at night, just think. There is a closet big enough for you to get out the New Yorker in, with 52 double-headed hooks screwed into the ceiling, like a flock of bats, and rows of additional hooks at 3 levels around the sides. Also built-in cupboards with sliding doors and drawers (bin like) in all 3 walls. In the room across the hall (Miss Garrett's, the one with the money) is an inlaid desk of many colored woods that I was only shown for a minute, but I saw the built-in mailbox it has with a slot, and when Miss G. dropped in a letter she'd written nobody could get it out but her! She kept the key. There are 5 chains with hanging tiffany-glass globes to light the room (the largest over the writing desk). The rugs, tables, etc. all Oriental. Then Miss G. has a closet—one even bigger than this one, it has a little wing.—I'm most comfortable, they are good to me, even breakfast in bed. I'm not asked to do anything but be available, and I'm being that right this minute. I like the girls very much, and the two faculty members who look after me [Laurence Stapleton and Bettina Linn] are kindness itself. So I seem to be blessed. I hope you are too, and as soon

as we can meet we can all bless each other. I loved very much your Virginia
W. review, it gave me joy.[68]

Love to all of you,
Eudora

William Maxwell to Eudora Welty, January [14], 1959

Dear Eudora:

When I was a graduate student at Harvard there were two bookstores,
one on the square, the Coop, which was all right, and the other, The Dun-
ster House Book Shop, on the way to the River, which I now dream about.
It has long been extinct, but I used to stand in front of the windows, and be
in a kind of seizure. The books were all folio, and more often odd-sized fo-
lio, longer than a line drawn on the diagonal of a quarto and extended to
folio size would have produced. They were always printed in England and
usually dark blue or plum colored. I never bought a single one of them, for
a very good reason, but in my dreams I go there as to any other book store
and discuss, with the proprietor, why he isn't in business any more. Appar-
ently though, he is. Otherwise, <u>where did you get that book</u>? The only clue
I have found is on page 84: "The crowded, ragged looking spike of grayish
green flowers is an unforgettable sight; the long curling lip suggests not so
much a lizard, as the extended proboscis of some moth. The whole plant
has a distinctly uncanny and sinister air, and were it more familiar, one
would not be surprised to see it forming part of the Freudian dream-patterns
of the surrealist painter. The sinister effect is not diminished by the plant's
odour, which is commonly stated to resemble that of a he-goat..." Surely
this is all very far north, as Mr. Ross used to say, and well over the line
into unreality. But marvelous. And it could only have come from that shop,
where every book was limited to, roughly, 1140 copies signed by the author,
and like this No. 783. It seems wrong not to take it to bed with me. When I
have become an authority on British orchids, would you like to take a little
tour with us, in the station wagon, of that rainy orchidaceous island, with
the dream book on the front seat, for handy reference? That settled, there
is only the question of how to thank you sufficiently for such a treasure.
There is no way, obviously. There are no words. Thank you will have to do,

until we see you. And if you ever have a moment's twinge of regret, as I often have for that now long dead collie that I brought Eric Nyland,[69] now grown and married, who fell in love with me and I with him, as I was taking him across Long Island—Well, if you do, say the word. Treasures are to be shared.

I wish I could share last evening with you, though it might have disturbed you as much as it did Emmy. We went to serve as props for a movie of Isak Dinesen reading a story. Before the shooting, we met—some eighteen people, in the "library" (Vincent Astor's calf-bound unloved books is what it turned out to be; he owns the place) of the St. Regis, which was a nice oval baroque, hotel baroque room with a big table and a small cocktail room next to it. She came in, in black, with a dark fur coat, not mink, and brown makeup on her upper eyelids (kohl?) and enormous brown eyes, as big as Emmy's, in a thin white face, the eyes glittering with tears, but not weeping tears. Old age, the cold? Anyway, she was so clearly royalty. The two people she most resembles are you and a Rameses—I think the second, with a slightly hooked nose. I know you know the one I mean. The other props, I'm sorry to say, really were props, though they seem to have fought their way into a party that was supposed to have been for ten; they none of them, except her publisher, had read her. Isn't that New York? And, of course, the whole city, and beyond that the whole country, full of people who worship her. Well, I worshipped her all through dinner, which I do not regret, but I also talked to her and made her talk to me, which I do, rather, because there shouldn't have been any dinner before the shooting, and it should have been done in the day time. The dinner party began at five thirty, the shooting, up on York Avenue, in the Rockefeller Foundation, which is making a movie to be shown, perhaps, on television, perhaps in Universities, began at eight thirty and last[ed] till after midnight, and she is old and frail (1885, the Cyclopedia of Names says she was born) and has been, she told me, mostly in nursing homes the last few years. She was impersonal, almost like a poker player, so bent was she on conserving her strength for the ordeal. But beautiful, wonderful. Pellegrina Leoni <u>not</u> being anything to anybody.[70] It took nearly four hours of takes, more takes, rehearsals, and retakes, to do eight pages of the Deluge at Norderney—you remember the story that begins on page 61, called The Wine of the Tet-

rarch. For nearly four hours we listened to that story, and looked at that extraordinary face, without for one second tiring of either one. And you could look because she never looked back. She looked at the camera as if it loved to hear stories more than anything in this world, and I certainly hope it did. She was able to repeat and recapture phrasing, cadences, pitch of voice, even fleeting expressions, time after time, as if she were an actress. She did not even look tired, until it was all, at last, over, and then suddenly when I turned around, she was sitting, in that black fur coat, but rather longhaired, not caracul or Persian lamb or anything ordinary, with a black chiffon scarf over her head, leaving a white wedge of face, with two burning black eyes in it, and the whole body in the posture of exhaustion. The nearest thing to it I have ever seen is Donne's effigy in St. Paul's, and he, of course, is grinning. She wasn't. She was cold. She is emaciated (always was, I think), and except among people she loves, perhaps, may have lost the power of being warmed. Not the Snow queen, though, because she feels the cold.

During dinner she told me that some of the tales wrote themselves, some were the result of hard labor. Writing themselves meant something different to her than it does to me—not coming sentence by sentence out of the typewriter, but in her head, entire, before she started to write it down. Can you tell me which ones wrote themselves. I said, politely, They all read as if they wrote themselves. Heat lightning. But only for a minute. But it wasn't the place to go into the difference between the Gothic and the Winter's Tales, and I could easily have been wrong. When she was 19 she went to Paris to study art, and walked the streets instead, looking at Paris. She was once in Rome in the autumn, when all the buildings turn a different color. I asked her how long after the war it was before people in Denmark had food and other things, and she said impatiently that they always had food, but that it was dreadful. Do they talk about it still? I asked. No, she said, but they feel it. It was a dead period in everybody's life. She is writing a novel. When she was living in Africa, and there was only a poor bookstore in Nairobi, that stocked mostly detective stories, she nevertheless found two good books by unknown writers, and wrote home to her friends about them. One was Chrome [Crome] Yellow and the other was The Sun Also Rises. She seemed not to know about contemporary American writers. She loved Colette, had met her twice but didn't know her well. Had I read Sido? I said if

she had to choose between the big novel, say Joseph and His Brethren, and My Mother's House and Sido, which would she choose. She couldn't, she said, with some anxiety. But in the end, she did. She chose Colette.[71] She has a passion for paintings, and missed them so, living in Africa, and when she went to Paris after four years, and could go to the Louvre, it was such happiness. She has given the estate at Rungstedlund to the Danish nation, for a bird sanctuary, and is moving into a house that is being remodeled for her in Copenhagen. "The smallest house in Copenhagen." Beginning with an hour long radio address, she raised, among the Danes, a hundred thousand kroner ($100000 roughly) for the sanctuary. No redbirds in Denmark, just nightingales. Just one kroner, she said. One kroner from everybody. And she got it. People walking past her tables in restaurants dropped kroners on their way past. Cab drivers handed her back the fare. The mail was full of kroners. In no time it was done. Forever. And of course water birds, don't you suppose. She herself at times looked so like a falcon. Though we talked all through dinner, she didn't do more than consider and reply to my remarks, until the dessert, and then something, I forget what, the fact that I had just finished making a doll house, perhaps, for my daughter, made her melt, and she talked to me—but still not personally, not as if she liked me or ever wanted to see me again. But in such a way as to make me love her forever. Her voice is so beautiful, the accent isn't either British or American. It has notes that are like cello music. It's like listening to Hayden. And those burning black eyes. It is several years too late to be her friend, but it is not too late to remember what she is like, as long as I live.

Kate sends you this picture [titled "Lady Snake"]. Emmy and Brookie and I send you our love.

B—

Eudora Welty to Emily and William Maxwell, January 14, [1959]

Dear Emmy and Bill,

You'd have heard from me before, but we've been in trouble. My brother, who's been sick for so long, died last Friday. He was only 43. Mother is getting along all right, we all are—the little girls are wonderful.

The cake was opened and eaten with joy when it came—as delicate and

wonderful as always and I'll be writing you and thanking you soon. I hope you have news from your father that is as good as possible, Bill.

With much love to you,
Eudora

Emily Maxwell to Eudora Welty, January 21, 1959

Dear Eudora,

Bill and I send you and your mother our love and all our hearts' sympathy. I am glad for the little girls that they have you! That will help them a lot always.

Bill came home just last night from Lincoln [Illinois]. His Father died on January 14th, and he spent a few days there with his two brothers and stepmother and all the friends of his childhood. He will be writing soon.

We both send you <u>much love</u>,
Emmy

William Maxwell to Eudora Welty, January 22, 1959

Dear Eudora:

We have been making similar discoveries, I suspect. Though perhaps you already knew. When I emerged from the tent in the country, I found myself looking into the face of the little boy I played with when I was five years old. And so concerned for me it was. And the next person I saw was the little girl I knew best, who was like a sister to me. Both strangers for thirty-five years—and neither in the least estranged. Such kindness, and such extraordinary surprises—about my father; even about my mother. So that I now find that a funeral is not the dreadful travesty I used to think, but one of the moments when everybody, quite simply, agrees to live on a plane of reality.

I wish we could be near you, and run in with food, and offer you surprising memories of your brother. I wish I could hold those little girls on my lap, and tell them that it is terrible but that one somehow lives through even the most terrible things. I wish I could answer the telephone for you, and sit

with your mother—I wish, in short, that Jackson was Lincoln, and that we had played together when we were little, and I know that because you are you, you will take the wish for the fact—

> My love to your dear, kind extraordinary
> mother, my love, as always, to you
> Bill

Eudora Welty to William Maxwell, [February 1959]

Dear Bill,

Your two letters were so wonderful that they made me feel very sane, in the middle of all that was happening. Did you know it worked like that? How are you? I'm sorry about your father—I was thinking what a journey that would be—But yes, there were those discoveries at the end, & how far back they did go. Our old yard man, who was old when Walter was a little boy, & who hasn't worked for us for years & years, paid us a call in his Chesterfield overcoat on that Sunday morning—had walked miles—"I just wanted to pay a call to say I hoped what I heard on the radio wasn't true." You must have had to fly almost straight out to Lincoln from Isak Dinesen— Were Emmy and the children well & fine when you got back? Brookie with her eye level just at the window pane—I hope all of you are feeling well, no colds—I feel guilty that it's such <u>spring</u> here! That's why I keep asking, I guess. Camellias & hyacinths blooming, quince, fl. Jasmine—red birds singing—sound & smell of the grass being mowed next door—I wish I knew a good way to send you & Emmy some flowers—If I could just string them, & throw.

The Dinesen reading and the dinner gave me the feeling of an old fairy tale (with engravings)—I'm glad for her she had you by her (one of you each side she needed) but I wish she'd had you on another day. She might have jeweled insides like a watch, wound up according to just how much she can stand—and reading like that might run you down. You should have taken her home. I was so glad to have that evening though—Thank you for sending it.

Are you working on the novel? I hope so. (Just nod, don't speak.)

I'm supposed to go back & finish up at Bryn Mawr some time in the spring, and hope to go. They'll set the time—All being well enough here, I'll take a week more for New York. A college boy who came & stayed in the house before will probably be willing to come back. Mother seems to sleep well & eat well. All of us have got along well, I think. The little girls are wonderful.

<div align="right">With love to yours, & Emmy & you—Eudora</div>

Eudora Welty to Emily Maxwell, [February 1959]

Dear Emmy,

Thank you for writing to me and I cherish the letters—They brought me in touch—I kept thinking about you & Bill, this comforted me, and about the little girls too. I'm so sorry about Bill's father. It must have been such a snowy trip—flying? I hope now all's snug and warm and everybody's sitting (several on the bear skin) before the fire, with pots of bloom in the window and some marvelous smell coming out of the kitchen, and you & Bill each with a glass of wine in your hands—and Kate just said something.

I was so pleased to know my name went in & out of the conversation like a butterfly through the garden. Well, I want to tell you that I'm forever saying "Kate" and "Brookie" and I don't know which one's my mommy either. Which one will be it for this afternoon? I'll choose her.

Since I didn't get to see Epitaph for George Dillon with you, I read it. It was a fine play, wasn't it? Only I thought the first act outshone the other two and had twice as much life to it—did it play as unevenly as I thought it read? I'm glad they were sensible enough to bring it back—a real play.[72]

I was in a friend's house this evening and right at my elbow, on the bookshelf, was a copy of They Came Like Swallows with the jacket on it, and there was a picture of Bill looking just like Brookie!

I tore this photograph of Paris out of a magazine (since I couldn't tear out the picture of Bill) for you all & Floribunda.

<div align="right">Much love to all—Mother sends hers too—

Eudora</div>

In the wake of Walter Welty's death, Eudora returned to work on the story that would become Losing Battles, *and she carried that story with her when,*

in April 1959, she managed to return to Bryn Mawr and then go on to New York. But in the midst of her New York stay, she was summoned home before she had a chance to see the Maxwells. Her mother had suffered a small stroke; had fallen, cutting herself rather badly; and was in the hospital.

Eudora Welty to William Maxwell, [May 1959]

Dear Bill,

Mary Lou in a little penciled memo out of New York wrote that you were "just out of the hospital." Better than just in the hospital, but tell me how you are. I hope it was brief and not bad in there. Write the news when you can, as this is all I know.

Mother is just out of the hospital, two weeks there after a blackout and fall (nothing broke), while I was in Bryn Mawr on my way up to New York. I came back of course and have been on hand, fighting the nurses in the hospital and since we got home being fought by my mother who is of no mind to be nursed. I'm supposed to watch her. Can you think of anything more foreign to the mind. I don't think it will last long, either she will fire me or she will outwit me. While things were at their most dismal, as they were for a bit, I had a wonderful dream that I opened the closet door under the stairs, where we keep miscellaneous, like the card tables, vacuum cleaner, double sockets and gift aprons, I don't really know what all is back in there—and there were you and Emmy, saying "We'll just be in here, in case you want us. Don't worry about us! We both brought thermos bottles, and we have an electric toaster." (The double socket came in handy I see). "Just open this door and we'll be right here." I'm afraid Kate and Brookie just weren't in the dream. Anyway, while I was dreaming that, who knows but what you were in the hospital room and it may have been something a good deal like that closet, and I ought to have been on tap with <u>my</u> thermos bottle. Let us straighten this out who needs who most.

How is your work, do you remember it? (I'm always pleased to be reminded, aren't you?) I hope it is going along well. I've almost got that long story licked, the sparrow story. Two parts out of four typed up and the rest I can get typed when all settled down. I do think it is better now than it used to be. I named the family Bunting—it has not only the whole sound I want,

and the country feel and everything, but it's the sparrow family, and I felt I had got the right name then, thanks to you.

Please give my love to Emmy and the little girls for me. I'd hoped for a glimpse this very month. Do let me know about your health.

<div style="text-align: right">

Love to you,

Eudora

</div>

I tore these pages out of a magazine named "Charm", which I bought in the supermarket because out of the oranges and tomatoes jumped the name Colette—and as I began reading it, I thought nobody would love that writer's work table as much as I do—except, of course, yourself, so here it is.

Remember the Spahi's cloak?[73]

William Maxwell to Eudora Welty, May 1959

On the train

Dear Eudora,

Well (now that it is over) what a winter. Mary Lou brought news of you to us, too, like a St. Bernard. In the midst of it I thought of you, we talked and wondered about you, and hoped to have an evening, <u>that</u> evening, with you and Elizabeth [Bowen], and dragged ourselves from one crisis to another, one indecision to the next. My hospital [stay] was not serious—I had a "huge big wad" of calcium removed from my right shoulder, so I could sleep after gardening. I was home in 3 days, drew numbers in the air for a week, and in two days of getting out of the hospital was knee deep in the apartment situation—for it turned up at that exact moment—and it is now ours for the next three years, but there were so many considerations—whether to move to another suburb where the schools were better, whether to buy or rent an apartment, and where to live. The first one we found that we liked and that was big enough to hold all five (six counting Florabunda) of us was on Fifth Avenue overlooking the reservoir from the 12th floor. It was as beautiful as Dante's rose, the view from those windows and financially it was wrong in six different ways—high maintenance, partially cooperative. So sadly we said no to it, and then couldn't like anything else. Meanwhile, Emmy was scouting schools—Dalton, Rudolph Steiner, and

Brearley—and taking Kate to be interviewed and on and on, and just before we found the second apartment, we decided on Brearley because the teachers seemed the most affectionate, and she hadn't liked nursery school this year where the teacher was all right but not particularly loving. In fact, we finally took her out because she resisted going so. All this settled in my stomach finally, and as near as I can make out what goes on there now is very like what goes on in the billboards of Times Square. I have been ex-rayed under various uncomfortable circumstances and am now on a drug which is supposed to do the trick in about a month. It all began March 14th, and I haven't had a cup of coffee since then. Poor Emmy. You can't imagine what it is like cooking for us. I skip all the colds, I skip when Emmy came down with the flu, I skip where Margaret had to go home to Scotland for a month because her mother was in the hospital, I skip the frost that almost got everything last night. No, I can't remember my book. Not at all. Whatever it was, it was a mistake, and what will I say to Alfred Knopf? That you are so near the end of the long story fills me with hope—for you, for me, for the world. Oh those Buntings! I cannot wait to renew the acquaintance.

And your poor dear Mother. How she must be fit to be tied, at having to bring you home, and then at having to be watched. We were both so distressed for her, and for you. If only we <u>had</u> been under the stairs, with our thermos and toasts when she fell! I know about fighting the nurses because I have so recently been among them. Such a pity to miss our visit with you, and for you to miss this stage of Kate and Brookie. Kate goes around the house singing "Goodby, my love, goodby!" to a tune of her own composition, in a minor key, with real feeling. And Brookie was heard to say, on her way to the Blumbergs'—"Sacred heart! There's Leda on the see-saw and there won't be any for Katie and me!"[74]

On the 19th of June we are driving to Martha's Vineyard. I will come and go till July 1st, and then we'll all be there during July. Then a month to get the apartment habitable (with luck) and (again with luck) we'll be moving into town around the first of September. The address is #1 Gracie Square and the living room windows look past Carl Schurz park up the river to the Triboro Bridge. It's just big enough, and kind of pretty, and 3 blocks

from Kate's school if she doesn't resist going to it. And Brookie is enrolled in Carl Schurz park, and when you come we can walk along the river.

Love from us both to you and your poor watched mother —

B

I loved the desk, the Spahi's cloak and the sentence I ringed — to the point of madness —[75]

4

"Stubborn Enough to Be a Writer"

BETWEEN 1960 AND 1966, Eudora and Bill led their lives in a sort of counterpoint. Bill would complete the novel he had struggled with since 1948: *The Château* was published in 1961, spent three weeks on the *New York Times* bestseller list, and was short-listed for the National Book Award for Fiction. Such achievements eluded Eudora. Since the mid-1950s, she had attempted to write two novels but finished neither in the first half of the 1960s. Instead, she cared for her ailing mother for more than three years before realizing that Chestina Welty needed a skilled nursing facility. Eudora chose the best available one, located fifty miles from the Weltys' home, and unless she had out-of-state work commitments, visited her mother there daily, jotting down notes for a story as she drove along a hilly, two-lane highway. To use Bill's words, Eudora was "stubborn enough to be a writer" and claimed whatever moments she could for her work. Bill, too, was stubborn enough to be a writer. Much of his fiction had been concerned with his mother's January 1919 death as a result of the Spanish influenza epidemic, and after his father's death in 1959, he revised *They Came Like Swallows* and later wrote "The Value of Money." Both the revision and the new story helped Bill come to terms with the loss of his father and with the difficulties

of their relationship. Eudora's fiction had dealt more obliquely with her fa-
ther's death in 1931, but the loss of her mother and the transforming of that
loss into fiction lay ahead. For now, she knew worry and sadness and frus-
tration.

While Eudora's and Bill's lives seemed to be counterbalanced, the bonds
between Eudora and the entire Maxwell family grew stronger and stronger
between 1960 and 1966. Bill recognized Eudora's difficulties, sought to en-
courage her writing, and enlisted his own secretary to help her with manu-
script preparation. Perhaps his support was key to Eudora's completion of
two powerful short stories about the civil rights movement. Both "Where
Is the Voice Coming From?" and "The Demonstrators" were published in
The New Yorker during this time. Eudora rejoiced in the success of Bill's
novel and in 1964 dedicated her only children's book, *The Shoe Bird*, to the
two Maxwell daughters. In a world where writers often prove to be imper-
fect friends to each other, Eudora Welty and William Maxwell were not.
Their mutual devotion was unfailing. So, too, was the devotion of Bill's fam-
ily to Eudora and hers to them.

Eudora Welty to Emily and William Maxwell, [April 1960]

Dear Emmy and Bill,

It was like hearing angels' voices—you probably didn't. But I believe you
did call. It was the finest thing to hear you and what a surprising amount of
news did come out—the book nearly ready, for one thing. I'm so happy
about that. I long to see even one word—perhaps more would be given. All
my love & expectations for the finish of it and happiness it brings you. How
are the girls, with Spring in Gracie Square? Wild? Emmy, I wish I could see
you in the dress Bill wrote me about.

There seemed so much to say, getting to be more. Every day in our liv-
ing room I see the Denmark candles. The winter black & white of Gra-
cie Square I have upstairs in my room propped on the mantle shelf—so
delicious—I wouldn't even be surprised to see it changing under my eyes.
I look at it so regularly, like the aquatint in the M R James story (only not
sinister changes, just going from bare limbs to leaves, to keep up with you

for me).[1] And the Japanese book—that's the secret you found out from me, I would rather see a book with beautiful snow white blank pages than almost any book I know—not all others—Bill, did this lure fasten on you in your own youth? Maybe it will never be written in, that is not the point—there are still books unfilled, that's it. And one tha[t] can be filled in from the back going forwards (just happens to be the way I write) is just beautiful. Since you have cast this upon the waters you may of course get it back one day. One day!

I thought of you when I read Isak Dinesen's speech "On Mottoes of My Life" in one of those handbook things—you probably have seen it already but I must be sure & am sending it. She might have been before me as you saw her & described her as I read this. It makes you cry.

It's so beautiful all at once here, is that the way it happened there? And at last[?] News here isn't very good—My poor mother had another bad time last week, making two bad ones since Christmas. She is at home with nurses, and today is feeling just a little communicative. I just this minute told her what I was doing & called your names, and she didn't say anything but smiled. She's come out of these things all right before, for a year now, & I guess she can again & looks to the doctor as if she's going to have to do it again & again & again. It is heartbreaking, just for her to perceive this, as she must be doing. But nothing "hurts."

Mary Lou must be in London about now. But from a letter I had, she isn't getting to see the very things she went over there to see—what kind of trip is that? Economical? It isn't though. I guess Agnes's grant has to be severely allocated, but you know Mary Lou would go without food, even marrons glacés, to be at the perfect point at the perfect time. I believe there is something dour about Agnes maybe.[2]

Do you like Henry Green?[3] I really am wild about him. I read nearly all his books again sometime during this past year. The starlings flying in at evening in <u>Concluding</u>—

Will write soon—I think of you all 4 so many times. I believe all will be better around here soon and I hope they're fine & stay fine around there. I count on it—It was 3 years ago? one day last week (my birthday) we had luncheon on the grass with prosciutto & melon & wine—Kate was in the

swing, telling a story swinging. We were listening, eating. 24 hours between my 2 last sentences, here comes this excuse of a letter. And meanwhile (in the 24 hrs.) I opened the New Yorker & read your Laurie Lee review, Bill. My! I can taste that book. And Sylvia T. W's beautiful story.[4]

Much love to all. I think of you & that's joy.

Eudora

I shall get back to work soon myself & still think that crazy story is a pleasure to work on.

William Maxwell to Eudora Welty, June 23, 1960

Dear Eudora

You have a letter coming up. I am out of the woods. Mr. Knopf has the manuscript. But this here note is to tell you that the New Yorker is bringing out another anthology of short stories and the story of yours the editors chose is "Kin."[5] The book is coming out in the fall and the royalties will be divided among the writers, as usual. Emmy and I had lunch with Elizabeth [Bowen] today. Your Elizabeth, I mean. Though not little E [Elizabeth Welty]. She was as fair as the day is long, and we left her at 3:30 talking to Monroe Wheeler about his Art Nouveau exhibition.[6] Love,

Eudora Welty to William Maxwell, July 24, 1960

Dear Bill,

I'm so happy about that novel I don't know what to do. <u>Remember</u> about the way they do get finished, when you're in the morass & and middle of the next one. (Part of a lecture I listen to from somewhere.) When & how soon?

It was good to get word from you about it.—Also thanks for putting in Kin—I always think of that story as something of a collaboration, happening all over the country, over the phone, & winding up in the Algonquin Hotel. Between you & me, I mean, & the other kin.

Is all well with you? I hope you & Emmy & the girls have somewhere cool in mind. Love to them.

My poor mother's not well at all, so low in her mind, & very opposed to

getting well, so when I & the help nurse her she's never getting her wish. I hope this part will change—her mind—the rest of her's better.

I've been trying out working very early in the A.M. before she wakes up—first week went all right. So good to hear word of Elizabeth and from you. I think of all of you so much & with love.

Wonderful about the novel! Eudora

Eudora Welty to Emily and William Maxwell, December 15, [1960]

Dear Emmy and Bill,

Thanks and love seem to be coming late to you after the way I left after my good visit & haven't written. The truth is, it's thanks & love every day, and I still will write a real letter—It was so good to see you all that it felt like a rescue—I don't know from what but I had needed that visit—not just any visit away from home, but that one.[7] It was good to be back with you for Hallowe'en!—& to think of the girls being old enough to cut a Jack O'Lantern's full smile with a knife—while Bluebell joggled the elbow[8]— The family dinner was simply a heart's wish, that's all. You know how much I loved being there, seeing the new house & how happy it goes—the view from the window, which compares favorably with the sketch Emmy—

And I can sit & wait for the novel to appear now, and can hardly. (Don't know how to correct or improve that sentence.) I'm so glad I did see the live proofs that night—[9]

Emmy, a delight to read the Children's book piece—your best yet, you know—[10]

I'll write again soon. Things go along here pretty well in all—Mother smiled with a good deal of self satisfaction to hear about Kate and Brookie, remembering Kate of course and remembering that she was told that Brookie was coming on the corner of 6th Ave. & 44th Street. Much love to you all from Eudora

William Maxwell to Eudora Welty, December 27, 1960

Dearest Eudora:

We fell upon the pears as if you had sent us, in a box, all of the twelve

days of Christmas! As in fact you did, by extension. The partridge, the five gold rings, the French hens, the maids milking, swans a-swimming, ladies leaping, etc. are all in the beautiful winy flavor. We had them ourselves, we had them for a dinner party for the Cheever's and the Truax's (pâté, oxtail stew, salad, your pears) and there are two a-ripening.[11] We both thank you with all our hearts. Pears are something all four are agreed on. Emmy carves and peels and the slices float around the table from mouth to mouth, while we argue who likes them <u>most</u>.

We have a darling tree this year, tall and slender and like a tree in the woods. The top didn't have to be sawed up and it is airy between the branches, and also there was the Accident, and finally it is the first tree the children have helped to decorate. Because of the dinner party, which was on Friday, we set the tree up and decorated it on Thursday. And Saturday morning, as E and I were getting dressed (Brookie has just gone out to the park in her <u>snowsuit</u> holding a large paper Japanese umbrella over her head!) we heard the most frightful crying from the living room—the way Kate cries when something awful has happened, usually to Brookie. I stood rooted to the bathroom floor, and Em rushed in and saw that the Christmas tree had fallen over. The breakage was indescribable (I mean I could describe it but I won't) and Kate was inconsolable. They had crawled behind it before breakfast and were I suppose playing house. Anyway, Brookie forgot and stood up and over it went.

After it had been stood up again, and the spun glass splinters and shards disposed of, and a little tidying here and there, we saw to our surprise that it was now, for the first time, just right. There had been much too much on it before!

At this age, to my surprise, I find it is impossible to guess how much carries over. They remember things from their remotest past, of course; and don't remember a thing about last Christmas. Hearing voices at daybreak I got up and tiptoed into the living room and plugged in the lights and went back to bed and waited for the patter of little feet. No patter. Nothing. They've gone back to sleep, I said, and promptly did likewise. And woke again and heard them still in their beds, and went in to see what was the matter, and Kate said "I'm so <u>tired</u> of staying in bed." They had been told

they must stay in bed till it is daylight, because weren't getting enough rest, but waking each other up in the morning, and they had not been told that Christmas was an exception. However, they didn't have to be told twice.

Brookie had left a cup of milk and three crackers inside the firescreen, and with it a note in some indecipherable language she knows, and sure enough in the morning it was all eaten and drunk, and there was a thank you note from <u>him</u> written in fireplace soot because nobody had thought to give him a Parker 51. All those lists are in pencil, and you know how hard it is to keep a pencil in a busy household.

Well, that was Christmas. We all send our New Year's love, and our love to your mother and hope every good thing for you, including a return visit, along about rose blossoming time.

Devotedly,
Bill

Eudora Welty, [New York City], to William and Emily Maxwell, [March 1961]

Dear Emmy and Bill, it's been like one of Kate's stories, the angels overhearing some bad fairy's wish and reversing things <u>immediately</u>, & so I say what is then said in the story—"Thank you." You've all four given me such joy & pleasure, & hope unexpected, along with love. I can't say thank you every day in life in words but you know I do. With of course my love.

Bill, the prospect of having this story [*Losing Battles*] something to be looked at in order is so marvelous to me and only you can possibly know how much so—Work at Vassar is going to happen in <u>spite</u> of the world being saved on all sides.[12] I'll telephone you Monday week from here again.

The Château goes up in my hand and will be a reward to me portioned out each night—I'm so happy with it—

Monday too perhaps I can get Kate's fish she gave me—

And Emmy said I might read her piece.

And here is mine on Henry Green.

And I am also taking up (I'm going in a car) the camellia branch with buds for my room at the Alumnae House. With love and wishes & thanks to you

Eudora

Eudora Welty to William Maxwell, April 5, [1961]

Dear Bill,

It was lovely to hear your voice and I still was feeling in all those ways in touch, seeing you, & Emmy & Kate & Brookie, & reading The Château all the way home & nearly without stopping, & then all this you're doing for me. It's all enough to make the angels sing. The Château is as full of living & light as running water, and with 12 years to go through before it all was what you wanted, and still (or more) to be like running water, is just one more sign of what a writer you are and what you are. And all the feelings of France and of Paris & of train rides through the countryside & of those moments of complete & unbelievable happiness, perfection that nobody but the traveler in a loved land ever dreams the depth of—and what these things all do to what we've brought, all the loads of our own, old feelings. The mystery was all just exactly as this reader would have begged to be given, if such gifts had been imagined. I loved the questions & the answers at the end, & there could never be such a novel again. The bicycle ride to the party! I feel much of this is the best you've ever done, & saying such a thing sounds pointless, since what is best when nothing is at all for comparing? But something has been carried the step further than it's been brought to before, possibly? It is beautiful, you know that, and I hope so much you're happy with it at last. Thank you so much for my copy—my two, so that I feel able to bestow it now.

I've come all the way from willow trees through dogwood to roses—all is deep in spring here. Mother was glad to see me and still seems to be— She is pleased about all I've told her and is even willing now that I take time working on my story since you have provided this wonderful chance for it— She does get a happy feeling at the mention of any Maxwell's name. So it's like a password to work at this moment. I've nearly finished Part II—and am sending it up when I get the print sheets—Miss Barbara Nichols is so fast till I can hardly believe my eyes—it is like putting the story in the Fax & having it come out all typed.[13] I've done what you say though & I know this is right, not looked back. She wrote me such an understanding note & made me feel easier about the awful job of it by saying she enjoyed the story! Here's a note for her. I hope she is not doing her work for you any harm in any way

in the least, ever? What this has done for me already is so much—But you more than anybody know this & very well. Thank you with my love for it all every day. I'm writing Emmy, give my love to her now—I'll send back her food piece to her at Gracie Square—Kate's fish is propped on my mantle. It has got a lot of suspense! Love to her & Brookie—Love to you.

<div align="right">Take care of yourselves—
Yours, Eudora</div>

My telephone here is Fleetwood-2-1668—I don't know any long distance number for it so far.

William Maxwell to Eudora Welty, May 24, 1961

Dear Eudora:

I feel that we should communicate with each other by tapping, since it is more than likely that you are far below the surface of the water and it is a simple fact that I am. Barbara thinks you weren't finished, and so you must have been interrupted. Well, as I learned from listening to Elizabeth [Bowen] describing my novel to me in the park, the thing about interruptions is that they don't count. If you are stubborn enough to be a writer in the first place, I mean. And it takes twice as much stubbornness if you are a girl, since the arrangements for you are somewhat made and certainly different. When you are able to pick up again, everything is ready and waiting at the end, and you can go on as before.

I am just tired with the emotions of being published. It seems to take so much strength to face all those copies in bookstore windows. As if some drama, on the scale of Paradise Lost, were taking place in my unconscious. Or as if I were selling the copies myself. All this is not complaining, since there is nothing to complain about, but explaining about Henry Green. I mean I had trouble with Concluding, worked hard at it, could not love it (except now and then) or quite love the Firefighting piece, and worked hard at loving it, and then Loving turned up and I loved it without working at it at all. I just sailed through it, smiling to myself, and that was that. Except that it won't do, of course. I mean, everybody loves Loving, and I am still on the outside of the circle of you and Elizabeth and whoever adores him, and I know this is my fault, but I can't think what to do in the present circum-

stances except wait for different circumstances, which will be occurring the last two weeks of July, when we go to Oregon for a family visit. There in central Oregon, with mountains all around me, and nothing whatever to do, I will pick up Concluding where I left off, and I am sure be amused by those two awful women instead of, in my tired state, just appalled by them. Just now I seem unable to read anything harder or more demanding than a British translation of Zazie dans le Métro. I read a good deal of it in French last year, but it is such French that I never could be sure what I was reading, since about one quarter of the words were in the dictionary, the rest being too slangy or too indecent.[14]

I didn't simply love Loving in a lump sum way, I loved scene after scene—especially the love scenes between the two maids, and the handing down of information from the Butler to the little boy, and the way the house didn't at all belong to the people whom it belonged to, any more than the zoo belongs to the animals in the cages, and the marvelous blazing scene when the mistress came home and the cook let all the calamities drop on her head at once, and the conversations at the servants dinner table, and the rotting peacock carcass, and the peacocks and the outrageous insolence of the last sentence, because of course they aren't going to live happy every after, he has something fatal wrong with him and will be dead in three months. Well, anyway, it is an elegant novel, and I feel sure that in the end I will find my way into the others as well. Or if I don't, that you won't hold it against me.

Just like last Spring, I keep bringing the country to Emmy in the city, because of her not being able to come. Last week it was the iris and the first forgetmenots and the lilacs. Also, I forgot to stir the spray for the roses, so when I got half way through the powder made the spray thicker and I may have burned everything with it. So I am afraid to go out this week and see. Your mother's rose was in fine condition up to that point, and since not every catastrophe takes place that could take place, maybe this one didn't. Some things are still recovering from the shock of the cold. The fig tree is alive, but just two tiny buds at the root. The strawberry shrub is green inside but no shoots at all. And that huge hardy seven foot golden wings [rose] died back, for the first time, to within a couple of feet of the ground. But, queerly, nothing really died, because there was such deep snow.

We will be in Yorktown after the first of June, but I lost my yardboy to I.B.M. and the present yardboy is pokey—the kind of conscientiousness that interferes with getting things done—and even he is about to turn into a life guard, when school closes. On the other hand, it is just possible that Kate is old enough to enjoy weeding. And just possible that she is old enough but won't enjoy it. I remember the distaste I used to regard the task of digging up dandelions for my father. And the money involved, five cents a hundred, didn't overcome my distaste, fond though I was of ice cream cones. Well, in time I got big enough to caddy, which paid better. I still have a half finished book of thrift stamps which I wouldn't part with for anything in the world.

How are you?

Love,

B.

Eudora Welty to William Maxwell, [September 14, 1961]

Dear Bill,

Just a little note to say I hope to pass through New York for 2 days beginning Sunday night Sept. 23, not a real visit but a chance I had to make a quick circuit (a meeting at Yaddo) free, and if all goes well I start out from here next Wednesday, to get back in a week. So could you and Emmy by the slightest chance find yourselves free to come to have dinner with me say Monday evening? I expect things go at a whizz there these days but I'll hope for luck. Anyway, if this trip tests out all right, I hope to come back for longer than just 2 days.[15]

I long to see you and see how things are with all of you. Well, I hope. Does Kate like school still? How is Brookie—it won't be too long till she gets that knife into another Hallowe'en pumpkin.

I've done a little more on the work [*Losing Battles*], and my secret wish is that it's enough for you to see and tell me something, viz. Is it alive?

I must go, but will first write to ask Barbara Nicholls if she will let me take her to lunch.

With much love to you and Emmy, Kate, and Brookie,

Eudora

William Maxwell to Eudora Welty, September 18, 1961, Telegram

=MY GOODNESS YES! YES TO MONDAY EVENING, AND YES TO MY READING THE WORK, IF IT TURNS OUT YOU ARE READY TO HAVE ME READ IT. LOVE=
 BILL

William Maxwell to Eudora Welty, October 4, 1961

Dear Eudora:

Well I find it very hard not knowing how they got the car down in time for the funeral.[16] Or what part Miss Footsie Kilgore played in the operation. Don't worry about the form. It has it. And don't whatever you do cut any of the physical descriptions of the place, the night, the moon, etc. The whole going to bed passage is so beautiful that it is like reading an opera. The mind supplies the music. Harold Brodkey has a theory that most novels run out of gas, that is to say the original inspiration, after the first seventy or a hundred pages. And then the novelist gets his second wind, with a different inspiration.[17] This doesn't run out of gas, but it takes on a certain musical solidity when they are at the table and begin to talk about Miss Florence Hand. Partly from the fact that they talk so long about her, and up until that point have refused to stick to any one subject for longer than three sentences. Anyway, it builds, all the way to the end of part III. There are a hundred remarks that delighted me they were so much like the people I remember. And made me laugh out loud. The only book I ever read that it reminds me of is Delta Wedding, it is so completely just like you and nobody else. It also has the richness of being the only thing you have been working on all these years. One feels that, more and more. Now what else can I tell you?

Love,
Bill

Eudora Welty to William Maxwell, [Fall 1961]

Dear Bill,

Thank you again for that letter, you know what it meant to me, and for

calling—so lovely to talk to you. If the ms is not in the way it's in the safest place on earth, there on your desk. I'm so glad Brookie's fine again, and all of you are well. And that I can hope to see you again so soon. I have to work 2 nights in Chicago, & a day & a night in Washington, then coming on to N.Y. ought to be by Monday Oct. 30.

Since Elizabeth will be in New York again, I want to have a little dinner somewhere with you & Emmy & her, & thought of Hallowe'en. (It just came to mind.) Could you? I wrote her this. And I don't want Emmy to be saying she'll work instead, you must let this be mine whenever the evening you can all come.[18] I'll make no dates ahead, but just wait & see how things work out. It will be lovely to see you all again—Heavens!

<div align="right">Love,
Eudora</div>

Saturday

Eudora Welty, Northampton, Massachusetts, to William and Emily Maxwell, March 14, [1962]

<div align="center">

SMITH COLLEGE[19]

MEMORANDUM

</div>

To Emmy and Bill *From* Eudora

In re selfish pleasure

Could you have dinner with me in New York a week from tonight? March 21st? It will be the night I come through on my way home—I'll hope. Our beautiful evening, and I never wrote to tell you, <u>was</u> so beautiful, and it also seems like 100 years ago. I came one weekend to N.Y. & saw Martha Graham dance & worked—have had a lot to do here but it's nice— and I've the surest feeling you're in Yorktown more now that the ice (thank God!) is breaking up, but I hope that somehow the Wednesday will find you in town and free and that it will be propitious—

<div align="right">I have to go to Holyoke this minute.
Best love to you from Eudora</div>

142 Green St.

N'hampton

Wednesday Will phone you from Algonquin

Eudora Welty, Northampton, Massachusetts, to Emily and
William Maxwell, [Spring 1962], Note card with image of
Edward Lear's Manypeeplia Upsidownia

Dear Emmy and Bill,

I think of you in the country, adding a little south to it. In Vermont, where I was last Sunday, the shad flowers were all along the lanes, with bits of snow deep in the woods, and here the apple orchards are all in full bloom. Last night I was taken to Mt. Holyoke to hear John Pope-Hennessey lecture with slides on Benvenuto Cellini and great crashing thunderbolts came in a storm during it and he never acknowledged them by the slightest—anyway, afterwards, driving home, there was the moon, and great ragged clouds black as ink rushing over and not Cellini or Mr. P-H was with me for a moment but suddenly Ibsen peeping out. I keep wishing for that cycle you made up for us all in London, Emmy—7 plays, 7 nights in a row.

I've been busy (see cover) but liking it—I meant to write & at times believe I have written to you—You know how happy it made me to see you—All such times seem snatched up like jewels to run out of a burning house with, somehow, except that sounds funny because while evenings would be the first thing I'd snatch up, jewels would be probably the last. At spring vacation I stayed home 2 extra weeks, domestic complications, but although there are still domestic complications—so that I can't linger in New York—Mother herself is well and writes long letters in her good handwriting.

Have you ever read a Mme. Zhitova's memoirs of the Turgenev family? It is what I want to give you if I can get hold of it—this copy is from the Amherst library. About Ivan's mother: "She at last deigned to read Dead Souls. 'It's frightfully amusing!' she praised it in Russian, 'but to tell the truth, I have never read anything in worse taste or more improper,' she finished in French." And of course what a perfectly hair raising woman, a demon. But a marvelous book.

I have to be in N.Y. at the Institute [of Arts and Letters] doings on Thursday & will call you, Wednesday probably, hoping to say hello & find out how all your healths are—Kate's throat is long since well, I hope. Love to all from Eudora. I am tired, really exhausted at times, but fine really.

In the fall of 1962, James Meredith sought to enroll at the University of Mississippi in Oxford. He was turned away on September 20, but on October 1 federal marshals brought him to the campus to ensure his enrollment. That evening there were riots on the Ole Miss campus; two people were killed, and seventy-five were injured. Eudora had long opposed Governor Ross Barnett, the ardent segregationist who fanned the flames that led to the Oxford riots, and she seems to have written Bill ruing the fact that all Mississippians were seen to be of the Barnett stripe.

William Maxwell to Eudora Welty, October 2, 1962

Dearest Eudora:

Worried about you is no name for it. Especially as your letter is dated Sept 30th, at which time all hell had not yet broken loose. But I am such a worrier, I peer at the television screen and remark "Eudora's house is quite <u>near</u> the center of town" and Emmy says "This is in Oxford" and so, for the moment, relieved that the smoking automobiles are there and not in Jackson, that you are not in sight and sound of the howling, I sit back and go on watching. What mostly bothers me is not that something awful will happen to you, because I know it won't, but how you must feel, the frustration of being misrepresented, helplessly. But you are right—at such times an aggravation is a comfort. Speaking of the press at the time of Faulkner's death, I read about it on the plane going to Oregon, some ten days after Emmy and the children had gone, and was able to satisfy my sense of slurring on the New York Times for printing an excerpt from your statement, which was beautiful, when the Washington Post printed it in its entirety.[20] What would they say in Jackson about you? In Lincoln, they say I write very well but am sorry for myself. Which was news to me. Though I saw after a minute what they meant. A taste for the sadness of life. Speaking of which, I had arranged for an interview for a young man who wanted a job on The New Yorker, and who was staying on the Baptist Church Road while the people who owned the house were away. I rode into town with him twice and saw him two other times, and all the resonances so to speak were just right so

I asked him if he'd like to see the personnel man at The New Yorker and he said he would, and wrote such a disarming funny letter, describing his life history, and four days before his appointment took an overdose of sleeping tablets from which he did not recover. My first thought was if I'd only known, I'd have talked to him about it, and then I realized to my astonishment that I <u>had</u> talked to him. We'd actually had a conversation on the subject of suicide and I had assured him that I was on my fourth or fifth life, and glad I hadn't judged life by the first and second. But he didn't believe me, apparently. Only how queer, how close to the edge things can sometimes be. What an analyst would say is the self-destructive impulse is perhaps indeed that, but it is also being in love with death, which it appears he was. The woman he was living with said he spoke of death as if it were a rose.[21]

I am so distressed about your mother's fall. It will perhaps permit her to skip the next six incarnations, but it doesn't make this one any easier. For either of you. Tell her that Brookie has learned to read. To see that fat little finger moving across the page, stopping at "Come" and "and" and "see"…"Come and see Rags…Come, Rags…" is enough to make my eyes fill with tears. She is so passionate about it. She reads herself to sleep with her reader, only it is awake instead, because she gets overexcited, and can't go to sleep. Kate says it isn't fair that Brookie learned to read the first week of the first grade and she didn't. Last night, being in bed with a cold, she (Brookie) made a book, on yellow paper swiped from the office, of words from "More and More Ant and Bee."[22] The newest one.

The roses have suffered from neglect. The puppies came in June and I stopped spraying on their account, and then after reading Rachel Carson, on my own.[23] Also, did I tell you I took up the piano? Well I did. I have had lessons from the concert pianist across the road, who made me (only no coercion was involved, it was all rapture) do scales from Hanon's The Virtuoso Pianist all summer, and when I had gone through all the parts of that I could at this stage, and suggested maybe Czerny, he, as Emmy described it, took me off scales and put me on music. To her relief. She has been angelic, especially considering that she doesn't even much like music. Just Verdi and Mozart. Nothing else, really. But she put up with it, and now I do those simple pieces that children play, and am enraptured when a piece of

harmony turns up. If you will come East for Christmas, I will guarantee to play you at least six or seven Christmas carols. Good King Wenceslas I already know, except that it slows down rather too solemnly toward the end, owing to my not quite knowing where all the notes are yet.

Emmy got cross at Thea[24] just after we got back from Oregon—five weeks vacation, so she took a four day weekend when a day and a half was coming to her—and fired her, and Thea quit, and then Emmy, the injured party was willing to talk and the injuring part wouldn't talk, so we have been without anybody until today. I am holding my breath. A 19 year old girl from Newfoundland. The New Yorker Children's book review is across E's path, so it is rather important. The fall has been trying—but no more than that—but the summer in Oregon was lovely, and just like last year. We have put in a whole boxful of bulbs, and if the children will only stay free of colds, will keep on going out [to Yorktown Heights] until cold weather. Edith Oliver expects you here for election day.[25] I think Elizabeth was in America this summer, but nobody I know saw her. It is terrible having such a tenuous hold on anybody you love so much. I am reading [Vladimir Nabokov's] "Laughter in the Dark" which is not a game but deadly serious. A paperback, with the paper turned yellow and brittle. Bought in a drugstore long ago, and for some reason never read. It is so queer reading first rate writing in such an awful casing. Oh the book! The Richard Hughes.[26] I will save that and the puppies for Emmy...Worlds of love,

Bill

Eudora Welty to William Maxwell, [October 1962]

Dearest Bill,

Thank you so much for your letter—it was wonderful. Of course this time I'm worried because of Emmy's family in Oregon.[27] Are her father and mother all right, and her house, and up in the country where you go in summer? I hope you've been in touch a lot by this time and that things are reassuring. Wind is the scariest thing of all the things Nature can do, don't you think—and when it blows out lights and tears down wires, and makes for darkness and not being able to get in touch, on top of all the other damage. I hope news is reassuring and things will be all right.

Also I hope the new help is proving good. Emmy and I will have to have a conversation to tell each other we know so well how it is. I hope everybody's well and the weather's holding so you can get to Yorktown Heights and have the leaves till the very last.

Awful about the boy. Something must have told you to talk about it and this probably added a day, two days, three days, onto his life however sad. The unfairness of it to you, too, after you'd <u>talked</u>.

It's very beautiful, very dry here,—we get along, good days, bad days. I might be a day or two in New York, 29th & 30th of Oct. but it's almost sure not to happen. If it does, I hope there'll be a way for me to hear Good King W. and then I'll play for you—Playful Kittens is my piece. What a happy thing, that Steinway in the dining room!

Much love to Emmy, Kate, Brookie, and you, and it was so lovely to hear from you.

With many wishes for good word from Oregon—this will be worrying Emmy in the middle of her Children Book piece too.

<div style="text-align: right">Yours,
Eudora</div>

William Maxwell to Eudora Welty, January 14, 1963

Dear Eudora:

I won't go so far as to say you missed your calling, because you haven't, but I do say that there is something you do almost better than anybody and that is spoiling people by giving them things they would never have had the imagination to give themselves. For years I have seen the <u>Observer</u> in my turn at the office, usually in doses of four or five issues, as somebody else finished with them, and out of order, and three months behind, and sometimes even with large rectangular neat holes where something interesting used to be. We have already had two issues, and the pleasure of seeing that brown wrapper on the hall table is more than I can begin to tell you. And on top of everything else, it is the only newspaper that comes into the house these days. We have almost forgotten what it was like to read the <u>Times</u> at breakfast, and as for Sunday—no book section, no Bloomingdales ads, no excuse for having a third cup of coffee. So you see, we <u>needed</u> the

Observer, terribly.[28] And thank you terribly, terribly much. I don't understand how this is so, but I read it from one end to the other, and then pick it up two days later and read an entirely different paper, and then again three days later a still different one. It always takes me three readings. (I usually read Tynan the first time, and maybe Harold Nicholson, Toynbee the second time through, and the political articles the third time.)[29] The truth is, I wish the Times only came once a week, and were as well written as the Observer.

We have had a long lovely quiet rainy Sunday. Poached eggs and three pieces of bacon apiece because it is Sunday. Then I had a spell at the typewriter and a spell at the piano, and Kate spent the morning cutting out a set of "Bluebeard the Pirate" for her Pollack's Toy Theater,[30] and then for lunch we had a wonderful soup—no, first marrow on toast and then the soup, made from the bones of last night's roast beef, and then I had a nap and Emmy had a rest, and I had another spell at the piano, and then Kate performed "Bluebeard the Pirate," at the top of her very good lungs, and Brookie complained that she didn't understand a word of it so I got her back in bed where she belonged by promising to read some of "Uncle Wiggly's Adventures", and now she is building a house out of Lego blocks, and Kate is getting up some new play, and E is doing needlepoint, and the lights are beginning to go on in the tall buildings, and Sunday afternoon is sliding down hill, and pretty soon it will be time to go get the ice cubes and the makings of two old fashioneds, and I wish we could have a month of Sundays, all like this one.

We had such a fine two weeks in the country, over Christmas and New Year's, arriving back in Gracie Square on Twelfth Night, with the little Christmas tree planted where it ought to get through the winter nicely, and in the spring it will be moved to the edge of the marsh, with the others. There was snow on the ground, and E and the children sledded, and I took music lessons day after day, and commuted just long enough to realize how much I enjoy not commuting, and we saw our country friends, and all in all couldn't have had better luck. No colds, even. Imagine.

I am glad that your mother is making progress, and that the piano is back and in proper shape.[31] Would you like me to send you some music— are you beyond the stage of "Easy Classics and Modern"? Or is the bench

full of good things? We have been only once to the theater—last week, to see the two Zen plays under the title of "A 10th of an inch makes all the difference," and they were both very good. E is reading and liking "Five Families" by Oscar Lewis, and I have finished [Joseph Conrad's] "The Secret Sharer" and started the [William Hazlitt's] "Liber Amoris." With Pritchett's "London Perceived" coming up. How I wish you could come once a week for dinner and reading it aloud, the way Elinor Hinkley's niece used to come to their house in Cambridge, Mass.[32] They got all through the Victorian novelists while she was growing up. And of course that poet <u>was</u> Ibsen's father...except for one <u>small</u> thing: what poet or writer ever resembled his mother and father's other children in the slightest? If I stood between my older and younger brother you would burst out laughing.

I hope the spring will bring you back to us. Love,

B

Eudora Welty to Emily and William Maxwell, February 21, 1963

At home

Dearest Emmy and Bill,

Your letters are things I carry around, which may be the next thing to answering them, only without the pleasure to me. Thank you for these from the day they came—I am so glad about your good Christmas—it did sound perfect for everybody in the family in every way. How are all your healths now? Love to each one.

How did you know about me and cards? There was a small shop near St. Germaine that had nothing else as I remember—do you remember it? I used to pass it morning & evening, old cards (tarôts?) and books on cards, gypsy cards. But these are the most elegant and captivating in their design that I've ever seen. Christmas morning I woke early & opened that one present as I drank coffee, and before I even took them in with my eye I'd shuffled a deck & laid out a game of solitaire just by feel—They are beautiful—Also, I've had an idea for a year now that I'd like to go back to bridge, for which I once had a passion—& had to cure myself of it the way dope fiends

do. But it would fit into life now better than most things would, and these beautiful cards are going to start me off. If you hear that I have disappeared in strange circumstances, you'll know it will be with those decks of cards and 3 other people,—only I wish as I contemplate that, that it could be with four other people for a while, all named Maxwell.

How goes the music? Bill, I want you to have a recital, when I come— Kate can arrange the whole thing—the program & program notes, the decorations of the entire house (Hallowe'en, again, if need be), who's to take bows & when, in what order, refreshments, favors, and prizes. You'd both better get to work on it, though there's no telling when I'll come. We get along but it will be better if Spring ever comes as won't it be for us all? I wrote a children's book "in my spare time," don't know if it's good or bad, but when it's typed I know who to send it to to find out.[33] Love to you all and take care. E

P.S. Those little books for the children were sent first-class mail as I remember, to Gracie Square—If lost, they were only stand-ins for a few Christmas lights.

William Maxwell to Eudora Welty, March 1, 1963

March 1 (and like a lion)
Dear Eudora:

Well you are amazing. I didn't miss Ivan Ilyitch, but I did suddenly put out my hand for "Invitation to a Beheading" and it wasn't there, and so I asked Jack Huber if he had it, and I asked Alix Taylor if she had it, and I asked Joanna Brodkey if she had it,[34] and they none of them had it and they are the only people who ever borrow books of us (You don't, we press them on you, in order to increase the weight of your luggage on the train) so I thought and thought and suddenly it came to me that it was you I had pressed it on, and I said I will order another copy because it is TOO MUCH for Eudora to have to think of returning books all the way from Mississippi, and will tell her to keep it, and within twenty-four hours of my having this thought the package arrived, so it was the oncoming package, no doubt,

that made me put out my hand for the missing book in the first place. But I do thank you, several times over, because I am not at all sure that ordering it would necessarily, after this length of time, have produced a copy. One has to grab books on the way by, on their way to the remaindering. It is too shocking.

As for Ivan Ilyitch, it took John Updike to point out to me that my own grandfather did the same thing—couldn't stand up in the face of suddenly getting everything just the way it ought to be, so he had what was called a nervous breakdown, and couldn't put his feet to the floor, and so kept them in bed, and died. All before even my older brother was born. And now I have gone and lost his beautiful tintype by putting it in a safe place that I can't for the life of me remember.

Emmy expects you to appear, suddenly. She bases this on her feelings. She feels you are about to come to dinner.

I go about reading aloud to people, and what I read aloud—to Brendan Gill, Janet Flanner,[35] Updike, etc. is the passage about your being taken as a child to see Mammoth Cave. If I had to choose between it, and Plato's allegory, I would choose it, though I am fond indeed of the allegory. But this is the way all writing ought to be, a marvel, a joy, a joke, an experience in itself, something seen in an Easter egg, a treasure, I cannot tell you how you enriched me by writing it. I come at the three papers from every which way, trying to approximate the way that they formed themselves in your head, which was not standing up in front of a lectern but at various times of the day, in various lights out of the corner of your eye, etc.[36] I also think of you every time I see Kate's head bent over a book. If you want her you have to go right down into the book and get her.

It is snowing again, and the view to the north is by Hirosnigi.[37] Love,

Bill

Can you not perform that experiment with the manuscript of the children's book yourself? Shouldn't you be the one to read it to them, I mean?

Emily Maxwell to Eudora Welty, April 25, 1963

Dearest Eudora—

For months I have been wanting to ask you whether you read Oscar

Lewis' <u>Five Families</u>, and whether, if not, you'd like us to send you a paper-back. I loved it so, and some of the people in it are so real to me, and have such worth and generous natures and real humility—that it's like having lived a part of my life there, and having shared with them the necessity of living from one meal to the next—and what inventiveness and energy they had to put into providing a single simple dinner. It's a cousin to <u>Let Us Now Praise Famous Men</u>—but there is the one great difference. That you were always aware of Jim Agee's presence & sensibility—whereas Oscar Lewis never shows himself. Maybe you'd hate it. Maybe you've read it.

I am sitting at my desk wrapped in my fur coat, just barely getting warm. We have had lovely weekends in the country—a slow, dry, spring—so that we could enjoy each thing that opened all by itself. And the children, who have been healthy, are beginning to love the country, and to beg for walks before breakfast. Someone gave them a rabbit, a baby and white for Eas-ter, & all Easter Day Brookie carried it under her sweater. We had to give it back after ten days because it put poor Daisy [the Maxwells' dog] under a terrible strain.

We have walked back in the woods to that monumental deserted build-ing which always makes me miss you especially much—and found King Cups and anemones and blood root—and we have lots of new little bulbs around. My favorite is the checkered frittilary, which never can seem to open before the wild rabbits eat it. It must be delicious!

Bill is writing fables, and Kate has written a 110 page <u>book</u> about some twins in the Middle Ages, which she first called "The Middle Aged Twins." It is very exciting when the Earl goes off to fight in the Hundred Years War. And she says that though the children loved their few books, it was hard for them to keep their minds on them when people went by in the street call-ing, "Throw out your dead!"—as this was the time of the Black Death. But you will read it sometime, and I mustn't spoil it. Brookie, not to be outdone, has also been writing stories, and I was going to send you her latest for the delight of her spelling (there was noone around to ask) but Thea has done something terrible with it—if it ever turns up again I'll type it and send it.

We miss you and love you,
Emmy

Please remember us to your Mother.

Eudora Welty, Austin, Texas, to Emily and William Maxwell,
[May 1963]

Dearest Emmy and Bill,

The train ride here, down the hypotenuse to Texas, is utter peace. When you leave the city goes away immediately and it's mountains, or valleys with beautifully ploughed fields and yellow barns till dark. There was the biggest thunderstorm I ever rode a train through, you could even <u>hear</u> the thunder through the roof & windows, but we were all enclosed and it was quite like added scenery, the wild heavens. After you leave St. Louis, you ride another good train, following the Mississippi from 4:30 till dark, as close to the water as the train used to go along the Riviera (it may still!). There's no very frequent sign of human habitation at all, and it's the way the river must've looked in the days of the Indians, or of Audubon anyway, so you imagine. Then that night, the whole <u>world</u> was lit up with fireflies. The train must have been going through wild country, hardly any <u>electric</u> lights, all darkness, and flashing, flashing from the ground to way up in dark trees, mile after mile. Then of course woke up eventually to oil wells—but not too many, because it's fairly green and full of trees, hilly, in East Texas. Austin is green, with huge live oaks, and oleanders, magnolias, gardenias etc. in bloom. The wildflowers along the tracks were so thick—gaillardias, cosmos, phlox, thistle, calliopsis, & of course bluebonnets. There is a wild clematis called the leather flower—dark ruby red—

So far I've not really begun to work (it starts in 20 minutes & goes on till Wednesday), but have seen old friends, one a painter whose work I like a lot and who is doing still more beautiful things than he did before, Kelly Fearing.[38] Desert rock, fishes, pools, children, saints, birds, snails, cats, poets all clear and jewel-like color and pure line. Well, I wish I could send you one. You would know how it restored me to see you and how happy I felt to be there. And that marvelous, marvelous dinner, a creation of a dinner. And Anna Gloria and Roger and Barbara and the Priest[39]—let's none of us forget that evening, keep it intact—And my love and thanks to you for making it happen—

Emmy, I still haven't read Five Families—Just like Anna Gloria & Roger trying to read the Gutenberg Bible & being distracted by the cries

of "Throw out your dead!" I was distracted by the fireflies. But all the better. I have it to look forward to. Love to Kate and Brookie, love to you, from Eudora

On June 12, 1963, NAACP field secretary Medgar Evers was assassinated at his Jackson, Mississippi, home. Horrified, Eudora immediately drafted a story about the atmosphere of hatred that had produced the assassin and led to such an event. She and Bill edited the story over the phone. "Where Is the Voice Coming From?" was published in the July 6, 1963, issue of The New Yorker.

William Maxwell to Eudora Welty, [July 1963]

Dear Eudora:

I thought you might want a copy of the story the way you wrote it, so here it is. Nothing but praise. Emmy shook her head in wonder at it, and Mr. Shawn stopped me in the hall to ask if I had talked to you and I said, "Yes, four times," and he said, "Does she know how good it is?" I expect you do, somewhere, if not exactly on top of your mind. Being brought up the way we were, it has to be that way.

I left home this morning in the midst of What is the matter with Mary Jane. Brookie, who loves play camp, refused to get ready to go and was sulking, and Emmy didn't have time to find out why because she had to rush Kate to the riding stable and get back in time to take Brookie and the Katz children to play camp, and as I walked past the bedroom door, I heard her saying in exasperation (see the N.Y. Times report of the weather—in New York) "Very well, I'll take the Katz children to camp and you can stay home with Ivy." Ivy[40] is Jamaican, and very black, and beautiful (only Brookie doesn't know it), and children aren't her strong point, though she has two (but left 'em in Jamaica), and every Monday night goes to beautician's school, and is among Brookie's undigested experiences, so I dare say she went to play school. So does life promote character, along with Anglo-Saxon attitudes.

Love,
Bill

P.S. I started to read [Joseph Conrad's] "The Duel" and stopped after 6 pages, because it has to be read aloud to Emmy, when I can get her undi-

vided attention, which will be August 1st, or thereabouts. It simply undid me, from the start.

Eudora Welty to Emily and William Maxwell, [July 15, 1963]

Dearest Emmy and Bill,

Just a little note to say Happy Saint Swithin's Day and I miss you—It really is Saint Swithin's Day, it really is raining, & blessedly, and I really do miss you—The Fourth was so lovely. It was first of all lovely to see you of course—and then it was the very nicest kind of visit—everybody doing what they had to do, but enveloped in the house, and meeting to eat, drink, & laugh—I realize it was no magic spell that put all those good things to eat before us—though I know you say, Emmy, "Deep Freeze" is a magic word, but I know how far that goes. But if you got back from the station with gas, Bill, all was as perfect a time as I ever hope to have—Thank you both, and thank Kate and Brookie. It's all down in my memory—with other times we've had, in the same general good clear neighborhood—speaking of my memory, not Baptist Church Road or Gracie Square—

Is Oregon being all you wished for? I think of you chasing around on horseback over green hills on cool mornings—

P.S. I opened this to say thank you for sending the story as you got it, I am glad to have it—What I ought to send <u>you</u> is the "poem" it started out as, with all the real names & places & quotes from living mouths, only I tore it up as I typed the story—

Went to Yazoo City (where Mother is) yesterday & read her the whole Profumo story out of the Observer, to refresh her mind from the surroundings—[41]

My novel is at present named The Honeycomb and is in 6 parts of which I have typed the last 3, almost the last 4, still unread & unspliced.[42] What I don't know now is whether to put the almost-end of the world in it or not—literally—but I've about made up my mind I can leave it out. I know I sound crazy with the heat. Hope your nights are cool when you get out of the train & ride home.

Love again,
Eudora

Eudora Welty to William and Emily Maxwell, August 13, [1963], Stationery from The Shelleys Hotel, Lewes, Sussex, with Eudora's autograph note saying "Let's pretend we are meeting here."

Dearest Bill and Emmy, are all of you all right? Are you cool and in Oregon? I have tasted your cantaloupes then, the last three days.

Love to you—We are pretty well here.[43] I work the early hours (story is tighter). As the sun rises they are nailing on new gutters (new roof next) and I am judging an Armenian short story contest. The gutters are beating the Armenians so far but there are 30 stories to go. It seems typical of August somehow! I <u>think</u> of <u>you</u>, that is where my heart goes a lot of the time. Mother asked me last night how you were—and how old Brookie was by now—and remembered again when you announced she was coming, Bill, on the corner of Sixth Avenue and 44th Street.

It was so lovely that night. I am thinking of getting a ukulele like Mary Alice, my niece, so that I can enter playing it if I ever get back and accompany the piano, WHATEVER you are playing. And we can go on from there. (What will Brookie pick up? A Tambourine?) Love from Eudora—I expect you've read these but wanted to be sure—[44]

Eudora Welty, Yaddo, Saratoga Springs, New York,
to Emily and William Maxwell, [Early November 1963]

Dearest Emmy and Bill—I miss you!

> Hallowe'en—Beware, beware
> From the shadow of Yaddo to Gracie Square
> I wish we could beware together,
> And can only tell you, by owl's feather
> Beware of witches & warlocks,
> And pogo sticks & sudden shocks—
> When it's the night for terrors vague
> Black cats & witches & Haig & Haig—
> When our round table in the Algonquin
> Turns into a Hallowe'en pumpkin,
> And when that turns into a rhyme

It's Hallowe'en time—[drawing of jack-o'-lantern]
Love to Brookie, love to Kate,
Puss-in-Boots and a Witch out late:
You frighten me, well, but I send you love
& Hallowe'en wishes on the wings of a dove
Dressed as a frightful witch who says "Boo...
What Kind of a Hallowe'en treat are You?"

We had 2 pumpkins on the coffee table after dinner, lit, made by Mr. Shavvon the caretaker or handyman—I passed around the delicious smooth glorious drink from my beautiful Pinch bottle—and offered chocolate pumpkin, but nobody cared to mix—Later on I ate the pumpkin (still have some) which tasted like an Easter bunny and was quite delicious—Shall have some with my lunch box sandwiches & grapes—[45]

Oh how lovely it was to see you—I can't tell you what a pleasure it was. A new start, too. Thank you for our darling party—

I'm working hard but am being summoned home by the old-time nurse crisis. "My dignity & self-respect will not allow me to stay" she [the nurse] writes me. And I can't reply "Yes they will"—So I can't stop over in N.Y. though I am sticking out my 3rd week here, working right through the big question-marks that parade through my head about Jackson—

Love and blessings—Wasn't it lovely with you both & Elizabeth [Bowen] & me all laughing the morning away?

Take care of yourselves—I'll be home Sunday the 10th—I think I'll have completed one whole section in last draft—Best love to all from Eudora

Eudora Welty to William Maxwell, June 1, [1964]

Dearest Bill,

You appeared in a dream here Friday night with the words, "But the dress rehearsal is at 7:30 and it's ten after now!" We didn't make it. I hope I didn't miss out on something marvelous?

A fine letter from Emmy said everything was going well and healths were good and the only trouble was no sleep because of being caught up in whirls this spring. Sounds lovely. In New York sometimes as a pampered visitor I used to get the feeling I had as a child that came from standing out

in the yard and turning around in place enough turns to make you fall on your face, very satisfactory—but you do need sleep. I worry about you without knowing how close they were to you when people at the New Yorker keep dying. Anyhow, their loss must mean confusion and more work. I knew Hamilton Basso a little, and felt drawn to what I knew.[46]

How is the country? I think of you as there. Here it's so beautiful just now—unseasonably cool! I've been doing the cycle of lecturing and typing and going to see my mother in the convalescent home.[47] The lectures are over all but two—one in Conn. in June (this is June—!) and one in Miss. in July. (I'll pass through New York coming back around June 30, but fear I cannot stay. But hope to find you there to speak to you.) It's been better planned this spring than last, but if I have to do any work at colleges next year I shall just try to get a job, I think, here in the neighborhood. When I get a little way further on the typing of this thing, I need to talk to you. I won't even say more now. But I need to. As you know, the normal way to have done this was one time—like a dive. I don't mean without my usual close revision. But I've done it as the whole single effort too many times. Anyway, you are the one who would know what I am just living to find out. Don't you dread it, though, because I may not have ruined it and I've kept the old.[48]

Tell Emmy I made her creme brulee the other day, after having lived for several weeks out of the refrigerator—can't tell you how good it was! That's the kind of test I like to give my cooking. Took some to Mother. The name Maxwell is still Sesame. I read her the children's story [*The Shoe Bird*] I was dedicating to Kate and Brookie and she said "Don't think much of it." Should have done something entirely different—I know it.

Will you be going to Oregon this summer? I have thought of you all so much, lately more than ever.

<div align="right">Love to you
Eudora</div>

William Maxwell to Eudora Welty, June 10, 1964

Dear Eudora:

We have just moved to the country and when that happens (though not

vice versa, strangely) I always feel like that old joke about the nude stat[u]e of G. Washington that is supposed to be saying "My body is in Mt. Vernon, my clothes are in the Patent Office." Emmy is sleeping better. I <u>think</u>. Not being awake to witness. Anyway, she likes being in the country, where she can hang things up on the line. And I think I have solved the rose spray dilemma. I have been using, all spring, bottles 2 and 3 of triogen, but not bottle one, which has the lethal chemical—endrin, I think—in it. And they are fine. The roses, I mean. There was some rotenone in 2 or 3, and that is apparently all you need.

You know that I am always utterly at your disposal, about that manuscript, but at your disposal with a certain amount of fear and trepidation, because I know—I have read—how you feel on the subject of neatness, and New Yorker editing is essentially a neatening process, and after twenty-six years I cannot utterly disassociate myself from it. So this you must be on guard against. What I have found is that you can trust the opinion of people who love you until the moment comes when you can't trust it, and when that happens you know, so perhaps it is not serious, what I am saying. I am sure you haven't ruined it. It is unruinable.

We are going to Oregon, about July 7th, so we will be here when you pass through and should it be possible for you to come out to the country want you there, where we can all talk to you at once, but count on hearing your voice in any case.

But you are mistaken about that dream. It was ten after <u>six</u> when I appeared and said what I said about the dress rehearsal at 7:30. I always allow too much time for everything. See Emmy on the subject. So we did make it, whatever it was.

Brookie has stopped sucking her thumb. The sight of poor Kate's braces did it, Emmy thinks. You should see the braces, but then you will. They're not just for overnight. They are both playing in their first piano recital this Sunday. Brookie's piece is called "Nodding Ferns" and Kate is playing two— a Mozart (but not <u>the</u>) minuet, and something else, a bravura waltz of some kind, by a composer I would rather not remember the name of. My music teacher almost died of pneumonia this last month, and I stood still (also my playing) wringing my hands, until he recovered, which he now has. Now

that it is time to plunge ahead, I find I have rather caught the habit of stand-
ing still, but never mind. We all send love,

B.

Eudora Welty, Suffield, Connecticut, to William Maxwell, [Late June 1964]

Dear Bill,

Thank you for your letter that I was so glad to get. And at about the same
time the New Yorker arrived with your story in it, which I absorbed just like
the grass out here by this barn after last night's rain—I feel much greener.[49]
So good and so plentiful with good things. I'm busy through most of the
day with this work here and if I had had to walk all the way from Jackson
and work free all the week through, I would have gladly because of Padraic
Colum.[50] Imagine having him in the same place as you and telling stories,
reciting poems of anyone anywhere any time in the whole history, and just
remarking. ("Emily Dickinson could have been a real artist but she didn't
<u>wark</u> hard enough"—thrown out to start an argument.) To think of his still
being with us and the liveliest one for miles around—the last link with all
that. Last night came his lecture in the barn, which is the Suffield Academy
Theatre, and of course it was so much more than a lecture—about grow-
ing up in his grandmother's house, with the peat fire which you look <u>down</u>
on, and so is so much better than other fires, and the greyhounds sleeping
"in a loop" on the hearth, and the story-teller coming, taking a seat (in his
grandmother's house there was always a pile of clean grass and leaves kept
ready near the hearth for any wanderer) and beginning "Now by the power
that has seized me, I will tell you:" (better than that, can't remember right
now).

Anyway, I'll phone you at the office and now I am hoping to remain
part of or most of the week of the 29th, so if you and Emmy could possi-
bly still have a free moment it would be so lucky—but I know this is late.
I have a reservation at the Algonquin though. Didn't get to work myself
here so no ms. to bring after all, but <u>what</u> has been coming into my ears! If
I can only (hopeless) remember the way to tell you about Brendan Behan
and the doped dog and the races and the rosary Marathon inspired by Billy

Graham and would the barking come at the wrong time. A precious person. In glorious command, too.[51]

<div style="text-align: right">

Love to all of you,

Eudora

</div>

Eudora Welty to William and Emily Maxwell,
[July 1964], Incomplete letter

Later[52]—during the [Republican National] Convention—
Emmy, one of Mother's nurses says "I consider Mr. Hatfield is just as good-looking as Dr. Kildare." The TV screen is hypnotizing me—paralyzing me—It is scary, for just one thing, that Goldwater has <u>no smile</u>—doesn't possess one. An unsmiling invitation to all the John Birchers to come into the fold has just been unsmilingly delivered.[53] And I'm being assured this benighted state is already in it—the fold—I wonder if you're in the thick of this in Portland or if you are, really, off in the clear woods (clear off, I meant) eating strawberries and sipping vermouth cassis. I pray you are.

After the good boost I got at your house, I'm still swinging, with this pile of pages. Bill, didn't you love it in Leonard Woolf's book on the train, when you came to the marriage ceremony and Vanessa took the opportunity to ask about changing her child's name and the Judge said "One thing at a time, please, Madam"?[54] [Enclosed was a postcard with a photograph of the Hampton Roads train.]

Best love to all—Thank you again—I told Mother that Brookie, not yet born when she was there, is now saying sentences like "It's almost completely transparent"—which gave <u>her</u> something to marvel at too—She is pretty well.

William Maxwell to Eudora Welty, November 11, 1964

Armistice Day
Dear Eudora:

From several days before Halloween on, we have been expecting you to turn up, and I now realize that you are being kept, and so I take my pen in hand to tell you how we all adored The Shoe Bird. I read it aloud, a chapter

a night, and we all four laughed <u>all the time</u>. It is and it isn't like your other things. I thought I detected a note of Bert Lahr, whom I have never seen — something theatrical, a kind of gag, only it comes off. Which is why I think it must be Bert Lahr. Along with all the other kinds of comedy. I don't know (because I couldn't find them) what places you were worrying about, but if you are still worrying, don't. It is completely successful, beautiful, moving, and terribly funny.

Love,
Bill

Eudora Welty to William Maxwell, November 21, 1964

Dear Bill,

On Armistice Day I imagined you and Emmy meeting for a movie — I was signalling from here. Thank you for your sweet note. I know I go slapstick when probably I ought to pray — you put your finger on the exact worry. And there were Kate's and Brookie's precious names on the flyleaf — that had been purest self-indulgence. Just so it was not all awry — and I drew a delicious clear deep breath at your note.

When you have time do let me hear a bit of what has happened or is happening about your text and Emmy's pictures. While you're writing just tell me everything. Did that rushing waterfall end up in a trickle over the dam — was the brook still there? I wondered about the roses and the corn — could you come into Gracie Square and have plenty for baths, etc.? How was Oregon?

It's been dry here too but we had water to spare in the pipes. A long lovely bright fall, and Mother's been up to going for short rides. She dearly loved the long piece you ran on Scotland, which I read to her — so did I.[55]

No, this isn't a year of travelling around, for I felt too out of pocket at times last year at colleges. A job teaching twice a week at the local college, for which I applied, is a godsend, and I'm working better now that life is in compartments of teaching and not teaching etc.[56] Were you able to write when you were at Illinois? I've got your Smith talk to read my children [students] some day when they can have a reward. They are nearly all darlings. But have they ever read anything? No, absolutely nothing.

Did you ever get the piece done on Leonard Woolf—and that other marvelous memoir that had only too much to want to tell?

Elizabeth Taylor's last novel delighted me so, did you like it?[57] Also I got very wrapped up—as I don't always—in I. [Ivy] Compton-Burnett in "A God and His Gifts." She has a grand time with writers.

Have a lovely Thanksgiving. Love to you all, many thoughts and wishes,

Eudora

William Maxwell to Eudora Welty, November 24, 1964

Dear Eudora:

Don't you have any worries about The Shoe Bird. That's my news to you and as Gloria said, What grand news! You have no idea how many sentences from it went straight into the family conversation. It is something that happened to us. Now if it will just make your fortune.

Nothing has happened about Bun and Emmy's pictures for it that hadn't already happened. I mean it just happened twice. The editor [at Knopf] all telephone smiles said I had misunderstood her letter and it was just a matter of a couple of sentences, so I went to see her, and there was the manuscript all edited and fixed and inserted and red ink here and more red ink in the margins, all ready to go in a You Can Learn to Read series, or something so like it I couldn't tell the difference, so I took it home and left it lay—the thermofax, I mean. She's still sitting on the original and the pictures. When I get the strength and organized and all, I will get it away from her and show it to Ursula Nordstrom, who will probably say the same thing, and then I can really let it lay.[58] Which is my inclination.

We dug another well in the country two years ago—265 feet—and so we haven't had any shortage, though if this kind of not raining continues, God knows what will happen. There are two gigantic brush piles in the back yard that I don't dare set fire to. Once in a while it rains a teeny bit, but never when we are there. It went directly from Indian summer into bitterly cold. The roses that are already in the ground are all in their mounds and the mounds in wire baskets. The roses I ordered from that madman in Scappoose Oregon [Roy Hennessey] haven't come, and when they do it

may be too cold to plant them. If so, I am just going to put them in a trench and leave <u>them</u> lay till spring. I am so glad your mother is better, and able to enjoy things.

If you mean when I was teaching Freshman rhetoric at Illinois a hundred and fifty years ago was I able to write, the answer is yes, book reviews. But that's all. But it's also more than I seem able to do now. I bogged down completely on Leonard W. [Woolf] <u>and</u> Lady Ottoline. And didn't even attempt The Journal of Jules Renard, though I was out of my mind with pleasure over it when I was reading it.[59] About Lady O, I kept thinking that there were so many people who knew her, and could write about her from first hand knowledge, and in fact had, and what was there to say more than that her book confirmed what had already been said? Renard defeated me because the original was in French and 1200 pages, and I couldn't even lay my hands on his other works, let alone read them, and it is so easy to make a fool of yourself in public if you are of an enthusiastic nature. <u>Also</u> when you do finish a review, you get so much pleasure from it, as if you had really finished something, which alas you haven't.

We are going through a crisis at Gracie Square—the wicked landlord, straight out of S. J. Perelman, with just a touch of Simon Legree and the Marquis de Sade—is co-oping the building, and so it is a case of buying the apartment, under terms that are entirely to his advantage, or moving, which is impossible. We have lain awake nights, tried not to be foolish, tried to distinguish between the foolishness of the head and the foolishness of the heart. It is all awful. I don't know yet what is going to happen except that we are going to <u>try</u> to buy it. But don't ask. It's like an illness. I'll tell you when it is over.

Brookie got knocked down in gym yesterday and whichever way she lay her head on the pillow it hurt, and Emmy came in and found her sound asleep sitting up in bed. Isn't that like her? Isn't that Brookie? E eased her down a little, and before I went to bed she was sleeping with her head at right angles to her body, but at least it wasn't a concussion.

E's children's book piece is done, and coming out in the issue of December 5th. The last page proofs were delivered this morning. Piano is going nicely. We are having Thanksgiving in the country with Uncle Jack Huber and the [Robert] Rushmores (Alfreda Urquhart remarried; when you

love couples do you ever get so you can accept them not the original couple? I even sometimes go to the wrong house, and often call the wrong telephone number and so does Emmy. Think what the confusion in the Ark would have been if the animals had got divorced.) I'm glad you are not rushing around. Elizabeth [Bowen] is here. Blanche Knopf told me she was coming—last Wednesday, for two weeks, I think. In heaven I am going to have her all to myself, but meanwhile I don't even attempt to capture her. It is quite enough just to love her.

We all send you our devoted garlands, two kinds of cranberry sauce, stuffing and everything—

B.

Eudora Welty to William, Emily, Kate, and Brookie Maxwell,
[December 1964], Incomplete letter

I'll be thinking of you all—The letters, the Christmas pictures on cards—so much more beautiful than Christmas cards—the mysterious box to be opened Dec. 25—and the first New Yorker from headquarters—all are here and around me—such a crowd of loving wishes!

Thank you Bill, Emmy, Kate, Brookie—I'm so happy to read, gaze at, & delight in them—The pink winter sky and the black trees are stood up against the mantle clock—pink-and-ink—and take me into the December moonrise every time I look to see what time it is, plus the intermediate times of looking on purpose. And what came next but Kate's shapely, dramatic tree—and what came this <u>morning</u> but Brookie's curly lamb, with well-placed thoughtful eye—I had to move Brookie's Baby in the Cradle over an inch to give the lamb room to see—I love this card very much too, which came with the yellow box.

It's windy and warm—72°—and the camellias just trembling headlong into bloom and gone in a day, too much for them. My mother sends you love. I took Elizabeth (home from college) and Mary Alice up to see her yesterday to start her Christmas off—

Before I realized the time might be not too good for ordering for Yorktown Heights I asked Armstrong to send you three roses—It will be all right if they come in early spring, won't it? There's a Mister Lincoln, on account

of Lincoln, Ill.—& Lincoln—an Eiffel Tower on account of Paris—and an Isobel Harkness just because. I know you like Isobel too and the first time I saw it in bloom was in Cambridge at the Vice-Chancellor's Garden Party for American guests, between showers—Isobel was 500% water that summer I suppose & perfectly ravishing. I was looking at the roses & nearby a baby was playing on a rug—"There, you see, is the difference between Oxford and Cambridge," hissed a voice in my ear. "At Oxford, a <u>baby</u> would never be allowed at a Garden Party."

Lehman Engel is home for Christmas along with other old friends, so it will be warming & nice—I'll eat turkey dinner with Mother—It's nice to be out of school, isn't it, Kate and Brookie?

<div align="right">

Love to you all,
Eudora

</div>

Fingers crossed about that.

Emmy, your words about my story [*The Shoe Bird*] in your New Yorker piece were so fine—I was proud. A monumental piece it was this year.

Despite the cheerful tone of Eudora's Christmas letter, worries about her mother's health and consequent unhappiness were intense as 1965 began. She confided as much to Mary Louise Aswell. Still, Eudora wanted to reassure her friends that she was coping with Chestina's physical and emotional plight and that friendship was crucial to her doing so. She wrote to Mary Lou:

Mother is mentally changed, though it doesn't often seem like a mental illness—just what happens to us all, I suppose, if we're 81. If she had her vision I believe she would be much more of a master of her situation. Anyway, I do seem able to comfort her. So this is what I work for. Sometimes when I can't comfort her, that's when I feel desperate, and your letter spoke to those moments and lit them up some, lightened them. But I feel ashamed of having caused you alarm for me. I am really a facer of facts by now, I think, though it took me a long time—took being a writer, perhaps, and of course it took being a reader—and I have had you and Bill and Emmy and Diarmuid for friends, and, after all, I have had my mother. Please don't feel uneasy about me—it would be unjustified, and

I would tell you if I felt I was slipping and all my friends could come and give me a good solid spank—that would be what's called for. So remember and don't worry.[60]

William Maxwell to Eudora Welty, January 15, 1965

Dear Eudora:

Clairvoyant is what you are. In the fall, having a yard boy who was six feet tall, and strong as all get out, I suddenly thought how nice it would be to have some new roses. So I got him to dig six holes, in the perennial borders, and wrote to that maniac in Scappoose, Oregon. Not Will Tillotson. You know the one I mean. Well, he wrote back that I ought to get this one instead of that, as usual, and then along came another postcard saying that he couldn't possibly dig a bush before Nov 10th at the earliest, and I wrote back all right, and then winter came and the ground froze, and still no roses sticking out of the mailbox. I assume they'll come along in May. But meantime, anytime that Armstrong decides to send Mister Lincoln, on account of Lincoln, Illinois—never mind Lincoln, Nebraska, it don't count and never did—and Eiffel Tower on account of Paris, which I dreamt about the other night, all in pastel shades, very beautiful, only it isn't really in color at all, the real thing, just grey, as I remember it, and Isobel Harkness because she is a friend of yours—there the places will be, all ready to pop them in the ground. And if Roy Hennessey—I knew I'd remember his name if I didn't try to—comes through with his bushes, that yard boy can dig three more holes. In any case, there will be a general perking up of the rose situation, thanks to you. Ever so many thanks to you.

I wish you could have been in Yorktown when E and the children were carving the linoleum blocks and printing their Christmas cards. It was as good as Halloween. Now E is doing some fresh illustrations for <u>Bun</u>, on scratchboard. We never got around to discussing the old ones with the editor at Knopf, because she kept saying it was just a matter of changing <u>two</u> sentences of the text, and then she leaned so heavily on her pencil that I didn't know my own style. In fact, I knew it wasn't my own style. So she not giving an inch and I not giving an inch, we politely parted. How boring

they are. She wanted to make it so that a child could read it, and apparently children can't digest compound sentences. The children she knows. Ours began speaking in complex sentences at one and a half, as you know. And in any case, a book is for the reader who can read it. Or wants to have it read to him. How glad I was to see the last of her. Though I don't look for any different anywhere else, we will try a couple more places.

Charles Shattuck who loves you came for the night, and I had the pleasure of sending him your record after he went back to Urbana. Once in a while you can give something to someone you are fond of that you know they will be beside themselves over. His wife is one of my oldest friends—from high school and college, and he is an old enough friend. If you can keep from being swept off into groups when you are in Urbana in March long enough to get acquainted with them, you will, I think, take to them both. Anyway, if one could pass along one's friends to someone, which I guess you can't, really, these are two I would pass along to you.

In her Christmas card one of my childhood playmates sent me a snapshot of some people in bathing suits, including me at maybe ten, bathing suit just above the knees, the face, to my surprise, the one I had when I grew up—same expression, everything. Everything is forecast in childhood, even middle age, it seems.

I wish you were here to go to the Moscow Art Theater's Chekhov with us. The Three Sisters and the Cherry Orchard. Nobody else is quite right.

Love, raised to the fourth power,

B

Emily Maxwell to Eudora Welty, February 4, 1965

Dearest Eudora,

By now you probably know that Elizabeth is here. We went to Blanche Knopf's last week for dinner, feeling as if we must be her idea of a good extra man, as we'd been there shortly before, and there, like a Christmas present, was Elizabeth. And afterwards she spent her evening with us here, with all our feet up, and we missed you terribly. She seems happy to be moving into her (as she calls it) 1962 brick house, with a view of village rooftops and

an edge of the sea. I've never looked down on rooftops (except in books) but it must be a charming thing to do. And to walk down a steep hill to the village![61]

We are off to the country tomorrow after missing two weekends—and those three weeks feel like 3 months to us all, especially Daisy, who's doing her best to transform all the surfaces in the house, including our clothes and shoes, to look like a blond Labrador's coat. She always sheds, but during February it gets so much worse I spend all my time brushing—I even have to brush the children's dark blue cotton jumpers before they go to school. The hairs are barbed like quills, and have tremendous magnetic force, leaping up three feet off the floor to reattach themselves to a nylon garment that you've just brushed them off of. It's great fun in many unexpected ways to stay in [the city], but I worry about the enormous colony of sparrows who live in our chimney-ivy in this bitter weather. Since birds have no flesh on them, I don't see how the poor things can live more than a few days without food, though we do our best to fatten them up when we're out there. Do you suppose that sparrows, like Indians, can fast the last part of the winter?

There's something from you in the mail this morning for the children, and it's all I can do not to open it, with the expectation of finding you inside. How is the teaching? Brookie adores her teacher this year, but that doesn't seem to have any effect on her application, which is marginal. I'm enclosing a poem of hers (she loves [Edward] Lear)—I find the spelling delightful, but I see I can't go on that way. Brookie feels that spelling just comes naturally to her, so she never studies it. I wish we could apprentice her to a wood-engraver at age ten. Kate is beginning to play tunes on the cello, an extraordinary feat to me, and to her, too.

I'm about to go out and look at two apartments. Without much hope, because we are all so spoiled. Lots and lots of love to you—and love to your mother,

Emmy

There was an old person of dover,
who consesantly chewed on a clover,
when they said: does it tast? he answered:
po! it's a wast, so they exiled that person
from dover.

Eudora Welty to Emily and William Maxwell, [Spring 1965?],
Written beside a copy of the first page of Flannery O'Connor's
"A Good Man Is Hard to Find"

Dear Emmy and Bill, This is the story I was thinking of when I spoke of it as "The Misfit"—when it has such a wonderful title—The first story of Flannery O'Connor's I ever read and it terrified me so, it was ages before I read any others—and before I understood too well what she was doing. I still feel terrified by it. Isn't the car trip wonderful? "The children's mother"—Mr. Edgar Adkins Teagarden from Jasper, Georgia—And the Misfit—"one of the latters"—

Love,

E—

Emily Maxwell to Eudora Welty, [Spring 1965]
Card with image of Emmy's original drawing of parents,
children, and dog moving to a new home

Following an orderly retreat, we are taking up a new stand, due northwest of our present position, at

544 E. 86th St.
N.Y.C. 28

William Maxwell & Co.

Eudora Welty to Emily and William Maxwell, June 7, [1965]

Dear Emmy and Bill, is the view from there just as good? Will I get to see it? One of my students found I was on the program at a writers conference in Conn. June 24 (where I was last year) and not to make a liar out of them I decided I could undergo the hardship of spending a week in N.Y. on the chance of seeing a friend or two on short notice—Terribly short notice, but could you have dinner at the Dardanelles some night with me? To wit, June 18 (date of arrival) or any night but Mon. (21) Tues. 22 after that, till I go to Conn.? If that's out, I'd try to stay over a day after Conn. (not sure how long they expect me for).[62] Are all of you well? I'm O.K., school's out, I'm work-

ing. Long to see where you live, as in my mind I've got you picked up (à la the drawing) but haven't put you down. I'll call from Algonquin & hope! With love from Eudora

Eudora Welty, Westport, Connecticut, to Emily and William Maxwell, [June 27, 1965], Postcard with photograph of Second Baptist Church, Suffield, Connecticut

Sunday, Conn.
A few bells to you, from one Baptist Church road to another. It was lovely seeing you, and the new apartment—even in the boiling city steam while I was hating your having come in & stayed in from the country, I was feeling refreshed and so happy being with you—

Love, Eudora

William Maxwell to Eudora Welty, October 27, 1965

Dear Eudora,

Here am I, sitting at gate 3 of the Boston airport, a victim of demonic possession. That is to say I told John Updike I would arrive on the plane that left NYC at 11 A.M. and he said he would pick me up at 11:50. But there are no taxis on 86th Street before 11, and I took the subway to the Morgan Guaranty, saw nice Mr. Colwell on the second floor about some bonds that had matured, and started to take a 42nd Street crosstown bus to the 37th Street air terminal in plenty of time to take the 10 o'clock bus from there to La Guardia. Only along came an empty taxi with a nice Negro driver who said it was cheaper in the long run (almost true) to go straight to the airport which we then did. He was huge and looked like a self-respecting pirate with very good gold teeth. 62 years old, going to retire in two more years, and take people fishing in his boat for $10 a day. He doesn't like driving a car but does like fishing and boats. And vacations. Each week he puts some-thing aside—a fund. This year he and his wife flew to Frisco and then to Hawaii. Came home with 100 left of the $1600 he started with it. Next year Nassau.

Well, we got there in time to take the 10 o'clock shuttle plane—you know about shuttle planes? They collect your fare on board, with a tea tray on wheels—It is all very pleasant and like the Automat—and 45 minutes later I arrived in Boston, thinking with respect of the force of example. <u>My father always got everywhere an hour before he was supposed to get there.</u> I came up to look at an exhibition of drawings and paintings by Nancy Hale's mother, who died a year ago, and was a very good portrait painter who had the misfortune (which I feel already I am sharing with her) to outlive her period, and so suffered the pangs of neglect.[63] She was also rather childlike in the simple dedicatedness of her nature and in sudden moments of out-spokenness. The paintings didn't find a gallery in NYC, so I came to them, and John is out of the kindness of his heart driving me to Concord, where the exhibition is, and back to the airport this afternoon. If there had only been a piano on the plane, I would have been utterly satisfied with the ar-rangements, and perhaps in time that will come, for those who don't want to look at the movie.

At this point I got up to see if Updike had come yet, and he had, so we went off to see Mrs. Hale's paintings. And wonderful they were, too, only we got lost in Watertown, and it's now one day short of two weeks later. I <u>think</u>. I've really lost all track of time, because I've been doing the galleys for my book of tales, and the children's book review is due next Monday, and it's Halloween—that much I do know (and where are <u>you</u>?)—and in short next week will be calmer. Perhaps. We both loved the speech, which has some of your best remarks in it, and needed saying.[64] And who also loves you is Eddie Newhouse's daughter Alison, who is not quite twenty and pretty as a picture and working in Brentanos.[65] She got them to stock up on all your paperbacks. Masses of them. But being young she likes the sad stories best. I can well remember when I did too. I also think Elizabeth [Bowen] is here, but how can you tell? Love, For sure, I mean.

Bill

William Maxwell to Eudora Welty, November 22, 1965

Dear Eudora:

I've been calling you, to tell you that we <u>all</u> think the story is won-

derful,[66] but all I get is the sound of a phone ringing in an empty house! drrrrr...drrrrr...drrrr

<div align="right">Love,
Bill</div>

Eudora's failure to answer the phone signaled a crisis in her family life, and her letters to Bill over the next month often crossed with his in the mail.

William Maxwell to Eudora Welty, December 1, [1965]

Dear Eudora:

The galleys [for "The Demonstrators"] are, or should be, just what you wrote. Reading through it slowly and carefully I came up with these few points, none of them important. If the suggestion is acceptable, fine; if you see the point but do not like the way it is attended to, another way will do as well. And if you prefer it the way you had it, also fine. In short, it is as usual with these things. And there will be another, final proof later, with Mr. Shawn's and the proofreader's queries. But sufficient unto the day is the literal-mindedness thereof. So first you get mine. The thing is that the story can only be treated as a poem, and a poem tends to become clear after you have finished it, not while you are reading it. When I had finished this story, everything was utterly clear. And I was even more deeply moved than when I read it the first time. It can't be true, but I feel that nobody is writing from feeling except you.

Now for the notes:

1) Do you hate dashes? Would parentheses be better? I thought for a minute that it was the young man who was locked up, ready to face home. Dashes or parentheses would lift that part out of the sentence, making it instantly clear.

2) Isn't all he would have thought simply that the street lights were out? The "tonight" starts a train of speculation about other nights, which you probably did not intend.

3) Or some such indication, since it turns out that they actually were all

men, but the reader has no way of guessing this until you say so in the next paragraph?

4) I didn't understand this sentence, and took it to the only poet I could lay a hand on in this office (Moss not being here Wednesdays), Mary Phelps, who said she thought it must mean that the girl looked as if she wanted to batter something with her head, the way sick people, moving their head (only she moved her eyes) back and forth on a pillow do sometimes. This could be the right explanation, but it is not what you have said. "Battering-thick" is where the uncertainty lies. Is it possible to make the idea clearer?

5) You haven't said that the child who came to get Dr. S was twelve-years old, and so this could be some other child, though eventually it becomes clear that it is the same one. If you put in "twelve-year-old" earlier in the story or changed it here to "little" it would remove all doubt.

6) Isn't it "<u>Out</u> in the back yard <u>there was</u> etc." or "<u>From</u> out in the back yard there <u>came</u> etc."? Strictly and pedantically speaking, I mean. In poetry anything is possible.
And this is poetry.

7) I kept wanting to know (perhaps from having a brother with a wooden leg) how she got her legs cut off, and you never say. Would you rather not say?

8) You've lost me. P is not near B on the typewriter, so it probably isn't a typo for "billowy", but I cannot imagine a pillowy glow. Once more I consulted Mary Phelps who sent up this sketch. Are we hot or cold? [Bill enclosed a drawing of "a pillowy glow" but said that it was "probably not close."]

9) Because of the order of the phrases, I read it that it was drinking from the cup that made him reel, and of course the cup has nothing to do with it. Does the transposition bother you?

10) The meaning of entertainment that instantly crops into the mind is always a performance of some sort. A vulgarization, of course. But would it work to say "this hospitality" instead?

11) If you leave it "<u>the</u> child" the reader has considerable reason to think that it is his sister's child you are talking about.

12) The grammatical antecedent of "her" is his sister Annie, but I sus-

pect that the person it really refers to is Miss Marcia Pope. If this is cor-
rect, what about making it "Now that he'd got by Miss Marcia Pope's dark
window, he smelled her sweet olive tree."? Or did his sister Annie live be-
tween him and Miss Pope and so it really was her tree? Anyway, you see the
problem.

We have been to Illinois for Thanksgiving. The gossip was much worse
than I remembered, the air simply marvelous. I don't think I thought about
the air very much when I was growing up. And of course I hadn't experi-
enced champagne, which is what it was most like. We stayed in the house
my father and stepmother built after they were married, and the children
had my old room, where (except for when I was reading A Tale of Two Cit-
ies) I wasn't very happy, but fortunately they didn't have to know that. My
stepmother has hardening of the arteries, and is heartbreaking. My mother's
sister is riddled with arthritis, and is heartbreaking. My mother's and my
grandparents' graves have all sunk level with the ground, and the cemetery,
now to all intents and purposes full, is so small compared to what I remem-
bered it as being. You could have them all to a New Year's party, and when I
was a little boy most of them would have accepted.

Love, from us all,

B.

Eudora Welty to William Maxwell, [December 2, 1965]

Dear Bill,

This is the first note I've written since I got yours—thank you for it, and
thank you for liking the story, and for taking it. I am so glad. I'd love to have
heard you on the telephone, but it's nice to have the letter to go back to.
Things are getting better but we've had a family crisis with two heads—my
mother had a stroke and my brother [Edward], several weeks earlier, broke
his neck and is in a hospital in Jackson—so they've been bad off fifty miles
apart, and of course neither knowing about the other. My mother's come
through it very well. I was told by the doctor she wouldn't, and the first
thing she said to me in a tiny little voice when she was able to speak was that
he was a moron. So I hope he stays wrong for a good long while so she can
get some strength back. The weather has been lovely—a long, warm, bright

Indian summer lasting clear up until yesterday morning, when it suddenly dropped from 70 to 20. I've been driving up to see mother in the sunrise, not my normal time to go, and it's all been so strange. I loved your letter written in the airport—and oh how well I know. I've thought before we were brought up by fathers who said the same things to us—always better to be an hour early, of course. It was after I was well grown that I learned it might not always be better for the other person. I was so glad to get that letter. All during the blackout I wondered if you and Emmy and Kate and Brookie were all in the same place—preferably at 544 East 86—and not you in the lobby of a crowded Cinema One holding up tickets and Emmy trying to find you when the lights went out, and the children at home with one of those nannies, all of whom scare me after reading that Fable. And the Fables—so happy and cheered to think of the book coming into actuality and my love to it.[67] Also love as usual to Emmy and Kate and Brookie and you, many thoughts, and delights in same.

Think of me as being relieved that things go better, and so happy that the story pleased you and is going to be in the magazine. Love, Eudora

Eudora Welty to William Maxwell, [December 1965]

Dear Bill,

Thank you for the wonderful letter and work with the story, and this is to say it will get back to you almost immediately. I am so glad you think it good. And for the tremendous check—I can't imagine how that much money could come for a story—and what is Cola? I'm thankful and amazed, and it could not have come at a more opportune time.

My mother is "holding her own" and my brother is doing about the same. I'll send the proof back right away—but did want to write you before starting off this morning.

Emmy's review was a great pleasure.[68] I liked the Beatle reference. The Illinois Thanksgiving sounded like something I know about too. It's good the air was like champagne—so restoring. Love to all of you—thank you again for all the generous feeling about the story, and thank the New Yorker for the astounding cash. Somebody just called me on the phone and asked me if I could identify a poem she had copied down in her schooldays and

read it to me <u>spelling</u> every other word—"P-a-r-a-p-e-t"—and I told her it didn't sound like anything I had ever heard in my life and she said well, it was understandable that I never had the time to <u>read</u>.

Love,
Eudora

William Maxwell to Eudora Welty, December 6, 1965

Dear Eudora:

I heard the silence, but heavenly days! Emmy said, "An automobile accident" meaning your poor brother's broken neck. I am relieved too that things go better, but so much room for improvement. And you the head of the family. And never getting any rest. But still writing better than ever. Cling to that. It's a rock. Perhaps it's because of the techniques of thinning the blood, and the medicines (violent) for controlling blood pressure, the pattern of strokes seems to have changed. I am glad your mother got her voice back. She would not (who could?) have liked not being able to communicate her dissatisfaction, and you would have been even more concerned to guess what it was she couldn't say.

We talk of going to Europe in June, and Kate has passed over the line (Brookie would just as soon not be going) and shares all the brochures, and digs up museums I have never heard of, and we both get each other so excited that we can't go to sleep afterward. If you know of any perfect little hotels in Paris like the Beaujolais, which Mary Lou sent us to and which is, alas, defunct, tell me. I am thinking we ought to be near a park, and preferably the Jardin de Luxembourg, for them. Then Kate and I can go to museums and Brookie and Emmy can sit and draw in the park. Brookie draws for money. Emmy has been paying her, I don't know how much. Ten cents a picture, I think [...] Her masterpiece is a white elephant with a howdah on it. Black howdah. Red and blue headpiece on the elephant. A marvel [...] Brookie just draws and paints and plays the piano and makes things in clay, and weaves, and cuts out, and makes moss gardens, and sews, as if she didn't have any mind. Just hands. Only she has, of course.

Shame on me for talking about my children.

Spare yourself when you can. And write when you are permitted to. And give your mother our love. And we devoutly hope your brother will be all right.

<div align="right">

Devotedly,

B

</div>

Eudora Welty to William Maxwell, December 7, [1965]

Dear Bill,

Hope you can read hand-written notes. First your numbered questions [about "The Demonstrators"], then your other questions, then some questions of my own. I'm afraid this isn't as good as I thought—it makes you turn through the galleys 3 times. My questions are nearly all changes that arise out of earlier versions—because I know you, like myself, tend to think there's something in the way it first came up. But I tried for tighter control in this than ordinary. Again my best thanks for all this understanding and help, and thanks to Miss Phelps—

<div align="right">

Love,

Eudora

</div>

Still December 7

1. Dashes I like better than parentheses—remembering Mark Twain's remark from somewhere, "He who would wantonly use a parenthesis would steal"—so if you agree, dash it.
2. "Tonight" belongs there, I think, because the lights, like the water supply, had been giving trouble. Also this particularizes this night, and its scenic effects.
3. Certainly should be inserted as you have it.
4. I ought to have said (Mary Phelps was right): Her forehead looked thick as a battering-ram because of the rolling of her eyes. Do you think that fixes it? I need to get home to the dictionary to be sure a battering-ram <u>looks</u> thick. If the picture's confusing, we could scrap it and just say, "Her eyes were rolling."
5. Yes and I think "little" is better than "twelve-year-old" for every time.

6. "From...came" helps a lot—I'm always weak on prepositions especially.

7. She got them cut off under a train, and in an earlier version I did say so, and had him pass by her house by the tracks. If you think I should say anything—beyond that it's a crossing with a bad record—I could with one word, couldn't I?

8. My clumsiness. I should have conveyed the reflection of pink on the sky as being in the <u>shape</u> of a pillow. <u>From</u> far down the railroad track beyond the unlighted town, a grass fire threw a pillow-shaped glow on the sky. Is this better? Sorry for the trouble to you both & you handled me too tenderly, I was inaccurate. I haven't changed it on the galley pending your seeing it.

9. Certainly, better transposed.

10. "Entertainment" just a local irony going back to the old days of "Mrs. So-&-So lavishly entertained last evening" etc. And still not good even at that—only one guest. Either "hospitality" or "gesture"? I wanted him to refer to it in a way to make little of it.

11. Certainly, <u>his</u> child.

12. Of course, use as you put it—It's rightly deducted—Miss M. P.'s tree.

Gal. 1 "Holden, <u>Miss</u>." is what he'd think and say. The whole word is so long in a long sentence. And I suppose just the sight of the world "Mississippi" written out tends to signal a certain kind of story these days & I unconsciously avoided it. Everybody <u>says</u> Jackson, Miss. Do what the magazine wants if it really matters—To me it's just a matter of sound & emphasis.

Gal. 3. Sure, <u>from the</u> kitchen.

Gal. 6 I meant the hand. Negro babies are often pale black—if that's gray—in the same way that white babies are pale pink. (There's a crazy sentence.) Hence the comma.

Gal. 11. Hence <u>your</u> comma. Sure.

Gal. 3. a. What do you think of this change? Would it mean paragraphing it?

Gal. 4. b. Do you think deleting <u>Elks</u> is better—to keep it to just one club?

Gal. 7. c. Instead of this speech, I originally had: "You sure ain't your daddy!" Which one's better?

Gal. 8. d. Here if you like could be added: She still lived by the tracks where the train had cut off her legs.

Galley 11

> e. This is of course an actual remark by a real man, if Ross Barnett is real. It was reported in the papers, I'm sure. OK to use it?

> e-x. "We are dramatizing your hostility." Any better? Or too much?

> f. Better to say "broken-up Coca Cola bottles" as more specific and self-explanatory?

> g. Do you think this helps enough to change it?

> g-x. (where, he'd heard, they were all giving parties for her). Add this?

Gal. 12

> h. Any better? If not, scratch it.

Gal. 13, 14, 15. i. Should the news idea be indented on the page? Otherwise, quotes, I suppose.

William Maxwell to Eudora Welty, December 13, 1965

Dear Eudora:

To plunge immediately into the story—Mostly out of curiosity I would be interested in seeing (but you don't have to bother with it now—on the proofs, when I send them is plenty of time) the sentence or so about the doctor's passing by Oree's house, on the way to the house where they were all congregated. It is alright the way—all right—mercy, some things die hard—the way you fixed it, but the other might be better. Only it also is probably true that you wanted to go straight to the house before you introduced any of the characters. My guess is that it is right the way you now have it. And I thought it would be keeping closer to your original intent to say..."rose the pillow-shaped glow of a grass fire" instead of "a grass fire threw a pillow-shaped glow on the sky", but either is all right, so be sure to say so if you don't like the first. I left entertainment in, for the moment. And Holden, <u>Miss</u>. And the Elks. Because I liked it. The broken up coca cola bottle I liked the idea of, but it played hell with the sentence as it stood, so I left it glass, and you can rewrite the sentence later with the broken up bottles so

it doesn't feel like a fixed sentence, if you want to. Up to you, really. And added about the parties for his wife. And the news item is printed in smaller type, instead of indenting, because the columns are too narrow as it is. If you would prefer quotes, you can have them. But you will see from the galleys how it looks. If it is plausible that she would say (I mean not too wild) "I bid that!," then it's fine, I think. I tend to take your word blindly for what a Mississippi Negro would or wouldn't say. Not fair to you perhaps. But there you are. I notice that Lilie Mae (from Virginia) speaks two separate languages, one a good deal more dialectical than the other. I don't know why she switches from one to the other, but when she switches it is like changing scenery, it's so drastic.

Cola is "Cost-of-Living Adjustment" and that has something to do with the statistics of the Department of Labor, but it is an effort to keep apace, in payments, with the rising cost of everything. It is with one exception only paid to people with—maybe two exceptions [with] no first-reading agreement. You are an exception, because Mr. Shawn respects and understands your reasons for not wanting to sign it, and since you would be grossly underpaid without the Cola, we pay for your stories as if you <u>had</u> signed it. That way there is no injustice.[69]

How I loathe the phrase "holding her own". They said it about my mother, during the three days when she wasn't, as it turned out. So it is engraved on my feelings like a scar. I hope the doctors are now telling you some different cliché. And that they are both improving.

<div align="right">Love, B</div>

Chestina Andrews Welty, Eudora's mother, died on January 20, 1966. Edward Jefferson Welty, Eudora's brother, died four days later after developing a brain infection.

Emily Maxwell to Eudora Welty, February 8, 1966

Dearest Eudora,

Bill and I wanted so much to call you, but couldn't tell <u>what</u> would be the moment, and then your letter came bringing you so close. I felt sure

you were getting all that love we were sending. I'm glad we had the joy of knowing your mother when she was well and full of happiness. And beyond that fragile afternoon's knowing, we know and love her through you, know the incredibly lovely person she must have been to have you for her child.

With much love,

Emmy

NO SIGN OF ELIZABETH

From the end of February to mid-May, Eudora was mostly away from home, hoping that work, travel, and visits with friends would serve as an anesthetic for her pain. In February, Bill knew the joy of publishing his collection of twenty-nine tales under the title The Old Man at the Railroad Crossing and Other Tales. *But on March 10, he faced another loss: his close friend, the Irish writer Frank O'Connor, died.*

5

"Your Heart Down on Paper"

AFTER LOSING her mother and her brother Edward, Eudora found herself for a considerable time unable to return to *Losing Battles*, the long comic novel she had begun in 1955. Instead, she traveled, seeing friends, taking in art exhibitions, going to the theater, hearing performances of great music. She sought to keep her mind busy, away from thoughts of loss. But those thoughts could not be denied. Ultimately, in order to heal, she had to return to fiction.

Bill well knew the way writing had helped him, but he also knew not to press Eudora on this issue. Instead, he advised her about revisions to "The Demonstrators," which *The New Yorker* had accepted in 1965, and he reminded her that his family was her family. In January 1967, during a phone call to Eudora, he detected sounds of despair and immediately wrote to her: "If what I heard in your voice persists, will you drop everything and come to New York and settle down in the back room and let us hang garlands of love around your neck, day after day, until you are feeling yourself again?"

Eudora did not settle into the Maxwells' back room, but their garlands of love provided needed encouragement from afar, and soon Bill's editorial skills would support her during a new writing project—one that directly confronted the issues of death and love and memory. She completed "The Optimist's Daughter" in 1967. *The New Yorker* accepted it that same year and published it in the spring of 1969, devoting almost an entire issue to it. Only after completing this novella was Eudora able to return to *Losing Battles* and finish it. Bill deemed the novel a triumph, and Emmy agreed: "It's as if you'd put your heart down on paper," she wrote. "I felt as if I was sitting up for a peat fire & listening to the voice of a master storyteller."

Bill's own writing languished a bit during these years. *The Old Man at the Railroad Crossing and Other Tales* was published early in 1966, and "The Gardens of Mont-Saint-Michel" appeared in *The New Yorker* in August 1969. But Bill struggled with a book of nonfiction he would not complete until 1970. The demands of his work as an editor, the pleasures of family life, the joys of travel (including trips to Ireland and Sicily), and concerns about his daughters' education were at the fore. Bill and Emmy enlisted Eudora to recommend Brookie to the Putney School in Vermont, where she was accepted, and Emmy credited Eudora as much as Brookie for this fact.

As they had long ago realized, Eudora and Bill were kindred spirits, and they continued to relish exercising their descriptive powers in letters to each other. Bill reported to Eudora on hearing Judith Raskin sing at the Met; Eudora reported to Bill on hearing Leontyne Price sing in Jackson. Bill reported on a midnight skating expedition with Emmy, Brookie, and Kate; Eudora reported on one niece's marriage and the other's debut. The two shared news of their reading and gardening, but beneath these easy exchanges lay a depth of feeling. The man who had written so powerfully about adolescent despair in *The Folded Leaf* was perceptive about his friend's emotional plight. The woman who had seen her mother's life restricted by blindness was anxious about threats to her friend's eyesight. In the wake of tragedy and in the face of difficulty, their friendship grew even deeper and became even dearer.

Eudora Welty, Bryn Mawr, Pennsylvania, to Emily and William Maxwell,
May 6, 1966

Dearest Emmy and Bill, your sweet note and your beautiful spring flowers made me feel so delighted and set up—so happy to know you were thinking about me, because it really was a great day—I'm staying here as Kathy McBride's guest (the president) and she said be sure to tell you how much she's enjoying your flowers. They were in the spot of honor for her dinner party last night. Tulips, daisies, Dutch Iris, poet's narcissus, stock, all the clear-colored & sweet things—Thank you for being my family on such a nice day—I basked. I'm taking the money home tonight and resting on it, starting right in on the novel.[1]

So glad you got to the Mellon Show—I felt somehow you were sure to —Today I got taken to see the Barnes—you know how hard it is to see, and now, as I felt nearly every step I took to stand before another picture, I wish for you to see it. Have you ever? I can't even send you a card with a reproduction of a single one, because no reproductions have ever been made. The Cezannes—50? 60? of absolutely radiant staggering beauty. And drawings!—the Monets—Picassos (Blues & Pink—Saltambiques (sp?))—a dozen wild Rousseaus—a Van Gogh Postman with a green beard and a sty, not my favorite painter, but just to show you. I felt drenched by the whole color of blue—and Matisse! Dozens, dozens of prime Odalesques & girls & goldfishes, lights & airs & chaises & [readers], & <u>you</u> know—It was a great feeling of being in the Presence just as I felt in the Presence of Turner that glorious morning—It is lovely to see pictures together, & I'll never forget having those all to ourselves—It makes them seem as incredible as they really are—[2]

How are all of you, and is your health all right? I'm fine now, after having the flu (I think twice) since I saw you & being unfit for human companionship or lecturing, so I cancelled (both). Went down to Agnes Scott [College] & Tuscaloosa, Ala., & Washington & now here, until the evening train. I loved every minute we had and thank you for all the goodness and pleasure. My love to Kate and Brookie, and tell them please for me it was a joy to see them & be thinking of them now—(acutely)

At home I'll write on the typewriter but I had too much to tell you— Thanks—flowers—pictures—treasures—love—never forgetting!

Love, Eudora

William Maxwell to Eudora Welty, August 29, 1966

Dearest Eudora:

If a book comes in the mail from Heywood Hill [bookstore], in London, don't send it back, it's a present. The children were good travelers; all that worry for nothing. Brookie was simply at home wherever she was, day or night. And they seldom got to bed before midnight, which, considering that 8 and 8:30 had until then been their bedtime, they terribly enjoyed. Kate could not accept at first the neon lights in the Avenue de l'Opera and no guillotine in the Place de la Concorde. She suffered in her historical sense, for about a week, and detested French cooking, and then helplessly began to enjoy Paris, and by the time we got to the Carnavalet [Museum] she was like a cat in a fish store.

Emmy and I fell in love with Paris for the third time. It is incredibly beautiful now. And in England we saw a marvelous Hamlet at Stratford with David Warner and an equally marvelous "You Never Can Tell" with Sir Ralph Richardson. Hamlet was not only Brookie's first Shakespeare but her first play. She took it like everything else, in stride. I let Kate buy and order any book she wanted in Heywood Hill, so she would remember me kindly when I am dead. And in Cerne Abbas we stayed in a place that I already knew the full feeling of from a recurring dream.[3]

When are you coming to New York?

Bill

Eudora Welty to William Maxwell, [September 1966]

Dearest Bill,

I was so glad to get your letter, and Emmy's postcard earlier from the rapturous boat trip to Finistere.[4] I thought of you all summer, and it's so satisfying to know your (that is my) visions must have started running true—it must have been pure clear joy for all four of you, and I would like to hear full four-

way accounts before the first bloom of telling is gone for you—it will still be fresh for me. The Concise Flora is my companion, and though I had had a day of supposing if it had got here by mistake, I knew it had come to the place that wanted it, and I wasn't at all surprised to know it had come from you.[5] Thank you for the steady and daily delight of it. That soul—when I think of the Rev. Keble Martin it's to see him welcoming the chance to do a life-work in his spare time, patiently retrudging the miles he'd gone in the morning so as to put back the plant he'd lifted to draw, so it would be safely in its own place—or a Better Place—by the next sun-up. The waiting for the rare specimen to fill the gap—then missing the post because he had to go preach, then waiting again. The love. I'm so relieved it wasn't from the fairies so I would not be required to deserve it or send it back. It is perfection, don't you agree?

Yaddo is having a board meeting on Sept. 24 and I am invited for the weekend to Saratoga. (You know of course I am in great demand as a board member by boards all around.) Anyway I get a free trip—in fact, if I don't go I get thrown off this board, since I've missed the meetings for 5 times or 5 years. I can stay a week in NY afterwards, and could I hear about the rest of the trip? About Kate's Carte Blanche? (Emmy, what about that for the title of a children's book, and are you too busy to go to see Diabolique with me, if it's as good as I remember it? I know that deadline.) It would be the greatest refreshment to see you. I'll come back into NY (Algonquin) Sunday night and call you Monday, 26th. Dolly is up from here now and I'm to meet her on Tuesday, otherwise any night at all or daytime, whatever.[6] I've been distracted and have to write myself notes to change my shoes, but I expect I can get away—this letter, writing to you, makes me positive I can. Much love to all of you, Eudora

Sunday afternoon
Do you know amyryllis advenum? It is blooming in the revived garden.

William Maxwell to Eudora Welty, October 12, 1966

Columbus Day
Dear Eudora:
This is scheduled for the issue of November 5 (Guy Fawkes Day?),

which means that we ought to have it back by October 26th at the latest.[7] The queries are either Mr. Shawn's (marked with his initials) or the proofreader's, and have mostly to do with punctuation. You don't have to move a bit closer to the magazine's standard punctuation, which is based on the N.Y. Times' stylebook—a thing designed for all purpose writing, not fiction—than you feel like. Do as you please, you hear?

Kate is home sick in bed with a bad cold, and I spent a happy hour reading The Ponder Heart to her. Not a single joke gets by her, and her laughter would do your heart good to hear. This time through, I keep thinking how like Lincoln, Illinois, it all is. While they are all talking, I can smell the surroundings. It is a marvel. Not one grey hair in its head. I will go to my grave bursting with pride at having my name on the dedication page. With Emmy and Mary Lou.

Love,

Bill

Eudora Welty to William Maxwell, October 18, [1966]

It says St. Luke's Day
Dear Bill,

It was the essence of pleasure to see all the family and I'll send a real letter to the house—where I hope Kate is all well again? Thanks for your letter, and also for your wire inviting me to dinner that Thursday, which was under my front door when I walked in—rather cheery, I would have loved living it right over again. As for the proof [of "The Demonstrators"], all looks all right to me, but there's one point where your advice, or decision is needed: where to break it on Galley 13. As set up, and I believe as I'd written it, the break comes when the dr. finds Dove and he says "Hide me." I thought this the natural place to break, but the night itself goes on for two paragraphs, then the proof corrector thought a break should come before next morning and the newspaper, and I agree that's a natural place too. But two breaks? I feel we ought to choose, and I incline to the dramatic rather than the time break, after "Hide me." But I'll accept that time break if you feel that's better.[8] You don't need to ask if I agree, I do, with whatever you think better. As you see, I marked the proof accordingly, so it may need

changing. I was afraid the story might sound dated in its events, being a year old, but I don't think it was quite explicit enough for that, do you? I hope not. Shall dash to P.O. now and write later. It was so lovely to see you. Love to all. It will soon be time to cut out the Jack-o-lantern. Thank you again for all on the story. Raining a little bit. I bought 50# cotton seed meal, 50# compost, sackload of sand and bale of peatmoss, and told yard man to start by spading up one of the old beds. Had to leave and when I got back he said "Couldn't get it quite <u>all</u> used up." I'd forgotten Mother said Reuben always used all of everything unless you stood right there. So I want it to rain considerable before I stick anything down.

<div align="right">

Love,
Eudora

</div>

William Maxwell to Eudora Welty, October 25, 1966

Dear Eudora:

Mr. Shawn decided that it was better to leave that sentence the way you had it: "It was the stink of sensation" (instead of "It gave off..."). And you can have the initial and break after Dove's "Hide me" anywhere you want it, or in short, the way you had it in the first place. But maybe it would be a good idea to change one thing. A story is datelined, but grammatically that "Datelined Sunday" modifies "headline" and (though anything can happen in Mississippi) I believe headlines don't have any date attached to them. Did this, anyway? What about the fix suggested in pencil on the galley? Would that do it? Mr. [Milton] Greenstein wasn't worried about the Barnett quote.[9] And the story (yours) is now scheduled for the issue of December 10. As usual, it is timeless; nothing to worry about <u>there</u>.

How dreamlike to open a telegram containing an invitation to a dinner you have already eaten.

We went to Annapolis last weekend to stay with Harriet O'Connor, in her parents' house, which had rooms to burn, and a pianola and was on a point of land across the Severn from the Naval Academy.[10] The yard man, colored, and named Gilbert, I wanted to steal. Very intelligent and proud looking, and given to digging things up out of the woods and putting them

in the spot where they would do best. I asked him where he learned all he knew about gardening and he said he went to work when he was eleven for a lady who had an acre and a half of rose bushes and when she didn't like one she'd dig it up and stick another in.

I was particularly looking forward to seeing the Hammond-Harwood house again, after forty-one years. I went home to Chicago and wrote a long poem about it, the first time. But either it or I have changed or more likely both. It was not at all as I had remembered it. Nor the street it stood on.[11]

But one other thing happened. When I was five or six my parents went to Kentucky to visit relatives, and my mother, being shown through a hunting lodge somewhere in the country, spied the remains of a set of Copeland willow, which the hunters were breaking at a great rate, and asked if she could replace it with a set from the ten cent store. They gallantly agreed to this, and so she got her great aunt's wedding china, all that was left of it, or almost all; her cousin's wife lifted the biggest platter and the salad bowl. Well, not to leave out anything, when my mother died, my father gave the Copeland willow to my Aunt Annette, and she often used to point it out to me on the top shelf of her china cupboard, and when my older brother married, he asked for two of the three most valuable (they weren't very; amethysts and pearls; you know) pieces of my mother's jewelry, because they went together, in his mind: but on the other hand, there were three sons. And the ring had been given to my mother on the occasion of my younger brother's birth. So, by way of compensation, my Aunt decided to give me the willow, which she did. And for twenty-five years I have been trying to find some more of it. There weren't any plates, and hardly any cups and saucers. And never have I found one single piece of it. (Copeland willow is light blue, cobalt, instead of the usual color of blue willow, and it doesn't have any gold on it.) And in the window of the antique shop in the main street of Annapolis what did Emmy and I spy but the butter dish, and when we went inside to see if there was more, there was. LOTS more. Plates, salad plates, dessert plates, the platter and salad bowl that were lifted by Cousin Wright Youtsey's wife. And all that we had already. Well, I was stunned. Wouldn't you have been? And it wasn't even terribly expensive. Somebody had died, in an old house in Annapolis, and the contents of the house had been sold,

and there it was. Only I keep thinking (a) that there must be some way I can get it delivered to my mother; And (b) of that Russian proverb that says "When the house is finished there is a funeral in it."

Love,

B

Eudora Welty to William Maxwell, October 28, 1966

Dear Bill,

Before I forget it again, let me give you my new phone number—601-353-7762—unlisted. I didn't see any further use in keeping my name in the book for those unwelcome callers everybody gets these days, and took it out on what a lady who lives on my street always calls "the spurt of the moment." You mightn't need it but I'd like you to have it somewhere around.

What a dunce I was not to catch on I'd datelined a headline—I missed it on the original galleys. Of course change as you've got it marked, and much obliged. Thanks for all the agreeableness from Mr. Shawn and you about sentence, break, and the rest. I'm glad if you think it doesn't date—as you know, I don't ordinarily have the kind of events from real life in stories that could be pin-pointed as to month or year, just not congenial to me, but anything with Negroes in it these days—there it is, but what I am terribly glad of is your telling me Ponder Heart doesn't date—oh, joy, that is delicious news. And you read it to Kate—and she laughed—and at the right places—of course a lot of that is you and Kate, but of all people it ought to be. [...] It's a marvelous story about the Copeland Willow. I am so glad you found it! And that now it's exactly where it belongs. I do explicitly know the feeling that there must be some way you can get it delivered to your mother, or get her told you have it all, safely, but that's a part of the adventure, like the little bridge on the china plate. Not sure I ever saw the Copeland blue—sounds soft and special. Once in a book on china by some English lady I read, about the willow pattern in general—I guess it was about antique china—that she'd received a letter from a gentleman who told her he had all his china in the Willow pattern, had also had his rugs woven in the Willow pattern, had covered his walls, chairs and beds and windows in the Wil-

low pattern—his house was called "The Willows"—and his question was, What did she think of the Willow pattern?

Are you having beautiful warm days and cool nights as we are? I don't know when I've ever seen it so fine, for so long, here—every day it holds. It's like the picnic day when I came out to Yorktown Heights and we climbed up above the brook and Emmy brought out melon and prosciutto and artichokes and all sorts of al fresco joys and when finally we were able to move on we found a golf ball—I was astounded to see we'd been right on the brink of another civilization, all that timeless delicious afternoon.

<div style="text-align:right">

Love to all of you,

Eudora

</div>

P.S. Let me ask you something—would it be improper if for a reading I have to give in Houston to a meeting of English teachers from all over, I read the new story? You wrote me it's now to come out in the Dec. 10 issue, and the meeting is on Nov. 26. I don't know what the proprieties are. I'd like to read them something they haven't seen. I read it once to a private group in Bryn Mawr, thinking that would do no harm, but this is a paid affair. (In fact that's why I'm going—Texas money, it will pay for having the house painted.)

About the novel, I'm still waiting for the leaves to fall, leaving the bare trees, but what started to fall were the leaves from another story and another time.[12] Perhaps it was taking the proper attitude all the time—down on my knees, I guess. I'll hold it—

Eudora Welty to William Maxwell, November 16, 1966

Dearest Bill,

It's the very best news, that Kate and her friend were standing on their precious heads—The weight of all this being taken away from you and Emmy must make you feel, I hope, just as light as Kate—I'm so glad— Thank you for letting me know.

It's nice & very generous of Mr. Shawn to say go ahead & read the story in spite of the date. Since you say to do it, I'll take him at his word—And I'm ever so much obliged. It's occurred to me that the Shattucks <u>might</u> be

there, since I gather this is some kind of super group—Wouldn't it be nice to see them again—

I have a hundred bulbs to plant, and soft fine days outdoors to do it, just too perfect—I sit up here & read Persuasion—Emma—I never can stop when I start—Really [Jane Austen]'s the only power to get me whole through some days I sometimes feel [and] willingly. It's salvation to adore how she does it. It's adoration, that's the best. "At one time Patty came to say she thought the kitchen chimney wanted sweeping. Oh! said I, Patty, do not come with your bad news to me. Here is the rivet of your mistress's spectacles out. Then the baked apples came home...."[13]

<div align="right">Love to all,
Eudora</div>

Emily Maxwell to Eudora Welty, November 23, 1966

Dearest Eudora,

I am in bed, with a cold—absurdly—because tomorrow is Thanksgiving eve and we're going to the country. The next morning we are expecting my brother & my dear old friend from Lexington, Mass., and her 3 children for Thanksgiving & the night. So my mind is cheerfully full of adornments for the stuffing, of branch raisins & black grapes & crushed pineapple for the yams, but my nose is red, my hair is limp, and it's too much trouble to blow my nose. I have just finished reading the profile of [Robert] Scull, the pop-art collector, in the new New Yorker. I liked it, did you? I like him. He appears to talk like theatre people, but it begins to seem as if all interviewers write the same dialogue. I like his gaiety, and obvious seriousness, and humility. It would be nice if he turned out to be the new American, but what will they do for Russian grandfathers who don't believe in working?

Kate's home, too, with a cough. And Brookie just breezed in cheerfully having remembered to get lined pads and unlined pads and Brearley belts at the store, but having forgotten Kate's homework.[14] So we had to send her out again! Tomorrow we are going to eat liverwurst sandwiches in the car so we'll get to the country in time for her to go riding with Leda, who lives next door.

I've also got a paperback of "Short Friday & Other Stories" of Isaac Sing-

er's—sadly, I sat next to him last year at the Institute luncheon, & hadn't read anything of his. I love "Yentl the Yeshiva Boy." In "Alone" he's so funny about Miami in summer and the storm is so Jewish. "The moon emerged extraordinarily large and red; it hung in the sky like a geographer's globe bearing a map not of this world. The night had an aura of miracle and cosmic change. A hope I had never forsaken awoke in me: was I destined to witness an upheaval of the solar system? Perhaps the moon was about to fall down. Perhaps the earth, tearing itself out of its orbit around the sun, would wander into new constellations."

You were darling to send the installments of "Flush" for Kate.[15] She is very uncatholic in her tastes—and I don't know whether she's ready for it yet—but I will let you know. You do want us to return the magazines, don't you? Life—or supplying books for her—will become much simpler when she begins to branch out. Dumas is what she likes, has a passion for. But it upsets her, too, so she's given him up for awhile.

Bill will be home soon, but has to go out to a big dinner at Columbia for Alfred Knopf, which he won't be feeling like doing.... Now it is later—Kate is reading word parts like "spec" over the phone to a friend, & they're trying to figure out what is Latin, what Greek. This is for a course called "Studies in Language"—odi is hate—skin in Greek? derma. What fun. Brookie has taken Daisy down to the dark street. Tele means from afar. (Greek) Kate says to her friend, sub means under. Brookie says, Oh I see! Submarine means you get under the marines and blast them. Here's Bill!

How was Houston? And did you see any of the small Lear watercolors?[16]

I think I'll send this out with Bill, with a great deal of love tucked inside. And thank you for all your thoughts of us. I can just see how beautiful those scrubbed walls in your house look!

Emmy.

I knew there was something I forgot to tell you. We loved the fig preserves!!

William Maxwell to Eudora Welty, November 30, 1966

Dearest Eudora:

Here is something. I hear nothing but the greatest admiration for the story ["The Demonstrators"].[17] Brendan Gill says it is a whole novel, and he

is very eloquent about "that poor man who has not one single thing in the world to live for."

Emmy and Kate were both under the weather at Thanksgiving. Colds. Emmy is all but over hers, Kate still coughing. Brookie's trampoline came at last, but with a square frame and a rectangular canvas. I put it up anyway and they bounced and bounced and after the weekend I took it in a plastic bag in a Bloomingdale box (just to confuse matters) to F.A.O. Schwartz,[18] and went first to the third floor: sure enough it was a totally wrong size, and then to the adjustment counter on the second floor, where the woman in charge said, "If it came in the box it's the right canvas," whereupon I said in you have no idea how loud a voice "NONSENSE!" It was my finest hour, and it stopped her. Which is not to say that we have the right one yet.

As you will see by this time, your story got into the right issue after all. How I was never told. I hope you had a good time in Austin [actually Houston]. Love,

B.

William Maxwell to Eudora Welty, January 9, 1967

Dear Eudora

I have put those treasures into the mail—the two Atlantics.[19] How they brought back my own past. But you must preserve them. It only happened once and never will again.

But something else. I heard from Sandy Campbell in the checking department that you did a review of Martha Graham's book for Life, which didn't print it. If that means it is home in a drawer, will you let me show it to Mr. Shawn, to see if it could do for the Book department of the New Yorker?

And something else still. I got up from the table at a luncheon at the National Institute on the 9th of December and went home and had virus pneumonia, all through the holidays, four solid weeks in bed, not particularly uncomfortable and very well cared for, and now I am up and dressed and at the office for the first time, but it is like Cinderella. I have just two hours and a half of strength, and when that is used up I dive into bed again and go on reading [Thomas Hardy's] A Pair of Blue Eyes.

And one last something: The fruit cake was the best fruit cake I ever et.

Your loving,

Bill

Eudora Welty to William Maxwell, [January 1967]

Dear Bill,

This color is what I wish you were in, the pink. Ever since I heard you had had virus pneumonia for four weeks I've felt I went right off the brink of 1966, which had already (so I thought) done its worst. It was so sweet of you to write, when I can't believe you had any strength left over after the getting to the office and the getting back still to go. It's wonderfully reassuring to know you have been to the office, though, it proves something though maybe just your recklessness of heart—I hope the doctor (preferably a new one, who doesn't take 4 weeks to know you've got virus pneumonia, if I can be rude about it) is seeing that you don't over-do, without knowing it. I also worry about when you do go out, there's all that pollution to breathe. I wish you could go for some weeks to one of the sunny places or dry places that might be good for you. (Mary Lou wrote recently that she was going abroad and maybe her new house would be just standing in Santa Fe empty—but I believe that's not till April.) Emmy must be making all sorts of restoring and delicious things to eat. I bet you can't use up too much strength on the piano so far, but hope you can spare it soon—but does it take much more than the typewriter? Please take care. If it would give you an excuse to stay right where you are at home and get some writing of your own done, all would be of a different color. (Pink.) It comes to you at some point when you've been sick in bed that you feel you're receiving rewards, or this is my childhood memory from once when I had to spend 4 months on the sleeping porch. It's not bad to have everybody wait on you, presently—Reading without having to stop. I also had a deck of cards and really did get so I could tell what every one was going to be, from the backs. Infant ESP. Time for all sorts of worthless accomplishments, and they can't blame you. But reading Thomas Hardy does sound inspired. Eustacia Vye![20]—Had read somewhere that Proust said that A Pair of Blue Eyes was of all the books in the world the one he would most happily have written? I bet the wish didn't

work vice versa with Mr. Hardy. I'm sure you have them on the home shelf but when I was in Houston, at the banquet I sang for my supper at, new paperbacks were the favors and I got Tess on my plate, which I might send you if it seems to be all there.

Thank you so much for the letters about the story, and I have saved a little bunch of them that came here, if you'd some time like to look them over. Maybe I'll just xerox some at the library so you can toss away. Thank you for the V. Woolf—you didn't need to send those back, but wasn't it amazing to know she could come out as a serial? I may still find the rest of it.

In Houston, where Mr. Shawn let me read the story thanks to you, I stayed at the Shamrock in a large suite—essential for the Texas way of life, I found. Was taken downstairs to a cocktail party beforehand and all were in dresses to the ground and glittering, yet schoolteachers, and husbands of were standing by. Long table covered with loose orchids, flown in from Hawaii. "Help yourself to a corsage, Miss W., or a lei." I had on short eve. dress, my usual, so I was pretty bobbed. At moment of marching in on the banquet, we were lined up in order, then doors opened onto a room with thousands of teachers in it, all applauding, and a band played as we marched the whole length of the banquet hall (like from 43rd St. to Brentano's) to the banquet table on a stage. That's what the long dresses were for. Ate under spotlights. The Menu listed baked alaska for dessert, which I thought was just a misprint, but when the time came, all the lights went out except for thousands of candles, the doors opened again and in came the head waiter and 3 or 4 behind him bearing flaming torches, and the band struck up a Sousa's march and the rest of the waiters followed bearing aloft either baked alaskas or dummies. They serpentined among all those teachers' tables and out again and then returned immediately with the servings. Hence I think they were dummies. But what a show—then they turned to me with my story and said "Go ahead."

Do you hear anything from Elizabeth, or know whether or not she is coming over? I hope all goes well with her.

There was a little inch in the Times last week that said poor E. M. Forster had fallen down in Kings and his condition was "poor," and I've never found another line about him—do you know any news of him? Katherine Anne wrote me she'd been in the Maryland University Hospital since De-

cember 12—but don't let me get back to 1966. She is now at home in Washington, word I got from the florist up there, so I trust that's a good medical report.

Gently raining. Camellias are blooming, it's cold. I'm enjoying my New Yorker you and Emmy are sending—it's so thin, as though the twins had come. A new Elizabeth Taylor to read!

Love to you and to Emmy, Kate and Brookie, and take care. Try to breathe purer air than other people, even if you have to leave NY for a little while, would it be possible? Emmy, let me know how Bill is, too.

<div style="text-align:right">

Best love to all

Eudora

</div>

It was wonderful to hear your voices just now and I do feel better about you. Emmy, I'm putting this in a story but you'll know it's true—a lady (old) giving a recipe for making calves foot jelly, begins it: "Take a pair of Percy's old drawers"—that's her husband, & to strain it. In case you need the rest of the recipe, I've forgotten it.

Eudora Welty to William Maxwell, January 24, 1967

Dear Bill,

Is it still better, and better every day? I have been believing it ever since you and Emmy called me up and yet if you are getting better every day and _yet_ it takes six months to be over it—well, I'll just ask you calmly what you are doing in the office. But of course you are taking care and looking after yourself and getting rest and not letting Brookie jump on your stomach, and this is not to add the worry of your friends to the other trials of the day. It's lovely to think of you reading Hardy once the day's over and Emmy bringing in all kinds of delicious and strengthening cupfuls, or bowlfuls, or gobletfuls & platefuls.

It was sweet of you to ask about the piece I did for Life and they rejected it. I only just found out recently they hadn't used it, then it took me forever to think of the man's name. I wrote and said I wished to return the money and get the review back. I turned it in a day late—simple mistake in writing down the deadline, piece of stupidity—but of course I don't know whether that or its lack of being what was wanted was the reason they didn't use it. I

don't believe the man's letter (will enclose with review) — Mr. Schermann.[21]
(He thinks he met me, but it was actually my mother, and she was standing
in the middle of our dining room with a big pine tree stuck through the roof
a few minutes after a tornado, all the lights out and plaster and blown things
everywhere, alone in the house (I was in England), and he said he was in-
terested in background information about the Natchez Trace and my use of
same. Mother complied.) (Not without some remarks.) Anyway, the piece
is probably far from anything you'd feel like showing Mr. Shawn, since for
one thing they held me to 300 words, but it would be a pleasure to me to
type it again and try to say some of the things I cut out, just on the chance,
and for what good this will do I'll mail it along. I felt so humiliated because
of old friendship, Martha's and LeRoy Leatherman's, and in fact I'd not
have tried to write it except for that.[22] I love Martha Graham and her work
but didn't feel for that reason I knew enough, and maybe this was the trou-
ble, though if it was, it's you that would know it at the New Yorker, not Mr.
Schermann at Life. But thank you for such a generous suggestion.

I'm also sending up some of those letters about the story — I didn't know
how to Xerox them for just the little paragraphs, etc., that you could skim
them over for. But don't worry about sending back — I mean to reply to
them, that was all, and I can address the envelopes first.

Beautiful day here — 70 degrees, spring sky, I have all the windows open
all over the house, two white Roman hyacinths in flower.

Best love to Emmy and the girls too, and all take care.

Love,
Eudora

William Maxwell to Eudora Welty, January 24, 1967

Dearest Eudora —

Last night — now what could I have started to say about last night?
The phone rang out and it was that dear Consuelo Putnam on the Baptist
Church Road wanting me to come out and stay with them because the air
(it is very mild — 50–60) would be so good for me to breathe, and she would
make me nourishing soups.[23] Such a loving thing to think of, but I am <u>pas-
sionately</u> interested in getting back that lost ground, without overdoing. It is

about as complicated as parchesi—and half the time the dice say "bed"—no, about a third of the time, and bed is where I accomplish all sorts of things I wouldn't be doing if I were vertical all day. I did a book review of E. Nesbit's life for The New Yorker, when they only asked for a half-page note, because for the first time in months I felt like writing, and <u>working</u> on writing—moving sentences here and there, and getting effects and making the imaginary reader smile—you know.[24] I have been to the office my usual 3 days a week, but for a much shortened day—11:30–2:30 and taking a cab, usually, both ways, so it has been quite easy. Actually the person who needs fresh air and nourishing soups is Emmy, who doesn't spend enough time in bed and has a cold and is generally tired. But she is going ice skating in Central Park with Edith Hamburger this morning and that always does wonders for her.[25]

It wasn't the doctor's fault about diagnosing—it didn't take him four weeks—He suspected some kind of pneumonia from the first, but I produced with real visibility the symptoms of the other kind, which I didn't really have—The kind that does react to antibiotics and lasts only a few days—<u>and</u> chicken pox, which I had when I was 8 or 9 and you can't have twice, and penicillin reaction, which I didn't have either, as it turned out, so, short of reading tea leaves I don't see how anybody could have diagnosed the trouble right off.

We are about to see a travel agent about taking your advice to go to a nice sunny place—Barbados—toward the end of February.

But at the moment I am too happy having everybody wait on me, reading without having to stop, and feeling—as I do too, that I am receiving rewards. There were a lot of claims on my time and energy that were not valid—people also who were not really writers but writing and requiring to be written to, and manuscripts bought with the understanding that somebody (me) would make them work by pulling a white rabbit out of an opera hat on page 8, and turning water into grape juice on page 15. I question, lying in bed, the wisdom of this sort of thing, and I plan to do less of it. When a piece of real writing comes along, it is nothing but pure joy to see it on its way into type.

It is no trouble to return the letters about the story to you, and that is easier than getting them zeroxed. How I loved your account of the banquet in

Houston. I suppose it is what we are coming to, but at the moment when we arrive there for good and all, I hope I will have managed to be somewhere else. Like the man at the end of Nabokov's "Invitation to a Beheading" who found there was more than one reality, and just stepped out of the one he was in, into some other that was more congenial. I see that, among other things, lying in bed makes me garrulous. But I haven't half finished all I have to say to you. I do not hear from Elizabeth ever. If I write, there is no answer. I know, from people at Knopf, that she is well into, and perhaps far along, in a new novel. The trouble is, her cast of characters, in real life, is enormous, as you well know, and I am too proud to pluck at her coattails. From time to time, fortune brings me face to face with her. She knows I love her, and I suspect she is fond of us. But Hythe is far away from 86th St. I didn't know about Forster. I will inquire of Edith Oliver, who ought to have news of him.

I have started Far from the Madding Crowd. That man is a magician. It is easy to pick him up here, so don't bother sending Tess, which, as it happens, we have a nice copy of left over from E's college days. I saw a review of The Collected Essays of V. Woolf in The English Country Life. Do you suppose if I sent to England for it, it would turn out to be just all the books I have so carefully collected?

You don't mention the Graham review, from which I deduce that there were impediments, so far as the N. Yer is concerned.

Your feeling about 1966, and fear for 1967, brought back the lowest period of my life — at the end of my sophomore year in college, when for about four or five months I really thought that the reason one thing after another turned out badly was that anything having to do with me necessarily would. So I decided on one last try, and if that didn't work I would not try any more, ever. I had nobody to room with in my junior year and I had been introduced to somebody in a revolving door who seemed like a nice enough boy, so I got his address and wrote and asked if he'd like to room with me, and he wrote back he would, and in the fall, when we met in the dormitory, it was not the boy I had met in the revolving door — I must have got his name wrong — but a boy whom I had never laid eyes on, who had had polio, and had a withered leg, so he always dressed and undressed in his clothes

closet, and he was a perfectly marvelous room-mate and from that time on everything worked out beautifully, for years and years.

What I am trying to say is there is no pattern in years, no constancy of good or bad luck. Who knows what the day after tomorrow will bring—the very thing we most wanted and haven't allowed our hearts to hope.

If what I heard in your voice persists, will you drop everything and come to New York and settle down in the back room and let us hang garlands of love around your neck, day after day, until you are feeling yourself again?

Devotedly,

Bill

Eudora Welty to William Maxwell, [January or February 1967]

Dear Bill,

It was so good to get your letter and thank you for it. What fine news that you're getting some writing done along with the luxuries of reading, and that the rest in bed is doing its work (I see about the doctor) and that you and Emmy are thinking about Barbados toward the end of February. All this is sure to work out to bring about good and new things—and not least your plan to do less of "that sort of thing," which drains away so much too much—and I say it knowing so well what you give to your writers, and also knowing you want to give it to the writers whose work you like. But the quality of mercy should be strained at judicious intervals. Love to all the plans.

I am really all right and ashamed of sounding as if I weren't. Not my health but my friends' had me worried, and rightly, but not to worry my friends with. [In the margin Eudora has written, "What the letter must have done for that room mate."]

LATER

Yazoo City, Miss., is a little town 40 miles north of me and right on the edge of the Delta, and all it wants to do is be another Greenville, your town. Some people [...] built a new house with a swimming pool inside it, and gave a reception. Not a cocktail party (their real speed) but an afternoon af-fair, ladies in long white gloves at three in the afternoon standing in a re-ceiving line. Colored boys in white coats to serve the refreshments. Well,

one of the boys entered bearing his silver tray and stepped right into the swimming pool—the hors d'. tossed into the air. Suddenly it was a good party! When pulled out and dressed down by his boss and asked what he fell in the swimming pool for, the waiter replied with dignity, "I was not aware that it was there." 2nd installment: [The couple] gave another stiff party, this one a dinner for the new directors of the bank and their wives, none of whom drink. The table was of course alongside the swimming pool. Very stiff. At a period of silence a tiny splashing was heard, and there in the pool was a mouse, swimming about. Without a word up rose one of the new directors, (the most infuriating) and laying his handkerchief over his hand he reached in, caught the mouse, with quite a gesture wrung its neck, and tossed it outdoors, and resumed his seat at the table. "The pool is ruined," says [the wife]. "First it was integrated, then a mouse went swimming in it."—The feeling is it would never have happened in Greenville.

You wouldn't have got that Tess anyway because it has a section of pink pages inserted in the middle like the order sections and index of the old mail order catalogues, and this tells you how to evaluate the characters, gives the meaning of "inexorable" etc. and supplies you with vocabulary exercises. I do believe I have heard that the Virginia Woolf Collected Essays is the same collection we have ourselves collected. (Vocabulary exercise, that sounded like.) And maybe it wouldn't have Vanessa's work on the jacket, couldn't have, could it? I was wondering how to get hold of this free description of wonders with stamped foolscap envelope, but the descriptions here are very nice, don't you and Emmy think?

<div align="right">Love to all
Eudora</div>

Have some "Demonstrators" letters—I left out some from our friends at the New Yorker itself! (Howard [Moss] and Edith [Oliver]) & on Xmas cards.

Eudora Welty to William Maxwell, March 4, 1967

Dear Bill, That was so sweet of you about the Observer wonders—but you shouldn't.[26] How I hope you're in the warm sun with your warm family around you and getting finer and fitter every day. I'm thinking of you on a green island and this is just a little thing to put on your stack at the New

Yorker for no matter how late a day—do you remember you invited me to send the Martha Graham review up to show the magazine. I enclose all pertinent matters, the original short review, letters from LIFE, etc. I realize how doubtful it is that Mr. Shawn would be interested. But I'd love on a remote easy day to know your opinion if you have one. I wish I could have been there for the present season, which I hear is galvanic.[27]

Well, if you didn't get away you got to hear the music. And I saw something in Virginia that I couldn't help thinking how much Kate would have enjoyed it—Monticello. Had to go to Hollins College, Va. (I got a medal in a cap and gown) and so took a day to see Charlottesville. I don't know when any house moved me so. Have you and Emmy both seen it? Every single thing, object, view, thought, plan, every use they were put to, were Jefferson's presence. There in his study with his swivel chair (he invented the swivel chair) between two windows with little windowledges on either side, one to hold a dictionary, one a telescope, with the University of Virginia he'd made across on another hill, visible to his eye—oh, I can't tell you how fine it was. Snow on the ground, soft day, blue hills, bare trees.—It's springtime here, daffodils blooming, redbud coming out, and I have been working hard but on the longest story (not the novel) and the reason I waited so long to type up this review was I hated to break in, but the trip did it for me. Love to all, and I hope everything's going absolutely the way it should. I had the poppy and its root and seed and all not framed under glass but mounted on a hard board, and hanging it up so it looks just the way it left Paris—just spectacular.[28]

I enjoyed your review of E. Nesbitt but was so amazed. (At her, not you.) It seems just the chances of a lottery that we ever got those treasures.

<div style="text-align:right">Love,
Eudora</div>

I will write to Emmy—Tell her yes, I took care about the letters.

William Maxwell to Eudora Welty, March 7, 1967

Dearest Eudora—

We're still here, still wanting to hear that we can go. The last two weeks in March is the time. I rushed downstairs with the Graham review the mo-

ment I had read it. What I thought was that she was brought very much alive —not that she is anything else—by the review. I heard her voice and saw that red flannel cloth tied around the door handles.* I longed to rush over and get tickets (it is the last week) and am restrained by the knowledge that night life is not yet for me. We tried it, and down I came with a cold. Now over it, Thank God, but still have one foot in bed, if you know what I mean.

We've never seen Monticello, alas, though I know it from pictures. But that's not the same as wandering through it. We will just have to go.

I am so glad you are working. Able to. I <u>think</u> about working. This idea and that. But don't take off my hat and sit down to it, for some reason. I almost had an idea in France last summer, but it faded away like the Cheshire cat's smile. But I tell myself if I keep on reading Hardy, it will come. I have just finished Tess of the D——. When Angel Clare found her in that seaside resort, living with Alec D'Urberville, and she said "Don't come near me," and "Too late, too late," and he went away, and she went upstairs to her bedroom and [threw] herself on the floor with her head on that chair, and said "O, O, O," and then "I can't bear it," it was she <u>and I</u> that couldn't bear it. I will never be the same. But what do you think they talked about, for those five days, in that empty house that didn't belong to them? Brazil?

E put the poppy poster in the back hall near the door of my abandoned study, where when you come on it it takes you by surprise. Just stuck on the wall with adhesive tape. I think glass comes between you and pictures, don't you?

And if you will root around in your correspondence you will see that I didn't write to Miss Warner about that free offer from the Observer because I forgot to detach the coupon when I sent the page back to you!

Kate is doing exams—serious ones, for the first time—with a not very bad cold, and Brookie is in bed with a runny nose and the sneezes. It came on her last Saturday afternoon when we were at the opera, seeing <u>The Magic Flute</u>. The Chagall settings were marvelous in themselves, but you couldn't tell what was going on, because of them, and quite a lot was, of course, so I'm not sure they were a very good idea.[29] More an interesting curiosity. Raskin sang like an angel, which is what we went for. And a letter from Wm Meredith[30] got us backstage, where Brookie had backstage fright, and it took a great deal of coaxing before I got her into the Queen of

the Night's dressing room. Roberta Peters. She was darling to B, and must be a nice woman. Kate and Emmy were taken to <u>La Boheme</u> on Sunday, and are going to <u>Butterfly</u> this Saturday. So that child is getting her heart's desire after all. For a while it looked as if she'd have to do with <u>Traviata</u>, having been promised six operas by the friend across the road, whose husband isn't well, so she couldn't do the taking. So happy to have your letter and to know that you have been out enjoying yourself. Love, B

*Also the sense of the company—how it's done, and all that.

Eudora Welty to William Maxwell, March 13, 1967

Dearest Bill,

I keep fingers crossed and hope you'll all be flying away to that warm island and that it will do you all the good in the world. Thank heaven the cold caught from that step into night life has gone—you just do need Barbados. I hope Kate with her sneezes feels like taking the exams in good form and that they all go like a breeze (not a draft) and Brookie feels better too— if she started sneezing at The Magic Flute, maybe she needs Eine Kleine Nachtmusik every night till she is over it—I hope she is already. Is Emmy all right? What a winter.

It's so lovely here at the moment I feel guilty to tell you—temp. in the 70s and everything bursting out. This doesn't mean we won't get another whack —we had one, and they say it got all the peaches—but with daffodils and red-bud and willow trees and spirea and now azaleas beginning, and the birds and all, I wish I could enclose a slice, neatly folded in a piece of sky-wrap.

I'm glad you got to the Magic Flute—not having seen reproductions of the set yet I am simply unable to put Chagall and Mozart together—especially since I like Mozart best—and Kate and all she is hearing and seeing! Yesterday afternoon Leontyne Price gave a concert in Jackson and I heard her sing the Dove Son[o] from Marriage of Figaro, along with a big work-out of a program—she was all radiance and glory, simply beautiful. The only other time she'd appeared in Jackson was when she was a young girl just starting to Juilliard, and it was private and invitational because it was in a downtown hotel and at that time you could only integrate privately and by invitation—she sang like an angel and was so astonishing that she was asked

to please just sing it over, she repeated the whole program because we just couldn't believe it. Yesterday the concert was in one of those big cow barns like the ones the U. of Wis. and Ill. used to hold concerts in when we were going to college, and all packed to the roof with white, black, yellow and what have you, everybody on their feet, and she must be at her very height right now, don't you suppose? I've missed her everywhere until now. She wore a beautiful Mediterranean blue chiffon gown with green and white shaded feathers around the top and green lining to a panel, and when she exited what a gay fling of that panel—she was so gay and loved singing, so visibly loved every minute.

I'm grateful to you for letting me send in the Martha G. review and for reading it with kindness—no matter what happens to it I'm glad you asked me about it, because it gave me some kind of pleasure to be able to put back in (as well as I could remember) what was there to start with and had to be whacked. How I wish you could have seen her—they wrote me this might well be the last season. They invited me up but I couldn't make it, but still feel sure and serene that there will be another season. Something indestructible about her.

Brookie having backstage fright reminded me that Kate did too, at the Old Met, didn't she? It's like being called up by the magician and being talked to out of the corner of his mouth and told what to do and yet, I guess, it isn't the same—the magician's magic never was real but Roberta Peters' & Martha Graham's is & stays that way. Good luck on things—Love to all,

Eudora

Your 2 letters about Observer came together! I didn't know which was first. Anyway, it was that page that was good as it was.

William Maxwell to Eudora Welty, [March 1967]

Dearest Eudora:

The red slip says all. Thinking to myself that if it was only in my bailiwick, I would work with you until you had it sufficiently in line with what is required of a book review, whatever that may be, I sat down a few minutes

ago to reread it, and after I had finished reading it, what I felt was a strong disinclination to change a hair of its head. As usual you know what you are doing. And my private opinion is that it would have done the New Yorker's readers good to read that passage about M.G.'s theater being like a moving boat on a river with the audience running beside it to keep up with it. It is for such observations as that that I continue to be a reader at all. Only they only drop in your lap every once in a while. If I were you, I would not put it away. A little tinkering and it will stand as an essay, with the book as the springboard. At all events, it ought to get into print.[31] Editors also do not always see the woods for the trees.

We have tickets, we are going. Last Thursday morning I tried to reach Anne Lindbergh, as a last resort, because her ex-sister-in-law, Margot Wilkie, who is her friend as well, and as well as ours, said that Charles would not help people get on Pan American airplanes (he being an officer of the company), but that Anne could do this and would. She had left for the city, at nine-thirty in the morning. Then Margot called to invite Emmy to her apartment for tea, to meet a Japanese roshi who was particularly darling, and said that Anne and Humphrey, Emmy's brother, and some other people were coming. Though not really searching for a roshi, and never happy at the thought of using people, E went off, with the flight information in her purse, at four-thirty. The thing was, we were on a waiting list and how to get far enough up where it would do some good. (Reflection suggests that there is only one way, to push somebody else aside.) The answer to why Charles won't do it. (And when the subject was broached, Anne said she could not do anything—This letter is as complicated as my sister-in-law in California, always full of facts about people we don't know—but she would ask Charles. Though he didn't like to. Quite enough for me to call a halt, if I had been there, which I wasn't.) But to get on with Thursday afternoon: Well, the reason E didn't take that telephone call herself is that she was off looking at the Wyeth show at the Whitney, and she came home full of that, so off I went to see them, after I had dropped my income tax file at the office and read my mail. And it was a lovely show. The things he painted had been looked at long and lovingly, and I am always happier looking at a painting of something. But along about four thirty or quarter of five, I be-

thought myself that Kate and Brookie would be at loose ends, both having colds, and their mother off having tea with a roshi, so I got in a cab and came home. And the elevator operator said "You have company." "Yes?" said I.

Well, in Portland, or rather just outside it, in Gresham Oregon, there lives a man named Jan de Graaf[f], whose name you probably know, because he raises lilies, and his wife is Emmy's mother's friend, though they are of different generations. Mrs. DeG is my age. Black hair, black eyes, very thin, very nice, very cultivated. And on their way back home from a trip of seven or eight countries, they had called, as usual, and been invited to tea on Thursday. Only I'd forgotten what day they were coming and Emmy had forgotten that it <u>was</u> Thursday. So Kate let them in. At that very moment the phone rang and it was the travel agent, saying that she could get us two tickets for Saturday or four for Sunday, March 19, and we'd have to let her know which right away. So Kate, being now extremely grown up, and knowing where her mother was, found the telephone number, called her, and told her the travel agent's number and what she said. But she is not entirely grown up, because it didn't occur to her to add the information that the de-Graafs were standing in the middle of the living room with their coats on, waiting to be welcomed to tea. When I walked in, they had finished doing the bookcases, and the mayor's house, and were looking at the Matisse lithograph, having made up their minds that they had come on the wrong day. Proving that one should always listen to the voice of duty. On the pretext of calling the travel agent I called Emmy, and got her away from the roshi, who didn't speak English, it turned out, but had though a very old man skin as smooth as a child and very bright eyes, and was fund raising. For a Zen establishment in California which Humphrey is under the impression was to be sixty thousand acres. That is several counties, surely. He must have got it wrong. E says she understood it was 240, which is enough, one would think, for a good many people to sit in the lotus position. Anyway, in she walked, and gave the whole thing cheerfully away with her first remark, and we had our usual pleasant visit with the deGraafs, which takes place year after year. That was Thursday afternoon. It is now Saturday morning, and in two days we have advanced far into spring. (I put my left foot in, I take my left foot

out…) Should we keep Kate home from <u>Butterfly</u>, because of her cold occupied most of Friday. The remaining time being occupied with should we go to the country. We didn't go to the country, we are keeping Kate home, and she is not bitterly disappointed because if she had gone to <u>Butterfly</u> tonight, she would not have been able to hear the broadcast of <u>Othello</u> this afternoon. B also has a cold, and E is tired. So it is just as well. And besides, shortly we will be in the sunshine. When E said to the travel agent, what about the return flight, the travel agent said, Oh don't worry about that. But I dare say when the time comes we shall. If you don't hear from us by Easter (which is when?) come and join us, wherever we are. And we'll all come home by way of Monticello.

<div align="right">Love,

Bill</div>

P.S. Sunday afternoon Kate's friend Kate Delacorte came over, and our Kate decided that it was the other Kate's birthday, so they dressed up, and invited all sorts of people. Verdi, Mozart, Edgar Allen Poe, the Brontes— fifteen people in all, and what with the doorbell ringing so loud and so often, it was all I could do to get my practicing done. And when I came into the living room, I sat down on Charlotte Bronte—by mistake. I never would have done it knowingly.

Eudora Welty to Emily and William Maxwell, March 15, 1967

Dearest Emmy and Bill,

What marvelous news! I'm so elated to know you're really going—I hope the warm sun & air & sea (?) do all the good in the world and you all come back rosy & fine—maybe with a new novel or story too, Bill—I imagine the place is looking sort of like an Easter nest?

Bill, thank you for all that trouble & kindness about the review—I wasn't a bit surprised it didn't fit, and thank you for taking your time, energy & all that I hate to think I let you spend on anything less than the best story I can write—

The chartreuse chains are hanging 5 inches long on the oak tree this

morning, and a Dutch iris opened a flower. I feel qualified to say Happy Spring, Happy Trip! & lots of wishes & love to all,

Eudora

In the spring of 1967, Eudora asked Bill for information about his friend Larry Woiwode, a writer from North Dakota, whom she wanted to recommend for a grant from the newly established Katherine Anne Porter Foundation.

William Maxwell to Eudora Welty, [April 1967]

Dearest Eudora:

Woiwode is in his early twenties and is married and right this minute living and writing in a summer cottage in northern Michigan. He was the protégé of a friend of mine—of yours too, come to think of it: Chuck Shattuck. He was in college an actor who wanted to write. He did Richard II and I think Hamlet, with great distinction, and I met him when he was still in Urbana, and kept an eye on him when he came to New York. The New Yorker has published five stories by him and has five or six more on the bank. I have sent you what seem to me the best, but you are welcome to the rest.

You asked about that idea I had for a novel in France. It went away. And so did another I wrote on the airplane coming back from St. Croix. In my mind. The whole thing. It's no good when that happens. It just means you have to be patient for a while longer. I have been more careful about editing. It isn't reading <u>you</u>, or any writer who is a writer, but trying to supply talent where it is missing that is wrong. I think. I'm not terribly sure about anything, to tell you the truth. All I know is that since we got back from the West Indies, if I see some manifestation of strangeness of the kind that before that used to make me wince, I just think, instead, Well if it makes him/her happy, <u>why not</u>?

Love, and please, please do come and visit us while I am still accepting the universe.

B.

P.S. I think you may have changed Nancy Hale's life.

Eudora Welty, Charleston, West Virginia, to William Maxwell,
May 2, 1967

Dearest Bill,

Thank you so much for calling me up. It was fine to hear you sound-
ing so well. And it's the help I wanted, your sending the Woiwode stories.
I remember your first telling me to watch out for him—and how I could
have let those stories slip by without using my eyes is a terrible warning to
me. The long one, "The History Lesson," is the only one still to go (reading
among the relatives, talking all over the house), but all of the short ones are
moving & real to me, with quite marvelous moments, & I'm so glad to have
them in a collection of my own, which, if I may, I'd like to take to Washing-
ton with me. How these foundation things come about I still have to learn,
but the main thing I wanted was a writer young & good to be my gift to the
givers. I do like his work so much.

It's my hope we can meet in NYC for I'm planning to leave Charleston
at the end of the week and be in New York by Friday night, then Diarmuid
had asked me to come see the new house that weekend, and I hope to be
in the city from Monday the 8th (Eight o'May, Emancipation Day, isn't
that right) till I suppose the next Sunday, 14th. Dolly Wells, old friend from
home, asked me to stay with her in her apartment at 31 East 12th St. and I'll
call you. So much to hear about.

Three Eudoras in one room yesterday. I have a lot of first cousins, but
mostly I came for the chance to see my mother's two remaining brothers,
both in poor health, one sad, one irrepressibly merry, and I've been shut-
tling. The mountains are in 20 shades of green & the dogwood on the river
("up Elk") is so thick that it's a roof over the road, and printed white all over
the straight up hillsides—I saw the fence of the courthouse where I used to
be chased by a Henry McLain who had long yellow curls (it was his father's
courthouse), and learned he is a well known attorney these days—saw the
bridges, the shoals, the houses, all such like, that I remember from <u>early</u>.
The uncles said they were too old to sing any more, but they did sing—
I saw the little hamlet on the river called Elkhurst where my father met
my mother and the boarding house where she stayed as the schoolteacher.

I guess only in a place like this would such things still be standing as they were —

Love,
Eudora

William Maxwell to Eudora Welty, May 16, 1967

Dearest Eudora:

I thought you wouldn't mind my showing the story ["The Optimist's Daughter"] to Emmy, who felt the same way I did about it. "What I liked best," she said, "was Mr. Allday, going through the whole house like hope and leaving everything worse than before." And today at lunch Diarmuid said he thought it was your best work, which is what I think. He also said that you thought it should not be published all by itself. My own instinctive feeling was that it should be. Don't make up your mind on this point in a hurry.[32]

Love,
Bill

Eudora Welty to William Maxwell, June 12, 1967

Dearest Bill,

Thank you so much for calling me. It was lovely to talk. And marvelous news that was about the story, though it was back in New York when you first read it that I got the real news on it. I was and am now so glad you liked it when you read it with all your generosity and care, and I'm glad Emmy wanted to read it and was sympathetic too. I must say—though it's fine to have any story accepted, sort of like finding a room and bath at the end of a long trip (but it's who meets you at the station you care about, isn't it?)—I wouldn't have ever supposed a story that long, etc., would have been really thought of for any magazine at all, and to have The New Yorker take it is still a bit hard to take in. (That's two takes right there.) Thank you for all you must have done to guide it in. I hope your own new story is as blessed as mine's been.

As you know, I generally work at more removes or with more disguises

from my own life than I did in this story, and I wonder if—with publication looking at me—I ought to do anything protective about it for other people's sake. The fact about the hospital is that before my brother [Edward] died last January, his frantic wife [Elinor] came to the hospital where he was stretched in a harness with a broken neck and hit him, according to the nurse, while she told me if I believed the nurse I was a so-and-so. As you see, I must believe it, deep down. I don't care about her feelings but do you think the story with relationship, city, illness, act changed is enough removes away to protect the magazine? Nobody else but me knows about this (unless she has told them) and since she says it is not true, it would be admitting it is true to find a likeness. But the idea of such a thing whether she did it or not just burns on, and as far as the story itself goes it doesn't matter either way, true or untrue. The West Virginia parts are all based on reality too, and I can't think the old uncles would mind, but I have not had experience with writing this close to other people's lives. I changed Mr. Allday's name because there is an only too real Mr. Day—I got his walk, and most of him. Illiterate, but that was easy to fix in case he heard. If there is anything I should do about changing anything, now is of course the time, the last chance.

It sounds busy as everything on Baptist Church Road. It makes me think of Emmy's drawing of everybody helping move—even Daisy, I think. Awful about the roses. Lightning struck a big pine tree out my window while I was looking at it—blinding light, puff of smoke which was jerked out of sight damned fast, like something not meant to be seen, telephone wire burned out, tree scarred top to bottom but may not die, windows broken, and the daylights scared out of me. Thought the house was on fire, such a smell of burning, ran next door and phoned fire dept., they came and said "Lady, we don't hardly see how you could <u>help</u> being on fire after that, but you ain't, but if you notice anything burning later on, don't hesitate to call us." Hesitate! I was in such a hurry to call them the first time that running through the lady's pitch black hall I fell flat as a Keystone Kop. What a displacing week in the world it's been anyway, so ominous and unpredictable when war started on Monday and still ominous and unpredictable with the war stopped.[33] Went out and painted the porch swing and chairs to keep steady while the news crackled.

I started you a letter in the U. of Maryland place where the meeting was for the Katherine Anne Porter thing—I can't find it, but seems to me it was mainly about what loud leviathan splashings [novelist] Glenway Wescott (it turned out) makes when he takes a bath, as the walls there are very thin—it was a sort of houseparty, with K.A. and everybody spending the night and next day. As for the reading I'd done, I'm glad I did it and glad I have Mr. W[oi]wode, but it was premature, because there isn't any money yet. It's all up to action by trustees and university custodians and the like —Katherine Anne doesn't have to die first, but arrangements of literary and legal affairs all have to go through. Only 3 people do all the reading, Wm Humphrey, Red Warren,[34] and me, so I'm relieved that at first there aren't going to be applications but invitations to submit stories, etc., and I'll be getting in touch with Mr. W. and any others I like by the time it's set up and there's money.

Well, you and Emmy know how good it was to see you, and it was the greatest joy you could manage it when I had such a flying visit and the time's always busy with you and the weather was so daunting, and yet we had our leisurely delicious Coffee House dinner, with everybody glowing, and one of our chases through the city, which I always enjoy, and after the movie that lovely ride to take me home, when you went to 86th Street by way of 12th. About the movie [Blow-Up], that old ham Orson Welles has some things to say about Antonioni in the enclosed clipping, which I cut out for Emmy—her letter follows—the night I got home, when I fell in bed and started opening Observers.

Do you ever have exchanges with Jose de Creeft at the Institute—I don't know if he attends much. Maybe you know him in other places. I knew him 20 years ago at Yaddo and adored him, and a card came saying to watch Camera Three last Sunday when a documentary on him at work would be shown. Not too terribly much of him came through on film and tape, but some did. It showed him in the middle of making a statue when all he thinks of at any time is "the stone, the stone," and how he keeps close to his farm with his wife even cutting his hair—did you possibly see this? He's holding the cat and singing, while she does it, and on impulse lifts the cat's long tail like the neck of a guitar and strums the cat to accompany his song. 82 now, and still having shows every year or so. At Yaddo he felt self-con-

scious as I did about being set apart to create, and we laughed all the time, weren't good for much work. I looked up and found a watercolor he did of me looking rather non-plussed, signed "souvenir de prison." "It is the spirit of the stone," he said with a nod he was trying for—he still makes his own tools in his own forge. In July, get Emmy to cut your hair, & play the cat, sing a song, and write your story, or at least write your story.

<div align="right">

Love to all, love and thanks,

Eudora

</div>

Please forgive me backsliding into not writing. I <u>think</u> right.

P.S. I couldn't hear what you said about "birthday"—whose, & when, & how many candles?

William Maxwell to Eudora Welty, June 21, 1967

Dearest Eudora:

Merciful God, the lightning might have been the end of you!

And Mr. Greenstein being still in Europe, I can't give you a definitive answer about the invasion of privacy matter [in "The Optimist's Daughter"], but I am pretty sure I know what he would say. You have disguised the episode thoroughly, and there is really no invasion. I will ask him to read the story with your letter in mind, and meanwhile I think you can just put it out of your mind. I will be sending you the galleys (unless I am prevented) before I go on my vacation, the 5th of July. I don't foresee much, and I would have had it done already, except an Austrian, who writes in German, submitted a story that was his first attempt at writing in English and was so good it couldn't not be bought, but had to have a lot of combing and currying. He's on his way to the printer, so I am now free. If you ever find that unfinished letter about Glenway [Wescott] in the bath, do send it to me. I have picked budworms off the roses until I am blue in the face, and I thought there would be nothing left of Spanish Beauty but there was. And oddly enough I sat next to Jose de Creeft at the Institute in May. On the platform. We talked cosily to each other—there was nobody on my other side—but not so cosily as we would have if we'd known we had you in common. He is still beautiful, and with all his buttons buttoned.

Brookie is going to camp on Friday, and I am taking Kate, and Philip

and Richard Hamburger, to hear Leontyne Price in the Masked Ball to-night. The [1st] two tickets were originally for Emmy and Brookie, but Brookie fidgets when it is Saturday afternoon, and would undoubtedly have had trouble staying awake, and Emmy didn't want to leave her so shortly before she goes away. I am looking forward so to it I keep worrying for fear she won't be in the cast. The garden is particularly beautiful because, since we are going to be away during so much of July and August, I didn't do anything but weed what was there. A foxglove seeded itself in the front, and there is a bright red poppy where there wasn't before, and it all looks like an old garden, which as a matter of fact it is. The shrubs around the house are all tied up in strings, waiting for the painter, and the house looks the way men do when they have just had a haircut.

Love,

B.

Eudora Welty to William Maxwell, [Late June 1967]

Dearest Bill,

Thank you for the letter. I'm glad you think the disguises are deep enough. I'd satisfied myself for my own sake and the story's sake, but my view was still not from the outside and I thought no matter how I hated bringing up that matter, it was better than letting you have something risky. It's dazing still that the New Yorker is going to publish it. I've sprung right back to my comic story now, just as I'd begun to think I was in spite of all going to let down my friends who had helped and hoped. Not to brag too soon.

So glad you still have a piece of Spanish Beauty left. I remember your big bush and the flowers so well, and Mother said she thought its other name was Madame Gregoire Staechlin—? Or is my memory right? Whatever it was, we got one, and later on it turned into Dr. Huey, on which it was budded. Hope you nab the wretched budworms and for keeps. How beautiful the garden must be looking with the volunteers—foxgloves, red poppies—I hope all of you have a grand vacation, and I'm so glad it's almost here. Best love to all of you, and good rest and good work and cool breezes. How was Leontyne?

Such a sight—I just saw one of those silver Rolls Royces—Silver Ghost?—go by with a neon-red bumper sticker saying Ross Barnett.

Shall look out for the Austrian's story. <u>He</u> must be amazed too.

Love,

Eudora

P.S. Diarmuid just called me about the payment—That makes 3 impossible things I've believed before breakfast—Well, I believe it but it was so impossible I can't remember how much it was. Heavens! Heavens, I'm going to have the outsides of my upstairs windows washed by the Jackson House-Cleaning Service, 12 men on ladders! Thanks.

William Maxwell to Eudora Welty, July 5, [1967]

Dearest Eudora:

This isn't me or even a reasonable facsimile. Too many last minute things have curdled my mind. But I did want to get these galleys to you so I could have them set up in regular type when I get back. I let the copy desk do the merest copyediting of a kind I didn't think you would object to, but I am enclosing a zerox copy of the manuscript anyway, so that in doubt you can look [and] see if they did it or you. And the usual trivial punctuation queries, and not many of those decorate the margins of the galleys. No hurry. Just when you feel like it. I have read it now for the third time, and feel it more each time. It's just simply unbearable. Like life sometimes.

Your loving,

Bill

Be back from Portland the 1st week in August.

William Maxwell to Eudora Welty, July 6, [1967]

Dearest Eudora:

Worse and worse. I did say, in yesterday's letter, that Mr. Greenstein said the only problem was not your sister-in-law but the hospital, which ought not to be named or be in the same city, if possible, as the real one? The real incident took place in—I assume—a hospital in Jackson, didn't it? I am not

worried, in any case. He was just being extra cautious, which is his legalist temperament.

Off tomorrow, if I live that long. And Spanish B is Mme. Gregoire Staechlin, as you remembered your mother saying. You must have it again. In fact, cut the flowers go rather nicely with Dr. Huey, whose name is the main thing against him.

<div style="text-align: right">Love
B</div>

Back July 31

Eudora Welty to William Maxwell, August 7, 1967

Dearest Bill,

I hope you and Emmy and the girls had a good complete change and a fine time all around. And find all well at home, paint job and all.

Here's this [corrected galleys], for whenever it's needed—with many thanks to you for all your care and help. I must say I was pleased when twice you missed something I'd taken out and I was <u>delighted</u> to put back in— sounds very dubious practice for an editor, other than you. Now and then I tend to think "The Optimist's Daughter" may be a better title after all, but maybe something better than anything so far will come up.[35] If you think of a good one, please communicate it.

They're taking down the tree the lightning struck—it began to die rapidly and the beetles got into it. Not a glad sight. Only good thing about losing it is the insurance will pay for it—several hundred dollars.

Love to all. Thank you again for all good help with the story. I hope you can get back to your own writing very soon.

<div style="text-align: right">Love,
Eudora</div>

The hospital in the story is not any real one—real one in Jackson. I didn't locate it in New Orleans where there is any real one that I know of. I didn't want any person, place or thing to come close in that incident.

P.S. I suppose you know the name of the assistant administrator of the Boston Museum of Fine Arts? See enc.

William Maxwell to Eudora Welty, August 21, 1967

Dearest Eudora:

Milton Greenstein wants me to ask you if you would check to be sure that there is no hotel in New Orleans named The Hibiscus. The telephone book would be sufficient, I should think. Have you got a friend there who could look it up for you? I know that you wouldn't knowingly call it after a real hotel.

The house in the woods: I know what Merl[in] felt now, willingly shut up in a tree. We swim in the pond at the foot of the hill before breakfast, and go shopping in Wellfleet and get fresh books at the library, and some fruit and fish and vegetables, and then walk through the woods to the sea. Kate plays Mozart and Schubert on the record player, and Brookie plays the Mills Brothers. I hope—I sincerely hope you know what the Mills brothers sound like singing "Don't Be a Baby, Baby," but how could you not know it. And sometimes it rains, but nothing like as much as it does down here. And some people who used to live on the Baptist Church Road have a house in the same woods, and all their children are home, with wives and children, and we meet in clusters, and walk and talk together and cross the line of generations in the most agreeable way. Emmy had eleven for supper the other night—of them, I mean—and we ate all eleven of us sitting in chairs and on the floor around the same square coffee table, and all in the same conversation. Brookie draws, whole books of drawings, and Kate reads, and Emmy deals with the laundromat, and I commute by shuttle plane to New York. Oh and I forgot, Bluebell and Maeve [Brennan]'s four cats are there, as in East Hampton. Tiny house, too, but not an all year round house, which is what I think makes it seem so happy.

Love,

Bill

Eudora Welty to William Maxwell, August 28, 1967

Dearest Bill,

It was lovely to talk to you. And thank you for your letter. All sounds just blissful.

The New Orleans phone book lists no Hibiscus, either under H or in

the Yellow Pages, so it seems all right. Where I saw that chained cat was at a dreadful place called The Cornstalk (after the wrought-iron fence) during World War II when I found the ballet was performing that night and it was the only bed in town. Think it may have been no telling what.[36]

So glad Brookie and I share a love for the Mills Brothers. I'm going to look up Baby among my souvenirs. In New Orleans the other night, first time I've been there in a long time, I went with my nieces to a jazz concert of the old, really <u>old</u>, jazz performers, in a room like a Sunday School room where you sit on benches or floor and no refreshments or other waste of time, with audience of about 40 cramming the walls—old and young, black and white, tourists and home folks—and Sweet Emma Barrett, the Humphreys brothers, Big Jim Robinson, all in their 70's let loose. They're Negro with nothing of Mississippi or Harlem, and some of them, like Alcide "Slow Drag" Pavageau—he's the bass player I've never caught—have the names that tell you why. The walls have their clothes hanging up, and the vibrations make their hats fall off the hooks, and they have 2 electric fans back to back, the extra one special for the bass and the drums, who need it most—all the players have canvas bags or grocery sacks at their feet with God knows what in them, Sweet Emma has her purse in hers, deep down. On wall a sign, "Requests, regular, $1. Other, $2. The Saints, $5." Basin St., Closer Walk with Thee, Down by the Riverside—A radiant evening. When Josiah ("Cie") Frazier takes his turn on the drums, Percy Humphrey (the trumpet) times him by his wristwatch which he can read while tooting.[37]

Frank O'Connor's piece touching to me and made me speculate.[38] By chance I just today came across a piece Diarmuid wrote years ago on his father and it is touching along with Mr. O'C's—you might like to see it. Love to all,

Eudora

Excuse unreadable looking note—thought it would be short.

William Maxwell to Eudora Welty, [September 11, 1967]

Dear Eudora:

I don't think Mr. Greenstein will have any more queries to plague you with, and I was delighted to read this piece Diarmuid wrote about his fa-

ther—delighted with him, because he writes so well, and with the piece
because it dovetails with the other, producing just the difference that is
so interesting about life—that no two people see somebody the same way.
Where Michael was simply dead to all forms of mysticism, though quite
capable of believing that he would meet his mother in the hereafter, Diar-
muid has a beautifully open mind on the subject. If I weren't fond of him
already, I would be from reading this. I have a copy of it.[39]

We moved to town yesterday afternoon. To an apartment with plastic
under-rugs instead of rugs, and dirt[y] windows and the ex dancer upstairs
whose tread shakes the ceiling, and the waterfall that is really the sound of
the air conditioners of the building across the street and that small cham-
ber music of fire engines, cars, voices, etc. that people enjoy (or don't en-
joy) whose bedroom is on the street. It always takes a week or so for us to get
used to the change from silence, crickets, and rain in the night, owls, cardi-
nals, whip poor WILL and Brookie going to the bathroom.

Love,

B.

*William Maxwell to Eudora Welty, October 2, 1967, Written at the top of
a letter he received from Diarmuid Russell concerning a title for Eudora's
newest work*

Oh dear how we are all fussing over you. As you know, I am mad about
The Optimist's Daughter. But when I went home and told Emmy about my
telephone call with you, she astonished me by saying, Of course it's a story,
not a novel, and should go with the other stories. But not, she felt, because
it was an exposure. Just by virtue of its form. So what I really think is that
as soon as you begin listening to what other people think you find yourself
walking along with the donkey on your back. TAKE CARE!

And love,

B.

William Maxwell to Eudora Welty, January 3, [1968]

Dear Eudora:

Here is the author's proof of Poor Eyes/The Optimist's Daughter. Nearly

all the queries are a matter of style punctuation, and you really do not have to make any concessions to the New Yorker in this matter at all. If some suggestion seems an improvement or is a matter of indifference to you, all right. If not, just scratch it out. Mr. Shawn wants you to have it the way you want it.

Such a queer two weeks in the country (where we still are). First of all, a few days before we drove out there for the Christmas holidays, a radiator in the room off the kitchen sprang a leak, and when the cleaning woman looked in, there was a small fountain of spray coming out of it, and a foot and a half of water in the garden basement, directly underneath. If there hadn't been a hole in the floor to let the radiator pipe come through, the water would have been all over the house. That was number one. Number two was the transmission blew (I am quoting Henry Thompkins) and sent the fluid through the manifold and the car caught on fire. On the way to the station, to leave [our housekeeper] Lilly Mae and pick up Harriet O'Connor and Hallie Og,[40] and with both children in the car. But the fire was after I had left everybody at the station; before, Brookie said, I smell something burning, and three times the lights and the ignition had conked out. It was lovely.* And snow. But anyway, I drove into a filling station, the motor gave out once more, and people started yelling "Get that out of here!" And I couldn't get it out of there (where the gasoline tanks were, with the flames shooting out from under the engine) because it wouldn't start. But in the end I did. And it is now sitting at Henry's and we are still waiting for the bad news.

Jamais deux sans trois, said I to myself and to Emmy, and last Saturday evening, when the Wilkies drove over from Katonah for tea, and I was sitting on the sofa talking to Peter Wilkie[41] about Paris, suddenly I was aware of flashing double parentheses out of the corner of my right eye. Flick, flick: parentheses of light. Since I had spent the morning working on these galleys, you don't need to be told what conclusion I drew.[42] I spent all yesterday morning at the eye doctor, and there is no retinal detachment, but neither did she know, after looking at me through the most elaborate and painful and I have no doubt expensive machinery, why the flick, flick. Which in any case is diminishing; only now and then. And perhaps means nothing

more than that you are a very powerful writer and I am a very suggestible reader.

How I adored our sending each other the same present. And of course, loving it insanely, we still hadn't got a copy for ourselves. As if we knew it was coming from you.

<div style="text-align: right">With love,
B.</div>

*It was ever more like No News or What Killed the Dog.[43]

Eudora Welty to William Maxwell, January 5, 1968

Dear Bill,

Let me know about your eye right away as soon as you have time, and meantime I hope it's only what I had when the same symptoms attacked me—turned out to be allergy. I was in the middle of typing up Delta Wedding and the flashes came from the sides and at exactly where I was focusing, the word, was a hole. People always tell you they had what you have, but I pass this on for every reason. Also my mother's eye was allergic violently over a period of years to things like eggwhite, the gas stove, above all, crysanthemums—and the pyrethrins (sp) they make from crysanthemums to put in garden spray. Maybe Mr. Wilkie had put some Christmas shaving lotion on—in my case it was cosmetics—that made him anathema to your eye, not meaning to sound unfriendly. I'll be anxious till I hear it's not only better but well—and I do know how terrifying those flashing signals are, showy as a railroad crossing warning. But they do say that allergies at least cannot damage the vision. I hope, however the nuisance, it was that and something temporary. And mercy, the fire—and the flood, or the threat of it—! For Heaven's sake take care—yes, how can you take care against bolts from the blue? Falling Rock Zone. But there've been three, and I hope the hurler of the bolts is a good adder, and now the blessings can have a turn. And now it is no longer 1967.

It could be in sympathy with your leaking radiator that my upstairs bathtub pipe did the same trick. I would take a bath and about the time I started

out the front door, the ceiling of the little doorway hall would be ready for me and I'd all but take the bath again as it dropped from above. I wrote Brookie about what happened when the man came to fix it, but I didn't know how old-hat water coming through the ceiling would be to her. How is Brookie? Emmy wrote she was having a touch of something, which I hope's clear gone now. Such a caring letter from Brookie, and from Kate, as well as from Emmy.

Yes, I do love that little book. You know once Emmy and I made each other fruitcakes too. I'd ordered this one sight unseen from Kroch's [bookstore] and on sight knew it was for you. And it's really so reasonable that thanks to each other we both have it. So much came from the Maxwells— it's like Miss Bates, how shall I ever recollect the dishes, and recollecting every one full well. I've begun Rosencranz and then sidetracked* (?) to Hamlet and read Hamlet again, and will now back in to where I left R & G. You may need to tell me how it sounds. I hear it goes very fast. I like the Langston Hughes very much and am so glad to have this to keep. He was an early discovery of mine in the local library, then I lost track of him, and now he is gone, and I was feeling I'd lost him. (It's odd, but in 1936 I too made a book of pictures and captions almost the same thing, only of course not urban, and I was able in those days to get pictures that were unposed or even unaware. It was one way I tried (unsuccessfully) to get something published in the hope of getting someone interested in my stories.)[44] I put the sandalwood bookmark in the Bible! It's in the Book of Job, whatever Job thinks. What on earth told me I ought to smell a bookmark? I did and it wafted at me. I enjoy it every morning—get up early, light the gasfire, make coffee, and take the bookmark out of Job and read of visions of night—since I'm still waiting for a thunderbolt of a title for that story to descend on me. I may send you a question on it later. (I did get the galleys with your letter—will attend to it, but ask you not to set your eyes on it again, however stupid that may sound of me.) And of course it was lovely to be told The New Yorker itself was coming too for the new year from you and Emmy. You've all given me so much and all of it what I delight in. The stars in combo together is one of my favorites of all the cards Kate, Brookie, or Emmy either ever made. Thank you many times again, and best love to all, Eudora

*These train track terms may be coming out because of a trip I made back to West Va. the week before Christmas when my uncle died. Only one of my mother's brothers is left now—he was wonderful about it, though! Then back home for my niece's debut—she's the younger of the two sisters, the one you gave your fortune to out of the fortune cookie—well, here it is. She is both beautiful and good.[45]

Eudora Welty to William Maxwell, January 8, 1968

Dear Bill,

I hope all is right again with your eye and that Brookie is well now. I'm about through with the galleys and they'll be back soon—thanks for all the careful work. I hope this is all right: I got a Christmas card from a young man I met four or five years ago when he interviewed me for his college paper and later asked me to visit his class, and his name sticker said he was Somebody McKelva Cole. I knew him as Mack Cole. Somewhere I must have retained that name from seeing his in those days. Names are in the public domain, aren't they? Will I have to add an "h" onto it? This state is full of Scots names on the same order. But when I saw it it smote me.

I loved your review of Leonard Woolf.[46]

Nothing looks more disheveled than a thoroughly rained-on redbird, do you think? I'm looking at one. (He's looking at me.)

Love to you,
Eudora

Eudora Welty to William Maxwell, January 11, [1968]

Dear Bill, thank you again and more than I can say for the aid you gave and for all the careful work. As you see, I left it "The Optimist's Daughter"—on looking over the quotes I took from the Bible I see possibilities now only in I Samuel, 29:11—that's "And the vision of all is become unto you as the words of a book that is sealed." Unless you see something better there? This is the hardest time I ever had with a title, and I've had plenty.

I hope all is well with you. Love,
Eudora

William Maxwell to Eudora Welty, January 16, 1968

Dearest Eudora:

The young man named Somebody McKelva Cole is not a problem.[47] Some-
times you didn't cross out the question mark beside a comma or something
else in the margin, but I assumed that anything you found acceptable you
just left, and the things that didn't quite do you wrote something about or
crossed out. If this is wrong, we will have to do something about it. So do tell
me. In a certain way, nothing you write is really ambiguous, but "sewing with
her fingers" didn't seem the perfect emendation for sewing on her fingers.
And just "sewing" left a lopsided sentence. (This is on galley 57—do you
have a copy there?) And so I wondered what you thought of something like
"We had to have a fire," said her mother, drawing the thread through the ma-
terial. Some such sewing action as that? Which the reader will see as hand
sewing? It has been so long—about five galleys—since there has been any
reference to where Laurel is, until the sentence in the same paragraph about
the matting (which doesn't need adding to, really, though the reader who has
forgotten would be grateful if it read "How could you make a fire on a raft?"
asked Laurel, here in the sewing room . . . instead of here on the matting. But
then you lose the matting, which is a pity, and here on the matting in the sew-
ing room, here in the sewing room, on the matting, are both enough to make
you cover your ears with your hands. Finicky detail, all this. But on galley
67, both Mr. Shawn and I were struck with what a strengthening effect on
the story it had if you cut the whole paragraph back to "It was a game for the
bereaved, and there wasn't much end to it." And then go straight from there
to the pictures over the mantel in the parlor. If you miss it on the clean gal-
leys I am sending you, by all means put it back in. Or anything else.[48]

The flashes are only at night, and only two or three times. I have not
only become reconciled to but also rather proud of them, since I learned,
in a letter from Miss Warner, that Virginia Woolf was beset by them when
she was finishing a book, and called them "electric ribbons". If I must go
mad (and I don't really think I am) nothing would give me more pleasure
than to do it in the same way she did, if you know what I mean.

<div align="right">Devotedly,
Bill</div>

Eudora Welty to William Maxwell, January 21, 1968

Dear Bill,

I think it finally has come to me, the title, and I hope it will suit you and Mr. Shawn and that it isn't too late—The Flickering Light of Vision. Is that it? I do want the title to refer to the whole story in one unit. I also thought of The Flickering Vision, but really a vision does not have that property, I guess? Anyway, I submit it.

Thank you for the pink galleys. I do agree about the cut, and thank you and Mr. Shawn for pointing out how much stronger that makes it.[49] I think my crossing out the questions was probably reflex and sometimes I didn't do it, but whenever I did not question you back I of course meant OK. Am I supposed to return these galleys, or are they a present? I'll check carefully down the pages this afternoon and write again if need be, but did want to get you this.

And to ask about your eye. I don't think much of this going along with Virginia Woolf THAT FAR. Keep in touch—good luck and I hate your having to do all this endless work on my commas and dashes. Oh, the matting. I think "drawing the thread through the material" and "here in the sewing room" just fine. Thank you (as people probably said to the saints, who put up with a lot of detail and second thoughts too).

Love,
Eudora

All that money came—the rest of it—Heaven help us.

William Maxwell to Eudora Welty, January 29, 1968

Dear Eudora:

You have until the week before the story appears to decide on the title, and whatever you decide is all right with us. Meanwhile, I will continue to tell you what I think, but not, you understand, trying to persuade you. I am still partial to "The Optimist's Daughter", because, by its ironic tone, it suggests a certain distance between the writer and the woman in the story, and because it also, again by its irony, suggests, matches, somehow, the full horror of the subject matter. The Flickering Light of Vision is, by comparison,

abstract, and to me less inviting. Also, I like titles that don't state the idea of the thing but are more oblique.

You are to keep the pink galleys.

I am seeing the eye doctor tomorrow, but think nothing has happened, one way or the other. Sometimes there is only one flick in twenty-four hours, and then flick, flick, flick, flick, flick. It seems to be when I am out of doors just after dark, in a taxi, passing lights. But why some lights and not others?

I just finished reading Passage to India for the fourth or fifth time, and am as always surprised by it. It wasn't what I thought it was. It never is.

Love,
Bill

William Maxwell to Eudora Welty, January 31, 1968

Dearest Eudora:

I've just come from a checkup at the eye doctor's and he says to forget about the flashes, it's nothing. Which I had begun to suspect my ownself.

Love,
Bill

Eudora Welty to Emily and William Maxwell, April 30, [1968]

Dearest Emmy & Bill,

It's 5:15 in the morning & I must hop from bed in a minute & start getting ready—but I'm ashamed to be so late writing you—however early in this late day—Anyway I have a trip to NY coming up (a small date at Vassar is my excuse) from May 1–14, with outside excursions inside that time. (Outside, inside—I'm writing this without my breakfast.) Will I be able to see you soon? Staying at the Algonquin. I feel stupefied with work, what I once heard somebody pronounce as bed-raggled. But the thought of seeing my friends is wonderful. I have felt like picking up this pen so many early mornings & just writing to you to say I can't write a letter to save my life so I'm just coming up for a minute, and so this time that's what I'm doing & here's the message. Emmy, I loved your postcard—That news sounded emi-

nently sensible though I'm hoping if the Ark isn't quite finished you're all still there—[50]

Much love,
Eudora

Eudora Welty to Emily and William Maxwell, [May 7, 1968]

Dear Emmy and Bill,

The voice on your telephone said you were expected home on Wednesday—tomorrow—and this is just to ask if there'll be a chance of seeing you anytime on Friday or Monday—I'm leaving now (Tuesday aft.) for Vassar & due back here at unknown hour Thursday, probably late afternoon or whenever they finish with me—and aside from the weekend (Katonah, Sat. & Sun.) I left things open just on the hope you were free for a little, or not worn from whatever trip—Ant and bee and Kind Dog <u>did</u> go around the world![51]

I leave Tuesday to be at Katherine Anne's 79th birthday party[52] on my way home—I do cherish the thought of meeting—I hope you can and easily —I want to hear where you've been, and everything—Much love, Eudora

Eudora Welty to Emily and William Maxwell, June 1, [1968]

Dearest Emmy and Bill,

The boring thing was I had to go to bed and take antibiotics after I got home—I think Washington polluted me—and this is tardy, when I did want to send love and wishes and Bon Voyage before you took off for Ireland, as well as so many thanks. Are you there? It was a wish come true to see you that evening, and to see all of you—the champagne and pistachio nuts, the ossibuchi [osso buco] and strawberries and rhubarb, Brookie's cookies— all the bestiaries, Brookie's and Bonnard's and Toulouse-Lautrec's and Renard's, with the sight of the sheep basket over there by the bookcase—and the delicious talk of London, and of all, that was all pure elixir—oh, but I was glad to see you. "The Pleasure Seekers"—isn't that the name of Brookie's book?—that must be what I am, because that's what I find there—and take away with me—I have it for a long time afterwards. Bill, your eye is the

thing I'm anxious over, and do let me know how things go with it, please do.
TAKE CARE.

You were absolutely right about there being no money to give away this
year—KAP [Katherine Anne Porter] had bought herself an emerald and di-
amond necklace to wear for the occasion, and so we'll have to wait till next
year, I take it. That Washington thing was so funny and so heart-rending
too, it was really something I'll have to tell you about from beginning to
end some day.—Bill, I don't think I really trust Glenway Wescott—has that
question ever come up?⁵³ This is nothing to start on here, when you're just
getting off to Ireland.

I can see you there. I can so well imagine you in all that green quiet,
with the racing sky, and the smell of sweet hay, or of the sea and the sound
of the voices, and of the wind at the windows, the whisky in round goblets
by the fire at night, white roads at night with streaking invisible bicycle rid-
ers without any lights,* the fuschia hedges, the horses in parks like fairyland,
the worn-down walls, towers, the beautiful children, the Tinkers and their
clothes drying on the hedges and their piebald ponies, the houses of the South
in many colors, and too many nuns in black—and Mary Lavin.⁵⁴ Do give
my love to her. (I really feel sure she never got my letters till she got home,
and it was so like her to make no provision for getting the answers to the
ones she wrote. But anyway, it is all right, but give her my love especially.)

Brookie's wonderful large tasty owl was eaten as a whole meal by me on
the train. The only hard moment was making myself take the first bite, even
knowing which end to start (I ate ears first, sparkles last) because he was first
a work of art. But he was made for a delicious meal too, and I thoroughly
enjoyed him (alone in my roomette). The ginger of him so refreshing.

Much love to Kate and Brookie and thank them for their company that
night, which was adorable, and if she will let me I'd love to see more of "The
Pleasure Seekers" the next time I come—this of Brookie's, and I would like
to see anything of Kate's and simply cannot imagine what by next time that
is likely to be.

Much love, bon voyage on the ferry, take care, have benevolent weather,
have a lovely time every day in Ireland, and among other things have some
delicious salmon, which would not be such a new treat to you, Emmy, from
Oregon, but those broiled salmon steaks right out of the Blackwater—Diar-

muid had something when he said once he only liked eating a fish that leaped.

More later.

Love,
Eudora

*Will you be there for Midsummer Night? Oh, Lord!—I was at Bowen's Court on Midsummer Night—a compelling experience—Be in the country if you can.

William Maxwell to Eudora Welty, July 10, 1968

Dearest Eudora:

I don't believe things could go wrong for anybody in Ireland, but they didn't go wrong for us. For one minute. From the minute I looked out of our bedroom at the Russell, and saw that Harcourt Street had a scrim over it, in the middle of the day, in broad daylight, I knew where I was. But what a city. And what a scale for a city to be. It was just like being in Lincoln. Sometimes we took a taxi, when we had shopped until our feet hurt and were in a terrible hurry to get home to meet somebody, but I always felt like apologizing to the driver, the distance was so small. When [Irish scholar] Dan Binchy came to take us to dinner at his club, he walked across St. S[tephen]'s Green from the club and walked us back and then walked us home again. All the places to spend money—Cleo (down in the basement) and Brown Thomas and Anna Livia and the bookstores—were so handy. Kate and Brookie would sail out together to spend their money first thing in the morning. And the weather being the most prolonged spell of fine weather in 20 years, we would meet Harriet O'Connor and Hallie Og for lunch, and sit eating cold chicken and that bread and fruit and figs, in the rented chairs in the Green, watching the children fall into the fountain. Do you remember the 100 foot long herbaceous border? And the round beds that had standard tree fuchsias in the middle and matching geraniums filling the rest? And the way people for some reason do not catch their death of cold from lying on the damp ground? And waiting under a tree for a shower to pass? And hunting through silver stores for teaspoons to match one you already have?

We were driven to Howth to see the cliffs of rhododendrons. To Glendalough to see the hermits cave and the round tower and the antiquarian ruins. To Blessington to have dinner and see the lake through seven degrees of increasing twilight until we arrived and the final one—the Celtic Twilight, of course. The mother leopard in the zoo in Phoenix Park walked around with her cub in her mouth, both of them looking like Colette. And I loved seeing a buffalo and prairie dogs in Ireland, of all places. We didn't get to Castletown, because it wasn't open that day, but we did get to the Abbey [Theatre], and saw the Shadow of the Glen, and the Shadow of a Gunman, and the first seemed far away and long ago to me, meaning Urbana in 1928, but Emmy liked it, and both of us liked the O'Casey, which had one actor so good you could put him beside the original company. Philip O'Flynn. Remember him. And Mary [Lavin] came to dinner at Dan Binchy's club, and Harriet and she were to arrange our coming to Bective, but we never got there because Mary herself was never there.[55] She was keeping away from her mother. From her description it didn't sound very real, the difficulty, but it was obviously real to her. And the last day she and I met on Molesworth Street, while Emmy was down below, buying more Avoca rugs and blankets in Cleo's, and we stood and talked for half an hour, and every person that walked by said hello Mary. Just like Lincoln. Or Jackson, I would guess.

And all this time a priest we knew in France, a friend of Harriet and Michael, was arranging our hotel accommodations for us, in the west. The idea was that we were to be shown Ireland by Michael, and since he wasn't there, Maurice [Sheehy] was doing it. Day after day passed, and I got more and more nervous as nothing seemed definite, and I thought of all the hotels filling up with Americans and no place for us, because though Emmy would like to travel with her things tied up in a red scarf and sleep in a bed of leaves, unless she has a room with a bath she cannot, as they used to say in Lincoln, go to the bathroom. And so after a couple of days I begin to worry about her. Well, I needn't have worried this time, because though some of the hotels we wanted to stay in were full up, others just as good or better were not. It all worked out. We went to the design center in Kilkenny, in the castle stables, and were given tomato sandwiches and tea because we hadn't had any lunch. And spent the night in the Cashel Palace

Hotel, overlooking the ruins, which I would trade for Mt. St. Michel any day in the week. And Harriet and Hallie Og went on to Killarney with us, and then took the train back to Cork. I refused to go to Cork because I was too eager to get to the West. Killarney is the one place I hope not to see ever again. The town, only. Everything outside was lovely, as usual. And even in the town there was something—the English edition of the Bride of Innisfallen, which Emmy and Harriet saw when they went out walking after dinner, and couldn't buy, because the shop was closed, and the next morning I meant to go get it and forgot until we were half way to Parknasilla. We drove on the left hand side of the road, and at first it was nervewracking, because we had a Vauxhall station wagon, to hold the luggage and six people, and that is too big a car for Irish roads. There were times when I shut my eyes and prayed. In Parknasilla something had gone wrong with the reservations, and they had put the children on a different floor, and when I looked upset at this, they moved us to "the apartment", which turned out to be a sitting room, two bedrooms, and two bathrooms, en suite, with plate glass windows overlooking Kenmare Bay. The hotel was charming, and set in gardens that were full of things that would be perfectly at home in Jackson, as perhaps you know. And islands to walk in, connected by footbridges, and motor boats, and so beautiful. And such good food. Salmon out of the bay, and that sort of thing. But it was full of English mfgerers [manufacturers?] and their wives, and after three days, we began to wish we were in Ireland. We went on to a guest house on a lake, in the most marvelous old garden I ever hope to see and that was full of German businessmen and their wives. So we jumped the tracks and went to Dingle. This experience, the high point of our trip, I will save, for your next visit, and you can tell us what made you uneasy about Glenway Wescott and we will tell you about Miss Siobvan Fitzgerald and the Canon's House on the rocks.[56] Where we were all four so happy I wonder we didn't die of it.

But now it is as if we had seen a ghost and were going around not talking about it. Do you understand? If you don't, who does?

And when you come we'll show you "The Pleasure Seekers" and then we'll all sit around being haunted together.

Kate has been in camp for ten days, which is much longer than we thought she'd last, and her most recent letters do not convey homesick-

ness, so I guess it is going to be (knock, knock) all right. Brookie is taking sculpture lessons and riding lessons and is, as she said of her year in school, "divinely happy." Between times, she and Emmy make clothes for B. She keeps Emmy occupied. "Today," she says at the breakfast table, "we are going to make Lasagna." "No, we are not," Emmy says firmly. But they do.

<div align="right">Love from us all

B</div>

Eudora Welty to William and Emily Maxwell,
[August or September 1968]

Dearest Bill, & dearest Emmy—

I don't know how many letters you get a day written out of friends' purses in the Bus Terminal but here's this one. I'm passing through on my way to Yaddo to a meeting that goes on this weekend, and am passing back through, spending Sunday & Monday nights with Dolly Wells (Rosa F. 31 E. 12, GR-7-3452). I don't really count this being a trip to NY, & hated to come just now, but I'll phone you just to say hello & get your news. Your Ireland letter I cherish, have it in my suitcase now, I may answer it right when I get to Yaddo. Thank you for it. I hope everybody's well. I am within sight of end of novel at last—dog tired, so that I was writing it in my sleep as well as while at typewriter, & when I had to buy a new refrigerator the other day I wrote that into the novel that night in my dreams—I'm sure you know the non-stop feeling[57]—I ran into your Mr. W[o]iwode immediately on getting off the train, in the 12th St. Longchamps—So very nice—What a piece of luck—Good to know his novel is coming out before long.[58]

Best love to you all, & hope to talk to you when I get back. I am hiding between 2 Chinese to write hoping I am concealed from other Yaddoites till Gate 2g opens. Love from Eudora

Eudora Welty to William Maxwell, October 7, [1968]

Dearest Bill,

I hope you've all been taking care and are well again—especially I hope you stayed home from the office and didn't get any more calls from those

Bill working at *The New Yorker*, late 1930s or early 1940s.
Photo courtesy of Kate and Brookie Maxwell

Eudora working at home, circa 1943. *Photo courtesy of Eudora Welty, LLC*

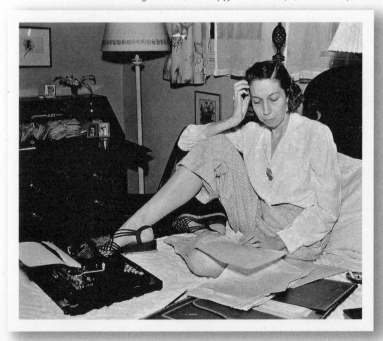

Eudora and friends in Italy, 1950. Left to right: William Jay Smith, Dolly Wells, Eudora, and John Robinson. *Photo by Barbara Howes, courtesy of Gregory Smith*

Mary Lou Aswell and Frank Lyell seeing Eudora off for England, summer 1954. *Photo by Louis J. Lyell*

Eudora and Bill revising "The Ponder Heart," 1953.
Photo courtesy of Kate and Brookie Maxwell

Bill and Kate Maxwell, Eudora and Chestina Welty, Yorktown Heights, 1956.
Photo courtesy of Kate and Brookie Maxwell

Christmas at the Welty house, 1953. Standing, left to right: Edward's wife, Eli-nor; Walter; Eudora; and Walter's wife, Mittie. Seated: Chestina, Elizabeth, and Mary Alice. *Photo courtesy of Eudora Welty LLC*

Bill and Emmy, breakfast alfresco in Yorktown Heights, late 1960s or early 1970s. *Photo courtesy of Kate and Brookie Maxwell*

Emmy in her studio, 1970s. *Photo courtesy of Kate and Brookie Maxwell*

Kate and Brookie at play in Yorktown Heights, circa 1967.
Photo courtesy of Kate and Brookie Maxwell

Agents and writers: Diarmuid Russell, Eudora, Bernard Malamud, and Timothy Seldes, circa 1972. *Photo courtesy of Timothy Seldes*

Eudora and Reynolds Price, Durham, North Carolina, 1988. *Photo by Daniel Voll*

Eudora and Bill at the American Academy of Arts and Letters, 1980.
Photo used with permission of the American Academy of Arts and Letters, New York City

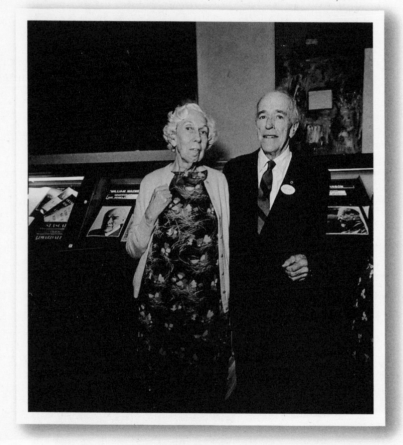

who were passing through and longed for some conversation from you, like me—since I had my lovely conversation—and it was so sweet of you, as always talking as though you had all day, and time for the news I most wanted to hear, when probably your taxi was just going by. Love to all of you. Don't take a chance on the health. Maybe this weekend you're all in the country, and looking around and appraising the pumpkins.

My week of riding mostly was good, and I found a copy of Elizabeth's book in Scribner's and had the whole ride home for it.[59] Isn't it a marvel—like a present to those who love her of everything that's most deeply a part of her temperament and mind and eyesight. I was so delighted when a note from her last spring said she hoped to be in New York for the publication—it isn't out yet, is it? And I wonder if she is coming, or has come? I would love to run back up and see her. Knowing how many more would be wanting to do the same.

At any rate, if I get the ms. finished when I had expected, I hope to come up by the end of the month or in November—I won't say anything about it, I've said too much and taxed you and Diarmuid too much. (I scratched out that ~~But.~~)

Had a note from Mary Lavin speaking of seeing you, and I could see you (from your letter) talking on the street, with Dublin walking by. So glad of a word from her—the rest of the letter said she couldn't write now—how well I understand, here I think if it would just <u>rain</u> I could write a letter, while thinking of my friends all day long all the time. But she is having me sent galleys of her new book, which I'll be pleased to see.[60] So thanks for passing us news of each other, on your wonderful trip.

Give my love to Emmy and Kate and Brookie and I'm so glad of the wonderful summer had by every single one, and now I hope everything goes fine for the fall. Much love, and I will write soon. A cool cloudy shadowless morning, but no rain—the sprinklers have to keep it up all day, just to keep the camellias placated—they all have big buds now.

Love,

Eudora

P.S. It seemed to me on the phone you said something about "galleys"—was it something about my story, & should I do anything, or know anything?—I don't. But of course you'll tell me if I need to switch onto it again.[61]

William Maxwell to Eudora Welty, October 30, 1968

Dearest Eudora:

 The mosaic of Elizabeth's visit can be guessed at from her last day, Monday. I talked to her on the phone about ten. She had told me to call her, with the idea, I could only suppose, that, we would meet somewhere, over coffee or lunch, and talk—a thing I couldn't quite imagine but neither was I going to leave the stone unturned. She was about to ruin her last day she said by going to the airplane office to get a new ticket, having searched high and low for the one she should have had and couldn't find. She was distressed, thinking it was the announcement of a crumbling intellect, old age, and all that, and grateful when I told her that it happened to me once a day, which it does. But we were to be at Bill Koshland's party for her that night, and would see her then.[62] I have since learned that she went to an afternoon party, and dinner, and changed for the evening one—Howard [Moss] told me. And was as fresh as a daisy. The blueness gone. And we had exactly one minute's conversation, as she was leaving to go home. There were only a dozen people there, and they tended to solidify, and the group around her was of course more impenetrable than the others, and I talked my way through the evening unworriedly thinking she'd be at the end, and miscalculated. But she put so much genuine interest and affection into that 60 seconds that, I didn't feel at all I hadn't seen her. We are to let her know when we go to Ireland next spring and she will join us if she can—a thing I have no trouble imagining whatever. In a way I think too many people is an impoverishment. Or to put it differently, who would talk to twenty-seven other people when they could talk to you or me? But I also think it is more seemly to take your friends as you find them. In J. R. Ackerley's "My Father and Myself" (which has wonderful things in it but I don't really recommend it to you; it starts off well and goes to hell in a basket, a rather tiresome and unpleasant basket) there is a letter which I suspect is from Forster, and in it there is this sentence, which gave me great pleasure: "Also if you want a permanent relationship with him or anyone, you must give up the idea of ownership, and even the idea of being owned." Which doesn't prevent me from grieving because my plan miscarried.

Here it is all but Halloween, and you not here, and the painter coming tomorrow. Count the next ten days out of our lives, unlived and unlivable. Probably the pumpkin will be under the kitchen table, among piles of books and records. But carved, certainly, and lit. But I am astonished by the Wallace News. Who writes it? Is that the way everybody speaks in Mississippi? Such a good ear for speech I never knew an amateur writer to have. I ask myself if she has made a careful study of your published works. To use those devices to set the reader's teeth on edge is remarkable, and more so if unintentional.[63]

All Elizabeth said, when I mentioned you, was that she <u>didn't</u> have any time (with a shadow across her voice, you know how she modulates according to feeling).

The Optimist's Daughter is scheduled to run at the time of Mardi Gras, and there will doubtless (to answer your question of some time back) be queries on the pages which will give me an excuse to call you a week or ten days before. But nothing as of this minute. We were in the country last weekend—Friday night, we came in Saturday to go to that concert I told you about—and still no killing frost. We picked roses and galliardia and nasturtiums and dill. Never since I have lived in Yorktown has this happened so late in the fall. I felt we were living in the South.

I simply can't bear the [presidential] election, can you?

Devotedly,
Bill

Eudora Welty to Emily and William Maxwell,
[December 1968]

Dearest Emmy and Bill,

The White Crysanthemum (I like it like that, it's more like crystal) and the Welsh poet of poets, and the Grave in the Rain of Kelly Fearing all seemed to come together for me—you sent me two and I'll send you the third one—to say thank you—The white Crysanthemum that with the visitor and the host spoke no word is carefully propped on my mantel shelf and indeed not a sound is heard—One of your loveliest—And Dafydd Ap

Gwilym! You remembered my love of the Welsh—I'd bought myself an early (Victorian?) translation in a secondhand shop in London, full of thou's and he was clear out of reach—I wish I had it to show you the difference, but later on I gave all my small Welsh library to Bryn Mawr (Kin)[64]—Now here is Nigel Heseltine—as alive and burning as a new rocket—I think the poems are superb, don't you? Of course the preface of Frank O'Connor's puts the poems just where they must have been always meant for in the land of rejoicing—for the readers, or hearers as he must have written for[65]—I'll read these many times again—Thank you all for such beautiful presents— And I haven't even got to the Irish scarf!

William Maxwell to Eudora Welty, January 10, 1969

Dearest Eudora:

Did I tell you I have taken to champagne? Whiskey is not my friend, and neither is gin, nor rum, though I love it in the summer time, but this year I tried having a split or a half bottle of champagne and for the first time in ten years I didn't have to give up drinking in the month of October. It may drive us into bankruptcy, but there are worse states. And the cooler with the champagne in it now sits on the Williamsburg trivet, a constant reminder of our affection for you and—why not say it?—your affection for us. When you come, I will put a half bottle <u>and</u> a split in the cooler, or perhaps even a whole bottle, who knows.

It was a lovely Christmas. I couldn't seem to do anything much about it before hand except get some books and records for the children and a strip of Krazy Kat which turned up in a knitting shop on E. 37th Street for Brookie because she is the artist of the family, well no, Emmy is, too, and so is Kate […], and a story for Emmy, but I couldn't bring myself to go to Bloomingdales or Bergdorf's or any of those places. Usually I get something for Emmy and I think Oh, dear it isn't enough, and so I rush back and get something else, which turns out not to be enough either, and when Christmas comes I am too tired of shopping to care. This year I just stood still and let it happen, and it was lovely. Christmas afternoon we went skating. I had given skating up for good two years before[,] after a spectacular spill on the Wollman Memorial Rink wearing rented skates. Sixty is time to give

up ice skating, I said, but I didn't want them to go off without me so I got my skates down from the top shelf of my closet in the country, and put on three undershirts, long underpants, three pairs of sox, a flannel shirt, two sweaters, two scarves, a windbreaker, and a stocking cap and gloves, think-ing if I fall at least I am well cushioned, and of course I didn't fall. So ev-ery day after that we all went skating, in all the ponds in the neighborhood. There was snow on the ground, but no new snow fell to spoil the skating, and the last weekend Kate had her friend Renate out, and Bobby Urquhart who is just about to turn 21 and the son of old old friends asked himself out for the night, and we borrowed some skates for him. He is six feet tall, and looks like a young poet in a story by E.T.A. Hoffman.[66] Blond yellow hair to his shoulders and yellow sideburns and muttonchops under his chin. And so gentle, but not effeminate. He never asks for anything he wants but he wants it so deeply that you—I mean Emmy does—feel it and then you have to pry it out of him, which we have learned how to do. Well he had been in England studying at the London School of Economics, and no skating there, and he was so happy to be on the ice. He skated beautifully, in a tan semi-military coat with the lining dragging and half the buttons missing and a vermilion scarf like the Toulouse Lautrec poster, and he has a long straight back and skated as if he was hinged at the base of his spine. Curious but also beautiful. Well that Saturday there was a full moon, and at eleven o'clock as I was <u>ordering</u> Brookie to bed, all other means having been ignored, Emmy looked out of the window and said "Why don't we all go skating." So we did. Including Brookie. We went to the pond across the road, and with Orion overhead and a flashlight to lace our skates by, and the moon, of course, and the white snow, and the woods all around—this sentence turns out not to have any ending. It was one-thirty when Brookie quieted down, and as we were about to go to bed Emmy felt that Bobby wanted something, and she said, "Did you bring some of your poems to read?" and it turned out that he had. So we read them, till two thirty, and then went to bed in a happy state of wooziness. And the next day said goodby to all that happiness and came into town and school and this and that, most of which is not unhappy either, but not the same as skimming across the ice like a bird. Like a bird who is well on the way to being sixty-one. A phrase comes to mind: a tough old bird. Do you think I can manage to be that?

I asked Robert Henderson[67] if your story was scheduled for the issue of February 12 or whatever that weekend of Mardi Gras is and he said that they couldn't run it because the issues were still too small, but that it was scheduled for the issue of March 1 or March 8, by which time they would be big enough to take it.[68] Maybe before that time we will see you. "Jules, est-il ladedans, quelle surprise…"[69]

<div style="text-align: right">

With so much love from us all,
Bill

</div>

Eudora Welty to William Maxwell, February 12, 1969

Dearest Bill,

It was so fine to get your call yesterday. I'm afraid I must have sounded like someone speaking from a stalled train in the Hudson Tunnel, but I was just in a stalled train in my novel, and you blew the whistle on me, thank Heaven. I was so glad to think you'd found a spot where I could be useful in the Institute—this could have been one of your first acts as president?—and at the same time give me trips to New York to accomplish it.[70] The happiest kind of arrangement, and so like you to know who would be the happy one. So thank you again, and I'll be just as free to do it as anything when this long long long ms. gets out of the house—I think it's long enough to reach from Jackson to New York already, and I could just walk up on its back. I'll tell you when I'm coming so we can do any needed thing on the proof at the proper moment. I know I missed something I'd so much have cherished doing when I had to say I couldn't write the O'Connor review. You know I would have loved to. Also I had to say no to the Southern Review when offered the new Mary Lavin book. I don't mind saying no to most things but these two I still think of with regret. When you do so much that it's unimaginable, the office, the Institute, all the world of your own life and your own work, and two houses and books and roses and flying to Ireland, and the opera and ICE-SKATING, and writing letters to the ones in your thoughts and affections—how did I begin this sentence—anyway I am amazed. Though not <u>surprised</u>, that you do it all, of course. How vast is this work at the Institute going to be? Will you have smooth-running and steadily available help—am I describing Miss Geffins?[71] It had been my wish that I could be

there for the occasion when you were made president, and I would have managed it just right, I think, finished my work and brought it up just at the moment, but for the flu setback, and then the date of it got away from me. They don't deserve you. (That would have been the message of this fairy, if asked for it.) I'm torn between the pleasure of speculating on the differences it could make in the Institute and the horror of the demands the Institute could make on you—none of which I know anything about. Well, now when wrong people get elected to membership you can have all their heads cut off, and when the right people are turned away you can call them back and restore their kingdoms. I wish I did know a little about the workings and elections and good ways to help there, and now maybe if I get to take my closer look, I can learn.

This most beautiful treasure from the Crock of Gold—the fringe is so light you can't even feel it in your hand. The fine, fine texture and the softness of the thread and the weave and the color—which all seem to be one softness—it is the loveliest thing to wear I ever put on, and I would almost rather look at it, spread out so I can see it all. It brings back of course the happy journey you and Emmy made and also it brings back my own, and it's so lovely to have so much in one. I'm writing Emmy today too—I expect she had kind thoughts about Smith for it, too—where I had to tell them I couldn't come, after all—but this will go with me anywhere and all the years, it's even likely to take me back to Ireland, or I'll take it, back to where it came from.[72]

Your Christmas in the country sounded one of the happiest—the moonlight skating, and the young people—and Emmy says you did some writing, into which some of that magic must have entered on its own.—And now this new snowstorm. Beautiful it may have been, with Brookie holding on so you wouldn't blow away, but when you are reading the paper about it, you shudder and feel anxious. I'm glad Emmy's doing all that vitamin-stuffing—all keep well and fine, stout and snug. (In Illinois do they say "stout" to mean "in good health"? And sometimes "fat and fine.")

We have had an early spring, flowering trees are out, daffodils and such, along with the camellias—all sorts of odd birds that don't ordinarily come here, so I'm told—I saw some evening grosbeaks, banana yellow and black and white, temperacious little creatures fighting one another around some-

one's feeding stand, beautiful and supposed never to winter south of Virginia, so I read. This ought to have made it apparent to me you were having the next thing to a blizzard on 86th St. I longed to send some camellias there—but I've seen how they look when they get to the end of their journey—ill-used. The way the Irish look when they have crossed from Dublin to Holyhead.

Best love to all, and thanks for so very many good things at once, and Happy St. Valentine's Day, & Lincoln's Birthday today—from Eudora

Eudora Welty to Emily Maxwell, February 12, 1969

Dearest Emmy,

The oak tree my window looks out into is alive with little kinglets—and some other tiny bird that flutters down through the tree like a spinning leaf and then spins up again. We'll have more cold—last year it snowed here on March 21, First Day of Spring—on top of all the flaming azaleas—but all looks like early spring, and I was horrified to hear of your snow storm. It must have been wildly beautiful while it was happening, but afterwards! Bill said you were filling the family with vitamins and all of you were well and fine—and I'm so glad. Your Christmas sounded one of the happiest— the moonlight skating and the cozy fire, and the young and dear around you. I was thinking of you, and the delight of my day was the opening of presents—I was in with flu but in full possession of my pleasure faculties— and when I opened the folds of this lovely thing as light as air and the colors of wind on grass or leaves on the water or little wild birds' eggs in the nest, I knew <u>where</u> it came from as well as <u>whom</u>. It is just beautiful. I love to hold it and spread it out as well as I love to wear it. It makes me remember yours and Bill's letters from Ireland and your love of the place, and puts my own memories with these. It is so warm, too—and I know you were surely thinking of Smith [College], where I had expected to be right now. (It's the first time I ever had to go back on an appointment, though I had always told them it depended on how well I could catch up on work and health, and it seemed I got more exhausted* instead of less, and I felt I could not give the job what was right. You can imagine how troubled, sorry, and ashamed

I was—and I'm so fond of people there. They were understanding about it but I still feel badly.)

It must have been lovely seeing Bill made President of the Institute. Do you think he will be happy with it? There's bound to be some stuffiness around him—and I do think one of the most demanding things in the world is stuffiness. But overriding that, I think it's a great chance for the Institute to have light and air and imagination and wit and poetry and youth let in through new windows—even doors. I hope to come up for more things now—and it will be fine for us out-of-towners to have new things to come for. I await Bill's first letter to the members as president. Allen Tate [the outgoing president] told us all to wear our rosette when mounting speakers' platforms—there is no use in Bill telling me that, I am going to wear my Irish stole, and not open my mouth.

The girls sound as if so much is happening for them, and with their wonderful, almost magical, responsiveness and their depth of feeling, understanding, giving back—you must foresee so much for them. All is not happy, all does not have to be happy, but how one wishes. Their sturdiness is one of the most beautiful things about them—it goes with great delicacy of feeling, above all, somehow—and it seems so rare, equally rare.

There's something in my house you would love—and tell Bill, he would love it too, and I came by it out of my New Yorker gains of course—a Bonnard lithograph, that was shown here in a visit of the London Grafica people, called La Coupe et le Compotier—of 1925—signed, in black, though he also made some in sanguine. A small, horizontal thing—it calls up all his paintings—an interior of course, two figures—one standing & serving the other, seated at a table—the gesture of the arm from the woman, most easy and beautiful, the man with head lowered over his dish—an indication of window curtain behind him, by daylight—so simple, so giving, and though I never meant to buy anything when I went to see their things, when I saw this I just brought it straight home. Now it's on the wall in my room—selfish, nobody else sees it—but it's where I work and live for the time being altogether. You may have seen it. I do love it.[73] I hope to see you about March? Thank you again for the beautiful Irish wool—my joy—With love to all,

Eudora

*I am on the up & up now for sure.

Eudora Welty to Emily and William Maxwell, March 10, 1969

Dearest Emmy and Bill, in the mail just now came a letter and book from my Welsh friend Alun Jones, the same Alun Jones that you let come out to Gracie Square and what a fine time we had and something told me that deep down on this desk of mine, under the letters, under the story, under the dust and the paperclips, there must still be a brown envelope addressed to you while I was in with flu and never had it left my house, about Dafydd ap Gwilym.[74] I wrote you after that and possibly before too—I can't even remember—I see it's dated Sunday. I don't know what's the matter with me—yes I do—anyway, here comes a little note very tardy. And unfinished too—

It was lovely talking over the phone so long, Bill, even if it was about hyphens. How can I ever let you know how much help came from you on the story, in all the other ways that exist <u>aside</u> from hyphens.

I hope all goes well, health, exams, and life. I'm working hard and hope works there go well, all departments.

Much love to all, and Happy Saint David's Day—Alun's book, Tea in the Heather by Kate Roberts, was a present for it, but I don't know when it is. (He mailed it in November!) Maybe it's today.

Love again from Eudora

William Maxwell to Eudora Welty, May 2, 1969

Dear Eudora:

Your kind gentle friend Don (?) Robinson turned up yesterday morning, on his way to Pisa, and said we could expect you in a couple of weeks.[75] Can we wait that long is the question. The disorder of my life went into a sort of geometric progression when I was called for jury duty, but I got off after six days, with no worse effects than that I found suddenly I didn't have the will to edit anybody. Fortunately I haven't had to. Much. And I haven't been able to finish that little book because I cannot bring myself to put the screws on various relatives who perhaps know the answer to questions it would be nice if I knew the answer to. My letters go unanswered, and I look at the phone and then go do something else. We went to Deerfield to see a daugh-

ter of a cousin of mine, who sent me home with my grandmother's scrap-
book, and promised to send a mass of zeroxed material, which so far has
not turned up. The scrapbook I was a witness to the making of. It is full of
obituary notices and thank you notes. As a girl my grandmother was taken
to Springfield to see the funeral procession of A. Lincoln, and it seems to
have given her a taste for assassinations. The first half of the book is filled
with clippings about Lincoln, Garfield, and McKinley, and even Mrs.
McKinley, who tried to rush into the grave after her husband, but lasted
on for almost a year. Also some lovely family pictures, and here and there
something I cut out and colored at the age of four. I will show it to you
when you come.[76]

<div style="text-align: right">

With love in huge quantities,
as always, from all of us,
Bill

</div>

Eudora Welty to William and Emily Maxwell, June 9, 1969,
Incomplete letter

Dearest Bill and Emmy,

 It was such happiness to see you—under all auspices & stars—the Cere-
monial, with the gift of the chair, that I was so unprepared for and did think
so lovingly of, and the evening that came after with the company you had
and the champagne and the supper—and the last evening, pure happiness
& pleasure and I guess quite necessary, for I don't know what I'd have done
without it—Awful to say that—I could have done without it, but afterwards
that's the way I felt. It was lovely to see Kate and Brookie around the table
again—and so nice that by now they don't have to leave so early & take
themselves off to bed. I want them there.

 It was the Ceremonial that I would have chosen to come to—for it be-
ing yours, and for it being Richard Hughes's time to speak—All seemed to
be going off exceptionally calmly & well, the exception to the exception be-
ing poor T. Williams, and it was for Lillian Hellman standing there that all
felt—though (I've just been reading her book) rescue was never anything
she much wanted. He seemed simply unreal.[77]

William Maxwell to Eudora Welty, July 2, 1969

Dearest Eudora:

I called Diarmuid about the zerox, and he said he would send it to me when he could spare it, and it hasn't come, so I presume he is still doing business with it. Maybe I will get to take it to Oregon with me, which would be the nicest of all. To read it unhurried by anything.[78] But if he is still doing business with publishers, you are still up in the air, which I hate to think is true. If it is, maybe you ought to descend through the air and write me a story as you come down.

Brookie is in camp at Kingston, on the other side of the Hudson, and I miss her terribly. It is just like looking for your glasses and not being able to find them. I have lost my glasses too—the extra pair—by way of enforcing the metaphor. One of Kate's friends went to the camp last year and the year before, and adored it, but neither Emmy nor I was very happy with what we saw when we delivered Brookie to her cabin. As for Brookie, her heart was turned to stone, not by what she saw but by the other girls, so happy and confident and returning to everything, where she was new. She never did say goodby, she just turned her back so that her mother would know she was supposed to go. And she was having such a good time at home. Emmy says, at the way I carry on, "What will you do when she marries?" I intend to be like Mr. Barrett and do what I can to prevent it. Then she will require a poet to carry her off and live happy ever after, and I will go and stay with them, which I don't suppose Mr. Barrett ever did.[79]

We read "A Sweet Devouring" aloud, with such pleasure. We met and had a long visit with the daughter of the author of Five Little Peppers[,] when we went to Concord a few years back. I am glad I was spared the Tales of Maria Edgeworth, though in general didacticism never bothered me at that age the way it does now. Now I simply can't abide it. And such a good joke about V.V.'s Eyes following you wherever you went.[80] At one point toward the end of his life my father decided the time had come for him to buy a work of art, and he and my stepmother went to a gallery in Chicago and all sorts of paintings were shown them, but what my father liked was the ones where the eyes followed you around the room and he found that they were so much more expensive than the other kind that he gave up and

came away without buying anything. Who would believe, very shortly, that parents could ever be the way our parents were? I was so happy when you found Mark Twain. I am reading Pudd'nhead Wilson right this minute. I like the quotations from the Notebook at the beginnings of the chapters better than I do the story, and they're very didactic, but they are also Mark Twain.

Kate is reading my accumulated correspondence. I mean the letters to me. She said a couple of weeks ago, "Daddy have you got any files of discreet letters I could read," and I said, "No but you can read the indiscreet ones." So she is. And maybe I will, as a result, not be the mystery to her that my parents are to me, but more than likely it won't change anything. It takes a great deal to change things. In a better way, I mean. To change things for the worse, all you need is somebody like Nixon, and there are plenty like him. I can hardly bear to read the Times and I can't bear not to read it, lest I miss some awful piece of new evidence against him. Nobody has been tolerant or broadminded in our family for five generations, if ever.

The young man who did Brookie's head in clay is now doing Emmy's, and she asked him yesterday if he'd mind if she had a permanent, so it wouldn't be such a problem when she went to Oregon. Needless to say, he did mind.

And I have finished part 3 (sixth or seventh version) and am starting on part 4 tomorrow morning bright and early. It is the watershed—the place where I can remember, though the dead seem more and more to have taken immense numbers of secrets with them. Not important ones, perhaps, but things they cared enough about to conceal from somebody.[81]

The roses are still blooming! Love from us all,

B

Eudora Welty to William Maxwell, July 16, 1969

Dearest Bill,

So good to get your letter, and I'll answer it soon, but this is just to tell you that with you at the watershed, starting on your part 4, it is the wrong time for my ms. to be showing up there and we both know it, so remember and don't fire until you are ready, Gridley.[82] And as you see (Diarmuid's

letter just now told me he'd sent you the xerox) if you tried taking that to Oregon, you'd have to leave your suitcase at home, or else take only xeroxes of your clothes. All this being said, I'm terribly excited that at some good free future time you will read this, and will tell me what you think. Emmy too, if the time and the inclination come together at such a busy summer. (I long to see the head the young man is doing. Brookie's looked so much like Emmy, to me, that I thought maybe the one thing sculpture can't tell you is age.)

Then when you finish yours and can, will you let me read—but I won't ask you anything about it now, in case that's not good luck. I'm happy for you though.

Yes, Diarmuid is showing the novel [*Losing Battles*] to 3 houses (Farrar Straus, Atheneum, Random (Albert Erskine)) wanting to do the best he can for me, and there was some leak so others have been after him, but we both feel that though others might offer more money I might be landed among strangers and might not like them very well either, and so it will be a decision among friends.[83] It's been hard on him and me, a bit, but I was sustained because Diarmuid liked it and it seems editors outside of Harcourt like it, and now if I can know what you think of it—at last—having seen all those beginnings and never given up on me and all the strength I took from all this, then I think I'll cease to wobble, and breathing will be back on a 24-hour basis. (but you understand that sentence) I enclose 2 pages that are missing and warn you about the title, as usual, being wrong, but mainly this is to say STOP—Don't read till something tells you it is exactly the right time. I hope Brookie is no longer of stone—is there perhaps a drawing class at camp? Love to all,

Eudora

William Maxwell, *Sisters, Oregon, to Eudora Welty, August 10, 1969*

Dearest Eudora—

Diarmuid and I are agreed—the book is a comic masterpiece. The only two works it reminds me of are "Tom Jones" and "The Tempest," and don't ask me why. I realized with the description of the baby rolling his eyes nursing that you had given to this book everything that you have in the way of

both feeling and talent. Nothing is skimped or held back for some other book. And the strangest of all is remembering the earlier version, so similar in action, and so totally different in effect. It is partly what happened to you in the intervening years that made you shift your essential position—not merely with regard to the characters but also with regard to life. "The Optimist's Daughter" is a dividing place in your work. This is clearly <u>after</u>. And speaking of which, I like "Losing Battles" as a title.[84] <u>It's what this book is about</u>! Once you realize that, there is no possibility of withholding sympathy. Anymore than there is with Charlie Chaplin. But my God how funny it is. I laughed continually—Emmy said she had never heard me laugh so much over a book. Not helpless laughter, not <u>tears</u> of laughter, but the quiet appreciative kind, as I hugged your jokes to myself. The best joke—even better than what happened to the judge's car, perhaps—is the condition of the bridges. I never could get enough of those bridges. Or indeed of anything. Only a very obtuse reader could want the book any shorter. I tried to make it last longer, and, alas, flew through it, promising myself another reading as soon as I could get my hands on a printed copy.

One of the things that moved me particularly is how rich they all are in their poverty. I believed in the poverty, all right, but the effect seemed to be that everybody shone with Everlasting Grace, which they would not have had if they hadn't been so poor. And how they got to be poor—<u>That</u> series of losing battles—is also haunting. They are on the way down, so far on the way, that they are also on the way up. But the up is not financial. I don't know how that boy is going to manage. I sometimes think I'll have to get on a train and go down there and give him a hand. Buy him a truck. Do something so it isn't such terrible odds. Which, of course, would be to spoil everything. But they are safe even from my spoiling. Their troubles are I feel sure as immortal as they are endless. They are in for a long space of being loved by people they can't know anything about, who know everything there is to know, practically, about them. One question: How did you do it?

E's parents are older and more frail, but all right in the head, thank Heaven. And this place is as yet unspoiled, though threatened like everywhere else.

We all send our love

Bill

Eudora Welty to William Maxwell, August 15, [1969]

Dearest Bill,

Your letter gave me so much joy. It unerringly went to just the questions I have wanted to ask you for such a long time and answered them—answered them yea and not nay, too, and in all generosity of understanding, so that the long sigh of relief I've been waiting to give has now been given. I don't care what critics or reviewers or any of them say, once the few I long all the way through to read what I'm trying to write have read it and told me their minds. What happened to it was time. I was writing it and writing it, all through life and other stories, with one hand while I drove the car every day to Yazoo City, before day at home. Time let them all (the different people) come into flower, insomuch as I could convey it, but I'm sure that was the reason for the strange experience that made me think I could still keep on. They still gave me pleasure—it was the only sign I could trust that they were still alive through all the work and changing. It was one of the key questions for you—you'd seen them at the beginning—had I lost them or had I found them. But more than that (the time) is the reality of that central element in the people that live in rural Mississippi—it's there to be seen by all—that character of the relish of life and its tales in the face of poverty and all it's done to them, and, heaven knows, relish of ignorance on some parts along with pride and the rest. Well, I can't put it into analytical words, but your question was a serious question (how did I do it) and the serious answer is I had it all given to me to go on, it's all there, and the feeling all the way through the writing was that it was making itself up—too fast for me. This makes me feel better about it than anything else—I feel proud of getting some of it in. And also you know I really love these people—the real ones and the story ones—even when I sometimes want to shake them and beat them on the head as a fellow Mississippian. I'm so glad you laughed. I love the bridges too, and <u>so</u> reluctantly cut a long section out that told of the ride up to the reunion the Moodys had because it went over about six lovely bridges, pure undiluted self-indulgence. If I can find them, I'll send them to you. And it's so fortifying to have you speak for that title. You know how helpless I am about titles, and the best thing that ever helped me was something you said once, just call it what the whole thing is <u>about</u>, which is plain

beautiful common sense and had never occurred to me. The "Losing Battles" was the last title I thought of, in point of time, and it <u>was</u> the answer to this question. I'd had the suspicion that I'd got it out of my own surrender to the book's being 700 pages long, and so it could have been more subjective than objective. Also it might really look self-defeating printed on a real thick book like that—I wondered if publishers might think that. But Albert [Erskine] said he thought pretty well of it, though if a better one struck through to any of us, he would still wait on it. I told him you thought it was good—he was on the phone last night. He also remarked that most good titles are ex post facto. We all say what a wonderful title Babbit is, he said, when at the time the ms. came in the publishers must have yelled, My heavens, can't he come up with a better title than <u>that</u>? I'm glad he's philosophical about things—a good sign. We are now both giving it a close reading and will compare notes in N.Y. sometime in September I guess. It has given me such a light heart to read your letter that I'll probably sail through the rest of it, making no changes but sudden or wild ones, like somebody joy-riding at 80 miles an hour on a rather tricky road. It's so funny, it's back to the time of my story again, and one by one all the August sights and sounds reappear as I work on my carbon—the locusts whirring, the yellow butterflies just today, the political season opening, and every day in the paper a correspondent's story of another big family reunion, all the who and where from, everybody gets his name in the paper. (My favorite sentence in any reunion account is deep in my memory, "Wanda Peavey held the napkins.") I miss writing that novel, it was teaching me things for such a long time, or such was my sustaining illusion.

Long letter about me and my work, which was really trying to tell you how happy your letter made me, and just before your letter came, here came the New Yorker with your story—what a burst of joy, I hadn't even known to be looking for it.[85] Everybody's own loves and own hazards and own memories—past, now, and future—ride together to a destination that ought to have been something better, had every right to be better because once upon a time it <u>was</u>, and the story at its heart and in the telling, the narrative, are so nearly one that it's perfectly beautiful. I love a story where nothing exists but as its own ray of light, direct or oblique, on the truth in the center—where every move, sight, saying, sound bears not only its relation to the theme but

a second and wonderful relationship to its fellow sights and sounds. Not only is the venerable omelette whisk listened for and not heard, but rock and roll on the transistor calls for ear plugs—the literal (but wonderful) example that springs to mind at the moment. And all these meet in the metaphor about the tide rushing in, don't they call it the *immensi tremor oceani* in the books? Memories of Eden while being hustled through Hades—but the earthly paradise, though eighteen years ago perceived by the two who were uncritical and all open to delight, <u>was</u> a paradise, the real thing. Now the Abbey's made into a prop, a dead monument, and the living monument is the old lady stranded in traffic, terror-stricken in the middle of Blvd. Saint-Germaine—it's so beautifully done. And the quietest thing in it bringing the most clamorous feeling, the vanished garden—the old walled garden of enchantment gone and not to be found anywhere. I love the "Trip sat up" sentence, and I can see her! I loved the <u>severe</u> light of the seacoast. And the voice of civilized man, when last heard from, was speaking your last sentence. A haunting deep true story. All so right that John Reynolds traveled with premonitions. A premonition, even if it was the wrong one, was the right thing to have. Only in the end it wasn't the wrong one, of course—something that's been allowed to happen that shouldn't have happened does most of its harm to the imagination—no wonder it's keyed to somebody getting run over. I hope you're still at Sisters, Oregon—delicious name—where things are still relatively unspoiled, and can stay a while. I'm glad you find all well.

I cherish your letter—thank you for calling me after page 150 too, and at a time when I was so nervous about it. And I'm so glad that now the novel has turned out all right at last.

Good luck on your new. Let me know when you can. My love to all of you.

<div align="right">Eudora</div>

Emily Maxwell, Sisters, Oregon, to Eudora Welty, August 16, 1969,
*Postcard with photograph titled "Source of the Metalius River,
Central Oregon"*

Dearest Eudora—As children, we got off our horses here & stretched out

on our bellies & drank the icy water where it comes up out of the ground. It's as delicious as the clear air & the deep blue of the sky. At night you can see very powdery stars in the Milky Way—Much love Emmy

Eudora Welty to Emily and William Maxwell, [Fall 1969], Incomplete letter

You knew that Elizabeth [Bowen] was to be at Princeton this semester? I expect you may have seen her—is she well? I want to write her soon because if I'm to be up that way in November it would be easy to run over & see her, if she could get free—I read Ivy Compton-Burnett's <u>Mother and Son</u> again on the train coming down, and when I read her I can't relish a line without thinking how much Elizabeth would relish it too—

This is being written downstairs—not yet in my room where I usually write letters, because workmen are in the house—You know my house, I told you, is built on a salt-dome (all the "best part of town" of course <u>is</u>) and when I got home I found not only the old cracks I was used to but a hole in one interior wall as big as a human head—(of triangular shape.) Rubble all over the floor. The time had come, fortunately I could get people, and now they're at it.

Getting ready for them I went through shelves, & drawers and closets, and in my mother's secretary a drawer I hadn't opened before had all sorts of letters & things, one of which fluttered out to say, from me, that you were going to have Kate—I'd gone to take you the Gruss an Aachen, & you gave me the news. I got deep in these things and that's why this letter's late. I hope all goes well with the work, Bill, you are keeping it, the part you were wondering about?

My love to all of you and my thanks for the happy meeting. Take care— Eudora

Eudora Welty to Emily and William Maxwell, December 9, 1969

Dearest Emmy and Bill,

Seeing you was so fine, both at the big grand occasion and at the lovely Coffee House Club where we had our chance to talk, and I could see your faces by themselves. Thank you for making both times possible, and for the pleasure it gave me to read to the Dinner Meeting—seeing so many old

friends and old acquaintances, and having the feeling of reading to many people of understanding and sympathy was its own reward and it was the first chance I'd ever had, I believe, to do something for the Institute, of my own.

I hope things go well with the household and I wonder if you've had luck with Putney [School] in the right directions. Has it snowed deeply yet in the country? The quiet of the snow must be so welcome too. I never found New York so loud and assertive and deaf, each to the others. We've had some cold, but many leaves still on the trees are holding their color— today's bright and getting warm again.

I need to warn you about a camellia—I sent you one, that is, Mr. Brent, the nurseryman, sent it—he crated it up and then found that Railway Express wouldn't guarantee getting it to New York under 12–15 days—by which time it would be asking for air, water, and somebody to see its flowers which might have opened in Saint Louis. So he sent it by Greyhound Bus, where it will be just like a passenger, put down in the station and asking to be collected—isn't that a terrible way to send you something? Is there any good way you can transport it (it's small, but is in a crate) from the Greyhound Station in NYC to 86th Street? Or have it done for you? I think you might even have to check the station to find if it has come, which it really should have done by the time you get this letter. I hope it doesn't give you more trouble than flowers, and I hope it will behave right, when it gets home to your apartment. It likes coolness and not being disturbed—just a little watering—perhaps from the bottom. (I'm not too familiar with growing them in the house.)

My niece Elizabeth is getting married—I hope it will be all right. She's 26, has known plenty of boys and has her own apartment (with some other girls) and a job, so I think she knows what she is doing, I trust her judgment—but it's that anxious feeling, of course, that I have. Fred [Thompson, her fiancé] has a small printing business here—prints county newspapers from all over, etc and I think that's a good sort of thing to do. The other thing he does is race sports cars, which scares me to death, but maybe he is going to give that up—I wonder if you can? Anyway, Elizabeth is terribly happy.

My love to Brookie and Kate, and the best of luck to them with their schools. All take care. I think of you a lot and send you love.

Eudora

William Maxwell to Eudora Welty,
December 15, 1969

This was written last Thursday and sat in my out basket over the weekend. The camellia is fine. So are we.

Dearest Eudora:

It's here! It's home being loved. The Greyhound office called Emmy and I went there and got it and insinuated into a taxi when the driver wasn't looking, and was back at the office before you could say Jack Robinson. Nothing to it, except the uncrating, which was most intricate. I was afraid I'd get too excited and break off a bud. Not knowing any better, I watered it from the top, but hereafter from the bottom is what it will be. It didn't any more look as if it had journeyed all the way from Mississippi than I do. If you'd sent it express it would have been dead as a doornail. Do you think gradually you could send us enough pieces of Mississippi and we could send you enough pieces of Yorktown Heights to alter the balance of nature? You have altered my feelings about Christmas, in any case. I was totally lacking in feeling until now. Something growing in the house that wasn't before. Only you could have an idea like that.

Love from all of us, and I don't think I will seal this now because there is some[thing] I want to tell you but I must discuss it with Emmy first. I just remembered the telephone. We decided that it would be better, if it is all the same to you, if you wrote for Brookie to Putney instead of for Kate. The person to write to is Raymond S. Goodlatte, Director of Admissions, The Putney School, Putney, Vermont, and there is no hurry. Anytime before the end of the year will do. Not that that isn't breathing hard upon us, but you know what I mean. Now I really will say

Love,

B.

Eudora Welty to Emily and William Maxwell,
January 5, 1970

Dearest Emmy and Bill—How is everybody? Bill, are you well of the chest cold? Is Kate back home? Is Brookie going to Putney? I've been only wor-

rying about the chest cold—I've been worrying about that damp ground in Central Park. All got back the way it should be again, I hope, and the blizzards subsided with all still snug & safe & doing well—so that it was a Happy New Year for you coming in the other night—I was thinking of you—And in good company here, because Elizabeth Bowen came down for the week with me, and I had my old New Year's Eve crowd in and we had a fine time. It was grand to have her back in my house again—can you think of anything luckier than the chance to have her?

I know you'd be glad she had some of your cheese—That heavenly <u>real cheese</u>—that Dragon cheese! I savored every bite I ate and have much more to savor still. It is the first I ever did taste, and I could so well imagine the fresh morning-sweet cow meadows where it all started—the clear springs in the grass, and the sweet water & tender grass & the flowers they ate—the cows. It is so good in our days to have something real & sound & pure left in the world, and I'm delighted I got it for Christmas! Thank you for then and now and yet a little while to come. (I just went for a cracker.)

And the double Christmas cards. Both so beautiful—Opening them both together was like seeing two fire-works both going off in the sky, those showery, flowery ones—the first one is miraculous, and the black-&-white one opens out so delicately too—Chinese fire-works. I love having them both—turning from one to the other—

Putney School <u>answered</u> my letter about Brookie—I never had anything like that happen. What nice people they must be & quite clearly B. is a favorite. I hope to hear all the family news when (if? I think <u>when</u>) I come up to the Grants Committee in a few weeks. It's right at the time of Elizabeth's—my niece's wedding, but that'll be over—it will be first.

Take care—Please keep well, also, & safe from the horrors.[86] I think of you & send my best love, along with my thanks, & many, many wishes—

Eudora

William Maxwell to Eudora Welty, April 5, 1970

Dearest Eudora:

Emmy thinks she forgot to tell you that Brookie got into Putney, I think

half because of your letter and half because of her dear self. She is terribly proud and happy about it.

We got home last night at midnight Sicily time and went to bed at ten o'clock New York time and tossed around all night trying to decide whether we ought to be up or asleep. Emmy got up to get a hotwater bottle at four o'clock in the morning (New York time) and went out to the living room and found both children playing the record player. While she was gone I got up and weighed myself. As a result of eating masses of pasta and bread—that is to say, marvelous Italian and Sicilian bread, I hadn't gained an ounce. Brookie thinks it is the magical aqua minerale. She hadn't either.

It was an utterly delightful trip. Venice is like Chartres, you can't re-member how romantically beautiful it is until you return and then all you can do is cry "It's too <u>much</u>!" As indeed it is. Add the Ravenna mosaics, and the fact that the ten days we were in Sicily we were only three times not with a balcony overlooking the sea, with gardens in full flower—no, that is not at all what they were like, they were like the drop curtain of the Majestic The-ater in Bloomington, Illinois fifty years ago—below us. Mid June the whole time. We we[nt] swimming twice at Taorimina. Or Toaramina, I never can remember which. Sicilians are an acquired taste, but we managed to ac-quire it. As we were leaving the plane in the Rome airport, to come home, Emmy exclaimed because she saw a young Sicilian woman struggling with five jammed string bags and a suitcase, her handluggage on the plane. God knows how much more was in the hold. Perhaps nothing. Anyway, without thinking twice, I turned back and forgetting both <u>Permesso</u> and <u>Posso</u>, said, as I reached out my hand, "Can I help you carry something?" and saw her eyes change shape and color as the full monstrousness of what I was sug-gesting sank in. In pure fright she shook her head and looked away. I think Sicily is not a country where it is safe to accept help from a stranger, not if you value what is in your string bags. But they <u>are</u> witty. And up to the age of four, perfectly beautiful. Then never again.

We have spent the morning, unpacking and straightening the house. To ease my mind I opened your book and read the first page, and felt as if I'd had a drink of spring water.

Devotedly,
Bill

Emily Maxwell to Eudora Welty, April 10, 1970

Dearest Eudora,

It does my heart good that you know when a letter of ours has gone astray. I did write, three & more weeks ago to say that your book [*Losing Battles*] had arrived, a very exciting event in our lives! I have only just begun it, because we went to Sicily with the children for the Easter vacation, and in Venice joined Harriet O'Donovan Sheehy & Father Sheehy & Hallie Og.[87] Together we took a sort of mosaic tour—driving first to Ravenna to see maybe the most beautiful mosaics in the world there—especially those in S. Appolinare nuova & S. Appolinare in Classe. Do you know them? The mosaics in Sicily were something of an anti-climax after that. Accomplished without the passion of the earlier mosaics, which were so full of joy & celebration they reminded me of St. Francis' unextinguishable happiness. The wild flowers in Sicily were beyond belief. Wild heliotrope, masses of yellow & blue flowers almost but never quite like anything that grows here—especially beautiful growing on the mountain slopes approaching the perfect little Greek Theatre, with a panoramic view on 3 sides, at Segesta. I longed to hear poetry spoken there. There was an old man or woman in a wheel chair at the top (all I could see was an ivory profile)—peacefully looking out over most of Sicily—surrounded by handsome happy young people who ran back & forth to the Volkswagen they'd all arrived in to bring their picnic up the steep hill. It looked like a story—by Thomas Mann?

Also I <u>think</u> I told you that Brookie got in to Putney [...]

We are off to the country—that's why this is written in such haste & I'm so happy to have brave and good Granny Vaughn under my arm![88]

Much much love from all—Emmy.

William Maxwell to Eudora Welty, May 12, 1970

Dear Eudora:

No, I didn't get a note from you asking what Barbara Nicholls' married name is (she isn't married; I think too many people were hanging around

her and she got tired of the whole idea. Why not?), but if you got Emmy's letter saying we were about to take off for Sicily (with the pictures of the gardenia?), then sooner or later I will get your note.

It's Field Day at school, and Brookie went off with eye-shadow on to play, I suppose, hockey and all that, and Kate got excused so she could go to her nursery in Harlem.[89] Emmy and I are having lunch with Mr. and Mrs. Victor Pritchett, and Edith Oliver.

And then we are having company—Kate's godfather and a young Frenchman, whose father figures in the Chateau. He is the man who disappeared down the Metro and we were so sad because we realized we were never going to see him again. Only we did, in Paris, and didn't realize that it was him because he had changed so physically, and then again in New York, in our apartment, by which time he had changed back. You know how people do. One by one, the members of that family discover the book, and get in touch with me, but don't tell anybody else in the family, which I think is terribly nice of them. And little by little the burden on my conscience is lightened as they confess that I did, in fact, get most things right. But it was so long ago that they are charmed to read about themselves as they were then.

I look forward to hooking necks with you at the Ceremonial. Would you like to have dinner afterward at the Coffee House with Cleve and Francine Gray[90] and Robert and Sally Fitzgerald and Emmy and me? Love, Bill

Emily Maxwell to Eudora Welty, May 15, 1970

Dearest Eudora,

I'm writing on my knee, under the home dryer. Bill & I are taking the plane to Boston, I think, to celebrate our 25th wedding anniversary—I'm not sure where we're going because it's a surprise. We're coming back on Monday, & on Tuesday I'm going to Oregon to spend a week with my mother and father. The day after I get back is the Institute lunch & ceremony, and I wish you were coming!

I've just finished <u>Losing Battles</u>. All I can say is, like the Banner School, it's beyond compare![91] It's as if you'd put your heart down on paper. I felt

as if I was sitting up to a peat fire & listening to the voice of a master story-teller. I could hear your voice all the way through, and at the same time all the characters' voices were their own. It has the sweep of a 19th C novel—Middlemarch comes to mind. In its commitment to life it stands out today like a bird in the Arctic sky. It seemed to me as if you were saying, well, if that's what you all want to do with life, if that's what you think it is, fine, but here's what I think it is—and then you spread it out like a bright cloth—like an Irish fairy shawl, with infinite care for the beauty and delicacy & color & gaiety of it.

Everything you tell of old age and death is so moving. The Delectable Mountain Quilt & the Song, Gathering Home, and Miss Beulah's infinite tenderness for her mother—& the fierceness of Granny & Miss J.M.—and the slow unfolding of Miss Julia Mortimer's character is one of the miracles of the book. Another is telling the whole thing through dialogue, and another is the vividness of the natural world around them, smells, sights & sounds. Do freshly-sharpened pencils always smell of jonquils? I can't wait to sniff them!

I'm sending you my very last Christmas camellia picture. Two others got lost with that letter that went astray.

Much much love
Emmy—Friday—

Eudora Welty to Emily and William Maxwell, June 10, 1970

Dearest Emmy and Bill,

What would I have done if you hadn't first made that time out of thin air and that dinner & the talk & the music out of your heads, like a story, (because everything <u>had</u> been packed up, I could see it) and I hadn't had that evening at your house? It was so lovely. It came & afterwards vanished like the soufflé we had, & was just as real, though, and so pleasurable & getting better every minute, like all good visits snatched from the jaws of time—I seem to be writing about 2 separate sets of jaws here. But I hope everything got moved in peace & smoothness then, in the middle of the night, and perhaps Daisy [the dog] drove. (If she can mail a letter!) I think of all of you on Baptist Church Road now, Brookie back from the wedding, and lovely let-

tuces coming up in the garden, mint & chives & cherry tomatoes, and the roses putting forth all over the place, and I can think how the brook must sound—

I got home still lucky—The Southerner got to Meridian 10 minutes early instead of 10 minutes late, so it was not necessary for me to highjack it & make it take me to Jackson, I made the bus. The house was still standing, & I could smell the gardenias blooming (although there weren't all that many) from the corner—The ride down was nice too—you could see the calves had grown some, in the pastures—The milk-&-wine-lilies were in bloom—and, where they've left any, the beautiful swamp mallows—

Thank you for showing me Robert Fitzgerald's poem—Everything was so restoring & lovely—My love to all of you, Eudora

P.S. I got my mail just now—the post office inspector's complaint, which is just wonderful. I was especially amused because a lot of those Oxford names are still going strong up there. What about Jimmy Jones, who was allowed to come back in the office & play cards, then cutting up over having to go to Bill's father to get a little mail? I was glad to know that with Faulkner you could always stand a sporting chance of finding your mail by going through the trash can in the post office. I Xeroxed this right away for my sister-in-law, who puts up the mail at Millsaps College—[92]

Many Thanks, & bless Wm Faulkner—all that mail was sacrificed in a noble cause, and I don't mean the Zip code. Love, E

Eudora Welty to William Maxwell, August 3, [1970]

Dear Bill,

You probably know this poem already, but I've just found it:

To E. M. Forster

Here, though the bombs are real and dangerous,
And Italy and King's are far away,
And we're afraid that you will speak to us,
You promise still the inner life shall pay.

As we run down the slope of Hate with gladness
You trip us up like an unnoticed stone,

And just as we are closeted with Madness
You interrupt us like the telephone.

For we are Lucy, Turton, Philip, we
Wish international evil, are excited
To join the jolly ranks of the benighted

Where Reason is denied and Love ignored:
But, as we swear our lie, Miss Avery
Comes out into the garden with the sword.
 —W. H. Auden

It came in the mail from a stranger—some boy in Wilkes-Barre. (He'd been excited to read somewhere that I had once met Mr. F. and so wrote me.) How are you? I keep thanking goodness you can go home at night to the Baptist Church Road, out from under that monstrous cloud black as a tar barrel that I see every evening on the TV weather map. I'm glad for both family and garden to be doing their breathing in a better place. I'm so happy to think of our both getting a new Gruss an Aachen—what a feat, and how wonderful that you found them.

What I'm hoping is the writing came to its right triumphant conclusion, and you are basking. I bask with you, from here to think of it.

I've been reading all those obscene books for the Grants Comm. Golly moses. I see them, the authors I mean, as certain-sure microphone seizers, for one thing. And they'll say it all to you.[93]

Didn't Howard write a beautiful review of my novel?[94] I was overwhelmed to see it. I was terribly glad he felt as he did about the book. And also so pleased it got reviewed in The New Yorker, which I don't think of as now being interested any more in just fiction in their reviews—and I wouldn't have felt hurt (like Elizabeth [Bowen]) if it had been skipped, since I realize this, but it is nice to be given that fine and generous attention in the magazine I owe so much to. I thank it again.

I'm going up to New Hampshire to get a medal—from the MacDowell Colony—at the end of the month, and after that I'm going on up into Maine for a few days with the Russells—and all without setting foot in the air. A train goes from Meridian, Miss. all the way to Boston without the passenger changing anything but cars, and then I go by car, by bus, and by ren-

dezvous with Diarmuid up into wherever it is. Nobody has made any suggestion or prediction as to how I shall get back, but I'm going to drop a little trail of pieces of paper and grains of corn and watermelon seeds from 1119 Pinehurst.

Best love to you all and wishes and luck, and I hope everything is going just as it should be. I think of you as reading the new volume of Leonard Woolf in the summer, there ought to have been another one—not that <u>he</u> didn't finish, but what are <u>you</u> reading?[95] I took down Howard's End, after that poem, and thought I'd begin it again right away, but before I opened it I thought I'd send you a word on a hot morning.

Love,
Eudora

William Maxwell to Eudora Welty, August 17, 1970

Dear Eudora:

It is supposed to be ninety-five and that's what it feels like. We are sitting here waiting for company to arrive. Harriet and Uncle Maurice and Hallie-Og O'Donovan. From Annapolis. They were supposed to come yesterday, and if they had we wouldn't have been ready for them.

I am not allowed into the kitchen (birthday cake?) and so can't make myself a glass of iced tea. It is thundering in the Dansereau's back yard, but nothing happens. In the way of rain, I mean. Kate is practicing. Mozart? Beethoven? Somebody's sonata, in any case. <u>Brookie has picked up her room</u>. And I have, sort of, finished my book [*Ancestors*]. That is I have shown it to Knopf, and got it back again, and have until the 22nd of September to fix this and that and whatever seems to need fixing. I was hoping to be allowed to go on working on it forever. The thing I was afraid of ("too much about the Campbellites") didn't happen. Though I know perfectly well there is too much about the Campbellites. But they interested me. I had such a narrow escape from being one.

What am I reading? "Murder on the Orient Express" and "George Meredith and English Comedy" by V. S. Pritchett. Both heavenly. I did know that poem of Forster's, and there is a poem I want to send you, but first I have to get Auden's Commonplace Book for Emmy's birthday, because it's

in there, a poem of Edward Thomas that isn't in his Collected Poems, so far as I know. Between the washing machine and the fan and the dishwasher and Chopin's waltz rhythms sprung for purposes of practicing I feel as if I am in the middle of the Cabinet of Dr. Caligari,[96] and I keep thinking it would be nice to have a glass of ice tea. Can you see the outstretched arm, as he came around one of the cubist corners, with the tea all cold and ready to drink?

I thought Howard's review was very beautiful indeed, and so is what happened with that book. And you don't mention coming home by way of New York. If you do, we will be here, and longing to see you, and don't let anybody drop your gold medal this time, and give my love to Diarmuid and Rosie and above all enjoy yourself.[97]

Devotedly,

B.

Eudora Welty to William Maxwell, December 1, 1970

Dearest Bill,

Gruss an Aachen came and was greeted back, a beautiful little plant, three strong arms, healthy roots, and it went right into the ground, where I hope it will be contented to live and bloom. How wonderful to have it—it's not often we lose something and it is restored—especially, and in every particular, Gruss an Aachen. It is a lovely present, and when it blooms I'll be thanking you all those times over. I hope your own is safe and tucked away now till spring.

It's warm still here, leaves falling fast now but still in their last fading colors. The camellias are blooming and those to come look very full and healthy—but camellias are more temperamental than opera stars, you never know.

The mail isn't coming and the train isn't running—that is yesterday we had NO delivery on Pinehurst Street, a Monday—and the train to NY is now only Monday, Wednesday, and Friday—I thought it would then come back on Tues., Thurs. and Sat., but it comes back on Mon, Wed. and Sat. (how?)—unless the strike comes, when I guess I'll be at the Algonquin the rest of my life, waiting on the Southerner. Anyway, I'll be in town for the

meetings at the Institute, from Tuesday 8th till Wed., 16th, with the week-end in Westport working on my photo book with Albert Erskine.[98] It's not like a real visit in NY, short and busy and everybody there in a whirl of course, Christmas so soon. I have to see you, though, and I'm coming to the Friday do too, so as to be present for Auden, and I devoutly hope to see you and Emmy first thing in the door. Love to all, Eudora

6

"So Much Honor Coming Down on My Head"

FROM 1971 TO 1980, both Eudora and Bill experienced major triumphs in their literary careers. Eudora at long last was able to publish a collection of her Depression-era photographs, *One Time, One Place* (1971). She revised and expanded *The Optimist's Daughter* for book publication (1972) and won the Pulitzer Prize for it. Six years later, a selection of her essays, book reviews, and occasional pieces appeared under the title *The Eye of the Story*. In 1971, Bill's book *Ancestors* — part family history, part memoir, part regional history — was published. In 1977, he published *Over by the River and Other Stories*, and three years later came his novel *So Long, See You Tomorrow*, for which he received the Howells Medal from the American Academy of Arts and Letters. Despite their common success, Eudora had become a celebrity and Bill had not. She was the darling of the college and university lecture circuit; she was tapped for membership on the National Council on the Arts; she appeared on national television with William F. Buckley and Dick Cavett; her novella *The Robber Bridegroom* was adapted for the Broadway stage; and previously obscure essays and stories were published as collector's edition books. Happily, fame did not go to Eudora's head, nor did it alter her relationships with friends and family. For his

part, Bill rejoiced in Eudora's acclaim even as he feared that it might distract her from her work.

The closeness between Eudora and Bill continued, and in their letters they shared their grief at the death of Elizabeth Bowen; their concern for Mary Lou Aswell, whose son had disappeared; and the joys of their European travels. They continued to report to each other on their reading and on family developments. Eudora told Bill and Emmy of her fondness for novelist Reynolds Price, whom she had come to regard almost as a son. And when Bill feared that Eudora's financial plight was dire, he offered her money, no strings attached. Eudora did not accept the offer, but she cherished the love behind it. There seems to have been one brief moment of discord between them. When Bill retired from *The New Yorker* in 1976, Eudora was distressed. She had already lost her close friend and agent, Diarmuid Russell, in 1973. She had had absolute trust in Diarmuid's advice about the texture of her stories. Now, she feared, Bill's advice also would be lost. But Bill was quick to assure her that other editors at *The New Yorker* would offer her wise counsel and that he would still be available as her reader. Despite this reassurance, Eudora would not be able to complete any new fiction.

The momentary sense of alienation between the two old friends is less surprising than a glaring omission that appears in their extant correspondence during this decade. One of the most important relationships of Eudora's life is never mentioned in these or subsequent letters. In 1971, Eudora met Kenneth Millar, aka Ross Macdonald, in the lobby of the Algonquin Hotel in New York, and the two almost immediately fell in love. Ken was married and faithful to his wife; he lived in Santa Barbara, California, half a continent away from Eudora. She and Ken had little opportunity for time together, but they began to correspond, typically sending each other long, loving letters about twice a month until 1979, when Alzheimer's disease put an end to Ken's writing. In Eudora's letters to Mary Lou Aswell, Reynolds Price, and William Jay Smith, there are many references to Ken, but in her extant correspondence with Bill, she never mentions him or his work. She doesn't discuss her love for Ken or her grief at his loss of memory. Why? This omission may suggest that Bill and Eudora's friendship did not extend beyond certain parameters, that she did not feel free to discuss this part of

her life with him. But surely she would have felt free to discuss Ken's work, if not her love for him. The absence of Ken's name in her letters to Bill may instead suggest that their communication about him took place in person and simply was not recorded on paper. Although this is possible, Eudora's visits to New York were widely spaced, and she was not comfortable with long phone calls. It is also possible that Bill chose not to preserve Eudora's letters about Ken. Certainly, Bill refused to read published letters between W. B. Yeats and Maud Gonne because he felt he was invading their privacy. Perhaps he likewise wanted to protect the privacy of Eudora's romantic life. But why is there no mention of Ken, or at least of his work, in Bill's letters to Eudora? She made no effort to censor or edit them. There seems only one conclusion to be drawn: for whatever reason, Eudora's relationship with Ken is not documented in her extant correspondence with Bill.

William Maxwell to Eudora Welty, February 1, 1971

Dearest Eudora:

The dictionary of phrase and fable arrived and is a marvel! I cannot tell you how soothing it is to my mind to read that Pliny says that loose-strife has a soothing effect upon oxen that will not draw in the same yoke, and that the Bug Bible is called that because of the verse "Thou shalt not nede to be afrayed for eny bugges by night", and that the leek is the national emblem of Wales, and that on Running Thursday, that is to say, December 13, 1688, a great many people ran for their lives into the country, and what a tucker is, and that the mandrake shines at night. It is incomparably better, and by this I mean more fascinating, than any book of this kind I ever saw.[1] It is the perfect book to take on a journey. The perfect book to receive from a friend. It follows us around the house like Daisy.

We have spent the last two weekends in town so Emmy could get rested up from the grippe, the double life being more strenuous than the single one. She had a curious bugge which hung on and left her without her normal strength. So we went to see the Walker Evans show and the Gertrude Stein collection and fifty centuries of masterpieces and The Petrified Forest—all restoring. And I who didn't need restoring fortified myself by

reading an Agatha Christie (Murder at the Vicarage) that Uncle Humpie sent Kate.

Kate is doing the synopsis of a Greek tragedy, and is reduced to tears of frustration because it isn't as good as she would like it to be—i.e. it compares unfavorably with Socrates. It is also, I think, a rather silly assignment. The form fights present-day matter the way oil fights vinegar.

I finally finished the galleys in the middle of January, and the revisions were so drastic that they have to be reset, so I will shortly have them back again, but not in time for Spring publication, it appears. So I don't really know when Knopf plans to bring the book out.[2]

At the Institute dinner on Thursday, Roger Sessions' son, who is a particularly handsome and sensitive-looking man, played one of his father's suites for unaccompanied cello, and then a trio played a very nice Copeland suite. Nobody got the fidgets, not even Malcolm Cowley. A number of people explained to me affectionately that I ought to raise my voice, so we are right back where I started, and Howard Moss (confidential) got elected.[3]

Do you have any plans for coming to New York? We have tickets for Midsummer Night's Dream, and after we have seen it I will tell you whether you must drop everything and come. I have the queer feeling that I am going to be the one person who wasn't happy at it. We were all three happy at The Petrified Forest. To see them all so young, and Bogart not even starred. He and Leslie Howard were like Sacred and Profane Love. To look from one to the other was a kind of bliss. Such a creaky play, and such totally uncreaky acting. What happened to Leslie Howard? Did he die young?...I went and looked it up: Fifty. Kate wants to talk about her opus. I'll be back in a minute. Ideas of good and evil. Kate has a way of showing me the total weakness of my thinking. And she, whose logic is impeccable, is, of course, lacking in experience. I am sorry not to have made a tape of the conversation in the living room. You would have then been in a position to help us both make sense to the other one.

Emmy came home yesterday with a perfect white rose and a bouquet of shasta daisies. And the masterpieces of fifty centuries show at the Metropolitan is as irritating as all their others tend to be, but every once in a while finding something in strange company makes it so vivid. A Memling hus-

band and wife. And the Breughal scene of the reapers. It was hung very low down, by a doorway, in a corner, and I was shocked at this treatment but as we stood looking at it, we saw it better than ever before. And discovered when we turned around that our passionate attention had drawn a crowd of people, come to see what we were looking at. The rose period Picassos at the Gertrude Stein show were too beautiful. The acrobat family with the baboon and Mr. Paley's nude against the pink canvas.[4] What made him turn his back on all that is beautiful, do you think?

How I wish you were here to help with Kate's play.

My love,
Bill

William Maxwell to Eudora Welty, May 5, 1971

Dearest Eudora:

The Mizener review was marvelous.[5] There is a kind of heat that doesn't look hot and is annihilating, I forget exactly what it is, but that [is] what the review was like. The last judgment. It also made me damn him to hell for spoiling the book for somebody else. Or perhaps you put the thought in my mind. I kept thinking of Francis Steegmuller who started off disliking Cocteau and totally succumbed to him and became his champion. As Strachey did with Queen Victoria. Anyway, you outdid yourself, as a critic, and undid him. Are you coming for the Ceremonial? I seem to remember that you are, and yet feel that there hasn't been a letter recently enough to have this information in it. What I mean is that I have quietly and fairly unnoticeably gone out of my mind, and don't remember anything. I hope you are coming because we all want to see you.

Love,
B.

Eudora Welty to William Maxwell, May 8, 1971

Dearest Bill,

Do you know what happened? Gruss an Aachen opened its first flower on the morning that my niece Elizabeth had her first baby—I took her the

flower, and she told me she pressed it and put it in a book. I thought you'd like to know it was a real and wonderful as well as lovely Gruss.

Thank you for writing—I've been starved for news of you and Emmy, and starved for writing to you. But all the while we've both been doing what you say, going quietly and fairly unnoticeably (are you sure?) out of our minds, I'm certain we've been doing it congenially. Yes I am coming up for the Ceremonial. Besides wanting to be there while you've got the thing in charge (this time, maybe I'll be ready for any microphone seizers—unless they are really any good, I could have my scissors ready and edge up and cut the connection, like the Good Witch). I also want to be there when Reynolds Price gets his award—sort of in the nature of his family. He is a good friend of mine whom I've known and liked since he was a student at Duke and I was there to read mss. and lecture.[6]

It is almost sure to be impossible, considering all you'll have on your mind and your calendar, but I would so much love to have you and Emmy come out for lunch or dinner on one of the days Reynolds is in New York. He tells me he'll be there the day before the Ceremonial through the end of the week. I'll get in this next Saturday afternoon, the 15th, and leave the 28 or 29—have to go home by way of Ohio and Tennessee—a hard day's Greyhound into night.[7] If you and Emmy could survive one more engagement in that whirl of a time and if you'd like to, do tuck it away in your lost mind, which out of my lost mind I still trust implicitly of course.

I'm so glad you liked my Ford [Madox Ford] piece (I really did believe you would)—I really wanted to kill Mizener, as you would know, and what I hate too is that now nobody else may write the biography that Ford deserves. Thank you for giving me good marks—as it turned out, I mistook the deadline date (over the phone) and had to write it all through one night and wire it in—a great deal too long, but they used it—I was beyond cutting, by morning. John Leonard is terribly nice to review for.[8]

Take care of yourselves. When I get to New York I'll telephone a Gruss— I'll be at the Algonquin—Meantime, much love to you and Emmy and the girls—and also from Elizabeth, who remembers how you sent us to see "Guys and Dolls" when she was nine.

Eudora

Emily Maxwell to Eudora Welty, June 8, 1971, Note card with
image of The Hollow Mountain *by Pamela Bianco*

Dearest Eudora,

Lunch at the Madrigal Restaurant has taken its place in the daisy chain of surprisingly lovely times we've had together. We both felt as if we'd known Reynolds Price forever, and how did you manage to subdue the restaurant, so it was just like home? It was there when we needed it, & gone when we didn't. I can still see that dessert-cart, like something out of Brookie's dreams when she was little.

We are going up to Putney to get her on Thursday. And oh how glad we'll be to tuck her into her own bed for awhile. It's been a terrible winter — missing her & worrying about her, and I hope I never hear the name Putney again.

I am haunted by Mary Lou's son. I hope some good news arrives from somewhere, soon.[9]

With much love,
Emmy

Agnes, Harrison's yellow & Mme Edouard Herriot are in N.Y. with us!

Eudora Welty to Emily and William Maxwell, June 12, [1971],
Note card with image of Studies from Nature *by Maria Sibylla Merian*

Dearest Emmy and Bill,

Seeing you was lovely and best of all was our evening, dinner at home, with Kate. You make finding the time for precious events seem so easy, when I doubt if anybody else doing half all you do could ever find a single minute — and never a minute like any of ours. And thank you for coming out with me so Reynolds could get to meet you and you could see him — he's almost like my child in a way. It meant a lot to him. Tell Kate: next time.

I just had wonderful news from Mary Lou and must tell you instantly — well, more wonderful than it might be. Duncan spoke to the friend he'd shared an apartment with in Haverford, over the telephone — the friend phoned M.L. (at 1 AM, four months to the day after D. disappeared). D. is

in some place he doesn't want known yet, with a manual job, is working out his own problems, and when he feels ready, he will communicate with his mother & sister. He's alive, and thinks of himself as having a future. Poor Mary Lou—the relief of just this much word, making as it does all the difference. It is like her that she held in all the trouble from almost everybody all the time it went on, and when relief arrives she lets all who knew about it know at once.

Bill, a letter is going to come when I finish the marvelous book. It is just enveloping. Am I the only one so far who read the beginnings of it <u>while going through</u> the Cumberland Gap? And in Lexington, Kentucky? I felt like telling the mountains, and showing it to the rivers. We were in a bus on winding country roads—At the rest stop they were serving corn-on-the cob. I'm down to you, now—It's a simply beautiful book—And the work! And the joy—[10]

I'm so glad you have Brookie back. (I almost feel she's been kidnapped.) Tell Kate I haven't found any Klimp yet—but still may. My love to you all, E.

I tried & tried to call you—then remembered it was Saturday & Memorial Day weekend.

Eudora Welty to William Maxwell, November 10, 1971

Dearest Bill,

I was so glad to get your letter and I want so much to see you and Emmy, needless to say one reason why I felt I had to come. I wish I could come either of those nights, but Tues., when I get there, I have a date made from here with a friend from home and Wed. is Diarmuid's birthday and I invited myself out to Katonah to eat dinner with them after the grants comm. meeting. Small chance as it is sure to be, I wonder if you could have dinner with me on Monday evening, 22nd? I should have asked long before, only didn't know for sure I could come. Whole weekend is in Conn., so most of the trip is work—must leave Wednesday AM, 24th.[11] We will, no matter what, see one another at the dinner meeting. Let's hold out hope for more in spite of all. So much to talk about.

The children. Riverdale—as Bertie just said in Jeeves & the Tie that Binds, you must have sung like a relieved nightingale.[12] And I'm so glad Kate has been considering choices for college.

Ancestors. I can't tell you how much I love that book, and this piece of yellow paper is a list of page numbers from it—am I asking you to write your own letter of praise? It looks that way—I've had it since the day I began reading. My right hand has played a trick on me—the bone dr. said it's worn out, isn't that the craziest thing? Two bones scrape together and make my hand feel broken. However, it's not as bad as I first thought—shots of cortisone help, and I've got onto typing with part hunt-and-peck. Meantime, whether I could do it or not, I did revise The Optimist's Daughter and get it in on time for spring book. It's the next subject after Ancestors. Lots more too. I'll get this in the mail for now, though, and it will be so lovely to see you, in just a little while.

<div style="text-align:right">With my dear love to all of you,
Eudora</div>

Eudora Welty to Emily and William Maxwell, December 15, 1971,
Note card with image of Mary Cassatt's Feeding the Ducks

The date it came December 15, 1971
Dearest Emmy and Bill,

So beautiful a thing to do, completely divining, because stirring up my cake was what always has told me it was Christmas, and I'd felt lost, really, without it—to look at, whiff at, wait on—Now you send it to me, made it for me yourselves—I was so deeply delighted and moved and all simultaneously barely restrained from taking a bite ahead of time. It is <u>beautifully</u> moist and fragrant—you may get a whiff of it back by this note. I've just been handling it—the plain fact is, it's a perfect cake—by nature and by deed. I'll be thinking of you on Christmas Eve—I hope you did make for yourselves one just exactly like it—so we can share cake as well as wishes & love.

This little picture is a copy I had made of a snapshot my mother took of her mother & me out on the mountain in West Virginia, "up home".[13] My

Grandmother Andrews, who was not very old but her life had not been easy. The first visit I can remember. An itinerant came through Jackson long ago & offered to frame any picture in a way that would "permanently preserve" it, between 2 sheets of glass—utterly unremovable—& this was the picture she (my mother) wanted kept. Black border could not be helped—it had to be photographed too. Much love to all of you and so many thanks—and hopes & wishes for you—and thank Brookie for her lovely card. Reading proof—letter coming—My love always, Eudora

William Maxwell to Eudora Welty, [Late 1971 or Early 1972]

Dearest Eudora:

The enclosed page is a typed copy of the first page of a letter of Sylvia Townsend Warner, whose handwriting is not always legible and in this case was—no, I think I will keep the typescript and let you puzzle the compliments out. More fun.

I don't think it is possible to be more interrupted than I was in reading the galleys of The Optimist's Daughter, and I haven't yet sat down and compared it line for line with the version that appeared in The New Yorker— partly because it wasn't necessary. I knew the other so well that all sorts of electric signals worked when I was reading new material. What I felt was that you felt that a story and a novel must be two different things, particularly as to their pace, so it was as if you had changed the tempo in playing a piece of music. The one has the rush of the most terrible anguish I have ever experienced in reading, and is really unbroken in its mood, its effect of staring down into a pit that has no bottom. The longer version is attached by threads here and there to the outside world. I was much struck by your ability to bring new incidents and characters to so finished a piece of writing. Ten years later, yes, but not something done so recently. And I will need to read it ten years from now to know which I prefer, or if I prefer either to the other. I was just with you. In it. And why do I keep feeling that the photograph you sent us for Christmas should be printed as a frontispiece? That treasure went straight to the mantelpiece and hasn't yet left it, but, shortly must be framed, because a snapshot unframed leads too chancy

a life. The gesture of the hand made me realize, as if I didn't already, all I had lost when the two girls left childhood behind. I wish I could say that it is what everything I have ever written was about. It is what everything I have ever written was <u>trying to be</u> about. That's how valuable the picture is to me.

I never got tickets to the Pinter because so many of my acquaintances, all Pinter fans, said, grieving, that it is a dead play.[14]

The pink rose that I told Brookie would never bloom because there is only one hour of sunlight (when there is any) in her bedroom in the city, where the windows look out between two tall buildings, is now blooming. She has dreamed about it over and over, and cared so much. And maybe it is that roses need, more than sunlight. One or the other.

I'm trying to put together a book of short stories, and finding it difficult. So many of them are either stuck fast in the copy of the New Yorker they appeared in, or in a period that isn't like now. I keep wishing that some-body (myself, for instance) had only said, "Couldn't you try harder?" A few are all right. But only a few. And what bothers me is that I didn't see this at the time.[15]

I hope your hand is better. I thought of it all the time I was reading the galleys. I almost forgot: Do you have a biggish book called a Dictionary (or maybe an Encyclopedia) of Roses? I got a review copy from Edith Oliver, and then somebody gave me a copy for Christmas, so there is one that I could send to you. It's nice in that it has quite a few pictures of old roses that I only knew by name, though perhaps Mississippi being a warmer climate you know them in actuality.[16] If you would like it, tell me.

We all send showers of love, on a day so foggy that I looked out of the window the first thing this morning and thought of Sherlock Holmes.

B.

Eudora Welty to William Maxwell, January 14, 1972

Dearest Bill,

There's one more slice of your cake still for the future—still moist, still heavenly and rich as Croesus, and the way I have treasured it (hoarding it and eating it at the same time) and meted it out is the only way I still have

one slice. Only my nearest and dearest had the chance of a crumb. (John Robinson is here from Italy—I gave him some.) Most of it, in case you haven't guessed the real truth, but you have, I've saved for myself—eaten peacefully by the window in the breakfast room where I can look out at the bird feeder and see the birds eating what to them may be fruitcake like mine, coming to them like manna out of the loving kindness of friends. But I know what makes my feast. You and Emmy are diviners, and so it came to you how for this year I couldn't beat and stir my cake, but then what made it even nicer was that you are so much better cooks! Not Better cooks than diviners—you aren't. Better cooks than me. I was so happy with that cake. It had angelica in it again, didn't it?

It was lovely to think of you in the country for Christmas. I knew you'd have real candles on the tree. Emmy's cricket is on its hob on the living room mantle by the clock, still, and Brookie's house aglow still stands on the mantle by the clock up here in my room. It smells like cake.

I'm so glad her rose bloomed. I remember how she held that slender little wand of it that evening. You may be right and love just as coaxing as daylight, to a rose.

I think that's what your stories do, too—coax the flower. Their gentleness is a form of concentration, and their strength comes out of what was intuitive always,—in the end they stand unprotected—that's the bloom. (It's hard to say it in so many words.) Don't worry. Being so full of truth, they're strong as iron. I'm glad of the book of them. And what's "contemporary" can keep its place (on a level lower than that of the verities) when it comes to your stories, just as well as you put it in its place when it comes to our stories, can't it? (Speaking to you as editor of your own.) I wish you wouldn't have any fears about the stories, but as one of the same kind of sufferers over my own I understand—that sudden dropping away of all confidence in any given sentence that looks you in the face. I guess deep down that's why I introduced those props into the Optimist's Daughter—but Bill, I took them out again. I wish I had known from Albert [Erskine] at what point you'd been sent the galleys, because I would have tried to get them right for you first. You were a saint to read it again—I wanted you to be that very saint, but I hope I have recovered the story now since you saw it from weaknesses both old and new. Some few new paragraphs I did leave in. (One is essen-

tial to me.) I did feel I had to face the existence and meaning of the hus-
band—but I think I've kept it just the lean bare fact it ought to be, but with
a clue to its force and reality. I would rather anything would happen to that
story than that I had done something to it that would disappoint you. Yes, I
think that little picture might be its lost or found real frontispiece—or the
story the picture's addenda. I'm so glad to have come by it. I know it's what
everything you've written is about, the gesture in it that's being so uncon-
sciously made—it's what all I've written tries for now too, and I don't know
what much more, what much else, there is, Bill, do you?

It was so lovely to be let read the page from Sylvia Townsend Warner—
I was thrilled to think of her looking at my pictures, and happy to think you
had sent them to her. "The floral quality of the young women"—and what
she said about the sun. I can say of her letter what she said of my pictures—
"I am glad to have got so far at last." Thank you for sending this to me and
I'll send it back in mine.

And you know how excited I was to read what Brendan Gill wrote. It
was hard to believe, how he'd found all those generous things to say, and I
hadn't supposed the book would find a place in the New Yorker reviews at
all—it isn't literary, for one thing. And then you know I was disappointed in
the quality of the reproductions,—but only to find that Brendan Gill liked
in the pictures what they had been made for, and what they showed, and to
him that made up for their lacks. In other words, he felt for the book like a
friend. And it was like you and Emmy seeing it, and like Miss Warner when
she sees straight to the floral quality. It was marvelous to have this happen to
my book.[17]

Thank you for that earlier review you mailed me from the National Ob-
server, which indeed I had not seen and was glad to see. And the inter-
view with Mr. [Padraic] Colum. Poor man, when I saw how the illness had
drawn and thinned that darling face, I couldn't be too surprised, or too sorry
for a man like him either, when he died this week. The Krochalises in Suf-
folk [Suffield, Connecticut] who looked after him so steadily and lovingly,
wrote to me twice after Mr. Colum was stricken, and I think from the letters
the memoirs he dictated would have been in good hands. I don't know if
you ever knew them (Ed and Jean Krochalis)—I did a little, only saw them

when I was in Suffolk [Suffield] too, to the same thing Mr. C. did every summer for years, and saw how he adored them and utterly relied on them in the most soignée manner in his every daily need. They would do anything for him, so I hope they will write well for him.

I had a dream one night in which you appeared—there were rows of bins and boxes and drawers all lined up, which were a sort of file system of ashes. Each one had the day of the week written over it. You said, "There is nothing at all that cannot be recovered, we only need to know the day it happened on."

Did you happen to get a Heffer's bookstore catalogue from Cambridge, the one with the library of E. M. Forster for sale? (After the bequests, etc of course). I have been reading it and making dream presents to my friends. The very book I had wanted to find for Emmy, as I told her, was there: "The Nature of the Physical World" by Sir Arthur Eddington—it's number 99, listed as "Presentation copy to himself: 'E. M. Forster from E.M.F. Xmas 1938.'" His old school prizes are here, you can imagine their nature, and his guide books to Europe, and his presents from other people, and all of them worn hard—how hard he was on his books! Spines broken, frontispiece hanging, corners bent, covers rubbed—of course I suppose they all spent a lot of time in his pockets.

Speaking of dream presents, I would so well love to have the Rose Dictionary if you do have two. I'd especially like those pictures of the old roses—only names but what names! to me too. If it's too unhandy to mail, I could carry it home with me—I'll be there in March for the committee meeting, I guess. And I've heard the same sad report about the new Pinter. So we'll spare ourselves.

My hand is better, and you see I can type which doesn't pain me though it may not look well, it may pain <u>you</u>, and it gets better all the time. I'm beginning to think about some new stories and think it will do its part—now if only the brain will.

My love to all of you. Take care. My thanks for so many things, so often thought about.

<div align="right">

<u>Happy New Year</u>
from Eudora

</div>

Eudora Welty to William Maxwell, January 22, 1972

Mr. William Maxwell, President
The National Institute of Arts and Letters
633 West 155th Street
New York, N.Y.
Dear Bill,

What makes this the finest is that it comes while you are president. The news you send me of the National Institute of Arts and Letters having chosen me to be given the Gold Medal for the Novel in 1972 fills me with gratitude and joy, humility and pride. The thanks I send you for your letter are deeper than I can say, and so I'm glad that you can so well imagine them, being close to the novels themselves as well as to me.

I shall very surely be there at the Ceremonial on Wednesday, the 17th of May, when I may have this great honor bestowed upon me.

<div style="text-align:right">

My thanks and love as always,
Eudora
1119 Pinehurst Street, Jackson, Mississippi
</div>

Eudora Welty to William Maxwell, January 24, 1972

Dearest Bill,

The joy and pride! <u>You</u> know this is the most wonderful thing that could happen, just as well as if I were the one that was president giving it and you were the one that was being given the Gold Medal, come next May 17th. I wrote you to the Institute and this is to the house—I feel like leaving you word at the New Yorker and maybe the Coffee House Club or the Century, just to make sure you get it, both early and often. (You know, they don't know about airmail at the Institute?) I'm so filled with pleasure, so grateful—really top-heavy* with so much honor coming down on my head. The real, untarnished, precious kind (of honor, not head). I can't help feeling I ought in honesty to tell them (you know it already) that in no case did I ever mean to write a novel, every one of them was undertaken as a short story. On the other hand, though, I could take the extra credit for that making it twice as hard. That still wouldn't make me deserve it enough. But you

make up for that with your blessing, and I'm happiest of all that this happens while you're the president. Thank you more than I can say.

I may write the news to Mary Lou, and Diarmuid—but Uncle Daniel is just wild to get it and spread it around.[18] About the things for the display case, has the New Yorker still got the ms. for "The Optimist's Daughter"? I give everything to the Archives here, and I can probably borrow some mss., but have the feeling that particular original is somewhere around your office.[19] If it's easy to lay hands on, that would already be there in NY.

Thanks for your second letter—I think yours and Emmy's imagination would be truer and safer for those pictures than anywhere else,—snapshots are nice evidence, but will never tell the story except when the right eyes are looking at them.

<div style="text-align:right">With very much love to all of you, and with my thanks—</div>
<div style="text-align:right">Eudora</div>

Do I seem not to have room to be glad for Walker Percy? I am.

Did I tell you I hope to go to San Antonio Feb. 4 to see Agi's exhibition, which opens a new museum—& Mary Lou and Agi there?[20]
*and at the same time light-headed—not impossible before breakfast.

Eudora Welty to Emily and William Maxwell, March 17, 1972

Dearest Emmy and Bill,

I hope Kate is safe home and that by now her toes, fingers, nose, ears, all the rest of her inches are warm. Love to her—I'm sorry I missed seeing her that lovely evening. Lovely inside, the fire, the talk, the dinner, the music, all warming my inches. I saw Daisy basking and could feel with her. Thank you for it all—that lovely shad roe, which I previously thought only came along in May, along with the darling buds. We had it like the strawberries, while rough winds did shake 544 East 86.

Sonnet 18. When I got to ask Katherine Anne my one question (as it turned out) during our afternoon together, I asked her that. "Either 53 or 57, darling," she replied. "Of course I knew all the sonnets by heart and could recite them straight through by the time I was nine years old, you know, but 53 I think it is."[21] And Henry's letter—I did find it. "Anon. Date unknown. 'O fat woman in white whom nobody loves, why do you walk

through the fields in gloves?'" So much better than I remembered it, and now I can stop looking for the author. Perhaps Louella got hold of all that information every week just to <u>rest</u>.[22]

Is the little girl still with you? I kept thinking of her, and of her parents. Wishing she could be given back her future. So indicative, isn't it, that she wants to hear Brookie tell her fairy tales—she may never go any farther now. But I was wishing her parents could know that she was under a good roof that night, anyway. Of course, I realize she would have no use for my sympathy—which is so much for you, too—having her there, until—?

Katherine Anne was in exuberant spirits, never stopped talking for 6 hours (there are some fairy tales going at the age of 84, too) and we sat in her dining room on gold chairs and ate catfish with gold knives and forks and drank champagne and we also had fresh asparagus which we ate in our fingers, holding them up dripping in melted butter (like grapes in orgies), then we moved back to her study, with the gold mirror—she's goldleafing everything, at the present—and with all her books and pictures, and talked some more. Her bed also is golden. She's happy carrying out wishes—who could wish anybody anything more?—and very gallant about her life which actually is that of an old lady with a broken hip behind her and cataract operations, and whatever heart condition necessitates digitalis every day. She has a big double apartment in a high-rise about 30 minutes fast driving out into the country, near Silver Spring [Maryland]. A nurse-companion-driver-housekeeper comes every day 9–5, and a secretary comes afternoons, and she keeps guest rooms there for a nephew and a niece, so I trust they come. She already has the outfit ready to give me the gold medal in—white Italian silk pants suit. Oh, I hope she makes it. She talked a good deal about death and dying, and is changing her will at the moment—I wonder how many times—and impatient because her lawyer of the wonderful name (Mr. Prettyman) is in the hospital having his gall bladder out. The photograph on the wall in her room is his (and he is).

Everything is in some shade of gold and green in the trees here, and the Banksia rose is in bloom—the late daffodils, the last camellias, some continuing azaleas. Dogwood is white all through the woods, I watched it coming out from the train as we came south. So soon, now, there—and I hope it's a beautiful spring and all will go well with all of you—everything unfold

exactly the way it ought to. So much love, and so many thanks, as always, and take care,

 Eudora

Eudora Welty to William Maxwell, October 23, 1972

Dearest Bill,

I feel so deprived, not to get to hear you—the Dinner Meeting comes right in between two trips I have to take to Washington. It just isn't possible. I miss you already, and Emmy. The envelope has been addressed and stamped for ages and the couple of pictures in it sealed up, either with or without a letter—I hope with, since I can't find it, but I'm living holed in in a downstairs room while a month's repair work goes on in my house. How are you? The appearance on this program seems a sign you're well & fine, or <u>were</u> well & fine till you said you'd be on the program. I hope all is thriving with all the Maxwells.

It's seemed hard for me to write this summer. The bad news over at Russell & Volkening froze me in my tracks. Now poor Henry is gone, and Diarmuid is very sick in the hospital in Mount Kisco. You know how close and dear to me he is.[23]

Julian Huxley's <u>From an Antique Land</u> has been a marvelous book to keep by me, do you know it & recently? I'm not too sure about wanting to jump into the Quentin Bell on his Aunt Virginia—have you done it? I loved your review of the Pritchett—[24]

The Washington trips are for meetings of the Nat'l Council on the Arts—Nancy Hanks' and Michael Straight's outfit, to which I found myself appointed—I'll have to <u>tell</u> you about it. They meet, as my mother would have put it, every whip-stitch.

The boys working on the house are named Calvin, Ronnie, and Earl, who're under a contractor named Jesse Parrish. They sing hymns from ladder tops, and keep buttermilk and Rainbo Pickles in my refrigerator. We've been living together for 5 weeks, they're sheet-rocking the walls so they won't look like George Price any more, or for 5 or 6 years anyway. Then painting, inside & out—all that's been put off for only too long. I'm writing this in my car, but sooner or later I'll be able to get to my typewriter.

My dear love to all of you. You don't know how many times I think back to the May meeting—moment of glory! But I expect you do know—having known all that went before & led to—

Naturally, I send Hallowe'en greetings—can still see Brookie at age 5 or 6 carving her pumpkin with that absolutely sure left hand—

Love again, Eudora

William Maxwell to Eudora Welty, November 27, 1972

Dear Eudora:

Such a long time to thank you for the pictures. I knew you'd understand, but even so. I was doing something on the Quentin Bell, and had to let everything slide.[25] And when I do that it isn't only things, it is the floor and the ceiling that get out of plumb. I finished writing out what I had to say at the Dinner Meeting by slipping away after the business meeting and cutting out the parts I didn't want, and reading the rough draft with interlineations, downstairs in Felicia's office, while they were having cocktails upstairs. It only seemed to take a minute, and when I got back upstairs they had sat down and the waiters were passing the soup. Lippold was extraordinary.[26] He described his earliest memory, which was sitting in his father's lap, and his father was a big man, and strong, and he liked being there, and his father wanted him to see the man in the moon, and try as hard as he could, he didn't, not any man, but he saw the moon, and realized it was something out there not him, (and that's how he came to do that wire sculpture in the Museum of Modern Art), and then about how his father made him a toy sailboat, which he loved very much but one day playing with some boys they got into a destructive mood and he broke it, and then he took it to his father and his father said would you like me to make you another boat, and Lippold said yes, and his father said all right, but you must sit here and watch me do it. Well it took a long time to make that little boat, what with the sawing and the planing and the string for this and the nails for that, and he sat there watching, and when his father finished he said to Lippold, "If you want to break this you can, but generally speaking, it's better if you destroy only things you can replace yourself." After this he spoke about the exaltation and misery of being in love with somebody who wasn't in

love with him, and then, returning to the sailboat, explained that in present-
ing his case before the draft board as a conscientious objector, he said "I'm
a constructer, not a destructer," and being an artist, not a writer, thought he
had made a mistake in English and changed the "destructer" to "destroyer",
but by that time it didn't matter because he had already broken my heart.

I missed you.

While you were having the painters we were too. The living room and
hall and Kate's room. She described the color she wanted over the phone,
an orangey-red, not orange and not red, you know, the color that's in Re-
don[27]...Emmy gave the painters a dust jacket from the Arden King Lear,
I think it was, and went off on some essential errand and when she came
back they had painted the room a quite different color, which we hoped
was what Kate had in mind, and Kate came home last weekend and said,
"It's just the color I didn't want, but I rather like it." The painters' names
I never learned, their first names, I mean, but they were both policemen
moonlighting, and very neat. And they went off with both my screwdrivers.

I was under the impression that Virginia Woolf also wrote in the car, but
nobody says so. It is something I heard when I was young. That he [Leonard
Woolf] took the house for the printing press and she had to write in the car.
Probably apocryphal. I mean she had that chair with the stuffing coming
out of it and that was all she needed.

We went to Oregon—that is, Emmy, Brookie, and I did—for the week-
end. Emmy preceded us and arrived Tuesday night. B and I came Thursday
night, and we all left on Sunday morning. I helped E's mother clean the
chickenhouse, and went for a walk with her father. In the house he walks
without a cane, and outdoors with two. We went for a winding walk in the
woods across the road, and it had been raining and the path was covered
with oak leaves, very wet and slimy, and at one point I said don't you want
me to walk ahead of you so you'd have somebody to grab and he said no.
Once he did slip and I cried out but he didn't fall and neither did he rep-
rimand me for crying out. On his eightieth birthday—he is now 87—E's
older brother and I had each given him a bottle of Chateau Latour '61 and
he had kept it for an occasion, and he decided that our coming was the oc-
casion, and so I ended up enjoying my own present. It was the best wine I
ever tasted, light and smooth and simple, a simple taste in layers, a land-

scape. Coming back, while I did editing, Emmy and Brookie both worked on the alligator side by side, at the same time.[28] Different parts of the background. We had ten minutes in Chicago, and it was raining, and I was sure we'd lose connection with our luggage. It took that time for us to get from F11 to E7, and it was dark outside and raining. But in New York, the first suitcase that came through the hole in the revolving wheel was mine.

I've also been to Lincoln, to my stepmother's funeral, but that's another whole set of stories, and they will keep. We all send love,

B.

P.S. And I never thanked you for the pictures. I do now.

Eudora Welty to Emily and William Maxwell, February 22, 1973

Dearest Emmy and Bill,

Just to be in touch, on learning of the death of Elizabeth last night. A friend in Bryn Mawr telephoned me this morning. I've had her so much on my mind lately, of course wanted to and meant to write her, too, without knowing she was ill, only I had not done it. She was here for New Year's Eve and part of that week, the winter she came to Princeton, a few years ago—It was just grand, too—I remember the lovely evening you had Elizabeth and me together at your house, Kate was just a child—night-gowned, hair hanging, a member of the party—The visits in Ireland. Would you like a little picture of Elizabeth at Bowen's Court? I can find you one.

Naturally, I have meant to write long before this sad day to thank you for the happy day when your Christmas cup arrived—It's beautiful, and I know it's Brookie's work—the shape uncompromising & good & plain, and the colors like a Persian miniature's or a piece of Chinese silk—I have been putting pale pink camellias in it (by name Bernice Bodey!) and looking at it, with or without flowers, dozens of times a day whenever I look at the clock, which I put it next to, on my mantle—Thank you for it, and also the falling snowflakes—lovely.

I've been up to Washington to a National Council on the Arts meeting,[29] and from there ran up to Katonah to see Diarmuid—I'm glad he felt well enough, and we had a happy couple of days to talk and look at the snow and the birds—I hope to come back, and then to be able to stay a little, on

the next trip—It must have been glorious flying out to Oregon and back and what a joy for your father, Emmy, seeing you both—was it a surprise?

Bill, I haven't had a chance to settle down to you on Quentin Bell on Virginia Woolf, which came while I was away, but I long to compare our feelings about the book. I'd not looked forward to the biography after the English reviews of it I'd read, but when I read it I was very moved by Mr. B's fairness, his care for the real & right word, his sense of perspective and proportion, and his feeling for the whole strange family story, and his restraint—a remarkable piece of work, to me, and throughout my reading there was a lot I wanted to remark then on to you both and to hear you remark on. I also liked a book of reminiscences that came out about the same time—you saw that?—especially the housekeeper's—and especially Elizabeth's—I'm back to where I began—[30]

Much love, that brings her in, missing her with you—remembering so many good beautiful funny things together, Indescribable friend—relishing every moment—of which something seems left—

Love to you both and to Kate and Brookie—I hope those girls are thriving, happy, & safe—

Oh, you are going to be invited to something strange & hard to explain—I'll write you later with the unlikely story—

Love again,
Eudora

William Maxwell to Eudora Welty, February 27, 1973

Dear Eudora:

I called you the evening I heard and you were out. Just to be in touch, as you said. I would love a picture of Elizabeth at Bowen's Court. I wish I had had the energy to write letters I knew would never be answered. But most of all I wish I could have kept her in my pocket. In the pocket of my plaid bathrobe, where I once kept a kitten whose mother was indifferent to her. But alas, kittens do not thrive in bathrobe pockets and neither would Elizabeth.

You are right: it was Brookie's cup. She turns out one chef d'oeuvre after another these days, and has, in addition, pulled herself up (with the help

of a young Tunisian tutor from Hunter College) from failing in math to
ninety-eight and a half on her last exam. And the snow flakes were Emmy's
chef d'oeuvre, surely. I think she is, comparatively, quite safe these days.
Kate is spending her vacation babysitting and taking music lessons of vari-
ous kinds, including the bassoon, and working as a volunteer at the For-
tune Society, which is, itself, safe, I guess, but it leads to an acquaintance
that sometimes gives us pause.[31] On the whole she seems to be sensible and
careful. What I mean is idealism is as dangerous as—but I don't need to fin-
ish the sentence.

When you read the Quentin Bell review you will be amused. At some-
thing, I mean. It is like dressing up in each other's clothes. I have just done
a note on Roger Fry's letters, and would gladly have launched off into ten
or fifteen thousand words about them, but a note was what was asked for.
His love letters to Vanessa Bell are so touching. Do you have her life of
him (VW'S, I mean) and do you remember his unfinished account, in that
book, of a trip through Italy with JP Morgan? He is wonderful on places,
which, naturally, made me think of you.[32]

To return to where we began, which is Elizabeth: I keep remembering
the time she invited herself to our house in the country, and on the train
riding out I found myself telling her about a knot I was having trouble un-
tieing, in The Chateau, and after dinner and the children were put to bed,
she settled back in the ottoman chair, with her shoes off and her feet up,
and E and I sat on the floor, in front of the fire, on the bear rug, and we
talked, till one, I guess. And at six the next morning I was awakened by the
sound of the waltz from The Sleeping Beauty, and sat up in horror and said
to Emmy "It will wake up Elizabeth!" You know how small the house is.
And then woke up a little more and realized where the record player was. In
my bathrobe and barefeet I knocked on Elizabeth's door, which was really
the door of Kate's room, when a voice said come in, I saw Kate on the floor
beside her record player, with the record going round and round, and she
was sitting on a pillow which she had taken from Elizabeth because it was
after all her pillow, and Elizabeth was in bed, reading a book about, I seem
to remember, Dr. Crippen, stretched out flat she was, with her head at about
the angle it would have been if there had been a pillow under it, and smil-
ing at me. Kate was three, I suppose.[33] She never failed to ask about her.

One thing more. We have had a tragedy. Brookie brought home a lost kitten last fall, and it was killed by a car last Saturday in the country, and we are all inconsolable. It was a tabby, with I suspect a coon somewhere in its ancestry, from the tail. And so strong and humorous and so nice to smell when you buried your face in its fur, and so brave and independent and it would only let Brookie and Emmy hold it, but it would jump up on the sofa and sit beside me while I was reading and lick my fingers. And it looked so much like my Aunt Annette that I wasn't absolutely sure that it wasn't. The first cat we had allowed ourselves to have in twelve years, because of Daisy. The cat loved Daisy, and played with her as if they were two tigers, but Daisy's character deteriorated ba[d]ly from having another animal in the house. Jealousy has very little to be said for it. One doesn't somehow get over the death of animals, but then I don't know that I am all that good at getting over the death of people I love, are you?

Love,

B.

I forgot to thank you for the poems, which we have read and reread. They are the real thing.

Eudora Welty to William Maxwell, April 16, 1973

Dear Bill,

It was so sweet of you to call me up, and such a pleasure to hear your voice and some of your news. I hope to be seeing you and Emmy at Ceremonial time, I want to be there for Felicia's honor and John Crowe Ransom's among other things.[34]

I knew you'd know my feelings about the Arts Festival day here.[35] At first, when they said to invite my best friends from all over the country, or maybe the world! I said it would be a terrible big thing to ask of them to come so far and for a day and a night—then I decided the only thing to do was just that, make an ideal list, and leave it to the friends to understand. It is lovely of them here to do it, and lovely of the friends who're free & able to come,* but it will be a crowd—which is not our best setting for a picnic out in the lovely open, where we can hear the living words of one another, and pass the tomato sandwiches without getting up. Remember: next March.

I loved your review of the Quentin Bell, as I must have told you. I loved the biography. It must have been so tantalizing to review, but you picked and chose so well and conveyed so exactly, and at what seemed to be exactly the right temperature. I just did a review of Vol. 1 of the Abinger Edition of E. M. Forster—they may not run it (John Leonard) because AGAIN I sent them twice the wordage they asked for, and with plenty of time to write it in—and now Walter Clemons isn't there any longer to cut it for me, he is such a congenial cutter.[36] (Do you read his reviews in Newsweek? He's one of the best going, if not the best, I think, with a special faculty of really understanding and caring about what an author tried for. Good reason: he's an author himself. He also never reviews a book without having read everything else the writer has published.)

Diarmuid and Rosie [Russell] arrive in two weeks, to stay a week, and I am praying all will go with smoothness and ease and give him pleasure and not fatigue. No hard-boiled eggs, no potatoes, and no shell-fish—starting from there, I can go North, East, South, or West.

It was good to see Howard's piece on Elizabeth.[37] I was so moved by a letter that came today. Bea Horton, a close friend of Elizabeth's (whom I knew when Elizabeth got me her London apartment one summer) wrote to me:

"I was on the telephone to her cousin, Audrey Fiennes, almost daily during the last two weeks of her life when she was in hospital and she, bless her, told me every detail of the funeral at Farrahy—that little graveyard at the end of the Bowen's Court demesne. Elizabeth, in a final will, written last December, said she wanted to be buried there. Alan is there and her forebears of the last 3 or 4 generations. Her heart turned strongly back to Ireland during this last year. The funeral was beautiful and moving—the country people came in crowds, with flowers—they looked (Audrey's words) 'dedicated.'...Charles was with her up to the last. He is back in Canada now[38]...I was sent the NY Times piece. Sad it was so full of inaccuracies, though very respectful." She sent Cyril Connolly's one from the Sunday Times, which she thought very fine, as did I. I Xeroxed it for you when I first saw it, long ago, and I'm sure you have seen it by now at least. I'll bring the little pictures. Best love to you and Emmy and Happy Easter and love to the girls—Eudora

*Charles Shattuck is coming—He may just go back on not finding you here, do you think?

William Maxwell to Eudora Welty, [Summer 1973]

Dear Eudora:

How firm Jill Kremetz is (see enclosed letter).[39] If you really want me to sign your copy of the picture, mail it right back to me. There isn't anything I wouldn't do for you, as I trust you to know, including autographing a picture of us, but it strikes me as somehow unnecessary and, well, operatic. It's a <u>nice</u> picture.

I can't remember when I last wrote to you but surely it was before Ireland, which was very happy and very green, with all the hedges in bloom, so that when I close my eyes I see the hawthorne. I loved staying in Dalkey, and found Shaw's cottage which looks like a setting from one of the early plays. And Nancy Allitt took us on a literary pilgrimage of Cork.[40] All the houses but one that Frank O'Connor lived in are still standing. We got inside the little house in Harrington Square, and even saw the orphanage where his mother was so miserable as a child that she was almost driven to commit suicide. But I felt the bulldozer in the wings, waiting to come on and make Cork up to date. In spite of the incessant architectural massacre, Dublin is still beautiful. Harriet's house looked out on the water—that is, down a terraced garden to the sea road, then Dalkey Bay, which is really a swift channel, then Dalkey Island, the near light house, the far light house, and Wales. E and I were taken out to Dalkey Island by the gardener, in a boat with an outboard motor, and wandered all over it, knee deep in wet Queen Anne's lace. The gulls scolded us, and I climbed a Martello tower, the better to understand <u>Ulysses</u>, while Emmy, who doesn't like even modest heights, wandered off and found a gull's nest in the grass. The eggs were putty colored with big black spots on them. There were four goats on the island, who stared at us, and a roofless twelfth century chapel, and some wildflowers, and a view of Creation.

Before we had had a chance to turn around twice we were in a plane flying to Chicago. Charles met us in Chicago, and drove us down to Urbana. We were made much of, and my hood has a white velvet band on it, and I

was so interested in hearing the citation that I shook hands with the wrong hand in front of 23,000 people, and Sunday morning Charles brought out the Ida M'Toy correspondence and read her letters and yours to us.[41] It was lovely staying with them, the scent of honeysuckle blowing in the bedroom window and long long breakfast table conversations.

When we got home Kate was there, waiting to be driven back to Bennington, on Monday, and we brought her things home the next day and she followed on Saturday. The garden is almost under control, and Gruss an Aachen is in bloom, and we are having guests this week end—friends of Brookie and Larry, with their two very small children.[42] After that I intend to sit down.

My love,
B.

Eudora Welty to William and Emily Maxwell, [Summer 1973]

Dearest Bill and Emmy,

You're safe home, and everything's been good—I'm so glad. Think of Ireland and Urbana and back again, and Bennington, and of course all that multiplied by pleasures and honors and everybody kissing you. I thought of you in the places you went at the times I believed you were there—I've read your letter about 3 times, Bill, and it will get a decent answer—this isn't a decent one—Nothing's wrong except I'm tired and guilt-ridden with about 200 thank-you notes to write that are still unwritten to those well-wishers who sent me cakes and lace handkerchiefs and flowers from their gardens and all manner of things here for "my day" in May—and to make them all different, you know—

It was overwhelming at the time and (numerically) paralyzes me now— As you know, I haven't written even to you yet after those hours of blissfully eating strawberries and drinking wine and talking and laughing and resting after the Ceremonial, and then coming away with the chapters Elizabeth wrote, corrected in her hand—which I treasure you know how deeply, and you know how gratefully—Those thought-messages were in the same waves with the ones I was sending you all along, to Ireland and to Illinois, in care of Chuck. Of course I was made happy by the photograph—No, I don't

need any arrows pointing to our heads, or names signed, I know that's you, Bill, and I think that's me, and I'm ever so glad to have it—that was dear of Jill, wasn't it—She's in such a perfect profession for one with her exuberant instincts—she's a hostess of a photographer—and she must really remember that she told me once, "I'm going to get pictures of you with all your best friends"—(even if she thinks one of them is Kurt Vonnegut, Jr.,—her best friend).[43] It was sweet of her to really go ahead and do it.—I'm sending you the little picture I took of Elizabeth [Bowen] on the back porch of the little hotel in Cahir, that she was so fond of (the hotel in Cahir) in about 1956, on a long ride in the country, the same day we went to Cashel. Have had it for you a long time—I have one for myself and love having it in view—it will seem a nice one to you too, I hope. Oh, Bill, how I wish I could have seen you get the honorary—what a day for them. (If you shook hands with the wrong hand, I did worse, though in front of just 200 Presbyterian girls—I bowed to them and my mortar board fell off.)[44] I'm reading the Chekhov letters. You too? My love to you both, E

Directions:

Write a conversational remark in the balloon,—then unfold.

It's a game my brother & I made up 25 years ago & played every week with Time magazine—Still good with Time.[45]

William Maxwell, Wellfleet, Massachusetts, to Eudora Welty,
July 20, [1973]

Dearest Eudora:

Printed cards: Miss Eudora Welty wishes to thank you for…200 of them. In my minds I I see them, and you delivered from that senseless burden. What I don't see is you doing it that way. But if they were engraved? People are always happy with anything they can run their finger over that's raised. Oh do think about it, if you haven't started in on that labor. Once started, you'd have to continue, I dare say. Even though Jackson isn't a small place. But what about the telephone? Is that worse? I guess it is. You wouldn't have any voice by the fifty-seventh call. But you could dictate a form letter, or several, and then have somebody write them for you to sign. One covering

cake, one flowers from the garden, with a space left for what kind of flowers they were, and one for all manner of things. As you can see the problem interests me. Speaking of flowers, in the current Vogue there is a wonderful article on the Vicomte [de] Noailles's ideas of gardening. Far beyond the likes of you or me to imitate, but adorable to think about.

The photograph of Elizabeth is a marvel. As Emmy said, she composed herself for it. Not the way people do when they want to be preserved for posterity, but for you, so that you would have all there was of her. And what, in case I should ever find myself in Cahir, is the name of the hotel in Cahir she was so fond of? Thank you for remembering and for the trouble it meant to get a print made for us. I have put it in the study, next to your photograph of [Virginia Woolf's home in] Rodmell.

I mean to read the Chekhov letters, but I am actually reading Pritchett's new book about Balzac, in case I wanted to do a review for the New Yorker, which I don't, I'm afraid. The pictures are wonderful, but the book is a potboiler. I didn't know he could write a sentence that didn't sound like him, but this sounds as if he had got some professor to do it, and then gone through the manuscript touching it up here and there. And Balzac, though dear, I don't find very interesting to read about. I read Malraux [actually André Maurois] to see what P left out, and like M a little better but only a little.

The Wellfleet woods are full of mushrooms and Emmy left her mushroom books at home, so we come back from walks with our hands full of mushrooms of all shapes, sizes, and colors, and then Emmy reads about them but so far no eating of em. But last night we had steamed clams and sea-bass, and E said why do people get so excited about lobster. It was marvelous, the bass, cooked in white wine and spices, in an iron fishpan.

The ponds are even better than before — not so cold as last year, and such perfect swimming. Also, when we had parked the car in order to walk through the dunes to the beach, Emmy said "Don't lock the key inside" — which put the idea in my head, of course, so we had to walk back to the house and found that we could easily do it and that it was so pleasant walking through the woods that we have stopped using the car. I am not too old for very many things, but I am too old to want to swim in the ocean when it is as cold as it is here. I would rather sit on a towel and watch the passing show.

The house welcomed us back, and now that I have cut and raked the poison ivy from the path through the woods, and made the upstairs toilet stop running, and learned not to walk away from the toaster, which doesn't reject the toast any more, and glued the rocking chair together that somebody almost destroyed—I see a large man throwing himself back in a paroxism of laughter at his own joke—with Elmer's glueall, I feel we are in total possession. But I wish you were here, and could sit on a towel next to mine, and we'd make up life stories for all the people passing by.

E sends her love, with mine,

Bill

Eudora Welty to William Maxwell, August 19, 1973

Dear Bill,

Here is a confidential read for you too—not exactly to match the Elizabeth-paper you let me have a copy of, but it belongs with what we'd like to keep of her, doesn't it—and has her voice in it. It was sent me, one of "two or three copies," by Bea Horton, Elizabeth's good friend (Spencer Curtis-Brown's sister) who produced the BBC interview with Elizabeth in 1959, unscripted, & edited for the broadcast, being very long, and after Elizabeth's death Bea had this transcribed from the uncut version which she had kept. It was so generous a thing for her to do and I was warmed. I feel she would not mind if I shared it with you, without asking, so I made you the Xerox—

You probably are better acquainted with what Knopf (or somebody) is going to bring out of her work now than I am, I'll just pass on what Bea wrote—Spencer Curtis-Brown is Elizabeth's literary executor, so she would be reliably up on it—She says he & David Cecil are going to select, and David Cecil to write an essay & introduction for, a book of what Elizabeth left, which she indicated to Spencer she would like to have published—this was not very much but brilliant what there was of it—as we know.[46] Bea did not know if a publisher had yet been approached. She felt all would be done well and as Elizabeth wished—as you know, D.C. & S. C-B. were among her oldest and most intimate friends—

It was so lovely to read your letter from Wellfleet and I've been feeling happy about you and Emmy being there in your house again—walking out

in the woods (for those far too mysterious mushrooms, don't swallow a one), swimming in the ponds, sitting on a towel & rejoicing—I can <u>see</u> that rocking chair before you put it back together again—that is, I can hear that fat man laughing it to pieces—

I'm so delighted you felt the picture was good, as I felt—What a lovely thing you say about it. The hotel in Cahir? You couldn't miss it. You'll know it the minute you see it. And Cahir's so little, I doubt if there's another one—just a castle, and a little bridge.

<div style="text-align: right">Best love to you and Emmy—
Eudora</div>

William Maxwell to Eudora Welty, September 25, 1973

Dearest Eudora:

I have had so much pleasure thinking of you holed in across the street, writing and hoping against hope not to be caught in the lobby. Zona Gale used to take refuge in hotels when she had a story she wanted to write. And also it gives me a chance to admire myself—that I have the strength of character not to call you.[47]

Any book of remains—for once the word seems to fit—<u>ought</u> to have that transcription of the BBC interview in it, it is so much Elizabeth. It even explained to my jealous heart why, to some extent, one person was (you always excepted, in her conversation and in fact) as good as another. It was part of her happiness in anonymity: "I hate to have to talk, I really would like to be—I would like to go into a comfortable, rather gay country inn for six weeks on end, like various writers who work frightfully hard all day and then come down into the bar, or the lounge, and talk with anybody who is around." What writer do you see doing that successfully but her? It is all adorable. Like her. I always wished I had a number of lives, so I could say to her, "Take this one and put it in your pocket and keep it." Instead of which, I had one life which seldom took me in her direction, even. I woke up this morning saying to myself, "Love is in the eye of the beholder." I'm not sure what it means, but at the time it seemed to account for a good deal, including out of sight, out of mind.

I don't think I told you (speaking of out of sight) that at the last minute

Kate decided to leave Bennington and go to CCNY. She wanted to study music in New York City. She has taken all her favorite books and records and a few clothes, and moved in with a schoolmate from Brearley, who was living with her parents (until they moved out) and her baby named Isadora, whom I think she found under a cabbage leaf in California, in a nice sunny apartment on Lexington Avenue at 94th. So coming home is a lot easier, and so is keeping in touch. So far she seems quite happy.

Brookie is in art school, The School of Visual Arts, on 23rd St. and also happy. I am driving Emmy back to the Art Students League, with whips and scolding, but so far to no avail.[48] Things have to be done (when haven't they?) and her brother is here, the one who lives in Athens. But next week, she says. I have finished a story and don't know whether it is what I meant it to be or not, and keep holding back from trying it on people, lest they wouldn't know either, and then where would I be? Anyway, it is odd. Which is something.

My love,
Bill

Eudora Welty, Chicago, to William Maxwell, October 31, 1973

Dearest Bill,

A joy to have your letter come just in time to cheer me on my way to Nebraska. I'm glad to know you're feeling incorrigible these days, because I'm sure as can be it's the only way we'd <u>better</u> feel, and I'm for it. This is a Chicago answer—I'm paying an old debt of a cancelled lecture—only reading to them, really, out of Losing Battles, & home tomorrow.

It will be grand to have dinner with you & Emmy—And I hope the 15th is still good—is it? I'm not free to attend the Institute dinner on the 14th either, as it's the night I'm down to give a talk, or reading, or something unsafe to define on "One Time, One Place" at the Museum of Modern Art. Think of being put on the program by them! You and Emmy are in fact invited (I have tickets to the talk for you just in case you're coming but I knew the Institute was a conflict) and Mr. John Szarkowski, who is putting it on, is having a few people in (somewhere!) afterwards. But if we could have our meeting on the 15th, whatever else transpires, that would be lovely. I'll

probably arrive at the hotel on the 13th—We'll be in touch—and how nice
& soon that will be.

I'll tell you all about Nebraska—& Emmy can tell me if she is liking
Willa Cather. I spent Sunday riding <u>all over</u> Nebraska on a finale-trip laid
on by the people there, & the Knopfs asked me to go along in the car with
them—That was fine—Helen and I talked about you & <u>Ancestors</u> for miles.
Alfred, at a luncheon in his honor, rose & gave an impromptu account
of his life as WC's publisher—you can imagine how good it was—and of
course he knows the things no one else on earth could—It clearly pleased
him & wore him out too—but I gather he's an indomitable gentleman—[49]

Thanks for the delicious Louise Bogan—

With love to you & Emmy & such looking forward to November—
Happy Hallowe'en! It's many a one, isn't it, I spent with the Maxwells?

<div align="right">Love, Eudora</div>

William Maxwell to Eudora Welty, [November 1973]

Dearest Eudora:

It is terribly good. I have always enjoyed her [Willa Cather's] books so
much I never put my mind to thinking about them, as you have done here,
and so I now see her differently. I never realized, before, that there is no
detail in her except the one telling detail, out of which the reader uncon-
sciously constructs all the rest. And the transparent style, that people speak
of, is also an illusion. It is no more transparent than Flaubert's, but highly
polished and certainly visible. The use she makes of the past, compared to
what Faulkner does with it—all that is so interesting. And do you remem-
ber when you couldn't flip the switch of the radio without hearing The New
World Symphony? It used to rank just under Beethoven. Emmy came upon
Steichen's picture of her last night and was dismayed; but that was because
Steichen was the wrong man to take her picture. Alfred [Knopf]'s brief movie
of her, with no sound track, but just her eye opening to a joke, was so differ-
ent. Steichen could never photograph the inside of an artist; only their fan
mail. And I keep searching and searching for a Dutch interior that has a win-
dow opening upon a view of masts or an expanse of water, and all I ever find
is a view of a street of houses or a canal, usually small, intimate, and narrow.

I think she has made it up. Out of her own misremembering. And the need to find a donkey to pin that particular tail on. The heart of your lecture and of the matter, surely, is what you say about the novels being concerned with the desire in one heart and soul to claim what is its own, etc. I cannot tell you how much pleasure this gave me, or how much it rounds out, finally, and I think forever, my understanding of her as a writer. For that particular thing you have to go to her. . . . Something happened, but what? Somebody called, I guess. Anyway, I've been in the attic, taking down Christmas ornaments, the card table, and so on. The electrician has been changing the kitchen light fixtures, and with the eye of my mind I suddenly saw what he would have done with the clothing bags that hang from a rod at the highest point of the eaves. There they were in a heap on the floor, just where I saw them being. Brookie is making a gingerbread—Next day: no, gingercake man, and only she could have got it out of the pan in one piece. Then the carpenter came to get his stepladder which he had forgot, and to return the key, and as luck would have it there was a leak (for it was raining like cats and dogs) in the living room ceiling by the fireplace. Then when we started to town the windshield wipers wouldn't work. Neither does the horn. Neither does the new icebox. Neither does something else, I forget what. But we went in the old Chevvy (1957) which has a hole in the back seat that Daisy fell through once, fortunately not when the car was moving. I put boards down, and E sat there admiring the road as it passed under the car. The reflections were so pretty, she said. Kate said she didn't want any things for Christmas, from which I deduce that she has now crossed over the line. She wants a drawing from Emmy and half a story from me. The other half next Christmas?

Thank you so much for sending the speech. It is a treasure.

My love,
Bill

William Maxwell to Eudora Welty, January 6, [1974]

Dearest Eudora:

I wrote this letter on the train, the day after Christmas, and it jiggled so I decided to copy it when I got to the office, only when I got to the office—I forget what happened. Anyway, we are now in the country again, and have

just reverted to daylight savings, and there is a beautiful snow on the ground
and more expected, so I keep one eye on the clock and one on the sky.
Speaking of which we saw Kahoutek over Madison Avenue on Friday night
and over the Blumbergs' barn last night. It looked like the evening star, and
not at all like the whisk broom I was expecting. Perhaps my eyes.[50]

I raced through the Forster epilogue, which was entirely new to me, and
then realized that enough time had elapsed for me to be able to reread (for
the third or fourth time) "A Room with a View." So I did. Oddly, the epi-
logue seemed to glue itself to the book. It's better, more finished, with it,
don't you think, though it couldn't have been written when the book was.
I do feel, though, that Lucy would have been happier if she'd married old
Mr. Emerson. But that bank of violets! I think that's what Greece was like in
the time of Pericles. Or a little earlier, perhaps. Speaking of missing rooms,
I lived from 1937–41 in a tiny apartment in Patchen Place, and not long ago
I went into the courtyard, just to have a look around, and found that noth-
ing looked right. It needed paint, and looked like a slum, which it certainly
didn't then; with Djuna Barnes on one side and ee cummings on the other,
how could it? Not to speak of Marion Cummings.[51] But my sense of scale
had changed, and I couldn't be sure any more even which entrance led to
my old apartment. I finally eliminated all those it couldn't have been and
walked to the top of the stairs and turned left: all wrong. Nothing was the
way I had remembered it. Was I ever there?

The view of London is what Pip saw when he rowed down the river to
that assignation with the convict. Beautiful but not Elysian. One senses the
coal smoke and the exploitation of the poor. It is a companion piece to a
scroll on spools that I got from Valentine Ackland a number of years ago.[52]
You wind your way from the countryside upstream through the center of
the city and out into the country again, about twenty years earlier. Where
on earth did you find it? Is Jackson, Miss, replacing Paris as the center of
civilization? Do you know a magician?

It is treasured by every member of the family, since we all read <u>Great
Expectations</u> together.

We had a lovely Christmas—mild weather, enough but not a morbid
superfluity of presents. And red ribbons around the neck of Daisy, Brookie
and Larry [Barth]. Crêpes for the vegetarian Christmas Eve dinner, so good

that nobody missed the turkey next day. And real candles on the Christmas tree, as usual. They always bring back the first time, when the sliding doors between the front and back parlor at my grandmother's house were rolled back and there it was, the silent glory.

It is so nice knowing that we are going to see you in six weeks.

E sends love, with mine,

Bill

Eudora Welty, Washington, D.C., to Emily and William Maxwell, February 7, 1974

Dearest Emmy and Bill,

The crabapple tree was coming out in flower, so were the daffodils in Jackson—and here I perch in a wool dress in Washington with my bathrobe on over it and a scarf tucked in—no, not to go out, just to write to you. (Here on an Arts Council session.) Forgive how long it's been. I was so happy to read what you both wrote me after you'd read my Willa Cather piece—your letters made me feel that everything I'd said or tried to say had rolled into place. (Am I thinking of billiards? I don't play.) Anyway, I felt the piece had got home, someway, after your reading it—your warm and generous words to me. I cut it for the Times and think probably I made it some better.—There's a picture book about Willa Cather—they got it out in Nebraska—but I'll tell you about that.

The beautiful Indian apple you sent me at Christmas I'm so used to having on my table by now that I actively miss it—and that's mighty late to be saying thank you. I do thank you, and do every time I pick it up. That's a lovely art. It's strange, but I have another piece of it—a small box—and while yours seems to have been discovered in a Greek shop, I believe the box came from Texas! (Neiman-Marcus)—It's like a fairy tale—enchanted apples & boxes mysteriously sent into the world to be discovered in widely separated places—if you know how. I love the apple above any example of it I could imagine. I also loved that wonderful tag with the insect on it—a fine announcer of a fairy treasure.

We have binders the size of the Manhattan Telephone Directory full of projects to go over—like Bottom-of-the-Bucket-But Black Street theatre

group—& voting money for everything, everything but Literature (my department. In fact, I'm the only one). You can see why we don't rate—We write by ourselves, and in the house, not on a stage or in a gallery or museum or street carnival, and it costs almost nothing. Nevertheless, writers need helping as well as anybody else—I try to think how—

After this, I go to Bryn Mawr for 2 days, then down to Hollins College (Roanoke, Va.) for 2 days, then back up again to N.Y.—to be there from the 16th till the 23rd. And there is the National Arts Club—and your Deed you're going to do for me.[53] How can I thank you—I didn't know they were going to ask such a thing of my friends—How good you everlastingly are—I'll telephone you when I come, in the hope that besides them, I might get you to come out and have dinner with me, some quiet place—

You're all well and fine, I hope. I saw in tonight's paper where Chuck Shattuck's Shakespeare is out—the Riverside [edition]—It'll be good to catch up on our news. Best love from Eudora

Eudora Welty, Burgundy, France, to Emily and William Maxwell,
June 24, 1974, Postcard with photograph of stone carving, Autun Cathedral

Dearest Emmy and Bill, you and your Guide Bleu brought me to Autun safely yesterday and how many times I thought of you in front of Gislebertus.[54] It was a mild day, softly raining, a Sunday, with music—choir & organ, Bach—As we were leaving, 2 family parties arrived with infants to be christened—the one in the longest dress cried the loudest—Outside, a parade of children with drum corps & home-made floats went by in the rain—Costumes of all countries—Mamas running alongside holding umbrellas, totally ignored—Vezelay tomorrow—Much love,

E.

William Maxwell to Eudora Welty, Paris, June 25, 1974

Dear Eudora:

I seem to remember that we were going to have a letter waiting for you at the Hotel des Sts. Pères, and Emmy may have written it without my know-

ing it, but if so she is a miracle, because we have had a week of solid social engagements followed by a week of houseguests, all very serene and happy, but no time for letter writing. It has also, during those fourteen days, rained forty days and forty nights. What satisfaction that used to give me when I was a child. Also, Kate and I have been to call on a whirling dirvish. He was visiting the next door neighbor in the country; and his entourage. The neighbor's son has been study[ing] at the University of Teheran, though that may well not be what it is called, and taken up with the Sufis. While he was learning to speak Persian. The dirvish was in his forties. I was summoned to meet him, and since Kate has also taken up with the Sufis, as you know, I said can I bring her, and was told I could bring anybody who wanted to come. Emmy wanted to come but only if she was invited. So Kate and I went. The dirvish was sitting in a chimney nook smoking a hookah. A quite big one. He speaks French (degree at the Sorbonne) and of course Pharsee [Farsi]. Neighbor's son was under the misapprehension that I spoke French like a native. Misapprehension having been corrected, he allowed his face to fall and relapsed into what appeared to be praying. There was I, set down three feet away from the dirvish, Kate on my far side, entourage consisting of five or six uncommunicative Persians whose gaze rested in the middle distance. Also a very small boy who was sitting on the lap of the other son [...] An escaped character from Losing Battles is what he is. It appears (though I didn't learn this from the dirvish, who smiled and laughed mysteriously but didn't ask that any of his remarks be translated for my benefit or in fact make any remarks) that Persian literature is crammed with works far greater than anything in English, and more profound than Dante. All untranslated, naturally. That most human beings are irredeemable. That there is no heaven in Sufi theology, but only man and his knowledge of or awareness of God. What else? Oh yes, that imagination is only the third highest order of thinking. I said beyond perception and imagination I didn't really care to go. And asked the translator to explain to the dirvish (because my remark was translated to him) that I had meant no offense. The dirvish smiled and said something in Pharsee, which took some time to say, and boiled down to the fact that he liked me very much. After which Kate, the darling, said, I think we should go now. I haven't been so far over my head socially

since we were in France in 1948. The compliment was ambiguous: he liked me because I was "fair" (fair?)[,] "honest," the translator corrected, about myself. He was a nice man; the dirvish, I mean. Very dark shining eyes. Also he chainsmoked. Which you wouldn't expect.* I didn't anyway. Terrible cough.

The rain has brought on enough roses for us and the rose bugs. Gruss an Aachen is just coming into bloom. Crimson Glory by the bushel. I am reading a book about Lord Byron called <u>Accounts Rendered</u>. It is a concentrated study of his bills, mostly unpaid, because of that dreadful solicitor who never answered letters and persuaded him to sell Newstead Abbey, which he swore he never would, when they were sitting on twelve miles of undeveloped coal mines, and from it I learned far more than I had from any other book on Byron, including the letters. Including the fact that his mother is much maligned. Anyway, it's all about money, who borrowed, who spent, who needed, who got it. In the absence of banks, everybody seems to have loaned money to everybody else, and ended up in the debtors prison because there wasn't enough to go around and nobody did anything for a living except loan money to people who couldn't pay it back because they had spent it. Riotously.

And there you are, living riotously, I hope, in Paris sixieme. Please take a walk for me on the Avenue de Varennes and look in all the courtyards, particularly the courtyard of Tallyrand's house. And pay a visit to the Cluny and the Carnavalet. And the Comédie-Francaise, and the Opéra, and every other bookstore you come to. And the Jardin de Palais Royal. Also the Luxembourg. And the Musee Guimet. And drink lots of coffee and eat lots of croissants.

We are waiting for you to return and tell us everything you ate and everywhere you went and everything that happened. This is only possible if we are the first person who sees you when you step from the plane. I know E would send love if she knew I was writing to you. She's drawing.

<div align="right">Love (oodles of)</div>

<div align="right">Bill</div>

*I mean I would have thought whirling would make cigarettes unnecessary. And unattractive.

William Maxwell to Eudora Welty, January 31, 1975

Dearest Eudora:

I don't give you much for the month of January. The first two and a half weeks I was in the jurors bullpen at 100 Centre Street, and then I had to catch up at the office and then I came down with a cold. Nothing you could talk about, just coughing and sneezing. I put my trousers on for the first time today, but I feel like my own shadow sitting at this typewriter. No crêpe paper crown and no WINGS to veil my face. How lovely that little book is. With lines going straight to much bigger books, that didn't then know they were ever going to get written. It is one of these meetings between an experience and an experiencer. And how noble the interior of the church is. The people are already known, and friends, but different in this different-shaped book. And Larry [Barth] has made me acutely aware of the charm and value of all hand-set typography and handmade paper. Not to mention #U of 26 copies lettered A–Z. This is something that is right now passing out of the world, if not forever for a good long time. It doesn't need to age to become a treasure.[55]

And thank you for remembering how much pleasure it gives me to read your uncut reviews. The quotations in this one are most particularly telling. "Never did I have the misfortune etc." first made me laugh and then made me hear the crackle of that [Elizabeth Bowen's] divine stammer. Your description of the opening chapter of the unfinished novel made me feel worse than reading the thing itself. Because if ever there was a book I wanted to settle down to and <u>read</u>, that was it. And you have caught it as beautifully as if you had aimed your WPA camera at it.[56] I have been trying to make myself read a book by someone named Robert Coles: Irony in the Mind's Life—can that be right? Ought I to go back and look? Anyway, it is about A Death in the Family, The Death of the Heart, and Middlemarch. And what it demonstrated to me is that people who can't write novels shouldn't write about them. But I liked equally what you had to say about the nativity play—have you ever written one? (Did I ever tell you that my earliest theatrical performance was as a daffodil, singing Pitter patter pitter patter on the window pane, Pitter patter pitter patter come the April rain, Robins sing

and bluebirds trill through the silvery hours, Pitter patter pitter patter Welcome, April showers…First grade.) It is also a model of how to write about someone one loved.

This has nothing to do with anything, but we went out to dinner the other night and were asked by the host, very tactfully, if we would mind autographing his copy of "The Ponder Heart." Emmy was stunned, but graciously obliged. What will posterity think? That we had lost our minds. If posterity knows how to read, and hasn't already lost its mind.

[…]

My love,
Bill

William Maxwell to Eudora Welty, February 11, 1975

Dearest Eudora:

There is something I want to send you if you don't have it—the references to Elizabeth [Bowen] that are in Charles Ritchie's War Diary. They add up to something I wouldn't have wanted to miss. The book itself was published in Canada and I found it somehow offputting, except in those passages, which indicate that, quite simply, she bewitched him. As she did everybody else.

Are you all right?

My love,
Bill

William Maxwell to Eudora Welty, February 1 and 2, 1976

Sunday morning
Dearest Eudora:

We are in the country and Emmy has just made garlic soup, because she has a gathering in her chest. Two whole flowers and very good it is, partly the Vegetarian Gourmet Cookbook and partly made up; you know. It cured my last cold in record time. I decided to have some too, though I'm the picture of health. It's good enough for a dinner party.

"Fairy Tale of the Natchez Trace" is a heavenly book. I don't know anything quite like it. I enjoyed it as much as "The Robber Bridegroom".[57] It was like being taken through somebody's house by them and shown what

was most worth noticing. And what quotations! And what a surprise. Because I had thought of it as a hallucinated story, and it turns out to have had its feet firmly on the ground. On one ground or another. Our Larry [Barth] has made me see all letter press books with a different eye, and this one is to be treasured. Some historical society, I say.

My new life agrees with me. And when I get the income tax figures off to the accountant, it will agree with me even more, for I shall have the afternoons to spend I don't yet know how. Your new editor is a Welshman named Derek Morgan. Unless you finish a story before you next come here and can let that stand as introducer, I will introduce you to him. And we are taking three vacations—one in March, a trip down the Nile on a Swan boat.[58] Wellfleet in July. And Wyoming in August. The colt kicking up his heels in the pasture. What I cannot quite believe, what comes over me as a form of absolute bliss, is that I shall never have to reject another manuscript as long as I live. It was the one thing I could never learn to bear, though I suppose the only alternative would very quickly have become unbearable too. Do you think it would be possible to publish a magazine first come first serve? You would like it, for one, because you like to read. And it would be every bit as interesting as the label on the ketchup bottle.

Emmy's painting is going well. Come soon.

Devotedly,
Bill

P.S. The next day. E was privately coming down with the flu, and is now in bed. Kate and two Sufis are here, unable to leave for Unadilla[59] as they had planned because there was a blizzard in the night, and the Thruway is closed all the way to Rochester. We 6-1212 says that it is forty below in New York City owing to the wind factor.[60] They have just discovered the wind factor. Anyway, nobody feels like going outdoors. The windows banged and rattled all night long. Did you grow up reading The Hollow Tree Snowed In Book?[61]

William Maxwell to Eudora Welty, March 20, 1976

Dearest Eudora:

In the midst of packing and mailing off income tax returns I had to stop

and allay the fear that you might come to New York and call us and not get any answer. We are off to London tomorrow morning to take, from there, a Swan's tour down the Nile from Assuan [Aswan] to Cairo, for two and a half weeks, and then about ten days more in London and a week in Amsterdam, looking at Rembrandts and Vermeers, windmills and (with luck) tulips and daffodils. With more luck, you will come to New York just after we get back, the last week in April, and then we can tell you every last thing that hasn't yet happened to us.

<div align="right">With love from us both,
Bill</div>

PS Emmy had the flu and has been over it a month but still runs out of steam constantly and doesn't feel like herself. I am counting on the hot climate (coldest winter in Egypt since Hatshetsup, if that's how you spell her).

William Maxwell, Cruising on the Nile, to Eudora Welty, [March 1976],
Postcard with image of mural in the tomb of Nakht

Dearest Eudora —

I think of "Life on the Mississippi" because there are no markings and when darkness falls we tie up at some mileage and wait for sunrise. Occasionally we get stuck on a sandbar. There is always something or somebody to look at. I feel I am in the land of Sunday School cards.

<div align="right">Love from us both
B.</div>

Emily Maxwell, London, to Eudora Welty, April 12, 1976,
Postcard with image of Randolphe Toepffer's Mr. Pencil, 1830

Dearest Eudora, I found this in the Tate, after my second visit to the Constable show, & it seem printed entirely for you. The Constable was wonderful — chronologically arranged, many pencil sketchbooks — some about 3 x 5 & those sometimes with 2 landscape pictures per page! The loveliest were the watercolors and pencil sketches. Toward the end of his life Constable said of Turner, "he paints like tinted steam". The Nile trip was so condensed & concentrated that it will take years to recollect it in tranquility. Every-

one had bronchial flu and dysentery, which made for a degree of suspense. Poor Bill is just recovering from a bad bronchitis—which spoiled the last of the Nile & the first few days in London—but his eyes are bright again—& we have tickets for [Ibsen's] "John Gabriel Borkman" on Wednesday. The hyacinths & primroses & camellias & daffodils are in bloom! Much love, Emmy

William Maxwell, London, to Eudora Welty, April 20, 1976,
Postcard with image of J. M. W. Turner's Hastings

Dearest Eudora—Our last ¾ of an hour in London—I could not shake off a bronchial cough and so we are going home instead of to Amsterdam. But we have had such a happy time in London, with Harriet Sheehy and E's brother Humphrey. The weather like Rupert Brooke's poem. And all the squares full of flowering trees and daffodils. There were five huge rooms full of Turners at the Tate, a big Constable show, and the original drawings for <u>The Tailor of Gloucester</u>—which drove me half out of my mind with pleasure—

<div align="right">Love from us both,
Bill</div>

William Maxwell to Eudora Welty, April 23, 1976

Dearest Eudora:

Emmy told me this morning about your calling back. The first call was a poor connection and it was like conversing from one cloud to another, but the last thing in the world I would have wanted was for you to be distressed by anything either of us said. In the first place you can say <u>anything</u>, and I would always know, we both would always know that it comes from love. As for my leaving the New Yorker, I didn't just turn my back on that job which I had loved passionately for forty years, I got ready to leave it by degrees, and not by letting go of my writers but by training those two gifted young men in so close and open and (so far as my feelings were concerned) exposed a fashion that I hoped whatever virtues I had accumulated as an editor would simply pass into them. More than seems reasonable, this is what

actually happened. I rejoice from 544 E. 86th Street, that you have finished a story, and I know that when it arrives at the New Yorker office there will be a similar rejoicing. Updike said, speaking of my leaving, it doesn't matter who I have for my new editor because any strictures they have about my work will be nowhere like as severe as my own are. The same thing is true of you. Will you bring a copy of the story for us to read when you come?

As for what I am writing, I have four beginning pages that are so nearly right I am afraid to talk about it: if you have a part that is right, I tell myself, then all that is necessary is to match the rest to it. I guess what I really want to say is that my turning wholly to writing brings us closer together, as being engrossed in the same occupation always does people. Think of the old women making quilts together every Wednesday in the tower of my grandmother's Christian Church. That's you and me.

<div style="text-align: right">Devotedly,
Bill</div>

William Maxwell, Wellfleet, Massachusetts, to Eudora Welty,
July 19, 1976, Postcard with photograph of boy flying kite on beach

Dearest Eudora—I hurry to tell you that nobody caught your germ. And that I am so happy you liked that story.[62] It was originally written as a birthday present for Em—and in that version you read the MS of The Ponder Heart to us. But that was for private consumption. I swam three-quarters of the way across a fairly large pond this morning before breakfast, so you don't need to worry about my health any more. Or Em's. Brookie is here, as happy as I've ever seen her. And we are in Wellfleet, just as you hoped.

<div style="text-align: right">Devotedly, Bill</div>

Eudora Welty to Emily Maxwell, August 26, 1976, Note card with vintage
advertisement for Atchison, Topeka and Santa Fe Railroad glued to card

Dearest Emmy, I made you this postcard to thank you for yours. How could you have gone wrong in sending the salt from the Great Salt Lake to me? I was delighted to have it—I bet it's exactly a tsp full, don't you? The stitching held. It's cheering too that the P.O. was willing to send it—a friend once

was refused when she tried to mail me a postcard from Paris that was en-crusted with sequins: "It would scratch the rest of the mail." Yours might have salted the rest of the mail. The paste under this is fighting my ball point pen. Your Portland trip sounds lovely—telescoped though the jour-ney home was. When I used to go up to N.Y. on the train in early Spring, I'd look out the window and watch the flowering of the trees folding right up, like a Japanese fan. I was so happy to know (on <u>Bill</u>'s postcard—a kite) that in the private version of that wonderful story I was in it, reading the Ponder Heart to him and you! Best love to both, Eudora

Eudora Welty, Boston, to Emily and William Maxwell,
[Late September or Early October 1976]

Dearest Emmy and Bill,

What a joy to know you'd both come out to see the Robber B. open! But it can't be on the 6th—it was postponed just now till the 12th (I think), because (at a preview or rehearsal) the Robber himself, swinging out on a rope, had it to break and pitch him 12 feet down to the stage, he's suffer-ing from "multiple hairline fractures"—I'd heard of the accident just be-fore leaving home, but at that time they said the show must go on etc. But Tim Seldes just called me (Friday night, I'm in Boston) to say it's off for the 6th.[63] However, I'm coming on down to New York from Northampton as planned on the 5th, and by then maybe more will be known of their plans—But now I have to un-invite my friends—and my sister-in-law [Mit-tie Welty] in Jackson—

But I'd love to come out on <u>either</u> the Thursday or the Friday, and we can talk then—After I get in on Tuesday, I'll call and see what suits you best. Lovely.

Brookie's line drawings for <u>Cue</u> are so full of life and her sense of design, and her detail—all those little feet under a table—made me feel sure it had started in that beautiful little house you had made, Bill. I'm so delighted to have these to look at—Thank you so much for saving them for me, Emmy.

And the Rose Stamps! So lovely they make you wonder how stamps could ever have anything but roses on them. Rosa Mundi! All of them—and their coming by way of the Nile, really—I cherish them—

And if I knew how to thank you for the butterfly hunt—What a marvelous account and so absolutely to be believed. At the same time it's almost like—isn't it?—an Edward Lear poem, one of those he wrote in the Tennyson meter. Every iota of proof of butterfly identity hanging on a little tag on a single wing of a butterfly a thousand miles from home. Only I guess then it was <u>home</u>.

I'm going to mail this when I can. This is out in the Chestnut Hill section of Newton, wherever that is. The taxi driver (a girl) who brought me from Logan airport had a CB radio to go by—"Come on, Snowshoes—Come on, Snowshoes—What do I do now?" Took her 1¼ hours to find it.

I'm so sorry about Wednesday—but I'm so glad to be <u>sure</u> of seeing <u>you</u>. With much love,

Eudora

There are no extant Welty or Maxwell letters between early October 1976 and late February 1977. During this time, Eudora published a review of The Letters of Virginia Woolf, *volume 2, but if Bill offered a comment on her review, that letter is missing. So, too, is a response from Eudora to Bill's July 18, 1977, review of the same book. The two friends reacted quite differently to Woolf's correspondence and perhaps chose not to voice that disagreement in writing, though months in advance of Bill's review, Eudora seemed to express pleasure that they both "liked" Woolf's letters.*

William Maxwell to Eudora Welty, February 20, 1977

Dearest Eudora:

It is presumptuous of me to ask, but how <u>can</u> you be "broke" with that musical running on Broadway? Every time I see the ad I think cheerfully Money in Eudora's pocket, and now it seems I am mistaken. Hasn't that incompetent young man ever got that contract straightened out? I start to get wild and then I think if what I think is true is true then Lehman Engel is already wilder than I could possibly get, being in the trade. Do send me a postcard saying—well I guess there is no good in your saying what I would

like to hear if it isn't true, but saying something. Otherwise I will lie awake at night grinding my teeth.

Love,
Bill

Eudora Welty to William and Emily Maxwell, February 21, 1977

Dearest Bill and Emmy,

Your calling up made me so happy, hearing your voices and learning some of your news. I'd been living in such contriteness about you and the letter I've been wanting to write and haven't written, but I took a leap right out of that and basked in the pleasure of present conversation. Thank you for calling up—I had the feeling of being back in your living room, and could see the snow falling as you told me, and the fire burning as I added to it while listening.

I'm glad you're well and the girls are, and that Kate is out of Turkey. It seemed to me everywhere I read anything about Turkey it was telling how freezing cold it was, there too. If it isn't being disrespectful, I thought well at least dervishes know how to keep warm, and Kate would have learned— Once I got out a magnifying glass to see if a tiny signature on a very nice line drawing in some magazine said "Brookie"—no, but I hope I don't miss one when it appears.

I'm all right—did have something like flu right at Christmas, but that didn't last. Before I go any further, I do want to correct a wrong impression I may have given on the phone when I said I wouldn't be coming to New York because I was too broke. This meant only that I'd be too broke <u>in New York</u>—I'm perfectly all right here at home—nothing to worry about. I made little or no money from my books this last year and have finished no new work yet, and that little play very properly didn't pay much money to me, ever, then folded. But I can always accept a lecture date when I want to, so I've been doing them here and there, which serves the purpose. There are the most still to go, and the writing work is bountifully upon me, so I'm feeling lucky, not unlucky.

Just the touch of this papyrus is so astonishing and mysterious, it's almost like receiving a little shock. To <u>think</u>. (I do.) It's almost lighter than air.

I haven't put <u>anything</u> on it, don't know when I can. I did put a flower on it <u>without</u> a vase—the open, soft, single flower of a camellia out of the yard— Bernice Bodey by name. It's a true color match for the Egyptian handkerchief you sent, and is also weightless. It is impossible to conceive how it was transmitted into cloth—that color pink—isn't it? Thank you for beautiful things, and the box they came in, which has Greek (?) writing on it. And for the dear letter, and the Beatrix Potter pen and watercolor from the Tate— "No More Twist", is that the needlework design in it? It sounds like a term from the vocabulary of Peter Rabbit, no, Mrs. Tittlemouse. I'm glad you liked the letters. Me too.[64]

Bill, I've been thinking about the possibility of doing something as you think I might about Elizabeth [Bowen]. And put a few notes down. I'm not too sure I can do anything that would be right enough, in your eyes, or mine, or God knows Elizabeth's. <u>She</u> did such a thing once, for Virginia Woolf, you remember, so she wouldn't have hated this idea <u>necessarily</u>. I've felt the abominations of what people have been doing to other people's lives after they're dead, so strongly, they have gotten worse and worse, haven't they?—that I just didn't trust, on sight and knowing nothing about her, the letter I received from perhaps this same biographer. (I'll start a hunt for it, and if I find will send you to see if it is the same.) (I am now in the throes of hunting records for the IRS, now auditing me yet again for my evidently peculiar income, it goes up and down.) I don't have to feel anything but happy on Elizabeth's account to think of the words you would write, and their value. This will have to wait a little while, I guess, on my part. I would like to send whatever it is to you first.

I was absolutely knocked flat by "The Duel", when I began reading Chekhov again all in a great feast and spread. Of course there isn't anything I could possibly say about him that is new, I only hope and aim to make it good, if the stories themselves give me the power. I go to Cornell to give it as a lecture in May (5th).[65] Would it be possible for me to see you on the way back if I stopped over a day or two in NY? (By that time I'll be ahead on funds.) The story I'm on, or novel—it's the shape that is defying me— is going speedily and sometimes in circles, somewhat like a philodendron. Someday I hope to send it to you for a true look.[66] I hope your work is going well, Bill. I wait.

Our own weather gives us anything on hand at the moment—6°, 72° (today), rain, ice, snow, and yet the camellias, who'd had their faces right down on the ground under the load of ice, are standing up and full of fresh open flowers now. When I see them I wish I could get them to you. Emmy, remember when you brought me (to the hotel in NY) an armload of camellia branches with leaves and buds all over them, just as <u>greens</u>—I'll never forget how lavish, and how in the vase the flowers began to open, though never expected to by anybody but your loving friend.

I hope everything goes well every day with you and you keep warm and well and thinking of something wonderful—a new story, or new place to be visited next time—or they don't have to be new. I'm glad of what you said, that we're always in touch, because I believe it. This means the earth doesn't open up under the feet. Much love to you from Eudora

William Maxwell to Eudora Welty, March 3, 1977

Dearest Eudora:

Is it possible that you have never read Beatrix Potter's <u>The Tailor of Gloucester</u> (which is where the expression "No more twist" comes from, and Emmy's card is one of the illustrations from it. They are hanging in the coatroom of the Tate)? Because that would mean I could give myself the pleasure of sending you a copy. Remember to tell me when you come.

And how like the IRS to audit you, of all people. And there is a new production of <u>The Cherry Orchard</u> that makes my hair curl to read about. As at Chichester, Firs is shut up and forgotten in a no-house.[67] But there are worse things. I have written your name across May 6, 7, 8, 9, and 10, just in case. When you know when you are really coming just send us a postcard of the night you'd like to be with us. I wish we could be at Cornell for the lecture. And before I forget it, if you ever should find yourself up against the wall—financially, that is, more going out than is coming in, or less coming in than is supposed to go out, will you kindly remember that, thanks to Emmy's father, we have more money than we quite need, and helping you would be a piece of great good fortune. I've been doing tax figures for the accountant and sometimes it makes me verging on hysterical, because I

can't find things, but this time I have been enjoying the fact that I can add and divide and multiply. If you had to invent a game could you invent a better one?

I am reading the bound galleys of a life of Turgenev by Pritchett and am confused because when I read Turgenev I mostly love him, but sometimes what other people write about him makes him boring, and sometimes (in the <u>Literary Reminiscences</u>) he is boring his ownself. Maybe if those minor Russian literary figures weren't merely names, but no, it is more than that. I thought I liked him more than Tolstoy, and I guess still do, but Chekhov is the one I really love. I guess it's my fault, and that I don't like ideas. As such. And, maddeningly, we seem to have all the novels and hardly any of the stories except the Sportsman's Notebook and First Love. We have three different translations of that. But I liked this: "From what one knows of Turgenev's father, the retired soldier who was both superstitious and a sportsman, he would have counted the magpies for luck and studied the edges of the woodlands for the first sight of snipe and woodcock and kept his eye open for pretty women. His wife would be watching the women working with long rakes in the fields, alert to see if any of her serfs were idle. For Varvara Petrovna her vast estate was a kingdom in itself; she owned all its villages and every person in them, every horse, cow, pig, goose, even the nightingales that sang in the trees."

I rejoice in the idea of your story that goes speedily and sometimes in circles. Just what I have always wanted to read, it sounds like. And day after tomorrow, with any luck, I will plunge back into my own.[68]

<div align="right">

With love from both of us,

Bill

</div>

After more reading I have come to the conclusion that I don't have the intellectual apparatus to deal with a book like Pritchett's, and that he probably does have it but is so driven by having to support himself by writing in an inflationary period that he doesn't give either the personality of the people he is writing about or the ideas that are an inescapable part of the historical period their just due. And also not knowing Russian. I mean suppose Francis Steegmuller had written about Flaubert and Madame Bovary without knowing French.

Anyway, I don't think I'll do it.

William Maxwell to Eudora Welty, New York City, [May 6], 1977

Dearest Eudora:

We were wakened in the middle of Wednesday night by a call from E's father: her mother had been taken to the hospital with they thought pancreitis, and it was serious. E left on the eleven o'clock plane the next morning and her mother died before she got there. I am going out Saturday morning, so we can't have that lovely Sunday night supper we were expecting to have. But there is more. Emmy was possessed that you see Lily Tomlin, who has the whole town talking about her, and is a kind of latter day Ruth Draper, but any way <u>terribly</u> funny, and through strings pulled this way and that managed to get two (possibly three) tickets for Monday night.[69] If you have an engagement that night that you can't break I will cover my head with my toga. I am going down now to see if I can pick up the tickets and leave them at the Algonquin. If they aren't in this envelope then you will have to get them at the box office. Under the name of Welty (it was your name that worked the miracle) and you are to let us pay for them or I will put my head even farther into my toga and perhaps never draw it out. I will probably be back at the end of next week, Emmy I don't know when, but we are both so sad at missing you.

My love,
Bill

Well they weren't at the box office yet. Monday, the man said, when I said they were probably house seats. Maybe if you call up Monday noon they would tell you how many seats are being reserved in your name. More likely 2. I hate to leave all this uncertainty in your lap.

Eudora Welty, New York City, to William Maxwell, May 11, 1977

Dearest Bill,

I'm so grieved for Emmy, and how hard it was on her, the long, sudden flight out and getting there to learn the news—I'm glad you went right behind her, and hope everything went as gently as it could. I looked for what kind of day it was out there and gathered it was raining. Anyway, I think of you both and wish there were something I could do—

To think that in the middle of all her distress & haste Emmy had thought of an evening for me, and that she & you took all that trouble about the tickets—Of course I was your charmed guest at Lily Tomlin—The tickets were there, and three in number, and you must have been psychic about the odd third, because Monday was the night the Kahn sisters[70] had invited me to dinner, so I took them—a theatre party. I'd read much about Miss Tomlin and fell for her talent, which is clearly bountiful & young & variegated (sounds like a plant for the garden)—Her presence is wonderful, and the quality of vulnerability which I suspected was the most deciding in her make-up made me admire her work a great deal. The audience that night was loud & obtuse it seemed to me, finding every act the same, cheering and going into gales every time they recognized anything—I wondered if it didn't bother her. The organist was my favorite—but we can all talk about her when next we meet. It would have been lovely to see her <u>with</u> you & Emmy—I could imagine that. Thank you both for now—& for thinking of it—

It was lovely at Cornell, where I was for 2 nights—It was pear-blossom, redbud, & tulip time in Ithaca—Everybody was a delight to meet that had anything to do with Chekhov. James McConkey, who I understand has published a short story in the <u>New Yorker</u> and is down for publishing another, and who has written a book on E. M. Forster (none of which I had come upon), is a fine and very sympathetic and interesting man—[71] He and his wife are your devoted readers of years' standing, and I feel you'd like their company as much as I did. Think of his idea of a Chekhov celebration: no centennial or reason to do anything, no group gathered, no professors or seminars, he simply invited 4 fiction & poetry writers—John Cheever, Howard Moss, Walker Percy—oh, and [Harold] Brodkey—and myself to come at some date convenient, by ourselves, and talk on any aspect of Chekhov we liked. A man who thought of it like that you're bound to approve of! and like. I intended to leave you a Xerox of my paper, but kept on writing it & messing it up after I started with it from home, so will copy it over first—

I'm having a nice couple of days—I miss you & Emmy, and think of you a lot—You know I send my love. Will write you a letter soon. From here I go to Atlanta, then Washington—

My dear love to Emmy—I'll write to her to New York, since I don't

know the Portland address, so you can give her my love for now. And much to you, I missed seeing the galleys and Brookie's jacket design![72] Eudora

William Maxwell, to Eudora Welty, September 17, [1977]

Dearest Eudora:

What a queer time summer is. So much about on foot and on horseback. And then September brings the first cold nights and suddenly you have the use of your mind again. The first use I want to put mine to is to tell you how much I like the Chekhov essay.[73] I think it is the best of all your essays, and what occurred to me to wonder is if the people who heard you read it forgot to breathe sometimes. I think also that it is the best thing I ever read on him. When you analyze one of his stories there is a faint double exposure: I see you seeing him. And it is doubly moving. When I finished I realized it was silly to feel guilty because one doesn't write as well as or in the least like him. Obviously it is what writing ought to be, but unless you are Chekhov you can't write like that. And there was only that one Chekhov. One might as well put aside one's typewriter and try to become a saint, but one doesn't become a saint (I believe) by trying, and the writer who puts aside his typewriter is lost, in any case. How you do bring out the beauties in him, though. What story is the Privy Counselor in? And what story is the one about the young man who was kissed in the dark? And is Granny chasing the police inspector who took the samovar in The Steppe? Which I read a long time ago and only partly remember. And the old man who danced at his son's wedding, what story is that in? And the little dog being trained for a music hall act, is that Valenka? There is something wrong with the sentence "No life is too brief or too inconsequential for him to be inattentive to its own reality." I think. For years I didn't know that in Constance Garnett, right next to Gooseberries, there was a companion story to it called About Love.[74] Bill Meredith told me. What would one do without friends.

Brookie and Emmy and I all love the moving picture book.[75] At first I couldn't make the fountains flow. Emmy had to do it for me. Page 25 surely makes up for the deficiency of page 13. I didn't realize until just now that the one on the back works too. When I was a child my father, being a fire insurance man, received a copy of a book with colored illustrations

of catastrophic fires—Troy, Ninevah, Chicago, etc. I found them again when I grew up, many of them being large canvases by a painter named Martin. Everything had a sweep and dazzle that was operatic raised to the nth degree. When I couldn't think what to do I would go and get it out of the bookcase and look at Aeneas helping his old father escape from the holocaust.

We had such a happy time in Wyoming. It is about 7,000 feet above sea level and full of rushing creeks and panoramic views, and sometimes the horses' hoofs stir up the odor of sage. Emmy slept out doors a couple of nights to watch the falling stars. Then we went on to Portland to visit her father, who is 91 and very much in control of himself and his life.

It gets dark now at quarter after seven, which it must not do yet in Mississippi. Emmy is trying the [Art Students] League both morning and afternoon, which may be too much for her but I hope not. Too much in the sense of what to do about all the other irons in the fire. The September roses, and especially Crimson Glory, are enormous. You'd think they were cousins of that dreary Peace. And there is a solid wall of morning glories on the west side of the vegetable garden fence. In the history of the world there has never been quite such a good vegetable garden as ours this year.

The books ("Over by the River") didn't arrive before we went to Wyoming, and I didn't want you to get your copy after publication day and the reviews, if any, so I asked Judith Jones at Knopf to send you a copy. Fourth class mail being what it is, I would be surprised if you had got it even by this time.[76]

My love—
Bill

Eudora Welty to Emily and William Maxwell, September 27, 1977

Dearest Emmy and Bill,

Your letters are cherished and made me so happy, both—Your summer sounded so benevolent & restoring—How healthy you both must be looking, so fresh from Wyoming and Portland—And the new book is out—and no, I haven't seen it yet but look each day for the Knopf sticker—Also I send you thanks each day that you liked my Chekhov piece—I so much

had hoped it would seem right to you, it seemed a necessity to me that you should like it—and if not I knew there wasn't a thing I could do about it, only mourn my hopes—Anyway, thank both of you for writing what you did. That sentence in there. Isn't it a mercy you put it in front of my eyes when you did, I can straighten it out in time. And you'll love the answers to your questions about which story—The story the Privy Counselor's in is "The Privy Counselor"[77]—and the story about the young man who was kissed in the dark is "The Kiss"—The little dog in the music hall act is "Kashtanka"—More later, but I want to try & find you a copy of the Viking Portable Chekhov, which has all of them and many others of the finest—it seems to have gone out of print but I got one & will try at the same place—But before I go any further let me ask you—this is really in haste—if by some miracle you are free on either Monday or Tuesday evening, Oct. 10 & 11? I'll be in NY—it would <u>take</u> a miracle, in October, to find you free, I guess. I'll be reading at Yale beforehand and stopping at the Warren's (Red & Eleanor) on the way down[78]—and in NY must do a day's chore at Random House—And Emmy, you'll be at the League—Never mind, I shall hope. We'll be talking to each other of course. I might reach you by phone before I leave here—which is before break of day on Oct. 6, (<u>Leaving</u> then, not calling then!)

I want to hear about being 7000 feet up in Wyoming and all the other elements of your trip, if elements is the comprising word. How lovely for your father, Emmy, and for you both that you were there. I always think of you riding your horse in the same place—and at the same hour (early morning) you described. I loved the postcard from the airport. Not only the knee-pants were different then, but the dogs were different! I long to see you and send love for now and for then, rushing ahead in my thoughts—Take care, & love to the girls too—Eudora

William Maxwell to Eudora Welty, December 29, 1977

Dearest Eudora:

What a most beautiful book.[79] The Book of Kells is the only one I knew before. I knew there were others but they weren't very real to me till now. In some ways I think it is the strangest book I have ever looked at. There

is never anything representational or at least not very, and yet it all comes through—the Crucifixion from the Durham Gospel Fragment II is agony itself, those symbolic animals are real, St. Mathew without any arms is even more St. Mathew than if he had them, St. Luke with a small calf resting on his halo is clearly the patron saint of vaudeville magicians, but how he got in and out of that robe I will never know. It is all beautiful, and all interesting. I feel looking at it as if I had passed through a door in a wall and come on some different shore of time. It is a treasure that I would love to pore over with you. And would you by any chance know where Saint John in the Book of Mulling got his slippers? They are just what I have been searching for, in Gimbels, and elsewhere.

Em went to town this morning, to attend a housewarming of friends, and I am stuck here in the country because the only time I could take the car to be looked at (it suddenly uses twice as much gas as before and I don't want to make the Arabs any richer than they already are) was 8 o'clock tomorrow morning, in Mt. Kisco. But after that I am going to town to join her, and have dinner with Robert Fitzgerald, who is down from Cambridge, and then we will drive back here on Friday, for New Year's. It has been extremely cold, down around zero at night, and squares of moonlight lying on the beds in darkened rooms, making me think of poor Chatterton;[80] but no snow. Should I confine my wild behavior to riding horseback in Wyoming, and leave ice skating to others, is the question. The silence in the house is deafening, but Em left me one of her best soups, and some short ribs of beef to heat up in the oven when the potatoes are nearly baked, and I will get through the evening somehow, but I must say it is no way to live.

Kate is home for a while, and apparently happy to be here. And Christmas was especially nice because of that. And Brookie meant to embroider Buffalo Bill on the lapels of a new bathrobe for me but being lefthanded it came out Bill Buffalo, which I like even better. Emmy quilted and had made into a pillow a square of the Swedish linen the curtains in my story were made of, and what with one thing and another we are so old fashioned that we might as well be living in the Little House in the Woods. Please find some excuse to come to New York early in the New Year and oblige your devoted

Bill

Eudora Welty to Emily and William Maxwell, February 15, 1978

My father's birthday. He'd have been 99.

Deazrest Emmy and Bill,

This is the first time this typewriter has written "dearest" or even "dear" and so even if it threw in a "z" I aim to send it to you. I just traded in my big Royal standard for this <u>electric Smith-Corona</u>, and pulled up my chair to write to you.[81] Much love, to start with. I've thought of you day after day, not writing but never feeling we were far apart. You've had such a terribly cold winter already, and I am frequently wondering which house you have been snowed in in, wondering which is more to be hoped for, the beautiful icy country where the power can go off, or the city where I can imagine the river out your window white and icy too (the way I can remember the Hudson when it froze over in the '30's) but I assume the building is kept warm, but I see on the National Newscazst people walking against the wind in the sleet, weaving and looking lost. Just so you are well, and nothing bronchial makes any least threast on your heads. (I do not see the key that allows me to backspaced.) Tell me if Kate is with you still. I was overjoyed to think of her there, most especially when the deep snows came to New York State and I felt that retreat would have been snowed in to the hilt. I would love to know her news, and to hear what she had decided on to do next. I hear from Joan Kahn that Brookie has done the most beautiful book jacket ever seen at Harper's for Suzanne Prou's new novel.[82]

Bill, Over Byh the Riverf (I feel that the typewriter is trying to tell me something. But it will have to learn that I was telling it something first, or rather telling yhou something. It could be that its when I slow down to think that it rushes in.) stays on my bedside table and I read in it at good times and it has become taken for granted there so that sometimes I see it anew and exclaim to myself "Bill's book!" It keeps its wonder either way. You already know how I love the stories one by one, and it is a second experience to have them in companionship with one another. All grow still deeper—the sense of the personal never leaving them, only illuminating every story in some way to do with its truth. When I try to think how to tell you, the typewriter makes a sound like the one you hear in your cabin on shipboard sailing at night. Or maybe any diesel. It says go ahead. I still love

"Over by the River" and "The Thistles in Sweden" more than any of them, but this isn't to say I don't value and feel the force of their differences—they are what make the new experience of the whole, for one thing. I can't tjknk of a Christmas present more beautiful than the pillow Emmy quilted from a square of that Swedish linen. You will be so grand wearing the bathrobe Brookie embroidered Bill Buffalo and the Swedish pillow at your head, or would it be your elbow, where you can enjoy it both ways—one as to the eyes (remember the Grreek accusative of specification? Dido was weeping as to the eyes.)

Joseph Cornell is beautiful to have all together in his own way too. I am so glad you sent me this book, which I did not know existed.[83] He is a part of my early years in New York, as I suspect he was of yours too—and there is something of magic-not-lost about his work that touches the heart as well as the imagination, don't you feel too? If we were all cooks, we would be often using the same ingredients. The most hypnotic ones to me are those with the constellations, and the globes, the mysteriousness of space present in a box. For myself, I always loved boxes and never found anything claustro-phobic about them, only the sense of something that will hold treasure, not in a miser's sense of holding it but a believer's. I love the Soap Bubble Set one of the Lunar Space Objects as well as anything in the book. And The Forgotten Game (the birds) and the Medici Slot Machine. I once heard Jack Baur (do you know him? He was at the Russells' often) tell about his visits to Cornell, I believe in connection with the Whitney show of 1962? and how much he came under his (Cornell the man's) spell.[84] One of the strangest things: a long time ago, I suppose it was late in the thirties, I had a letter in the form of a collage come to me from Joseph Cornell—this seems hard to believe, but when I find it I will send it to you to join in my astonish-ment (which no one else ever did). It had some written words but I have for-gotten them all—what I can see now is the pasted-on figure of a man in ro-mantic costume coming out of a brick chimney, along with a LOT of sparks and smoke, such as comes out of a steam locomotive—and walking out into the sky. I can think of only one connection between Joseph Cornell and a beginning writer in Mississippi—Charles Henri Ford. At about this time Charles Henri was editing a little magazine in Columbus (the Depression) and I believe I sent him a contribution—forget now. Or maybe it was when

View was being published.[85] I remember feeling awfully shy over this visitation and I wonder how a recluse like Cornell ever got it mailed? I was probably so far away and remote to him that it was all safely surreal? Of course it is somewhere. I'll keep looking.[86] It could very well have been put away in a box (underlined). In the book Cornell is quoted as saying "Everything czn be used—but of course one doesn't know it at the time. How does one know what a certain object will tell another?" You see how your present has been acting and acting on my inner life. Thank you for it.

I'm so glad you like the Celtic book—so do I. Yes, I have one too—I sent you the first one and ordered it again for myself. I would love to talk about both these books when we are all next in the same room again. (I'm still doing too many trips and readings, but I have finally had the sense to take the advice you paged me to tell me over the phone one morning at the Algonquin, and resigned from the Council on the Arts. I knew it needed to be done—in fact tried to once, but N. Hanks prevailed on me to stay.[87] Maybe I can get up for some time in May, but that is far ahead. Meantime I did get the non-fictiom book turned in and it will be oujt in late Apil I think. I called it after the essay on KAP [Katherine Anne Porter], "The Eye of the Story." The reason I'm so late writing is just the travelling about to Ann Arbor, Sewanee, Atlanta, Columbus, O., etc. etc. which I need to do to get some time purchased, and shall be keeping on at a lesser rate during the spring. Then quitting I hope for good and all, so as to use this time. better,.

I am going to copy a poem (again byh Seamurs Heany, Emmy) to send you but I need to type better for Seamus Heaney. My dearest love to you. I hope all your news is good. I think of you and Kate and Brookie—I hope the classes are going beautifully, Emmy—So much more to say! Next time— Yours always, E

This bears a strong resemblance to the way words come out in my galleys— Is Knopf any better than Random?

Eudora Welty to Emily and William Maxwell, March 1, 1978

Dearest Emmy and Bill, This is a little oddity which came of a student publication of the University of Montpelier in France that is got out as a labor of love for Southern writing in the U.S.A. An Englishman writing on their

behalf (from U. of Sussex) had seen this little item in a bunch of unpublished stuff in the local Archives & asked if <u>Delta</u> could publish it in the issue they got out on me. Must have been written about 1936 or so and it was 100% rejected, so now here it appears.[88] It's everything a young writer does to begin, I guess, though I don't know if you did, Bill—I feel you knew better where your bearings were. Everything in this story was an unknown quantity to me—Europeans, acrobats, incest, etc, the Catholic church,—everything except Smith Park, in Jackson.—And the family—Anyway, they sent me a few offprints of the story—the magazine not yet. Love, E.

William Maxwell to Eudora Welty, March 14, 1978

Dearest Eudora:

The reason that story ["Acrobats in a Park"] didn't get accepted is that it is considerably ahead of its time. I said, when I was a few pages into it, why it's Picasso's pink period saltimbanques dropped down in a park in the middle of Jackson! And that's what they were to me. I also thought that the reason Byrd couldn't make love to his wife was that she was not a member of the family. And Ricky's arm broke because he wasn't willing to hold up the weight of that unborn child. Did you mean the reader to think those things? In any case, they are so alive that one has theories about their inner workings, as if they were real people, one's acquaintances. It is so visual, as Emmy with her painterly eye pointed out. It is also full of things I treasure, such as "The family is very quiet in the park" and the third paragraph, and the fourth and fifth paragraphs after that. And the description of how Nedda stands during the performance. And it isn't true that everything in the story is an unknown quantity, to you. Surely the story is also about the artist as balancer of one thing against another, or ten others, and in that sense acrobat. The two paragraphs on page 7 about Ricky's sense of physical perception, the strength with which weight is borne, the timing of contact, the lightness of falling, etc. and that he can think of his wife only after the moment of the drumroll, and how he felt when the pyramid gave way are all <u>knowledge</u>. Of a kind that no writer but you has ever been known to have. I am so grateful to you for sending it to us. I feel about it the way I felt about

those letters in [Elizabeth Bowen's] "A World of Love" that decided it was time somebody came up to the attic and discovered them.

Emmy's father is doing very well, not quite as strong as he was before, but getting much stronger all the time. We may (unless it is too much for him) all go out there for his 92nd birthday. And between April 30 and March 25 we are going to be in London and Amsterdam, and in between these trips we are trusting to have a visit from you. Our spring visit.

It is raining cats and dogs. How I admire the person who said that for the first time.

Devotedly,

Bill

William Maxwell to Eudora Welty, April 11, 1978

Dearest Eudora—

I've been taking The Eye of the Story with me wherever I go. The subway, buses, The Passport Office, and so on. And everywhere I go is transformed by it—when I don't forget where I am. It strikes me as a really substantial book. And so much an expression of your deepest beliefs—which one isn't allowed to express, only to convey, in fiction. I continually hear your voice while I am reading. And was so delighted that you had bothered to correct the misprint on p. 9. I rather hated to give up the idea that she was jumped down the steps by Captain W. to unlooked for misinformation. It has so much the suggestion of the fortune teller. And also raises an interesting question: is most misinformation looked for or unlooked for? I like particularly having all this variety brought together—Jane Austen and Katherine Anne and Elizabeth and Ford Madox F. and Mr. Forster & Isak Dinesen and E. B. White, Virginia Woolf and Ida M'Toy—in a single volume. To be treasured, on the shelf next to the fireplace.[89]

In my last letter I forgot to thank you for the poems by Seamus Heaney. Both of them are wonderful, and aroused in me a desire to read the rest. Which most contemporary poetry would not have done, I'm afraid. I particularly liked "Like a child's tongue following the toils of his calligraphy etc." and wished I had written it myself. Or that you had. What you write I can claim as all in the family.

Did either of us tell you that we are going to be out of the country most of May? To London on April 30, and home from Amsterdam on May 24. I worry for fear we will miss your Spring visit. I also worry about how we will keep warm. I talked to Miss Warner yesterday and she said it was snowing on the daffodils.

My love —

B

P.S. Did your mother say "receipt" or "recipe"?

Eudora Welty to William Maxwell, April 24, 1978

Dearest Bill,

It's your letter I carry around with me. I can't tell you how happy it makes me to know you think it (the book) substantial and can take delight in it. Always claim what I write as all in the family, or I'll pray you can. I knew you would like my invited or invoked company — I put Ida M'Toy in special for you and Emmy, and of course Charles Shattuck. And it eased my mind that you could look at "misinformation" in place of "misfortune" in a really pleasurable way — it makes me feel less obliged to correct every single copy Random printed. Their galleys were the worst I ever did see — in a quote from Forster, they changed "after the laughter has departed" to "after the daughter has departed." I asked to see page proofs but was denied because I live in Mississippi not NYC. They said the proofreading was all done by "freelance proofreaders." What a calling! There are more mistakes in the book than this, but they too can shelter under your wing, and I don't think it will upset you as it did a clergyman friend of mine who wrote me "P. 186, read Bozrah (Jer. 49:13) not Bozrah (the capital of Edom) (cf. Isaiah 63:1)"[90] This is my old school friend George Stephenson, who also told me a really bad mistake I made in "The Optimist's Daughter" about the count of the weeks around Mardi Gras, by which I'd marked the time of the Judge's illness. I'm keeping this error (<u>my</u> error) a secret.

There's so much we both and all of us need to talk about — and I'm hastening now just to write you before you take off for London, to say what a wonderful trip I hope it will be. And to wish that the snow won't be falling by April 30. I don't suppose the Constables will still be all at the Tate, but

whatever Constables you see, think of me. What <u>will</u> be at the Tate, I won-
der? It's so, your trip will be at the same time as mine to New York, and it
will grieve me not to see you—but I'm absolutely sure I'll be coming back
when you are back too, so as to see you then, because I want to see you terri-
bly much, to hear all and be shown things like what Brookie has done since
the Vitamin B-15 ceramic cityscape with Super-Vitamin vaunting over it—
it's marvelous,[91] and it must be a new medium invented by her altogether,
isn't it? The Chrysler Building was just made to be a model for her. I like
B-15's laced-up shoes a great deal—he must have to give a big jump in those
to take off so healthily. Please give my love to both the girls.

And I hope the visit to your father—the second one, after he was well—
came off as planned, Emmy. I'm so glad he made such a sure, prompt re-
covery. (Almost as if Vitamin B-15 in Brookie's NY scene was headed for
Portland to him.) I wrote you a piece of a letter in answer, it was "over Min-
neapolis," but what became of it I do not know. I blame the North Dakota
Writers Conference I was part of which was really strenuous. Maybe it's just
that I've been talking too much to too many writers in too many colleges—
well, I know I have, but I mean maybe it is having the effect of making me
lose my little ties and claims to sanity (my letter to you, though brief, was
one.). I like young people and really am stimulated by the back-and-forth,
but they just don't want to let you go. In a moment of desperation I thought,
I bet that was what happened to old Orpheus in the end, he was torn to
pieces by the original Writers Conference—this is pretty ungrateful of me,
because I undertook these things knowingly and knew what would happen
except I forgot how old I am. The last time I did this was 13 years ago and I
got along fine—I forgot about the 13 years. Tomorrow I go to Texas, next to
Virginia and that's the last—it's after that that I spring up like B-15 (I really
am crazy about him) and land right in that ceramic city in the ceramic Al-
gonquin, for about a week or a day or two more. I'll think of you every day,
in the double view, East 86th Street and England. Sending love and thanks
to you, wishes and probably anecdotes.

It was warming to have you write to me about my "Acrobats in a Park."
For the first time, the story appeared to me in its reality—it had found
its readers. Your saying Picasso was hitting the nail right on the head, all
right—I was in love with his Saltimbanques and was wishing they were set

down in my little Smith Park, like the girl in the fairy story who made the
wish and the table spread was set down before her under her tree. ("Little
Two-Eyes"?) Thank you for your letters—I cherish them—

And Julietta the Badger is so unbelievably true to the English bad-
ger, and the English badger must be what she is, and the English hand
that wrote the account—I have read it with pleasure so many times, once
aloud—it is perfect of its kind. I do wonder what happened to Thready?
The boar—the sibling who took up his residence at the local pub. I wonder
if he ever found an old rug and draped it around him and charged up and
down the public room, or found the proper person to have a bullfight with.
He may have taken to drink, though he wouldn't have needed to. Julietta
did so remarkably on praise alone.[92]

Dearest Emmy and Bill, I'll write better next time—This brings all my
love, and wishes for a beautiful time in England—

Eudora

Eudora Welty to William and Emily Maxwell, [Fall 1978]

Dearest Bill and Emmy,

Our evening stays with me—it was so lovely. Thank you for it all—and
thank Brookie—I hope you found you could take up the leaves again right
where the last one had fallen when you had to leave all that glory—

Maine was tantalizing because none of it could be seen inside the Hol-
iday Inn, where we were trapped—but there was the ride up from Boston
with Elizabeth Spencer in her car, and the ride back to Boston with Louis
Rubin, and we played hooky during somebody's paper to run up the coast
to L. L. Bean—And late one night, from my 10th floor window, I saw a
beautiful, white, lighted ship move out of the harbor and out to sea—

Road sign in Maine: "CHOICE—Left, Highway 95, RIGHT, Rt. 101"—
That'll stop you! A tavern sign outside Boston: "Cabaret. All New Girls."[93]

I couldn't resist Xeroxing a little Henry Green for you—It's a Paris Review
interview, which I came across one day much later than it was published
—It's the way he talked, one of the ways—I'm off to Agnes Scott College
early in the morning—but that's an easy one. My love to you—E—

Eudora Welty to Emily and William Maxwell, November 23, 1978

Dearest Emmy and Bill,

The dinner dance is right upon me—it's November 30, and I've been holding onto the big hope we can meet on an evening after that—Since you'll probably go to the country on Friday, I'm hoping you'll be back, and free, on the Monday or Tuesday? (Dec. 5 & 6). I have to go on Wednesday—Of course it doesn't have to be in the evening—If you'd let me take you to lunch some place you could bear, it would give me lots of pleasure. Anyway, I'll telephone you on the morning of the 30th—if it isn't too early, before a business date I have in the morning. What it is: I'm to do a new recording for Caedmon.[94] I wish I could have you there with me to read <u>to</u>!— which I guess is very selfish and not even feasible—

Is it still warm and strangely mild there, as it still is here, on Thanksgiving Day? I ate dinner with my nieces & their families—the youngest, whose name is Elizabeth Eudora White, is 8 months old—she can stand alone, but still hasn't any teeth—That doesn't sound quite safe, does it?

Much love to all of you, Eudora

Eudora Welty to Emily and William Maxwell, December 14, 1978

Dearest Emmy and Bill,

It was a heavenly time together in your living room (with the anemones) and around your table and it lives on in my memory as indelibly as the pheasant's reflection in the fountain—in needlepoint![95]—It was good to see your faces happy. I enjoyed seeing Humphrey again and hearing his and Mr. [John] Heliker's two versions of Greece side by side. The delicious dinner!—There were so many things said and waiting to be said and expecting to be said, and surely must've been <u>partly</u> said, I can't remember how far we got, but it was all happily the same. Emmy, going home in the taxi (Mr. Heliker rode to the hotel to take me back, kindly), I listened to your praises all the way—Mr. Heliker told me how highly he thinks of your gifts and your work. I was so stupid that I didn't know till after we'd left you that he had been your teacher at the [Art Students] League. So I went home in a

glow too, after having had to say goodbye to you and Bill—Champagne was the right thing in our glasses—

It was a delight to see Brookie's reindeer on their trek over land and sky, in and around the landscape of slippers & shoes—Their wings, no wonder they worked—They (the deer) appeared to elevate with no concern at all, just ceramically—The babies lying together with wings folded were a pure act of creation—I hope Christmas is lovely in the country—snow (and not sleet) and a beautiful fire and talk and music—Kate will be able to come, I hope? Much love to all of you—I always think of you on Christmas morning when I wake up. This is the rest of the little book I sent you a poem out of once[96]—with love—Eudora

William Maxwell to Eudora Welty, [Christmas 1978]

Dear Eudora:

My eyes fall on [Henry Green's novel] "Party Going" and I know you were here. Reading it is going to be my Christmas present to myself. The Fats Waller records are delightful. Humphrey and Emmy go searching earnestly for their favorites. It is all new to me, or practically, since I was an opera buff at the time when I could have been listening to jazz.

We are in the country and it is raining cats and dogs, and tonight the temperature is going to drop and there is going to be sleet and snow and drivers advisory and icy roads and who knows what else Santa Claus. If I was him, I would start a little early and beat the rush.

Devotedly,
Bill

William Maxwell to Eudora Welty, January 7, 1979

Dear Eudora:

Seamus Heaney and getting in the mail a copy of Robert Fitzgerald's brief speech about those, about how he first read those two ravishing poems of Wallace Stevens, have set us, has set us, off, set fireworks off in both our minds. Why, Emmy asks, meaning it, haven't we lived entirely for reading poetry? All I could say was that when I was young I used to. So did she.

Robert said he delivered his speech "with special efforts not to swallow my words because who should be there in the front row but Eudora Welty, who had come with Bill Meredith, and he sitting on my right." I see it all. A youngster who is the son of an old friend and in his own right dear to both of us had come down from Cape Cod partly to look for a job and partly to hear you read, and said he called up at ten o'clock to find out what time the reading was and was told 10:12. And he on 22nd Street at the moment. He couldn't believe that anything so important would take place at that hour of the morning. So to console him I sent him off with our old copy of the recording of Why I Live at the P.O. grown scratchy with the years, and recently replaced. It was nice to feel you were near, and I hope you had a lovely time with Mary Lou.[97]

The paperback containing [Henry Green's] Loving, Living and Party-Going has arrived from the Madison Avenue Bookshop and I should send Party-Going back to you but can't resist reading it for the first time in that Hogarth Press edition, unless you have some immediate need for it. I embarked on Living, and was so beguiled with it that I went back and started reading it to Emmy, who also adored it, but when I read aloud to her it is usually at the end of the day and she does what I do when she reads to me (see the Mad Tea party) and if I am especially gripped (and I was) I forget to keep asking if she is awake, so she missed the whole second chapter and had to go back and read it herself. Tonight, Chapter III. Oh my God it is so funny. And Updike's introduction is very good too: "His observations of the world appear as devoid of prejudice and preconception as a child's and it is as a child—an ideally attentive and unnoticed child—that we seem to be present…"

A Christmas package arrived from Harriet Sheehy, in Ireland, and in it a paperback of Elizabeth [Bowen]'s Irish stories, which pleased me as a sign. I don't know what, except powerlessness, made Alfred Knopf allow her work to go out of print in America. I like to believe that the right things keep poking their heads up like daffodils, no matter what. If they don't, we are finished and it doesn't matter what happens. But I hadn't realized that she wrote so few stories—nine, it seems—actually set in Ireland.

I finished, in a manner of speaking—I mean I felt the weight of an albatross fall from my shoulders and thought with surprise, It's done—that long

story I have been working on for the last two years. It isn't, of course. But nearly. I wanted to read it through in a clean copy and left it at The New Yorker before Christmas and still haven't got it back and so impatiently have been doing other things. There is only one thing more I want to do, but how to do it, when it doesn't work that way, because of this and that. Sleight of hand is the obvious answer. Too much comes out too soon, if you know what I mean, and some of it has somehow to be placed farther along, providing more to arrive at, where more is needed.[98]

Emmy's brother went back to Greece just a few days before Christmas, carrying with him an indelible impression of you. He never stopped talking about how you read that story, and about Ida M'Toy herself. I expect the Greeks are hearing about it right this minute.

Ever since Christmas I have had such an appetite for reading that one thing leads me off to another, to the point of madness. I was writing a note to a woman who lives in Berkshire, near Newbury, and that led me to wonder about Newbury, so I got out Muirhead, where I found that "the blameless and the brave" Lord Falkland was buried in a church there, leaving me no choice but to get out Clarendon's <u>History of the Rebellion</u>,[99] a Victorian edition with engravings, that once belonged to my friend Eleanor Hinkley in Cambridge and before that to her father, and so discovered that Falkland was raised in Ireland, and his eyes were as far apart as Kate's and Brookie's used to be when they were children, and his grandfather passed over his father, who was extravagant, and left everything to him, at the age of twenty, and though he had a passion for London he wouldn't go there until he had learned Greek thoroughly. Having read all the Greek historians he set off for town, but also loved learning so much that he attracted others of like disposition and his more than comfortable house was a kind of school. His ideas of honor seem to have been nice to the point of exasperating, if you were Charles the 1st, but he did let himself become Secretary of State in his early thirties, and once when some fool in parliament, of which he was a member, proposed that each member stand up in turn and salute and also wave his hat at somebody present who had distinguished himself by doing what he was supposed to do, Falkland stretched out both arms and clamped them on the top of <u>his</u> hat and kept them there. At the age of thirty-four, in a battle near Newbury, he was shot in the stomach by a Roundhead hiding

in a hedge, and that was Lord Falkland, but can you see why people do anything at all but read? With a little time out now and then to play Schubert and Fats Waller.

Somebody came to see me who is writing a life of Frank O'Connor[,] a nice young man, not a fool, and O'Connor must be like the Duc de Guise, that is to say larger dead than when he was alive, because the Irish are still making derogatory remarks about him and his work. I kept saying, as I drove the young man to the station, "But he was a <u>great</u> writer…" But he isn't on the list of great writers at the moment, so I am not sure he heard me.

Kate came home for a week or more and is coming again on Thursday. She seemed the happiest we have ever seen her. As if she had come into some sort of immaterial inheritance. As I rather think she has.

We went to the country on Friday, woke up to a Japanese snow, the quiet kind, and talk of more sent us back to town, but it was rain by the time it arrived. Emmy has balanced her checkbook and I am about to go do something about the pile of records that nobody but me is ever willing to put back where they belong. We were thinking of going to the south of France in April, somebody having offered us a house there, but then Emmy got to thinking about her father and how important it is to his housekeeper to be able to pick up the phone and talk to her, so we decided to stay here. In some ways the most beautiful journeys are the ones you don't take. But anyway, only you would understand Emmy's reasoning.

<div align="right">

So much love from both of us,

Bill

</div>

William Maxwell to Eudora Welty, June 12, [1979]

Dear Eudora:

I hope you weren't being polite when you asked to see this. The typesetting is a little peculiar, because of its coming out in two parts in The New Yorker. Those headings ("A Pistol Shot" etc.) are really chapters and in the book will be numbered. The thing I am really proud of is the unpunctuation. I wanted originally to call it "The Palace at 4 AM" but unfortunately Howard Moss had used that title for a play. Does this title seem all right?[100]

There is no hurry either about your reading it or about your mailing it

back to me. Just treat it like the printing on the ketchup bottle, and read it when you have nothing better to read. I hope you are now able to stay home and do all the things you have been wanting to. I hope most of all you are writing a story or a novel.

I have been having such an interesting time pursuing the letters of Sylvia Townsend Warner, in particular her letters to Anne Parrish, which means finding out where Anne Parrish's papers are, possibly (I learned two minutes ago) in the Atheneum in Hartford.[101] I could use some help from Sherlock Holmes. Mostly people write back that they will be happy to let me see copies of their letters and then nothing happens. Or a truckload arrives, in a single fat envelope. I begin to suspect she wrote as many letters as Horace Walpole.[102] Often there is a steady stream of letters to a person she met only once, and those are usually the best.

The night before last there was a full moon, then it rained all day, buckets, and now it is cold and clear like Eastern Oregon. It is so nice when Sunday evening comes not to have to drive back to New York City. Tomorrow we are going in for a dinner party and to pick up the mail.

All winter long I worried because there were no birds, and now there is such a racket you can't hear yourself think. A robin is raising a family in the snowball bush outside our bedroom window, and for the first time in years there is an oriole.

As we are here less and less of the summer because of being at the Cape, I have let the roses get fewer and fewer. Such as there are are just coming into bloom, rather smaller than usual because of what they went through last winter, I suppose. But Frau Karl Drushki cries out for a lady's hat, circa 1916, to go on. And there is one pink peony blossom that is beyond belief.

We both send love,

Bill

William Maxwell to Eudora Welty, August 9, 1979

Dearest Eudora:

We had breakfast with you this morning. Emmy and I outside on the deck, and you and Dick Cavatt inside on the kitchen table.[103] Part I. For the first time. Part II we saw when it was originally broadcast. I don't sup-

pose TV stills exist, but there were moments that were the best pictures of you I have ever seen. When you abruptly stopped reading "A Wide Net" I thought I would break, I was so prepared for you to go on right straight through to the end. The next time you come, will you read it to us? It was marvelous.

The conversation about strange names reminded me of Zona Gale, but your letter had already done this. She was, as you know, my fairy godmother from the time I was sixteen. In the summer of 1933 I took the manuscript of "Bright Center of Heaven" to her. I wanted her to tell me if it was a novel. When I went to see her she said yes, it was. She also said that she had had insomnia and got up in the middle of the night and went downstairs to her study looking for the last chapter, and couldn't find it. Had I forgotten to give it to her? Instead of asking what it was that was missing, I said, No, that's all there is. Truthfully. Twenty years later when I reread it for the first time after it was published, I perceived what it was she went downstairs looking for. That forty-six years later you, who are in certain ways very like her, should have got up in the middle of the night to finish my story pleased me as only repetitions of a central experience can please. I don't expect another reader to see so completely what I was up to, but one such reader is enough. It tells you that you haven't been deluding yourself. That it is really there. I thank you with all my heart. And those blue mailboxes have been painted green, the way I then of course remembered that they used to be. I still grieve over the fact that it cannot be called "The Palace at 4 A.M." All substitutes remain forever substitutes, don't they?

Listening to your distinction between the short story and the novel this morning, I thought of all the passages and even whole chapters that ended up in a shopping bag under the grand piano because they weren't part of the general tautness. That farm woman who came to keep house for Lloyd Wilson—I had the hardest time keeping her from monopolizing the conversation, and even from being too interesting.[104] Because of course she found out what was going on.

What you say about houses is all true. And unconscious on my part. When I was a child I looked at them as I looked at picture books. I still do. Frank O'Connor used to be so amused at my interest in houses. What was the <u>house</u> like, I would say when we were working on his autobiography or

on stories even. What was it like <u>inside</u>? At that stage of his career he had developed rather rigid ideas of what the short story should be. He was after the aural. The visual hardly interested him at all. But he would look at me a moment, smile, and then indulge me by writing in a description that brought tears to my eyes.

I try to imagine signing William Maxwell six thousand times, and I am not sure I could. Six thousand bricks would be child's play. Did your family name finally begin to lead a life of its own?[105] It is possible that the person you corresponded with at the Franklin Press was Peter Wilkie, who is the stepson of a close friend of ours. Also a friend of mine, himself. He is a very nice young man and speaks of you with worship. I am so glad you won't be coming home to the builders, as we came home at the end of July, from Wellfleet, to housepainters. Emmy is doing the Bates method eye exercises,[106] some of which are rather strange, like holding a yardstick to the end of your nose and staring down it. And she finds it unnerving to be stared at at such moments. And there is a head in every window, like the last act of <u>Rosenkavalier</u>.

We will be celebrating my birthday in Santa Fe, and Emmy's birthday in Portland, Oregon, and Labor Day in Yorktown Heights, after which we are going back to the Cape for the rest of September. So far as I know. One speaks with such confidence about the future. Out of necessity, I suppose. Once you admit how unprotected by anything all human life is you are almost obliged in self defense to take refuge in madness. So instead, I say, confidently, that we both look forward to hearing all about Oxford when you come to dinner in November.[107] Or whenever.

<div style="text-align: right">My love,

B.</div>

Eudora Welty to Emily and William Maxwell, October 2, [1979],
Postcard with photographs of the Tower of London and Tower Bridge

Dearest Emmy & Bill,

This is really from Jackson, not the Tower of London—but wouldn't it be lovely in a slide lecture? Try it in the dark. (It may be toxic.) The Acad-

emy-Institute has called me for a meeting on Oct. 9—I'll be there from 8th to 12th and pray that somehow you might have some time I could hope to see you (any night but Wednesday). Have you had both birthday celebrations? When is the book out?

With my love—Eudora

William Maxwell to Eudora Welty, October 18, 1979

Dearest Eudora:

I have committed larceny. I didn't like the jacket copy [for *So Long, See You Tomorrow*] that Knopf sent and so rewrote it. At the end of two days (it being much easier to do something than describe what you have done), at my wits end, I helped myself to a sentence from your letter in order to get the bloody thing out of the house: "It has an inner force that never lets go". And without giving you credit, since that would be the same thing as asking for a quote, which I would rather put my head on the railroad tracks in front of an oncoming train than do to my friends.

Are you working hard at getting rested? I don't want to pick up the morning Times and read that you have died of natural causes.

I have raced through the E. Nesbit, wishing I was the age I was when I read Prince Prigio for the first time, and am about to settle down to Miss Bird's travels in the orient.[108] It doesn't seem correct to say that we miss you after one evening together, but put all the evenings together and it is perfectly reasonable. Anyway, we do.

My love,
Bill

Eudora Welty to Emily and William Maxwell, December 17 [–?], 1979

Dearest Emmy and Bill,

I found your unanswered letters in my suitcase, they've been going with me to the Blue Grass, to Ohio, and to Princeton, where they protected me from academics and added to all that gave me joy—and of course that (finding them) didn't substitute for what I mean to do (answering them)—I

mean, on paper. Especially did I want to write to you from Versailles, Ky. An old friend of mine, who used to teach English at Vassar—Susan Turner— went back there to live in her family home, and had me to spend a long weekend in it, along with Caroline Mercer, also from the Vassar English Department, now living in Louisville.

Versailles (pro. Ver-sales) is in the real country not far from Lexington, an adorable little town—Susan's house is right across the street from the girls' academy where she went to school, and the courthouse is on the Square a few blocks away—everything is tree-lined, everything is yards and porches and backyards with gardens and pear trees. The railroad track runs not far in the distance of course and you can hear the whistle—even if it's not the same whistle of memory or the same train. The Kentucky River is at the foot of nearby wooded hills, rounding its bend, <u>clear</u> to look at, too. The family farm is out there too—not a horse farm, like most in those parts, just a working farm, big barns, one hanging with tobacco—I'd never been inside a tobacco barn—they were big and still and brown as tapestries, those big sheaves of leaves. Guy Davenport, from the U. of Ky., where I'd been working, drove me to Versailles, and we got there after dark. Susan and Carrie heard the car, the door opened wide and streamed with light, and they came out laughing—inside was a fire and a tray with Jack Daniels and silver goblets and a bowl of picked-out black walnuts from the tree in their yard, and then wonderful ham and all. Upstairs my room was just what you'd imagine, big and no foolishness, a big high bed and lots to read, and that's where I thought I would write to you. But it was too welcome, I fell asleep, every night the same. We talked all the time, they had both been to Jackson to see me at different times but I had never been to Versailles. Oh, the first night, Susan said, "I've just read William Maxwell's novel, and was so excited I telephoned a friend in New York about it—"[109] We agree about what we love it for. They brought out some pictures of times when Elizabeth [Bowen] was at Vassar—bright summer, outdoors, garden chairs, the same silver goblets. This was an oasis in my trip—the next 5 days I was at Denison University and had (counting in awful self-pity) 22 different sessions with groups of students. My own fault. Next year will be different. It's not that I don't like students. It did come back to me, something Elizabeth said one time, "They drink your blood."

Dearest Bill,

My heart sprang up when I opened the envelope and saw the book had come before Christmas after all, and saw it in Brookie's jacket. The figure, the color, the hour, the act of the book, beautiful and beautiful together. She caught the essence, as she did the terrible youngness of the reaching and just balancing boy. Her photograph is remarkable too. And well, you know what I think of the inside, and my belief that it is your masterpiece, which is what many think too. (I was so happy that you let me contribute anonymously to the description on the jacket, my words as chosen by the author.) Thank you for the book. I want to go straight to it, read it again as I did the first time, without a stop.

Would you tell Brookie for me how much I love her jacket?

Enclosed with these two letters was a third, handwritten at the bottom of the first.

Dearest Emmy and Bill, this letter waiting in the typewriter got a permanent wave—I'm going to send both the letters unfinished or you will never hear from me before Christmas—I <u>have</u> to tell you how happy I am in receiving the book—

Enclosed is the paper of wonderful information I picked up inside the <u>Camera Obscura</u> in England for you—at Bristol. My old and dear friend in England, Edward Malins, who took me there, is also the editor of one of the Irish books I was sending you for Xmas—The other one, by Tomás O'Crohan, is something else—I'd ordered you a copy from Blackwells in hardback but when it didn't come I sent you mine, just a paperback, but it's glorious—a wonderful present (!)

Early yesterday morning at an hour before sunrise, expecting to see the conjunction of Jupiter & Mars in the South/Southwest skies, as foretold in the paper, I rose & started downstairs to the landing where the best window is and lit on the landing ahead of time—saw stars but not Jupiter & Mars! Nothing bad came of it but wouldn't you think after living in this house since 1925 I could go downstairs to see a simple conjunction of Mars & Jupiter without landing on my tailbone! I have one more chance tomorrow morning. All is well here, and I hope all's well there—

I miss you. When will we read aloud again!

With dearest love to all of you. A better letter soon. I'm sure there isn't a day when I don't think of you, by any of a hundred different ways it might be. HAPPY NEW YEAR.

Eudora

William Maxwell to Eudora Welty, December [19], 1979, Letter was enclosed in a Christmas card with Emmy's original design

Dearest Eudora: How I wish I were twins so one of them could stay home and do all the things that need to be done here and the other could get Emmy some wicked bitter chocolate at Kron, and arrange for Brookie's subscription to the Paris Vogue, and buy Kate some precious book of Sufi je ne sais quoi and myself a je ne sais quoi too, while I am at it. I tried and tried to reach you by phone, over a matter that I decided was not all that important. The book is on its way to you, all wrapped up in Knopf's best typography and Brookie's accomplishments. Emmy has done a wonderful painting of the same rooftops as this card. If you must leave home, I hope it is to come to New York, so we can take up where we always take up, which is where we left off.

B.

William Maxwell to Eudora Welty, January 5, 1980

Dearest Eudora:

When we went to Ireland the first time Kate asked us to bring her books by Lady Gregory. You remember what that precocious child was like. And "A Book of Saints and Wonders" was one of the two books we brought back for her, and she loved it dearly, and somebody else must have also, because it disappeared from her bookcase some time ago. When I unwrapped it, she cried out with pleasure, at being reunited. I have been following the career of Brigit (the book being left here, for safe keeping). I think I have never read a better story than the one about how Brigit spread her cloak and almost achieved the independence of Ireland. It is a heavenly book, in both senses of the word.

I have just peered into "The Islandman" because of the intense sociableness of the past two weeks, but what I read, about how they swam into

the cave and killed the seals and brought them out to the waiting boat, I read with my heart in my mouth the whole time. It is very different from "Twenty Years A-Growing". And reading it is like listening to the conversation of Frank O'Connor. I remember sitting on a cliff with Nancy Allitt and her two poodles, looking off at the Blasket Islands, with the amethyst cliffs of the mainland on our right. Nancy almost lost her life there, climbing on a precipitous path.[110]

Now if I am just let alone, I will not raise my head from this book until it is finished. It is, as you say, a glorious and wonderful present. And while I am reading Lady Gregory, I have the added pleasure of thinking that it is a dear friend of yours who wrote the introduction.[111]

Did you succeed in seeing the conjunction of Mars and Jupiter? And were there really no after effects? My father-in-law once startled me by remarking that both his mother and his favorite aunt lost their lives through inattention. He didn't explain. But since I am the most inattentive person I know, he didn't really have to. DO BE CAREFUL! REMEMBER WHERE YOU ARE AND WHAT YOU ARE DOING AND THAT YOU ARE INEXPRESSABLY DEAR AND IMPORTANT TO US!

The heavy snowstorm prophesied has turned out to be not all that heavy, but we stayed in town for the weekend because of drivers advisory (is that the right word?) and because Emmy was on jury duty for this week until she came home dismissed last night, and to plunge straight from New Years Day parties to Centre Street rather brought both our lives to a standstill. Anyway, she is sprung. And actually, she enjoyed it very much. Interesting people, and an interesting change from remembering that we are out of domino dots [sugar cubes].

I am engaged in putting my life and my study in order so that I can go full steam ahead in four different directions at the same time. This, as I don't need to tell you, is much too like building a house of cards. And some of the disorder is internal. And E says I need a part time secretary. And somebody who will go and be photographed while I am deep in the letters of Sylvia Townsend Warner.

The book [*So Long, See You Tomorrow*] came out during the week before Christmas, and appeared to be doing well, but what is happening now I have no idea. It is all so accidental. Larry Woiwode wrote and asked the

Times to do it, and then had to go off for a family funeral and when he came back called them because he hadn't heard, and was told by the editor that somehow his letter had got detached from the galleys and somebody else was doing it instead and he was sorry. And unless that somebody is more intelligent than the person who reviewed my book of short stories, I am going to be sorry too. But you can't say that anybody is to blame. Only that the editor of the Times Book Section's life is disorderly too, and he no doubt has a full time secretary, engaged in losing things that are attached to galleys. Ah well, maybe it won't be as bad as I think, or if it is, it won't matter all that much.

I am so glad you had that lovely visit in Ver-sales (as in Jow-liette, Illinois) and I will undertake to keep my study in better order (not to mention my life) if you will undertake to say no oftener, to people who only want your life's blood. I said, yesterday I said no, to a nice man whom we often meet jogging in the sandy roads of Cape Cod, a psychoanalyst, who wanted me to read a thirty-three page story, by his thirteen year old son, and evaluate it, and help him find a publisher. Politely. But I SAID it. And what I can do you can do. Better. If it is a matter of money, just tell me and I will dig around in the back yard in Yorktown Heights until I find you some. My love, and Emmy's until she gets around to sending it herself, and Happy New Year and thank you for the treasures.

Bill

Can you feel the house resting more securely on its expensive new foundations?

The vicissitudes of that camera obscura: How I would love to see it. It must be as good as having a tree house.

Eudora Welty, Chicago, to William and Emily Maxwell, April 19, 1980

Dearest Bill and Emmy,

This is from your home state, Bill—I'm in Chicago, on my last (4th) college visit of the Spring, a week at the University. I ask people every day what has been going on at Mount St. Helens (no way to get news in a dormitory) but you know they don't keep track in Chicago of volcanic erup-

tions in the West or floods in the South. But I'd read earlier that the great cloud of smoke could be seen from Portland "40 miles away" and I was glad you'd be far enough away to be safe and hoping you'd be near enough to see the awesomeness of a volcano in living life—Has even your [Emmy's] father ever seen it go up before?[112]

I've thought of you in regard to other things besides volcanos of course, and day by day—you know that—and carry a letter from each of you around in my bag, which is a substitute of sorts only to me for writing back—Please forgive me. Is your spring as it should be? We never really had our spring— the only one in my life when the old reliables (like the crab-apple tree) never made it into flower—the temp. dropped from 70° to 15° overnight, and like that. The bulbs were beaten down by torrential, repeated rains, the Banksia rose never bloomed, unless it did it & faded away while I was 5 days in Randolph-Macon. Most of all I missed the bloom that never came to the magnolia fuscata outside my bedroom window—those less-than-an-inch long creamy flowers that smell like bananas when the sun is on them or you hold them in your hand. We used to carry 3 or 4 of them to school wrapped in a handkerchief and sit at our desks with our noses buried in them. When I left last Friday, the azaleas were blooming, tardy & out of order, and dogwoods in a hit-or-miss way. I felt <u>confused</u> by spring. Arriving in Chicago from Charleston, S.C. (the Citadel Military College!) which was a mass of bloom, I was met by snow. But today is bright and fresh—I work quite hard and like the students, and have old friends here too, so life is made smooth & interesting for me. Tomorrow I move back to the Quadrangle Club, and am being taken to hear Solti conduct the Symphony—A Japanese student asked me if I would please sign my name in a large notebook filled with Japanese writing. "You have signed my diary," he said, frowning very hard at my awful handwriting. Too late then <u>not</u> to. Emmy, I loved bee that you sent me—what life in that child's drawing! I have it on my mantle shelf in the bedroom (at home), to start me off on my day.[113] I don't know where ant is, but I just saw ladybug, coasting along on my skirt which I just took off after coming in from the campus. I let her run onto my finger but when I tried to push open the window I found it still fastened down from winter. How will she ever get home?

This envelope had some odds and ends (or as my yardman says, ends and odds) I'd stuck away for you. More at home, no telling exactly what.

Much, much love to both,
Eudora.

Eudora Welty to Emily and William Maxwell, [Mid-April 1980],
Incomplete letter

The previous place I visited[114] was the first citadel I'd ever been inside. A solid mass of white buildings that looked not solid but 2-dimensional & like papier-maché against the sea-coast blue sky, and set along a line of live-oak trees, facing the 4 sides of a big flat bare green rectangle. That's the way it looked from spectators' chairs when we attended a parade for some general. At a signal, from behind us, the cadets started coming out through archways in the walls, pouring out in marching lines over the field, about 2000 of them—the band played, bagpipers in kilts among them, they were inspected by the general first, then they paraded around the field & before him—Much jumping up & down by the spectators from their seats, according to the tune, like in the Episcopal church, and when at the finale out came Dixie, then yells and hands over hearts—I can never not shed tears to hear it—Then the firing of a 19-gun salute (if that's what it's called) for the general, out of a <u>cannon</u>—I never heard anything so loud, it did rock you on your feet besides kill your ears, and I lost count—It was terrible. We had <u>our</u> stuff inside—Our cannons were Cleanth Brooks, Andrew Lytle,[115] Sally Fitzgerald, & me, and <u>we</u> all said "Sh!" or so I felt like saying. I missed Cleanth and Sally because my plane was late. It was nice to meet Sally for the first time, we had a good chance to talk there and afterwards when we took the same plane as far as Atlanta. I heard some good tales in Charleston. There was a man went on a visit to Huntsville, Ala., (an old, fine little town that thinks pretty well of itself too.). He looked ill—His friends said "We're going to pray for you." But he said "No thank you. They're praying for me in Charleston."

Later.—After the week's work was over, we celebrated by going to the Symphony last night. You must have seen Solti conduct, but I never had. Act III of <u>Siegfried</u>—He has so much drive & energy he looks like a wizard in mid-spell, moves so instantaneously & absolutely so fast that you see him

first in one position, then in another, but your eyes can't catch up with him, can't see the motion. So demon-like, crouching and pointing and fixing a player—He has Dracula ears (seen from behind—[drawing of head and ears]) bald head, but you've most probably seen him, in London or some-where. A young man from Tupelo, Miss., was the Siegfried—Couldn't hear too well how he sang, because of Solti—Thundering—Leaving we ran into his wife in the lobby—She recognized me because she used to work in a bookstore in Jackson. (It never fails—Mississippians turn up everywhere. I didn't know about Dennis Bailey or have any idea he was from home.) It was a strange juxtaposition—Solti & Tupelo! A most beautiful day today— Spice bushes (I'm told they are called—do you know them, Bill?) Large shrubs with mimosa-yellow bloom on bare branches—Against the stone University buildings, lovely. Boys immediately stripped to their shorts, hi-fis came out of open windows, frizbees sailed over your head everywhere you walked, couples spread out on the not-yet green grass, and one young man went running carrying off a girl, who wasn't minding it. The Lake soft blue and benign. That night the city was sparkling in clear air, stars too—moon too—Spring has arrived in Chicago.

I'm sorry for the handwriting & the poor letter but will write a less scat-terbrained one when I'm home after all this.

William Maxwell to Eudora Welty, April 23, 1980

Dearest Eudora:

We flew past Mount Saint Helen's on our way to Portland. It was send-ing forth a long, long plume of smoke, like an old-fashioned railway train except very much larger and longer. In Portland we couldn't see it except on the front page of the paper and on tv. Business there had to come to a stop and people talked about nothing else. Emmy's father's house had been broken into about six weeks before and the burglars made off with the sil-ver, including a Georgian creamer and sugar bowl and a sideboard tray that my father-in-law was particularly attached to and he still was troubled by this. I could not help reflecting that when their car is stolen people collect the insurance and go buy another. The loss of silver appears to be irrepa-rable and to some extent is when, as in this case, it has come down in the

family. Otherwise he was in splendid form and when we went out to clean
up the woods a little he took the ax from me and wielded it to better effect
than I could. Very impressive for ninety-four, and it was nice having Kate
and Brookie with us. And Uncle Humpie who came from Greece on the
first of March and stayed until the middle of April. With us, I mean. It is
the longest family visit I can remember since I was nine years old and my
great aunt came from Greenville, Mississippi, with her entire family in or-
der to provide me with material for a novel.[116] It is very melancholy about
your spring, especially since ours has been so unusually early and beautiful.
When we were in Portland a neighbor brought a huge branch of camellias
in bud or in bloom to Emmy's father and we put some of them in a suitbox
with damp newspaper and brought it home on the plane. For several days
all went well and then suddenly as if the buds had realized they were in the
wrong place they all fell off on a coffee table.

I have never seen Sir Georg Solti conduct. The concerts in New York
are always sold out before I even learn they are going to be. But Tupelo,
Mississippi—the very thought of Tupelo makes me sad because Brookie
brought home a wild coon-cat which was living in the woods behind our
house in Yorktown Heights and it got run over by a car. It could not bear
to stay indoors at night and one morning Emmy, returning from the super-
market, saw it lying in the road. It was a heavenly creature and loved to lie
curled up in her wash basin licking the drops that fell from the faucet. It
also liked to lie curled up inside Daisy's paws, a situation that Daisy put up
with rather than enjoyed since she had a thing about cats.

We have thrown our hat over the moon and are buying a little house
near the ocean in the Wellfleet woods. It is a little pavilion looking down on
the moors and protected from the winds off the ocean. We have been try-
ing to get it for two years—ever since Emmy, walking along the road to the
beach, saw the chimneys above the treetops and had hot flashes of intui-
tive ownership. I once had hot and cold flashes when I saw a horse named
Building Trades at the race track in Chicago. It paid twenty to one but by
that time I had lost all my money. In less than a month we will be seeing
you. What luck.

Devotedly,
Bill

On May 21, 1980, at the American Academy of Arts and Letters, Eudora presented Bill with the William Dean Howells Medal for fiction.

Eudora Welty, New York City, to William and Emily Maxwell, May 22, 1980

Dearest Bill and Emmy,

I hope you're still in bed and will be feeling altogether restored, Bill, when you get up. I think of you taking on a lot more of Emmy's glorious soup today for one thing, and both of you drinking it among the irises. It was so good to be called last evening and I didn't feel as anxious about you afterwards, but being noble and being in front of people giving a beautiful speech while having fever was something to go to bed for afterwards— which you did. It was a wonderful day all the same for me, I'll never forget that I was allowed to hand the medal to you (previous to the box too) and my feeling about it. Here are the scripts—It was just that it's hard to put down words for the public about something so close to me, but you will both very easily understand that. It was restoring to see you, & Brookie—All take care—

My love & wishes,
Eudora

Eudora Welty's presentation remarks for the Howells Medal:

On behalf of the American Academy of Arts and Letters I am honored to present the William Dean Howells Medal for Fiction to William Maxwell for his novel <u>So Long, See You Tomorrow</u>.

The most important facts in our experience, answerable or unanswerable, never go away. William Maxwell has written his best novel out of his comprehension of this. A family tragedy, past or present, is a magnetic field of everlasting, imploring questions. The novel searches them out. It takes him back and forth in time; it does not waver, and it cannot flinch. It has its divining rod; it is direction and destination in one.

<u>So Long, See You Tomorrow</u> is a vision which has taken on a verifiable construction, spare and plain, but no more simple than a house. In the writ-

ing, the novel's tension is finely strung and unremitting. Its quiet carries its own reverberations, so accurate and true that in the end they shatter the crystal: We are face to face with other people's mystery and with our own. There is nothing between us and the realization that without love and without death we should never have come into the presence of human mystery at all.

William Maxwell to Eudora Welty, May 28, 1980

Dearest Eudora:

We were both so happy to have your pieces of paper with the speech on it. I think I must still have had a little fever, because each sentence as you spoke it fell straight into my heart and made me happy. But I didn't know afterwards precisely what you had said. It was the way it used to be when I was a youngster and went to see Zona Gale. For an hour and a half I moved in bliss and after I had said goodbye on the front steps what remained was the memory of bliss without a single detail. I also think of you getting up at six in the morning to improve upon the first draft. If you knew how much I didn't want the medal to be given to me by someone else.

I'm feeling fine now.

My love,
Bill

The Shattucks' address is now 707 West Pennsylvania Street, Urbana, Illinois 61801

Eudora Welty to Emily Maxwell, June 13, 1980

Dearest Emmy,

I hope so much the next news that came about your father was good, and that your minds are enough relieved so you can relax once more about his wellbeing—He's such a remarkable gentleman, I've long realized, that recovery is what you <u>expect</u> of him, it's his specialty—I hope this marked another triumph—It's hard on you being away, & far away, and the two brothers both out of reach, and it gave me concern when the morning news reported Mt. St. Helens erupting again and I wondered if you could get

through well enough on the phone. But I'm concentrating on all being relieved by now, and hoping you and Bill are bound for Wellfleet—and the new house?—and the good clean Atlantic air and blue water and fish out of it—and raspberries ready for picking.

Thank you so much for sending Bill's beautiful speech—Now I can read exactly, word for word, what I <u>knew</u> was beautiful when it came into my ears, but needed to have before my eyes to hear it again. That was a wonderful time—something coming true that should have, since the beginning, was what it felt like, and I could see you smiling with the same thought.

There <u>were</u> a couple of places I went to after New York, the U. of Tenn., where I did a reading (etc.) job and Kenyon College, where I was given an hon. degree (in Latin: "hanc Eudora Welty") and stayed with a very old friend (the friendship is old, but I'm older than him, Robert Daniel). Then Memphis, to Southwestern U., where they gave me a ride on the Mississippi in a houseboat at sunset, lovely. Next day after that I was in Washington, where along with Red Warren, Tenn. Williams, Roger Tory Peterson the bird man, Ansel Adams, Beverly Sills & a few more, I had the presidential medal hung around my neck by Mr. Carter, an occasion really full of grace & feeling, and lunch at The White House afterwards. I am proud of this medal and respect it deeply but it is not true gold and not like the one <u>we</u> have—Now I am indeed home, and can't tell you how early I woke up this morning with beating heart at the prospect of time to myself and the summer ahead to work in. It's true I found the proofs of the Collected Stories had arrived, to read first, but they have to be out of the house by June 19 so that's not bad.

It's lovely to start off my freedom by at once sending a line to you and Bill. All does go well with you, I hope—healths being restored & spirits up where they belong. Tell me when you can.

<div align="right">Much love to all of you,
Eudora</div>

Eudora Welty to William Maxwell, June 13, 1980

Dearest Bill,

It's early in the morning, I'm having coffee by the breakfast room win-

dow looking out over the backyard (not a garden any more, but what it is) where a towhee has hopped out, as he does every morning at 6:45, and thinking about your speech, lying open on the table. It seems to hold not only all you said in it but the whole reason and cause of it and the living moment when you were speaking it, and I'm so happy to have it here on paper like this. It's good to be able to think too that having been so rising-above your fever, you didn't have any harm from that come to you. It really wasn't safe for you to have come out in that rain and endured that crowd, I know. But you did—and how happy your being there made a lot of people. I feel its glow of happiness now as I did then, actually beginning at that same ten minutes after three—It was good to all talk on the phone next day—Thank you so much for your letter now. I'll keep thinking back to that time.

And thank you for sending me the Shattucks' new address. There is much I have been wanting to write Charles. I hope Susan keeps on doing better.

As I was just saying to Emmy about her father, I hope relief has come to your minds by now—with him <u>much</u> better, the way he's achieved it before, and with you & Emmy not needing to fly out, worried and through that volcano smoke. I hope you're on the way to Wellfleet, with that house of your own in view—

I also hope the horrendous amount of editing & writing letters about S.T.W. did reach its end, and that you feel good & content about it. And now can go just as you feel like it into your own again. How could you help needing the clear good air and the undemanding hours at Wellfleet after all this last year. My love to what you do next but not a word about when.

I look forward to trying to straighten some mistakes out in a story too long & hopeless to mention, but I do to you—I'm really filled with delight at the chance to start in on it—hoping to dig out the weeds and find & separate the true things I could swear I planted! That's to make sure about. Meantime I have the galleys of my Collected Stories to proof-read—from the beginning through "The Demonstrators" will be 622 pages & I've peeped. Heavens. Aside from the 5 or 6 of them I use for the readings I've been doing, I haven't read the stories since their own day. I don't know what the whole of them will be like to go through now, and at one blow. Maybe it's a protection to have a new one waiting on me, regardless of how weedy it is. It's still possible to make that one better (or worse).

I'll think of your summer in my summer & hope it's full of blessings too — Much love, E

Here is the text of Bill's speech at the Howells Medal ceremony. Eudora had just received it in a letter from Emmy.

Miss Welty has just slipped me an empty box. The catch is broken and she was afraid the medal would fall out. When <u>she</u> got the Howells Medal a stranger came up to her afterwards and asked to see it. Miss Welty obliged, and the stranger dropped the gold medal and, since it really <u>is</u> a gold medal, it cost fifty dollars to have the scratch removed. My medal has been in my pocket since ten minutes after three.

There is no empty box that I could prize as highly as I do this one, because of what it stands for and because of those writers who have had it before me.

I believe that it behooves the living, for our own sake, to keep the memory of the dead alive and vivid, and so I would remind you now of Louise Bogan — of her ravishing formal poetry and her literary criticism, so free from intellectual display and so on target. Because of her encouragement at a critical period of my life I stopped being a full time editor and went back to writing novels and I therefore have her to thank for the fact that I am standing where I am this minute.

In a talk that she gave at New York University in the nineteen sixties there is a precise and moving description of the creative process. Actually she is speaking of poets but it applies equally to every artist who, after many years of effort and apprenticeship, has at last come into his own talent. The passage concludes:

> ...a poet can never be certain, after writing one poem, that he will ever be able to write another. Training and experience can never be completely counted on; the "breath," the "inspiration" may be gone forever. All one can do is try to remain "open" and hope to remain sincere. Openness and sincerity will protect the poet from...small emotions with which poetry should not, and cannot, deal; as well as from imitations of himself or others. The intervals between poems, as poets have testified down the ages, is a lonely time. But then, if the poet is lucky

and in a state of grace, a new emotion forms, and a new poem begins, and all is, for the moment, well.

William Maxwell, Wellfleet, Massachusetts, to Eudora Welty,
July 29, 1980

Dearest Eudora:

We start home to Yorktown Heights the day after tomorrow, and Emmy is going through the kitchen like a whirlwind. Fortunately it is a grey day and so she doesn't feel abused at missing the ocean. We have had a marvelous five weeks, with constantly beautiful weather. We arrived rather run down from colds, and are now ready to pose for a 4H poster. Also, to make up for the beautiful house that we didn't get to buy after all, we have rented for next summer a very different but also beautiful house on the next pond from this one, and a little nearer the ocean. The water is about twenty feet from the living room door, it is secluded from the road, and when you go swimming you walk down an aisle between banks of water lilies. The nearest neighbors are a family of otters. It belongs to Anna Hamburger's brother, who built it himself. We went through it carefully yesterday looking to see what wasn't there and all the things we expected not to be there were there. The fog was rolling in from the pond and the birds sound happy, and I expect we will be too.

This morning on the way down to the pond to swim, Emmy peered into the bushes, and said Is that a towhee. Could it have been yours?

I am so happy to learn that there is a story that has some mistakes that need straightening out and that is too long, which could mean, of course, that it is not long enough.[117] If I had my way, I would disconnect your telephone and discontinue the mail service and make the people that want you to come and address them or read to them walk to Jackson to ask you to do it. And when they did I would fix it so you weren't home that afternoon. And though I think we have all the collections we don't have the uncollected stories, so there is that to look forward to, when we get the 622 pages. What a lot comes of just putting one foot in front of the other. When it is a definitive collection there is not much choice but to arrange them chronologically, I would think. With Over by the River, I arranged them over and

over, this way and that, and finally they all clung together and wiggled off like a snake. When it isn—the telephone rang and I don't know now what it was I wanted to say.

I am still deep in the [Warner] letters, but everything of importance is gathered in, that I know about, I mean, except the correspondence with David Garnett, which hasn't been an easy trout to land, because of his great age and one thing and another.[118] With any luck I will get it, though, and can then begin the preliminary choosing. Just when I was sure I had failed, a cousin of S.T.W. took it upon herself to get in touch with him, and they met in London and he agreed to let me have them, but actually getting my hands on the photocopies is another matter. I hold my breath and sit with my fingers crossed. I have enough without them but there are a hundred twenty-two letters from two twenty-year periods, and her letters to men were usually more interesting than those to women, for reasons I don't understand, but perhaps George Sand could tell me. I have a limit of 90,000 to 100,000 words, including the index and notes, to work within. And time is breathing down my neck (a good thing) because the price of publishing books in England keeps rising, as the general quality goes down. It is very melancholy. When you think of all the dearest books on our shelves, The Hogarth Press, etc.

We got tickets long ago to fly to Portland at the end of August, and then Emmy went earlier, when her father wasn't feeling very well, and after that he said she was not to come this summer, and in fact made her promise that she wouldn't, but she thought before we cancelled the tickets she ought to try to find out if he really meant what he said, and so she wrote and asked him whether he would really like us to come in August and he had forgotten all about telling us not to come and was delighted at the idea. I think Nature knew what it was doing when it made the old forgetful. I don't want to [be] marooned by Mt. St. Helens but otherwise look forward to the trip. He fails, I think, steadily, but to such a slight degree that he may go on quite happily for years to come. The only thing we dread is the thought he might be bedridden. Isn't that a wonderful word? Why ridden? I would look it up but I have packed the O.E.D.

We both send worlds of love,

B

William Maxwell to Eudora Welty, December 26, 1980

Dearest Eudora:

In the morning paper Mr. Jovanovitch discussing his policy, his new policy about returns. Emmy said last night "What a marvelous preface to 'Acrobats in a Park.'" "So is the story," said Know-It-All. This morning, I have been sitting in my study reading the preface, in seventeen layers of clothing; even though the radiators are frequently hot to the touch, the windows are large and give a fair idea of what it is like at the North Pole. I think it is maybe the best introduction I ever read to any book. It makes me realize how important it is for writers to live a long time after they have come into their own—long enough to turn and identify what they have done.[119] Mr. Jovanovitch must have been talking about a different species of object, more like a baseball or parchesi. With (certainly) different rules. I wish I could find for you what I think is the first short story I ever wrote. It was published in the Lincoln High School magazine, I was fourteen at the time, and the protagonist was an aristocrat who hid in a grandfather's clock to escape the guillotine. I had been reading "A Tale of Two Cities" with my long black stockings in front of the space under my bedroom door so nobody would see the crack of light and tell me to put out the light and go to sleep. It is a far far better thing that you wrote in 1935, but on the other hand you weren't fourteen. Wouldn't you like to be able to go get your fourteen-year-old self and take her to hear something she'd like? What you said about the fleetingness of Galli-Curci,[120] Blackstone the Magicians, et al, made me understand as never before how similar our childhoods were. At eleven or twelve I was taken to see Otis Skinner in "The Honour of the Family" and we (my uncle and aunt and I) sat in the fourth row, and when he pounded on the table with his whipstock I jumped straight up in the air. It was the first time I ever saw a play from the orchestra. Usually I took myself and sat in what was universally referred to as Nigger-Heaven. A true heaven, if there ever was one, but I don't remember ever seeing any black people in it.

Bye-Bye-Bye Brevoort is kin to the skit Virginia WOOLF WROTE ABOUT Mrs. Cameron, Tennyson (when the electric typewriter decides to fling itself into caps there is little you can do about it except pull on the reins) and their friends on the, I think, Isle of Wight.[121] I wish I could have

seen the performance. It reads as though it would act beautifully, and I can almost hear the laughter. It also reminds me of the wonderful sense of being let loose from probability into something more convincing that I found in "The Madwomen of Chaillot". The man who emerged from the Paris sewer with a copy of "The Brothers Karamazov" under his arm. How happy it made me. So does this "bauble" for the same reason. When Fortescue says "Not in the corridor" she speaks for all the old women I have ever admired and loved. As for their outward form, sewed as they are, and on that paper, they are going to <u>last</u>.[122]

In The New Yorker, Christmas issue, there was a brief book note about a book of recollections of the Powys family, which had a sentence that bothered me. It ended "...David Garnett, Jacquetta Hawkes, and the late Sylvia Townsend Warner." Late, said I to myself. Why <u>late</u>? I don't remember ever reading "the late William Faulkner" or "the late Elizabeth Bowen" or even "the late John Galsworthy." When this walnut was cracked open it revealed a belief unconsciously held that good writers do not die, they simply pass into their works and go right on living. In short, they last. If they work hard, and they are supposed to do that in any case.

Thank you, and love from us both in the beginning and right straight through to the end of the New Year,

Bill

7

"What There Is to Say We Have Said"

BETWEEN 1981 AND 1996, Eudora and Bill more intensely felt the pressures and limitations that advancing age brings. As a stay against time, they both turned to the past in their writing, Eudora in her memoir *One Writer's Beginnings* and Bill in first-person narratives about his youth in Lincoln, Illinois. And in defiance of time, they both sought to seize the moment. Eudora along with two friends took the *Queen Elizabeth 2* to England in 1984, and she ventured back to England by herself, this time flying, in 1990. Between 1981 and 1993, Bill and Emmy enjoyed an extended stay in France and three times visited Italy. Eudora spoke at colleges and universities across the country, took the trans-Canadian railroad from Montreal to Lake Louise, and relished her trips to New York City. Bill and Emmy continued to maintain residences in Manhattan and Yorktown Heights; to visit Wellfleet, Massachusetts, each summer; and to find joy in their daughters' achievements. In 1987, Eudora watched the Iran-contra hearings with fascination, and she and the Maxwells all rejoiced in the 1992 election of William Jefferson Clinton as president.

Bill was still writing fiction during the 1980s and into the 1990s, but Eudora found herself unable to do so. Although honors for her fiction contin-

ued to pour in, her ability to transform her experiences into stories had vanished. This irony was tormenting. Eudora ultimately found ways to accept the situation, but she experienced some dark moments along the way, the most intense of which she confided to Bill. His reply assured her that she was not alone. "Who hasn't, at our age," Bill rhetorically asked, "at some time turned his face to the wall." And then he encouraged Eudora to turn away from that wall, to come into the Maxwell home, and to let them drive her despair away. An actual stay with Bill and Emmy didn't prove necessary, but the love that prompted Bill's offer was sustaining. Later, when Eudora and Ronald Sharp jointly edited *The Norton Book of Friendship*, they included Bill's story "The Fisherman Who Had Nobody to Go Out in His Boat with Him." In this story of a fisherman whose miraculous singing saves a fleet, Eudora must have seen an image of Bill.

The exchange of letters between Bill and Eudora eventually came to an end. Eudora's last extant letter to Bill arrived in 1990, his to her in 1996. Eudora's bouts with arthritis and compression fractures, Bill's recurring lymphoma, and Emmy's ovarian cancer took center stage in their lives and restricted their correspondence. But the friendship endured. As Bill wrote in a 1993 letter, "Dearest Eudora, what there is to say we have said, in one way or another. You know how much we love you." And the Maxwells in turn knew how much Eudora loved them. Written words were no longer necessary.

Eudora Welty to Emily and William Maxwell, [Late March 1981],
Note card with image of a bespectacled rabbit about to drink from a beaker

Dearest Emmy and Bill,

This hare is about to drink some <u>swich licour</u> (correct my Chaucer), and I am about to go on a <u>Pilgrimage</u> to Vassar—April 8 & 9—with a few days after that to spend in N.Y. Chores to do there, but if you're not away on a Pilgrimage of your own, could you find a time when I could set eyes on you? I'll probably talk to you, if I can reach you, before then, but I know it's so late either way. (My college visits. I really am tired, & far behind, and need to have every vein bathed in swich licour like that rabbit.) I hope every bit of news is good with you, and with both the girls. I think of the pear trees on Baptist Church Road—How do your roses look? It's dogwood time here—

So I'll be at the Algonquin—reaching town from Vassar on the afternoon of the 9th—Is the 9th any good for you?—My friends from Washington, John & Catherine Prince with whom I went to France, phoned me they were going to be in N.Y., in what turned out to be the same several days, and I hesitate to make dates before I see them. They're planning to leave on the 15th, as I was to do, but if the 15th happened to be a free evening with you, I'd stay over. I'll try to call you tonight from home—Forgive the lateness and I will pray for luck—If—when—<u>whenever</u> I see you, I'll tell you about being with Victor & Dorothy Pritchett in Nashville and Leontyne Price in Hattiesburg, Miss. After N.Y.C., I'll be in Chattanooga, Tenn., seeing Walker Percy. It's <u>really</u> Spring when I lay eyes on you—My Banksia rose is opening up, I ought to bring you a lap full. With my love, E—

I didn't want to write around the rabbit—with those spectacles on. A crowded message—

Eudora Welty, Chattanooga, to Emily and William Maxwell,
[April 1981], Postcard with photograph of the blessing of the fleet,
Biloxi, Mississippi

Dearest Emmy and Bill—The ranunculus rode home on the plane with me and almost the minute they were back in water they straightened their beautiful stems again and were their same beautiful selves for 2 more full days—They brought my mother's "borders" back to me so, it seemed to me blooming in the house as well as in the Algonquin was part of their birthday character—It was so lovely to see you, and Kate with you! Thank you for the evening, the flowers, and everything—

I'm in Chattanooga, Tenn. on a 2-day thing. Walker Percy is too, and he sends his respects. He was saying how tremendously he admires <u>So Long, See You Tomorrow</u>. This postcard is of the Blessing of the Fleet instead of Lookout Mountain because it fell out of the book I'd brought along ("The Inimitable Jeeves").

Much, much love, and thank you again for the evening I treasure—Take care of yourselves—Eudora

Eudora Welty to Emily and William Maxwell, [Late April, 1981], Postcard with photograph of two horses in crocheted costumes pulling a buggy with two men in it, titled "4th of July Parade Early Twentieth Century"

Dearest Emmy and Bill, here's a souvenir of my visit to the U. of Ala. at Huntsville—(really a wonderful town) with love from Eudora

> Black mares paired, each in mother-hubbard,—
> Crochet-canopied, fringed-around fillies—
> Hitched to a pony-cart with high wheels rubbered,
> Pulling a couple of Huntsville Sillies—
> The mare going last is decorous as can be.
> But the one going first is laughing, isn't she?

Eudora Welty to William and Emily Maxwell, August 20, 1981

Dearest Bill and Emmy,

Here's a good novel waiting for your return from the shore. I loved the writing. And to be so exhilarated by somebody around 80 years old! Only the Irish could do it. Molly Keane was a friend & neighbor of Elizabeth's— (I was taken to her house once, in the 50's, & can tell you a little about her sometime.)[1]

The summer has gone well for you, I hope—And the burden of the S.T.W. book off your shoulders, Bill, so that everything's been lightsome— where did I pluck that word from at 6:30 in the morning? It's cool at this hour and hot from 8:00 on—I'm ashamed to say I haven't cleared the decks so as to get down to work as I'd vowed to myself I'd do—By decks I mean the dining room table, in addition to my desk and all—covered with undone tasks, unanswered mail and the rest. When I ask company to dinner, I have to carry the old mail off the dining room table and hide it on my bed. Isn't that one of the cardinal sins? Sloth, I mean. I <u>suffer</u> from it. Well, anyway, it will get cooler, & some of the mail will expire. I can't <u>write</u> letters, as you see. Just put this on some back porch table & leave it.

The trip I expect I mentioned to you on the lovely train across Canada is still on, I think, in spite of plane uncertainties—I fly to Montreal to board the train. Then fly from Calgary to N.Y. My decision to spend a week in

Banff by myself to try to sort out a story may not do what I hope, but it will be new & strange to be there. Margot Wilkie wrote & invited me to a party in Katonah with the delicious word that you were coming, she hoped, too. That's at the end of next month, isn't it? It's better to look forward to seeing you than to seeing Lake Louise—I hope you're able to come. There's all your summer to hear about, & how the girls are, and everything. Much love, Eudora

William Maxwell to Eudora Welty, [January 9, 1983]

Sunday the who knows what of Jan because we're in the country with no NY Times

Dearest Eudora:

A couple of days after we talked to you, the book arrived.[2] I thought I was seeing things, because in the picture of my mother with her younger sister, aet. 6 and 4, that is on my dresser, my mother is wearing that same bonnet with the ruff that is on the older child on the dust jacket. It beats anything, this whole book. I thumb through the pages and read the text and sigh for I don't know what exactly. For all that innocence, maybe. My mother's doll, residing in a drawer in Emmy's studio, keeps turning up in picture after picture. The way the book cuts across all social classes (or so it seems to me) suggests that, poor or not, the children's photographs had to be taken. Somebody told me recently that the oxford shoe for men only came in in the 1920s, a thing I have trouble believing, but it is true that when I try to remember the shoes I wore as a child I remember the pinch of the button hook. For some reason the unidentified little boy on page 207 particularly beguiles me, but then I reflect upon what he probably turned out to be, and it wouldn't be my kind. What I'd like is to be running an orphanage with all of them as the orphans. Black and white. Butterfly nets, blocks, balls, parasols, artificial curls, lace, fans, striped stockings, velocipedes, et al. Do you think children have the same faces now? Because I somehow don't. There exists in the family, though I don't have a copy of it, a picture my father had taken to commemorate (I can only think) the death of my mother. He is holding my younger brother, aged three or four months, on his lap, and my older brother, at fourteen or possibly just turned fifteen, is sitting beside my father,

looking as if he were about to recite "And if thou sayest I am not peer to any man in Scotland here, Highland or Lowland, far or near, Lord Angus thou has — etc."[3] And I am wearing a norfolk jacket and spoiling the effect by looking cheerful. The photographer was a terrible fool and kept telling us to look for the birdie. My poor father's expression I won't go into. In a still earlier picture I have my thumb in my mouth. One thing I am sure of, from looking at this book, is that as the exterior of American houses has got worse and worse, the interiors have got better. I really wouldn't like to have lived in that house on page 52. My cousin Maxwell Fuller was easily the prettiest child ever born into our family, and there wasn't a house that didn't have him, aged three, with long blond curls, in a petticoat, usually framed in a horizontal series, like a yard of pansies or kittens. Little Lord Fauntleroy, of course.

Oh dear, what a lovely present. What an understanding friend to know who would so absolutely love it. If you will look at page 35, you will see what I mean by the pinch of the buttonhook, but of course you remember it, that is to say, your ankles do.

The sun is shining, and it is very cold, and Emmy is going for a walk, and in a minute I am going to take a custard she made to the old woman who lives across the road from us. She had a double stroke a year and a half ago, and ended up in a nursing home and when we went to see her we would concentrate on her upper eyelids, to see if there was some sign that she understood what we were saying. Little by little she has fought her way back, and is now in her house again, with some part-time help, and pulling all the things out of cupboards and drawers, just the way she used to. She also calls up people in the middle of the night, and is full of secrets, which show around the edges of her conversation.

I don't suppose you take the magazine Prose or can find it in the Jackson Library, but there is a very fine piece on Gertrude Stein and Toklas in number 7, fall 1973, and as writing it got me excited, at the beginning of the week, and at the end of the week, meaning last night after supper, I was reading aloud to Emmy a story by William Plomer called "The Child of Queen Victoria". It is from a book of his I didn't know about, called Four Countries, and I came upon it in Barbara Howes' paperback anthology of "23 Modern Stories" and it is <u>wonderful</u>. You know how good he is anyway. This even improves on second reading, though we were bowled over by it

the first time. It is like Conrad if Conrad were William Plomer. If you know what I mean. Now I must take the custard across the road but I will be back shortly.

Hours later, after a false start to town. Last weekend Emmy announced that there was something under the car, some liquid, in the parking lot last weekend and rather than believe that our dear car had a leaky radiator I put the whole thing out of my mind, so successfully that not until yesterday morning when I saw a damp patch on the floor of the garage did I think about it. To the extent of putting newspapers on the floor of the garage to see if it was coming from the car. After which I forgot all about it until I was packing the car to go to town. I took a mayonnaise jar of water just in case and kept my eye on the temperature gauge which suddenly shot up into the red, about five miles from home. So we are back, and will be watching The Good Soldier[4] here instead of in town, so that I can go to the garage in Mt. Kisco first thing in the morning. Why must this sort of thing always happen on the weekend when the garage is closed, I complained, and Emmy said, We only use the car on weekends. But it is true. The refrigerator broke down last weekend; neglect, neglect, all the motors are saying. They don't really love us, they live somewhere else. If I haven't cracked the radiator, and if I haven't cracked the cylinder block, I expect the garage can fix it, with a little bit. If not, well one thing at a time. But I am charged with adrenalin.

And E has another of those tumors on her eyelid, that may have to be taken off, since soaking doesn't seem to be doing much good. Otherwise we are fine. If we had more trouble in our life we wouldn't, I wouldn't, be upset over a possibly cracked radiator. It is really only that I love the car like a person. Or the way I used to love my bicycle.

I also think it is going to snow, but we have snowtires. Did you ever read a novel by Sherry Mangan called Cinderella Married? When she needed to speak to her godmother she flushed the toilet and out she came and settled herself on the bowl and inquired what the trouble was. Emmy bought a copy of the Enquirer, and it seems that Prince Charles and Princess Di are not getting on too smoothly. She doesn't want to sit around in wet duckblinds and he doesn't want to stay home and dandle the baby. I don't see how either of them could have foreseen this, do you? And what about the tear that slid down the Royal cheek when the Archbishop said, Do thou,

Charles take this, etc.? They had an argument <u>in public</u> and the Queen gave the Princess a cold look. Aren't you glad not to be mixed up in any of that? Nothing but trouble. Better a cracked engine block, though I don't like to put the words on paper. With my fingers crossed for the young couple and for this old couple and everybody,

<div align="right">Your devoted,
Bill</div>

PS The garage said do you want to leave the car and I didn't, so I got the radiator filled with antifreeze and off we went to town, and nothing bad happened, but there is a leak somewhere that will have to be attended to, and better soon, of course, than later.

And come to think of it, if you find you would like to read that piece about Stein/Toklas, or the story by Plomer, there is no reason in the world why I couldn't mail it to you. It wouldn't even entail a trip to the postoffice.

Emmy's eyelid seems better, and there is a sentence that gave me pause in the introduction to the book, p. 34: "It was the eve of the 1880s and 1890s, when technology would plunge the country into even more changes—great railroad networks, telephone and telegraph lines interlacing distant sections of the land, electric lights and streetcars, expanding industries, exploitation of natural resources, the rise of the department store (<u>zing</u>!...) skyscrapers, metropolitan centers, adding machines, fountain pens, typewriters, flush toilets, cast-iron tubs with enamel finishes, phonographs, cameras, big city newspapers, magazines, automobiles, and eminently, the middle class." In short, many of the things we think of as old-fashioned, were, not all that long ago, terribly new. Including the class I sprang from.

There is a huge, dismal new history of Logan County that my cousin just sent me and that depresses me to be in the same room with it. It is the third, and if you didn't have the first and second, you wouldn't have a clue to where the things and people and money and land all came from.

William Maxwell to Eudora Welty, February 21, 1983

Dearest Eudora,

Just a note to say how startled I was to find myself a candidate for the Gold Medal for Fiction. If I were betting, I would put my money on Mala-

mud.[5] And if he gets it, feel a slight burden of guilt removed, for no ratio-
nal reason. I once served as a fiction judge for the National Book Award
and, having talked the other judges out of giving it to By Love Possessed, I
proceeded to talk them into giving it to The Wapshot Chronicle. Francis
Steegmuller thought it ought to go to Malamud for The Assistant, which I
also liked very much. The other day I found a long, intelligent letter from
Francis explaining—at the time—why The Assistant was a novel and The
Wapshot Chronicle was not. The distinction didn't interest me much, and
doesn't now, really. I feel a novel is a long piece of prose narrative with the
breath of life in it. But anyway, I was afraid that The Wapshot Chronicle
was the only novel John [Cheever] would ever write. Afterwards, I realized
with some guilt—for I didn't stop talking until the other judges gave in—
that both books should have had the award. Has there ever been one, a joint
N.B. Award, I mean? As for the Gold Medal, who gets it is less important
than the pleasure of being in the running.

All that is left of all that snow is mountains of garbage waiting to be col-
lected, and more filth than usual in the gutters. I say to myself, when I have
done this and that and that and that and that, and the figures for the tax ac-
countant, I will be almost caught up. But of course I won't. We are going
to Oregon as usual at the end of March for four days for my father-in-law's
birthday. We are expecting you to come up with the daffodils.

<div align="right">With much love,
Bill</div>

William Maxwell to Eudora Welty, April 12, 1983

Dearest Eudora:

I saw Bill Meredith at the Institute dinner, and it seems that that din-
ner party has been moved forward to the evening before the Ceremonial.
They would be enchanted if you could come, but it also leaves us free to
have our usual quiet supper after the shindy, here at home. I sort of had the
impression that you would not be in New York the evening before the Cer-
emonial, and were not even sure about whether or not you would make the
luncheon. Anyway, whatever you do, don't write. Surprise us.

I read [Elizabeth Bowen's] Look at All Those Roses aloud to Emmy the

other night, and was left with a longing to have you confirm our impressions, which were that the girl's father <u>was</u> in fact buried under some rose bush, but I wished—except that she is always right and knew what she was doing—I was left wondering what he did that injured the girl's back. She would have been seven at the time. Dropped her. I guess. But he would probably not have been murdered for an accident (once, in Yorktown, on a very hot day, I was sitting with my feet on a mossy step leading into the Lewissohns' pond, with Kate as a baby tucked under one arm and in the other hand a manuscript of a life of Dillon [Dylan] Thomas, which I was reading, and I stood up and my feet went out from under me, and I went through a series of extraordinary efforts to regain my balance, and when it was all over, both Kate and the Ms were dry, though I was wet and covered with scratches. I have no idea how I managed it). Did he do it while he was drunk, do you think? I guess it just pleased Elizabeth not to say. Tucked in the book I found a letter from her. I was under the misapprehension that I had never had a letter from her, and so affectionate that it made me very happy.

Such a nice piece of slapstick: When I was twenty-seven I spent the summer at the MacDowell Colony, and sat for my portrait by a painter my age named Charlotte Blass. At one point I thought it was very good, and then she went on painting (they always do) and I thought spoiled it. Anyway, she died last fall in El Paso, Texas, and left the contents of her studio to the MacDowell Colony. Including the portrait of me. I think Brendan Gill is on the Committee, but anyway he wrote and said it was there and would I like to buy it? I said could I see a photograph and he sent one and it looked pretty much like what I remember myself as looking at twenty-seven, so I said yes and sent a check. The picture arrived before Christmas, in New York, I mean, and Brendan said the director of the Colony wanted to meet me and so he planned to make an occasion of it when the Director came to town. That was the last I heard so this past week I jogged Brendan's elbow delicately, and yesterday he called and yesterday afternoon they arrived—he and Bill Banks, who was in town for thirty-six hours, with a large crate, which we took to the pantry. While the other two were having at the crate with a chisel and claw-hammer, Brendan was telling me about Charlotte Blass, who had been a pupil of George Luks, and had also done a portrait of William Rose Benet.[6] As the crate fell open, revealing a lot of opaque plas-

tic wrapping, he remarked, "Wouldn't it be awful if it was the Benet portrait instead" and of course it was. Meanwhile, all her other paintings, including the portrait of me, were auctioned off in San Francisco a month ago. Would you like to bet one way or the other on how it is going to turn out? And wasn't it odd that Brendan said that? What is one to think, except what one has always thought.

Oh I do hope you come. It will be so nice to see you.

<div style="text-align: right">Devotedly,
Bill</div>

Eudora Welty to William Maxwell, April 23, 1983, Postcard with photograph titled "Kiss of the Muse," c. 1867, by Julia Margaret Cameron

Dearest Bill,—I think he is under a rosebush, and that he dropped her. An effect of the heat, do you think?

I can't bear that about your portrait. About "effects" I trust no one—if it's something so rightfully somebody's, they don't get it. You will recognize that I speak sadly from experience, though it wasn't my own altogether. Well, it was Hubert Creekmore's things, marked with names of family & friends, and his executor said Sorry, but the night before he was to ship them off, a burglar broke in & took them all—that meant letters, mss., bits of pottery, autographed books from his friends. Have you any art acquaintance in San Francisco who could look for you? I think I would recognize you at 27—Oh I do hope you recover it. Or you could advertise in San F. papers "Will Exchange:"—It saddens me to miss coming to your house after the Ceremonial, especially now that it's so unexpectedly possible a free evening after all! But I'll be gone from N.Y. on the 15th—But, I'll be in N.Y. May 2–15! We can see one another then, can't we? And soon? We have so much to hear & tell—I was so GLAD to have the letter from you. I couldn't write back because I was (still am, frantically) working against time to get my 3 Harvard lectures done. I go up at 7:30 AM tomorrow to Cambridge. Pray for me. Much dear love to all of you. I just long to see you.
Eudora

Eudora's three Harvard lectures were a great hit. A year later, after she had revised them and published them as a book, Bill described the lectures to readers of The New Yorker: *"The audience was, for the most part, Harvard and Radcliffe undergraduates, many more than the hall could accommodate, with the overflow in other rooms that were wired with speakers. After the last lecture, bringing flowers, they waited in long lines for the privilege of speaking to her. Not bunches of flowers. Just one flower."*[7]

Eudora Welty to William and Emily Maxwell, August 13, 1983,
Postcard with image of "tulip with a nodding flower" from
John Edward's A Select Collection of Flowers

Dearest Bill and Emmy,

I wanted you to see how this ended up. Forgive the way it looks—I can't reach the point where I can let it alone even yet. (I've worked just about ever since I saw you—happy days!) And I haven't even had the grace to write you. You may be at Wellfleet—and I hope you have missed the heat or the worst of it—Bill, I was so glad to read your piece that snuffed out that biographer of Frank O'Connor—It showed the truest friendship and it made me feel that he knows—Take care of yourselves.[8] I send you love every day, trusting you to receive it every day too. Eudora

William Maxwell, Wellfleet, Massachusetts, to Eudora Welty,
September 9, 1983

Dearest Eudora:

There were enough similarities in our two childhoods to make me feel, reading the lectures, that we grew up on a tandem bicycle.[9] So much came back, beginning with the buttonhook. Adorable, that introduction. And why did they have so many clocks? In Emmy's father's house in Portland there were two grandfather clocks, one in the downstairs front hall and one almost directly above it on the second floor landing. The Reading Circle books I didn't actually own, but posed for advertising copy. Aged nine or

ten. Dorothy Nichol's father, who was the superintendent of schools, had something to do with it. I still have the picture, of nine children reading in a half circle. I have long black stockings on.

The Victor Book of the Opera Kate took over from me. If you gave me a bedsheet, I could wrap it around me as Galli-Curci wrapped Gilda's cape around her. Farrar as Manon I could not imitate.[10]

Speaking of eloping with Dickens, Emmy's mother in her will left me a very beautiful set of Dickens, under the impression that it had come down in her family, whereas it had come down in Emmy's father's family instead, and though he was punctilious about all other details of the will, Dickens' name never came up, and the books remained on the shelf. Shortly before he died[11] he asked me if there were any books in the house I wanted, and I said I'd rather read them out there, and now we are expecting several packing boxes of books, (and no empty bookshelves!) including Dickens. Beautiful paper, and the Cruikshank illustrations are very sharp and black.

Now I know where Miss Edna Earle came from.

In case you were lost, struck a responsive chord in my soul. I was lost, or thought I was. In Peoria. My mother was shopping in Block and Kuhl's department store and thinking I was sufficiently absorbed with the toys I wouldn't notice her absence, whipped up to the floor above to look at linen sheets, and when I turned around and she wasn't there, it was as if a pit opened in front of me. What tears. There I was far from home. No mother. I sometimes wonder how I got through the remaining seventy years of my life.

Glenway [Wescott] is enough older than we are that he remembers Halley's comet. It looked like a whiskbroom, he says.

It is true about the empty seat in the carriage. I never realized why we always took the Donalds driving with us. On the other hand, we never took the Kiests, who lived on the other side.

When I took Emmy home to Lincoln for the first time, I took her to the sewing woman, who by that time was a fitter in Landauers' Ready to Wear. She was German, and like a Christmas cookie, and I had only to ask and the children's pages in the fashion magazines were mine to cut out and paste.

It is so touching, that scene of your mother telling you about the death of her firstborn child.

I have often thought that my having led such an overprotected life was a serious drawback to writing, but you comfort me with the idea that daring comes from within. Daring I sometimes have been. I mean it was rather daring to throw up my teaching job at the U of Illinois in the year 1933, with no prospects whatever.

The King of the Golden River I read dozens of times, and was very fond of. But it had no previous billing, to exaggerate my expectations.[12] For my birthday, this summer, Joanna Brodkey gave me a copy of [Frances Hodgson Burnett's] Little Lord Fauntleroy, that she found in an antique shop, and I am ashamed to say I read it with undiminished pleasure.

The rapid beating heart I have had since college, and finally it got serious enough for me to be put on digoxen permanently. Now I have no symptoms whatever. I used to turn greenish.

Undoubtedly you have got the title of Darwin's book right (p. 40) but I question it because I always get it wrong.

Do you remember that your mother reading Time and acting out the wolf in Little Red Riding Hood is part of the evening when we became friends? At Mary Lou's, was it? I remember laughing over it till the tears ran down my cheeks.[13]

Do you still have the tambourine?

I have mislaid a hymn, and it occurred to me that you might know it. I don't know whether it begins, or the chorus begins, "Blessed Surrender, so happy and free…." When I tried to track it down, all that came back was Blessed Assurance, not the same thing at all.

On 42, and again later, you repeat the facts, or some of them, about Dorothy and the Old English etc. Does it matter?

I was called up on the stage by a vaudeville magician at the Majestic Theater in Bloomington [Illinois]. In a whisper he told me exactly what to do and when I did it he made a fool of me in what he said to the audience, and I went right on doing what he told me to do, and the audience laughed and laughed and when he was finished with me he said, "Tell your brother you did fine," and I went back to my seat in amazement. How did he know I had a brother?

The facts about the founder of your father's insurance company occur twice, on 45 and 91, but I am sure you have caught it by this time.

Fumigating the notes in the hot oven reminded me of my mother's sealing off our bedroom when my brother and I had recovered from chicken pox, measles, and what not, and burning formaldehyde candles, which must have been every bit as efficacious as the oven.

I will never get over Walter's letter as long as I live.

Dr. Caligari on Saturday afternoon reminds me of [a] children's matinee at the Comedie Francaise (s) of Phaedre. They sat listening to the horrors and gently kicking the back of their seats with their heels.

Since you love processions (my wonderful uncle in Bloomington always managed to let me see the circus procession <u>twice</u>) don't miss La Nuit de Varennes.[14]

My temper departed forever when I was fifteen, and without my doing a thing about it. Perhaps my brother's going off to college did the trick. I have often wished for it back. I am not sure I understand the parenthetical "But that was it" that follows, on page 51, your mother's saying "I always get hurt." I mean, it suggests several possibilities and I am not sure which one you mean.

As for Where is the Voice Coming From, you can doubt that it comes off if you want to, but I have no doubt whatever. The ending, the very thought of the ending makes the hair on the back of my neck rise.

The frayed ferry rope in West Virginia made me think of that Chekhov story about Easter ["The Night before Easter"], and the ferryman who never got to see the service.

The idlest kind of curiosity makes me long to know why your mother was using crutches when she rescued her Dickens from the burning building.

I didn't have a candle in my room, so when I wanted to stay up and find out what happened to Sidney Carton [in Dickens's A Tale of Two Cities], I put my black stockings across the crack under the bedroom door, and read on undisturbed till past midnight.

What does Chessie stand for? Not Charlotte, or Cassandra. I looked in my Collegiate Websters, but it was not helpful.

The arrival in West Virginia, the summer dawn with the brothers waiting on the other side of the river, the mist, and the ferry boat and the iron bell your mother rang—what a present you have given me.

I wish I had known, when you brought your mother out to see us in

Yorktown Heights, all I know about her now, but it was also nice knowing nothing, because we were so attracted to her and charmed by everything she said. Irresistible is what she was.

Grandfather Carden losing his eyesight in prison is the equivalent of a whole volume on the Civil War.

I long to read a story about the brothers' coming down from the mountain to live. Unlike the story of the piano, it does seem as if there must be more.

Whenever I hear crows I think of the farm in Wisconsin that became my second home.

A[nd] wasn't it odd of people to name their daughters after Salome? I guess they just thought it was, divorced from its context, a pretty name.

My father also was interested only in the future. Was it something to do with their generation? Or with the fact that they were both in the insurance business (the tandem bicycle).

Emmy also used esq on letters to her father, and to him only.

Yesterday Emmy's model turned up with a young man from Minneapolis who spoke with an inherited Norwegian accent, and whose strongest exclamation (speaking of pshaw) was "Oh my."

Thank you for the buggy the hens nested in. And for the chronology of revelation, which is as much true of these three speeches as it is of your stories.

Only because I loved the brothers so, I wondered about "Carl is writing letters to different ones that he thinks might come to school." Was he teaching, at that point?

And it took me some time to get past the Wandering Aengus to the dolphin torn, the gong tormented etc. Do you know High Talk in "Last Poems"? Silly questions. You'd be the last person not to know it.[15]

It is so sad, that your father didn't know what you could do. My father knew, but not what to make of it.

If I didn't love you already, I would for "The very soul of our human transience is its inherent dignity."

W[hen] next we meet, will you tell me about the earthquake that made the Miss River run backwards, please?

I liked very much (it is the only cut I questioned) the paragraph that has "Hide the encyclopedia" in it. Is there a reason for cutting it?

That you were present during that blood transfusion stopped me dead in my tracks. How many times in the history of the world has such a thing occurred. Not often, I would think. I thought at first you were describing it at second hand, until I (I read it first out loud to E.) reread the whole ms. Though I doubt if you meant to imply it, the switch to the train departure suggests (to me) the voyage of the soul after death.

In a closet off our summer kitchen there was a grocery carton full of letters from my father to my mother, which as a child I had no curiosity about, and which he must have thrown away when we moved. She couldn't write to him, because he was always on the move. Anyway, she didn't. Or perhaps she did and he didn't keep them. But this I somehow doubt. I mean I would have seen her writing to him.

What a story, the soldier who simply stepped off the train that had halted in the midst of nowhere. It is a kind of homage to Chekhov. Who said, details, not generalities, are what matter.

Webbie. It's enough to bring tears to your eyes.

And how I loved the paragraph about coming home, on p. 86.

And Elizabeth [Bowen]'s pronouncement that physical detail cannot be invented has settled a question in my mind. Wonderful last pages. Wonderful portrait of an American family!

This really too beautiful morning, Emmy decided to take tea and muffins to the ocean, and have a swim and breakfast on the beach. So we packed everything and set off in the canoe, across the pond, and walked over the dunes, and were met by hundreds of flies. Some shrimplike creatures had washed up on the beach by the thousands, during the last few days, and the sand smells like dead fish, and the flies may have come from as far as Hartford Conn. Anyway, we ran like Adam and Eve—no, we had a swim first and then ran for the canoe, and the flies clung to Emmy's shift and blue hat, all the way across the pond and into the house. Did you ever hear of such a thing?

Today is the last Friday. We are starting home on the fifteenth, to Yorktown, first, and then to New York, which is, the apartment is all torn up for the painter, who didn't keep his word. What painter ever did?

I am returning the xerox of the ms, because you will surely want to show it to someone else. I wouldn't have been able to part with it, if I didn't have

the expectation of getting [it] back in the form of a book. I have worked on some very brief stories, nothing to be very pleased with but to be writing stories instead of editing is happiness. I have to escape somehow from what I have been doing for years to something I haven't yet imagined doing.

We both send much love,

B.

Eudora Welty to William Maxwell, [September 1983]

Dearest Bill,

It was so wonderful to read your letter. I want to answer it line by line. We were more in tandem than I knew, though of course right from the start we knew we were sort of. It was a need to me for you and Emmy to read the piece, more than even in the case of most mss. It's been strange in a way working with the Harvard U. Press, because they were reading the thing without knowing me. You and Emmy restore me, and I am more exhausted than I could have dreamed I'd be after writing it—I wrote about twice as much as appears in the ms., which is in turn about twice the length of the lectures I suppose. (The tambourine is out—in the interest of continuity—and the organization of the whole is a little more lucid now than when I impulsively sent it to you. No, I don't even have that tambourine now.) I can't find "Blessed Surrender" in my Cokesbury Hymnal either but can ask among churchgoers here. One of the things the Harvard copy editor changed (along with deleting 2,000 commas, approx. She <u>added</u> one comma = "Tidewater, Virginia") was "ran it in the oven" (Mother with our notes) to "ran it <u>through</u> the oven." To the sentence about a Welti pushing through the St. Goddher [Gotthard] Tunnel, she wrote "through what?" I wrote, "The Alps!" I remember full many a time and oft (as Bertie Wooster would put it) how you used to go down the margins of my galleys erasing the queries before I had to deal with them. Took me a week to get my commas, paragraphing, spacing, etc. back in place.

One main reason I had to send this to you and Emmy was the meeting my mother had with you and how well you all three liked one another, and I'm so glad my mother came through to you in the piece. She was on crutches, I think, because of the long convalescence she had from septice-

mia—I'm sure it was that, because I don't know of any other time she was on crutches. (All before I was born of course.) Chessie stands for the unlikely name Chestina, she was named for her mother's sister, and where it came from I have often wondered. A corruption of Justina? A feminine form of Chester? When that Chesapeake and Ohio RR began using the name "Chessie" and applied it to a cat, my mother wasn't too well pleased about the cat part.

My last poems of Yeats don't include the truly last ones, because "High Talk" is not in my book, so I must take remedies. One thing I can get immediate hold of for you is an account of the earthquake of 1811—in J.F.H. Claiborne's (b. 1805)[16] Mississippi as a Province, Territory and State, written from a lot of first-hand accounts. If you have great big magnifiers on your specs—it's back in the appendix. In those days, a trip was really a trip, and if you asked somebody to "tell me your trip," here was what you got (especially if taken by one of the Knickerbocker family named Roosevelt) except this account is better by being told by Hon. J.H.B. Latrobe, "a savant of Baltimore." I hope you like it. As of course you know, New Madrid (accent on the Mad) is the early name for St. Louis.

I love the train departure suggesting the voyage of the soul after death, and possibly it was trying to suggest itself to me, and now that you have it elates me.

It's like knowing a ship has made it into harbor to know what you and Emmy feel about the book. I'll write you better when some of the chaos I'm living in (I mean the rooms of my house, full of stacks of things everywhere and my growing uncertainty of just where some little piece of paper I need is. (Harvard needs to correct that sentence.))

I hope and pray your work goes the way you want it to—my love to it.

Oh yes, I put that in about Mother and the Wolf and Time with you and Emmy and our meeting in mind. I'll check up for sure about Origin of Species—that same book is still lying around the house though not in my pantry. Which is scarcely odd because I haven't got a pantry. All at once, the heat went—is it the same there? It got to be cool and bright and clear— shivered in bed, with the blankets downstairs in their cedar bags. I hope all's lovely in Yorktown Heights and on East 86th St. Mary Lou is not very well and I'm going out for a long weekend in Santa Fe on the 28th.

My love to you both and my thanks for all your letters said—I'll write better soon—

E—

William Maxwell to Eudora Welty, September 19, 1983

Dearest Eudora

We're expecting <u>lots</u> of books from Oregon, and nowhere to put any of them. So I have been playing Russian sleigh. It seems most unlikely that you don't already possess a picture book entitled "William Faulkner: The Cofield Collection" but if you don't I would much rather send you my copy than simply dispose of it to some second-hand book dealer. The enclosed card is to save you time and trouble, and if you write me a letter you will defeat my intentions. We both send love on a day that is hot as blaizes.

B.

William Maxwell to Eudora Welty, January 9, 1984

Dearest Eudora,

The glass globe reminds me of a poem I couldn't have got through college without, beginning, "My candle burns at both ends," for it does indeed give a lovely light. But also did I ever thank you for that marvelous account of the first steamboat on the Mississippi? I think the difference, in reading matter, between what gives you pleasure and what gives me pleasure is so slight as not to be worth thinking about. A friend (Harriet Sheehy) brought us from England a Commonplace book that has this very odd and beautiful poem in it. It is by Charles Cotton, who was the friend and collaborator of Izaak Walton.

> In this cold Monument lies one,
> That I knew who has lain upon,
> The happier He: her sight would charm,
> And touch have kept King David warm.
> Lovely, as is the dawning East,
> Was this marble's frozen guest;
> As soft, and snowy, as that down
> Adorns the Blow-ball's frizzled crown;
> As straight and slender as the crest,

Or antlet of the one-beamed beast;
Pleasant as th' odorous month of May:
As glorious, and as light as Day.

Whom I admir'd, as soon as knew,
And now her memory pursue
With such a superstitious lust,
That I could fumble with her dust.

She all perfections had, and more,
Tempting, as if design'd a whore,
For so she was; and since there are
Such, I could wish them all as fair.

Pretty she was, and young, and wise,
And in her calling so precise,
That industry had made her prove
The sucking school-mistress of love:
And Death, ambitious to become
Her pupil, left his ghastly home,
And, seeing how we us'd her here,
The raw-boned rascal ravisht her.

Who, pretty Soul, resign'd her breath,
To seek new lechery in Death.[17]

Brookie, as I think you know, is mad about dancing and shortly before
Christmas did one too many turns and broke a bone in her foot and went
through the holidays with a styrofoam cast halfway up her right leg. Over it
she wore a black wool stocking with bright designs appliquéd on it by the
artist herself. It was removed a couple of days ago (the cast, not the stock-
ing) and her foot seems to be all right, though not quite ready for dancing
on. Kate has an apartment all by herself on West 92nd Street between Cen-
tral Park West and Columbus. The back half of the top floor of a brown-
stone. A nice white marble fireplace, but very shallow closets, which in any
case are full of books and records so that her clothes have to shift for them-
selves. It is, I think, the first time she has ever lived alone and she seems to
be enjoying it.

We are almost through dealing with the furniture, china, and books from my father-in-law's house in Oregon. By some sort of ill-luck a tag fell off the chaise-longue that was in Emmy's mother's bedroom so that it didn't get taken with the first shipment and is arriving in a few days and must somehow be dealt with. And the roads at this time likely to be all snow and ice. The only place in the apartment where there is room for it temporarily is the living room. I have seen chaise-longues in libraries, but never in a living room. Have you? Maybe if we pushed it close to the bookcase. Or maybe it will arrive during the January thaw. Last year there wasn't any. The less said about this winter the better.

We have cockroaches in the kitchen and keep missing the periodic visits of the exterminator. It is my private opinion, since Emmy never leaves food around, that they have taken it into their heads that they are lemmings and they are looking for some sea to throw themselves into.

It was so odd about Vogue and Barbara Ascher. She sent me a xerox of her interview, and I thought it was very good indeed and that any magazine would jump at it. I also was under the impression—no, that's not true, I wasn't really under that impression. When I was very young Edmund Wilson[18] sat in my office one day and gave me a lecture on the editorial fallacy which, he said, was changing things for the sake of changing them. So naturally what you said got changed to something you didn't say. I haven't heard yet where the piece ended up, but end up somewhere I know it will.[19]

I am making myself go to the January dinner at the Institute and excusing myself from the meeting that precedes it. So many of the older people that I loved or found interesting have either died or are ill or just stopped coming. I hope something brings you here before long. I am perishing to talk to you.

B.

William Maxwell, Wellfleet, Massachusetts, to Eudora Welty,
August 18, 1984

Dearest Eudora:

I rejoice to see that book still on the best-seller list like a bird on a branch and I think now, surely, you will not be obliged to go about the country un-

less you feel like it.[20] I groan when I think about the income tax and how in Ireland writers don't have to pay any. But still in all if there is such a thing as a well-earned windfall this is it.

I have written a story which is now being typed and which may not be what I wanted it to be but at least it is done.[21] The little house that I rented in town so that Emmy wouldn't be distracted by the sound of my electric typewriter when she was painting, she took one look at and claimed for herself, and has gone there nearly every day. It is just barely large enough for one doll to live in. Two dolls would get in each others' way. But it has a deck so that she can paint outdoors and it has made her so happy that I feel we must somehow find a studio for her away from the apartment.

As I was having that opinion sheet xeroxed for you I realized that there was a conflict of loyalties. Editorial opinion sheets are written in the assumption that they will not be read by outsiders and it would not be right for me to ignore this so I am sending you only what I wrote and I think that it shouldn't go into your archives but into the wastebasket instead.

[...] Brookie was coming up for the weekend with a friend until they found out the price of the airplane ticket from Boston to Provincetown. The circumstances were such that we couldn't offer to pay for it and the weather, alas, is perfection. E. would send her love if she weren't in her little house painting.

B

In late 1946, Bill had urged The New Yorker *to accept Eudora's story "The Whole World Knows." The magazine declined to do so, and the story was published elsewhere. Bill's hesitation about making his editorial opinion sheet public was based on a concern for the magazine (see his letter of August 10, 1987), but happily* The New Yorker *has now granted permission for the opinion sheet to be part of this book. It follows.*

We're in a position to pull off any experiment we feel like. The magazine has always reserved the right to surprise its readers, and it's when we don't surprise them for long periods of time that the complaints get

loud. There will be readers who will complain that they didn't make head nor tail of this story (though it is not unintelligible, but just a difficult piece of writing, requiring slow careful reading) and there will be others, possibly just as many, who will respect and honor us for publishing a work of art.

After spending a whole evening with this piece and making all kinds of notes I've arrived at the conclusion that it shouldn't be changed, and that we ought to print it as it now stands. If you change it even to the extent of making the narrative more orderly you take away seriously from the total effect, which is of a man teetering on the edge of a breakdown. Many things that aren't instantly clear become so in the next paragraph or by the end of the page, and at the end of the story it's all there, everything in its right place; even the unprepared switches in and out of the man's consciousness seem to me to have their reason and to be right as she has done them. The piece violates every canon of this magazine and it's absolutely first rate fiction with wonderful things all through it which raise it, for me, above anything we've run in years. No matter where it's published it will be admired and remembered, and its excellence is so undeniable that no explanation or apology will be necessary, any more than they were necessary for the Hiroshima article.[22]

There must surely come a time with any magazine when the usual editorial canons have to be laid aside in favor of a work of the highest quality. We have been getting clearer and clearer, and more literal and more literal, while the world all around us gets foggier and ambiguous to the point of nightmare. The cult of clarity and literalness pushed to its logical conclusions (where we are rapidly pushing it) will end eventually in a kind of monotonous, mediocre, factory-made fiction that is completely divorced from life, without richness or poetry or (in any true sense) meaning.

Eudora Welty to William and Emily Maxwell, [December 1984]

Dearest Bill and Emmy—I was in NYC and didn't call you—I began to feel sinking-low, it was all in my spirits, and you'd know this on sight of me, so I waited—and <u>was</u> all right next morning but had to make my plane—It was a quick trip, to be given an award by NYU, and you know I've just had

too much awarded me—I can't bear not seeing you, and getting to do that that might have been my cure, but I just stayed on the bed (though dressed) reading your Christmas present, which I brought with me & was going to tote you, as you see—I won't do this way any more. A letter soon because I wanted to say so much about how I loved the wonderful story. That wonderful story! I thought you'd found a sort of golden perspective to see everything from—some perfect point—[23]

All my love and wishes for Christmas,

From Eudora

I hope you do like Seamus Heaney as I do—I've read this one a number of times—Faber & Faber brought it out in paper in England and I read it on the boat.[24]

William Maxwell to Eudora Welty, January 2, 1985

1/2/985, no 1985
Though maybe I wish it were 985.
Dearest Eudora:

If I were to say what I was prompted to say when I read your letter, you would think, quite reasonably, that I hadn't understood a word of it. I do understand. Who hasn't, at our age, at some time turned his face to the wall. We both worry about you—about the never quite going away tiredness. And about the way you are plucked at by people all over the country wanting something. Wanting you. Wanting you to do something for them. They don't mean to be heartless, and, of course, don't know or can't imagine about the others, but the effect is the same as if they were. I was even struck, at the library that day, by the fact that a purpose not entirely honoring (meaning PR) is sometimes served by the giving of awards. Dr. Gelbenkian or however it is spelled, had read the book.[25] With the others it was doubtful. There is also the matter of living alone. If you live with somebody you are saved (often by petty irritation) from having to confront despair. But anyway, you did it, and got through it, and got home safely. Which is the main thing.

Night before last I was aware that Emmy who usually follows me to bed

by half an hour was taking longer than usual, and finally I got up and went to see what she was doing. She was reading Seamus Heaney, at one-thirty AM, that's what she was doing.

I assume that you got a photograph from that girl who took our picture on the steps of the side entrance of the library. I thought it was very good of both of us. And so nice to have.

What I was going to say, and felt it made no sense to say, at the beginning of this letter, is that there is this room with the four-poster bed, very comfortable, Kate's room no longer occupied by her, and it would have made us so happy if you had rung the bell and said I am at the end of my rope, will you take care of me till I get over it? We would have put you to bed in that bed, and driven that despair right out of the apartment. Remember that this is possible, won't you?

Once long ago, when we were in Oregon, Emmy's brother arranged for us to stay in a motel when we came to Portland from the beach, and I didn't too much like the sound of it, and so when one of Emmy's childhood friends offered us the house of a friend of hers who was in Iran to stay in, we cancelled the motel reservation, and drove up from the beach on a day when it was 103° — Emmy and I and the little, very little Brookie was, girls, and Margaret McBride, from Scotland. And the house we were expecting to stay in was full of fleas, because the dogs had been taken to the kennel, which alarmed Margaret McBride, since they apparently don't have fleas in Glasgow, and everywhere we looked there was either a bottle of something poisonous, or something sharp that young children could hurt themselves on, and we couldn't reclaim the motel reservation, because they were dearer than hen's teeth, and there we were. Until I thought of the woman who lived next door to Emmy when she was a child, and whose two daughters were Emmy's playmates. I bundled everybody into the car and drove to her house, and rang the bell and when nobody heard us (she was rather deaf) walked in and called up the stairs "Margie, we <u>Need</u> you!" It turned out there was a bed for every last one of us, and no poisons and no sharp instruments. Nothing but love.

<div style="text-align:right">So as I say, just remember.
Bill</div>

William Maxwell to Eudora Welty, February 28, 1985

Dearest Eudora,

 Thank you so much for the copy of the Paris Review with Robert Fitzger-
ald's interview in it. I not only enjoyed it for what it said but because it is so
wonderfully lighthearted. I can't remember whether I wrote you about his
funeral. It took place in a fairly ordinary Catholic Church in New Haven. At
the front of the altar there were baskets of spring flowers which didn't at all
have the look of funeral flowers. I sat in a pew in front of his family—that is
to say, Sally [Fitzgerald's second wife] and three of her grown daughters and
a grandchild—and could hear their responses to the Mass. The coffin was
covered by an embroidered white cloth that went to the floor, and the three
officiating priests wore white surplices. There was a Requiem Mass, with
music which Robert had chosen, and beautiful voices to sing it. And one by
one the children, the three grown sons and the three grown daughters, went
up to the lectern and either read from the Bible or from Robert's poems.
And then Penny [Fitzgerald's third wife] talked about his life. One of the
stories I had never heard: When he was in Choate and had his first poem
published, Dudley Fitts, who was on the faculty, came up to him and said
(as nearly as I can remember) "If you are going to be a writer you will have
to learn that G O E T H E does not rhyme with L E T H E."[26] It reminded
me of the struggle I had at the age of seven or eight in pronouncing the
name of Richard Wagner. At the end of the service the priests came down
from the altar with their incense and holy water and stood around the cof-
fin, and instead of feeling that it was going to end up in a hole in the ground,
I could believe that he was being taken into a sublime mystic fraternity, like
the one in The Magic Flute. It has been the greatest comfort to me.

 Yesterday, a young woman came to tea who is on the editorial staff of
The New Yorker and who had Robert for her tutor during her final year at
Radcliffe. She wrote poems under his eye and, as in the interview, he was
strict with her but also lighthearted. One of the things he told her was that
he used to show his poems to John Berryman. And when there was a weak
line somewhere in the poem, Berryman would put his finger on it and say,
"Tsk!Tsk!Tsk!"

Brookie's 42nd Street is now on display I believe through March and April in the Port Authority Building.[27] Though I do say it that shouldn't, it is worth your coming to New York just to see it.

<div align="right">

Devotedly,

Bill

</div>

Attached but not reprinted here was Bill's February 25, 1985, New Yorker piece discussing volume 5 of The Diary of Virginia Woolf.

Eudora Welty, New York City, to William Maxwell, [March 1985]

Dearest Bill,

Here is an article, under the heading "Miscellaneous," from <u>The Lady's Almanac for 1859</u>, which I just received yesterday—the opening paragraph is arresting enough:

<div align="center">

STITCHING MADE EASY.

</div>

"From the day Mother Eve performed the first needle-work, in the garden of Eden, down to this enlightened Nineteenth Century, our sex has been doomed to toil and slave with the needle, at the expense of health and life. The invention of the Sewing Machine, though long delayed, has at length afforded the needed relief; and womanhood rejoices in her emancipation from the slavery of the needle."

How to sew it on the sewing machine, with "engravings," follows. Also in this Almanac is the most hopeless set of directions I ever came across— Also under "Miscellaneous," for October—"How to Mount a Horse." (for a lady). At the very beginning of this useful book, there is a list of Eclipses in 1859, every one of them, almost, turns out to be "only visible in a small portion of the Southern Ocean" or "invisible in the United States but may be seen in the Russian Possessions and the North Pacific Ocean." The partial eclipse of the sun, July 29, results in this: "Only a part of the Sun's southern limb will be visible in Boston." A partial Eclipse of the Sun, August 27th & 28th, will be "invisible in America, Europe, and Asia. But a small portion of it will be seen at Cape of Good Hope. It will commence in the vicinity of Madagascar and end near the South Pole." Women just have to take what they can get. There are advertising pages, including that of Dr. J. R. Dilling-

ham, Dental Surgeon, featuring a letter of recommendation from <u>Daniel Webster</u>, on Dr. Dillingham's leaving Boston for California.

We'll miss you so much this evening. I hope you'll be feeling much better tomorrow. I'll be hoping to hear your voice over the phone before I go back. I saw Mr. Shawn at a party at Joan Kahn's last night and he was saying how much he hoped you & he could have lunch before long. We had a good conversation and I was so glad to see him. — What a soul-satisfying review you did of the Virginia Woolf—

Much love, Eudora

William Maxwell to Eudora Welty, April 23, 1985

Dearest Eudora:

It was a masterly reading. All those <u>people</u>. The storm. Dover, Mississippi. That darling wife. I kept thinking <u>How does she do it</u>? <u>Where did they all come from</u>?

Devotedly,
Bill

Attached was the introduction Bill gave Eudora at her April 22, 1985, reading of "The Wide Net" at the Poetry Center of the 92nd Street Y in New York City.

In reading fiction there are two demands we can reasonably make of an author—that his characters have the breath of life in them and that behind the interplay of action and ideas, perhaps at times even intruding on it, there is a presence we feel, often in the very first sentence. No matter what the author's intentions may be, there is this unintentional unconscious thing we look for, a voice that is woven into the words on the page. The greater the literary artist, the clearer our recognition is of the presence, the voice, the invisible signature of the mind in which the whole fancy took place originally. About the beautifully transparent stories of Eudora Welty what more needs to be said except the thing we are all agreed upon—that they are a national treasure. And hearing her read one of them compounds the delight and wonder.

William and Emily Maxwell, [Urbino, Italy], to Eudora Welty,
May 25, 1985, Postcard with image of Ideal City, *often attributed to*
Piero della Francesca

This is what the Ideal City of St. Augustine looks like during the siesta.
The roads around Siena are lined with acacia trees in bloom and I never
dreamed there could be such roses.

<div align="right">

Love
Bill and Emmy

</div>

Eudora Welty to William and Emily Maxwell, June 1, 1985

Dearest Bill and Emmy,

Piero's Urbino just arrived — It was such a happiness to know you were
in the Ideal City when you wrote the card. And it let loose feelings of mine
about a story I've been working on off & on for 2 years, or 3, going back to,
despairing over, and earlier this year tearing up probably 100 pages of — a
story in which that very painting has a central part, thumb-tacked to an ar-
chitect's drafting room wall. And here Urbino came back to me, recalling
its own wonder, its persistence in the mind & heart, through everything,
and I felt that coming from you it was a sign.[28]

It's lovely to think you're having such a fine Italian journey — I hope to
hear more when we meet on June 11. I get to NY on the weekend before,
the Pritchetts come on the Sunday.[29] We'll talk at the earliest possible mo-
ment — whenever you get back to town?

<div align="right">

Much, much love to you both,
Eudora

</div>

Emily Maxwell to Eudora Welty, [Early 1986], Incomplete letter

Dearest Eudora,

What a lot of beguiling layers your Christmas present had! Still on my
desk in the living room is the yellow & gold Bolivars box which once con-
tained bonbons fait des grains de café en chocolat dédiés au grand Conquis-
tador Colombien, Simon Bolivar, and inside it the little plastic dish with

the Light Green Bird (I might have been in doubt about the coffee beans but I'd have known who the Light Green Bird came from) and inside that The Little Store, the loveliest little book ever printed, with its marbleized end papers, its moss-green leather & gilt edges, and the dearest story inside.[30] I loved your writing in it, & I am putting it in the glass cabinet with my mother's netsukes and the lacquer eggplant I got in Japan. There it will be happy because there's always a small glass of water inside: It is said ivory must have humidity. I had a little volume of King Lear from Sylvia's friend Valentine [Ackland]'s shop in their front room, but the leather turned into crumbs. (Oh! I knew I'd forgotten a layer: the 3 boys in turquoise sailor blouses saluting Santa! From a postcard of 1912? (Bill's magic year))

Did the sign—our card to you last May from Urbino—persist in encouraging you to go on with the story I so much want to read?

Just after we heard from you about the library being named for you, we received an invitation to attend the opening. I can't think of anything that would give us more delight. Now I'm afraid we'll never see you in Jackson, or the camellias in bloom in your garden. I don't know whether you heard that Bill spent 10 days of the month at the Cape last summer in the Brigham & Women's Hospital in Boston. It started with an emergency attack of kidney stones. He still has the k.s., but once they began to examine him they found other troubles. Bill's conclusion was, "Never give anyone a urine sample." We saw the Warrens [Robert Penn Warren and his wife, Eleanor Clark] in the corridor of the hospital so we knew he wasn't well. After the tests were repeated in NYC when we came home, they diagnosed the problem, which was serious because it could lead to kidney failure, as too many lymphocytes in the bone marrow, for which they are now giving him chemotherapy in a mild form in pills. It doesn't bother him at all. The only difference in the way he feels is that he gets tired more easily, so that's why he doesn't feel up to the trip. They keep on testing & he is very patient about it, though it interferes with his time for work. By spring (late May), if he is enough better, we plan to go to Corfu to see the opening of my brother Humphrey's film called "The Girl from Mani".[31] You know though he has lived in Greece for 15 years we have never been there, and this means a lot to him. He was here for the past week of bright days, warm enough for [...]

William Maxwell to Eudora Welty, January 12, 1986

Dearest Eudora:

I am thinking about where to put "The Little Store" where it will be safe from the fairies.

Reading it aloud to Emmy I was struck, as always, with how very similar your childhood was to mine. If you want to look at where my mother sent me, go to the foot of Ninth Street hill and turn left. Except that it's gone, of course.

Living in a city you tend to forget how people sometimes have no choice but to vanish, like that poor storekeeper and his family. There were two when I was growing up in Lincoln. One was grotesque [... He] organized a great Love-Thy-Neighbor-As-Thy-Self parade. The whole town was swept up in it. My mother's friends, wrapped in sheets, were allegorical figures on a float. I forget what I was. I expect I marched with the fourth grade. The day after, the organizer of all this mutual affection was obliged to leave town. He had been molesting his landlady's little boy, and the little boy told.

There was another. In my class at school was an Austrian child, very pretty and delicate. I was invited to her birthday party and on the ice cream there were little American flags. This was at the beginning of the First World War. One day her seat at school was empty and they were gone. I know now what must have happened—that mass rounding up of aliens.

Not the least of our pleasure was the way you had wrapped it!

I have been working on a story all week, and hardly know my own name. Not that it is all that much of a story, but getting things placed right, and choosing the exact right word. You know. It is done, all but going over it for repetitions of phrases and sloppy writing.[32]

Right this minute I am waiting for a call from Brookie, who is meeting me at 47th Street Foto to get a zoom lens for her camera so she can shoot zebras and giraffes in Kenya. I don't much trust travel in primitive countries, and wish she were planning to shoot sheep and cattle in Ireland instead, where there is less likelihood of malaria and tsetse fly.

Emmy had the prevailing stomach bug for two days but is over it. I hesitate out of superstition to add that I have been feeling fit as a fiddle.

I am sorry we missed you when you were here for the PEN.[33] There is

to be, as I am sure you know, a reception for the delegates at the Public Library, given by the Institute/Academy. I am going to stick my head in for a minute, but can't imagine enjoying an affair of that size, or why all those writers were willing to leave home.

I rejoice that Reynolds Price is surmounting that disaster.[34] Lightness is his element, air, courage, all that. He would surmount, where someone else might not.

I lost, in a manner of speaking, Judith Raskin and Robert Fitzgerald last year. When I was a young man one of my mother's friends said to me, "I have never become reconciled to her death." I thought, how strange. It doesn't seem so now. One doesn't want to become reconciled. When you come I will play Judith's recording of the Pergolesi Stabat Mater. They both go right on being part of my life. From our living room windows you can look into the Raskins' apartment, which used always to be lighted up and now isn't ever. [Her husband] Ray cannot bear to be home. Since the beginning of the world this has been going on, hasn't it.

<div style="text-align:right">With much love,
Bill</div>

William Maxwell to Eudora Welty, March 3, 1986

Dearest Eudora,

I have been reading through the Centennial edition of the Lincoln Evening Courier. It was published in 1953 and consequently the paper has turned brown and brittle. I thought the enclosed photograph [a 1908 picture of a family with horses and buggies] would give you pleasure. Also, there's a runaway that I wanted to share with you. I used to see the fine horses being exercised on my way to school.

As for Don and Dewey, the most vivid memory about these bay horses was the time they broke during a fire and dashed four miles from the scene of the fire. It all happened in 1917 during a fire at the Lincoln House at Broadway and Chicago Streets. It was about 3:00 a.m. when Don and Dewey were standing near the fire plug. Watson had made the connection and Otto Sikes, the night policeman, was standing in front of the team.

Just about this time an early morning train was pulling into Lincoln on the Chicago and Alton Railroad. When the locomotive came up to where the horses were standing, hissing steam poured out and swept under the feet of the animals. With sudden leap they broke loose and unraveled 1400 feet of hose as they dashed north on Chicago Street.

The animals, pulling the wagon, ran to the Illinois Terminal line and then to the North Tower. Here they turned onto the tracks of the Illinois Central Railroad and proceeded two miles to a 400-foot-long bridge. Horses and wagon miraculously crossed over the ties as the gait of the horses was so in unison that all four legs of each animal missed the empty spaces between the ties.

FELL OFF BRIDGE

After crossing the bridge the horses approached another span and here they fell off, wagon and all. Neither of the animals were hurt, and firemen found them resting after their four-mile jaunt.[35]

Thinking of your mailbag, I hesitated to send it but remembered the pleasure you gave me with that burning steamboat on the Mississippi River. In any case, I forbid you to answer this letter. We will see each other in God's good time and that's enough. Emmy went down to Centre Street for jury duty with a frightful head cold. Last time she made a delightful friend. I hope she gets on a jury because otherwise the waiting is intolerable.

We went yesterday afternoon to a concert performance of Cole Porter's "Jubilee" at Town Hall. You must have seen the original because you saw everything. The young woman who sang "Begin the Beguine" didn't have the voice for it, and I suspect scenery and elegant clothes would somehow have disguised the inaneness of parts of the book. It was a full house, standing room all sold out, and the audience almost entirely over 50. What I liked best about it was that I didn't wish I'd brought along earplugs.

Devotedly,

Bill

In mid-May of 1986, a crew from the BBC arrived in Jackson to produce a documentary about Eudora. She traveled to various Mississippi sites with the crew. One of those sites was the Mendenhall Hotel, L'Marie Erven, Owner.

Eudora Welty to Emily and William Maxwell, [May 1986],
Postcard with interior photograph of the Mendenhall Hotel,
Mendenhall, Mississippi

Dearest Emmy & Bill,

Okra, corn pudding, butterbeans, turnip greens, beets, sweet potatoes, English peas, black-eyed peas, red beans, Cole Slaw, squash, fried chicken, fruit salad, cornbread, relish, iced tea, pineapple betty. The tables spin both clockwise & counter clockwise—Dishes are constantly being exchanged for hot ones newly brought in as everybody continually (especially the children) helps his plate. L'Marie is the daughter of the original owners & really doesn't [as the picture suggests] play the organ while you eat, she's bringing it in. In the lobby stuffed deer heads, mounted catfish with open mouths as big around as gravy boats, hat racks & rocking chairs. It would have been good in the Beulah.[36]

Love,
Eudora

Letter Follows

Eudora Welty to Emily and William Maxwell, May 27, 1986, Note card
with image of Ah! Mon Beau Château *by Maurice Boutet de Monvel*

Dearest Emmy and Bill—we just have to meet! I've been thinking of you, and your letters to me—unanswered on paper but only unanswered like that—and with your postcard this morning, Emmy (which came wonderfully unsplashed on through a downpour right on top of the postman) I thought: I can be there as early as June! Can you? In New York, I mean, so we can sit around your coffee table? The date is when Random House is going to tape my reading of The Optimist's Daughter for their Audio Books, and offered to do it here, but I said "There!" It's set up now for June 23–27, reading some hours every day in a studio near the Algonquin. I want to stay on a little, on my own, and in the meantime I'm not planning on anything at all (in the evenings after work) in the hope there's some time you can keep for us all to meet during the week.

I was so disappointed that I couldn't come for the post-Ceremonial this year! I was wandering around the weedy ghost town of Rodney, Miss. sitting on the steps of the Presbyterian church there, while the BBC was taking me reading a bit of The Robber Bridegroom—isn't that the unlikeliest reason you ever heard for not being with <u>you</u>?[37]—It's still pouring rain, and now it's lightning & thundering, but it feels so happy & comforting to be writing to you, even if I haven't got much said. I wanted to say I hoped Brookie was safe back from photographing giraffes in Kenya?—I need to say how I cherish all you've sent me to nourish the mind & heart and to hope about the new story that it's going to bless you, Bill. I love Louise Bogan, through the years and now. Thank you for her.

<div align="right">All my love—
Eudora</div>

P.S. These enclosures are ones I've saved for you from different times. Did I put in the name of the man on the drunk drivers list? Quo Vadis Rain Dance.

The other night I came into the dark kitchen for a glass of milk and saw the flashing of a lightning bug moving in the dark, from refrigerator to cabinet and soaring over the sink. I caught it lightly in a Kleenex and carried it through the house to the front door, flashing all the way, and let it out again. "You may have 3 wishes," it might have said, without seeming any stranger—

Eudora Welty to William and Emily Maxwell,
September 3, 1986

Dearest Bill and Emmy,

The splendid speech by Walker [Percy] came about because of a chair at the local Millsaps College being endowed mainly by Walker's brother LeRoy, & named after me, and was inaugurated by the perfect one to do it—I thought you might enjoy it—It has a lot of good Walker in it. (My comment has a typo in it—just try to pronounce "pyhysician." Luckily, my bit was only written, not spoken.)[38]

The times I think of that evening in the courtyard at Barbetta's [Restaurant]!

All is going the way it should, I hope—

I'll get to come to NY for a few days the latter part of October—I'll pray to see you—Love, E—

William Maxwell to Eudora Welty, September 13, 1986

Dearest Eudora:

Bill Smith called to invite us to dinner with you on the 18th of October, which will be lovely, but not prevent us from seeing you again in non–dinner party circumstances if there is time. I fell upon Walker Percy's speech, and it is still reverberating in my mind, as it must in yours after hearing him.... The exterminator interrupted us: carpenter ants in the ceiling of the screened "tent." Speaking of which, when it rained and rained and rained I found myself thinking of the tents at the Chautauqua grounds, that used to collapse on people when the rain loosened the tent pegs... I am struck with all that goes on in Jackson. It may be just you or on account of you, but it more and more begins to seem the center of American civilization. Everywhere else about what is being celebrated the less said the better. Unless it is by Walker Percy. Such a beautifully made little book. And that fact that you wanted us to have it reinforced an idea that occurred to me recently, which is that we have become your family. I hope this is correct.

It has been the most heavenly summer. The first time we have been in Yorktown all summer in twelve or fifteen years. Emmy brought back the flower garden and the vegetable garden, by a combination of love and fish oil. In case the deer ate the flowers in the perennial border (isn't [it] strange how suddenly typewriter ribbons give out these days) we planted flowers among vegetables, and encouraged by the rain everything has grown and bloomed lavishly. There are so many nasturtiums it is almost a chore to pick them every morning, and our bedroom windows look out on a wall of blue morning glories. Beyond the tomatoes and zucchini there is a vista of cosmos and gloriosa daisies. And why does no one ever talk about zenias. The pure color, especially at dusk, outdoes even roses.

Alec Wilkinson was made very happy by a letter from Reynolds Price

about his book about a North Carolina moonshine agent.[39] A really beautiful letter: he was so pleased he read it to me over the phone. Speaking of your family,

We both send much love,

B.

William Maxwell to Eudora Welty, December 18, 1986

Dearest Eudora:

Dearest is an insufficient word for it. I hope Jackson and its camellias and you all escaped the cold we have been having. It was 8 above last Sunday morning when we woke up in the country. Fortunately I got the roses covered. On the front lawn, in front of the front porch, we had a new septic tank put in last fall, and the man who filled in around it and planted grass seed above it didn't use enough soil or pack it hard enough or something, because it has sunk around what appears to be the grave of an extremely large ladybug.

The cat, the dear cat, doesn't care for ice and cold weather and is happy to stay indoors and doesn't complain about the city, all of which relieves our minds but then (at 2AM) the thought occurs to me: how will he manage if we go to Capri and Naples and Positano as there is talk of doing, next May or June? No doubt he would adjust to Naples as he has to everything else, but there is probably a quarantine. When we are undressing for bed he jumps up on the comforter and settles down for the night, somewhere in the vicinity of my shins. If I thrash around too much he plops off and finishes the night in his favorite living room chair, but comes with daylight to claw the bedroom rug and remind us that cats need to be fed, preferably at the earliest possible moment and often. He has a vocabulary of at least twenty-seven different heartrending miaus. Enough of cats.

We celebrated Kate's 32nd birthday by taking her to dinner and both girls to La Boheme. The music is too familiar, because in college I had a recording, on 78s, which I played constantly, along with the second act of Tristan, for variety. But it is lovely all the same. The Zefferelli settings[40] were too clever by half, and the second act was a whole Paris street, on the upper level, with side stairs for the sixty-five-piece military band to march

down at the rousing conclusion, and lighted recognizably Parisian houses, and hundreds of supers walking around and another street at stage level, and a wall slid back revealing the Café Momus. Well with all this and a great deal more, it was hard to keep track of where Musetta was, until she began to belt out her famous waltz. We had good seats at the front of the dress circle, but the Met is so huge that even with my distance glasses on, things often seemed rather far away. The production at the Chicago Opera House seemed, to my recollection, much more tender and more exciting, but then I was young and it was all brand new.

Brookie has prepared a surprise for the city of New York on Christmas morning. She is making body casts (I think of four friends: they seem to be prepared to do anything she thinks up) in plaster clothed in muffin pans (this is hard to imagine but I am sure it will all be clear when we see it) to be set up in Central Park where they can be seen from the windows [of] John Lennon's apartment in the Dakota.[41] Privately I wondered if the Park police would have ideas on the subject but B doesn't discourage easily so I kept my ideas to myself.

Last Sunday (again with the help of friends) she took a group of home-less children that she got to know last summer at the Bear Mountain camp to the Historical Society to see some dancers from the NY City ballet dance part of the Nutcracker. The children, as it turned out, were terribly inter-ested in the fact that during pirouettes you could see the (oo look!) balle-rinas' underpants. Later, they taught the grown people who were there to prevent them from tearing the museum apart break dancing, in the Audu-bon room. It was touch and go, Brookie said, whether they would go crash-ing through the glass that covered Mr. A's birds, but the guards did nothing to stop them, not, probably, ever having seen anything quite that excit-ing in the Historical Society's halls before. One of the friends, friend of a friend, took two of the children home without telling anybody, and when they counted noses, there was a frightful to do. B said she woke up the next morning grey-haired, but on the night of the opera it had reverted to its usual color.

We all four send oodles of you know what.

Bill

Eudora Welty, Bryn Mawr, Pennsylvania, to William and Emily Maxwell,
April 6, 1987

Dearest Bill and Emmy,

 This is in a room in Wyndham, the guest house [at Bryn Mawr Col-
lege], and the desk is one of the antiques in it, a large inlaid and brass-fitted
and galleried and decorated (flower baskets and garlands and butterflies) af-
fair, with a mail slot at either end, into which you drop your letter after you
write it. Some Hand is supposed to collect it at the other end of a chute,
which has a door with keyhole to keep it unseen by any Eye. It is part of
the old Deanery furniture I remember from 30 years ago, collected by M.
Carey Thomas's friend Miss Garrett. The wardrobe is almost ceiling high,
with I don't know how many shelves and doors, drawers of different sizes,
and the main door is decorated with carved starfish, or comets (as you like
it). I put a small traveling bottle of bourbon inside it and it immediately was
swallowed up, lost in a cavern, just didn't belong in there. I'm here all week
to meet with students and read, on a cause of friendship—There's been a
gift to the college in the name of Bettina Linn, a teacher, who first invited
me to Bryn Mawr on the first Lucy M. Donnelly scholarship back in the
fifties, and I was invited to be on the program in honor of the one for her.
What a sentence, when she was a scholar. Her friends are my old friends
now, as is her sister who came. Elizabeth Bowen used to come at that time
too, and once we coincided in the Deanery and had a fine rowdy time—
what a shame they tore the Deanery down anyway, it had seen Henry James
and W. B. Yeats and the whole flow of the grand. Miss Garrett's clothes
closet was as big and deep as a tunnel, with turns along it, and studded with
hundreds of double clothes-hooks from walls and ceiling, like a cave of bats.
Her wardrobe must have been extensive, she was such a souvenir packer &
world traveller. Camel bells were roped up into a swing in the Blue Room,
and the beds are Asiatic—so much brass, I remember my first night ever
in bed there being frightened by a thunderstorm, expecting to be struck by
lightning. Wyndham is conventional, and as you see I've been given a type-
writer and my mornings are free. I feel free. It's been a while since I have
written, I know, and now it would be so wholly wonderful if there were a

chance I could see you—I am coming on up to NY to stay from Monday night 13th till the 21st of April. I wonder if you might still be there, or have you left on your visit to Italy? I hope everything is going well with you, and with whatever plans. I'm glad you were out of the way when all that New Yorker carrying-on was carrying on.[42]

All this that's happening now about the Dial Collection[43] and the battle over its dispersal by auction at Sotheby's is very dismaying, infuriating, isn't it? My friend Laurence Stapleton here turns out to be not only the one who discovered this—it's being sent from the Beineke at Yale to Sotheby's—but the one who is the single hand that's started off (This is three days later) the fight to save it, keep it together. She is physically an invalid but from her chair and telephone she started in calling all over the country to the scholars and libraries and institutions she knew to alert them as to what was about to happen and put them to work. (She says "I grew up on the Dial!" She's also a Marianne Moore scholar and has written a book on her.) The best bet to save the Collection at the moment (letters of all those contributors, manuscripts from them, letters of the entire history of the magazine, poems written out in the hands of Eliot, Pound, Yeats, the works) is (to end the sentence) Dr. Vartan Gregorian. Who is the right one, don't you think? He has been working like a demon to see if the money can be raised— the deadline with Sotheby's has been Friday, tomorrow, but they have indicated, though not promised, that if an offer promising enough is made by then, the execution may be stayed. You may know much more than is now known here about the fight at that end to save it. I have a lot of faith in wonderful Dr. Gregorian.[44]

This weekend I'm going to be not very far from here, in farm country in Pennsylvania at John Ferrone's farm, where I've been a number of times before, and expect to rest and look out and walk around in the Spring.[45] Since I've been here, I've seen my second Spring arrive—and my wish that the Japanese Weeping Cherries would be in flower has come true—every day the 24-hour's change, the deeper color, the longer the fall of tears. These trees here are old, old, black and tall and graceful in the Japanese way— along with the cherries you see the white magnolia stellata and plum trees, and daffodils—today the first tulips. We might be a little ahead of Yorktown Heights. Yours is to come.

Must go again—this brings you a whole load of love. And the hope to lay my eyes on you. If you can come save me any evening, I'd like to take us to dinner, or whatever other time suits you. I'll be so happy to run to meet you—Love, Eudora

Mailed <u>outside</u> the desk

Eudora Welty, New York City, to William and Emily Maxwell, [April 21, 1987]

Dearest Bill and Emmy,

This is just a line out of my purse, out at the airport—Even though 2 Jackson ladies turned up to wait on the same plane I am concentrating without effort on the wonderful Easter Day on 86th Street. It was one of the happiest times I can remember, the only ones approaching its pleasures, I believe, are other ones with you—one an early picnic in the woods near Baptist Church Road, with <u>artichokes</u> for lunch (though not the only course)—beside a brook. This was before Brookie. All the family news was so cheering this time. Bill, the sight of you & Emmy & Kate will be doing me good for a long time after I get back. It was a pleasure to see Julie too, and how kind it was of her to see about a ticket for me to Bill Irwin and see that I got there with the ticket in my hand. I loved the performance. Did you ever see anyone change size before right in front of your eyes? There was an element of magic there. Changing size is <u>hilarious</u>. I hope Julie's play comes off to please her.[46]

I thought of Brookie painting buildings as the taxi ran through the slums on the way out here—But it was more reassuring to me to think of her coming there for tea on Easter Sunday with her newest young man. Did we leave them any champagne—or strawberries and all? They had the tulips & daffodils to see—I'm enclosing the snapshots of Bill that I found I'd run off with, in addition to the one you'd given me, Emmy—It might have come of having a hard time choosing. It's grand to have Brookie's photograph, which is going up on my wall, along with Victor Pritchett's, to do me good. One of the ladies just showed me a snapshot of her grandson at the age of <u>ten minutes</u>. I may have to mail this in Atlanta, but love now from LaGuardia. Have a wonderful holiday in Naples & Rome—E

Eudora Welty to William and Emily Maxwell,
July 26, 1987

Dearest Bill and Emmy,

You're bound to be on Baptist Church Road—how could you be any-
where else in this awful heat? Or—I forgot this was as late in the summer
as it is—you might be in Wellfleet which must catch a still more valuable
breeze? Anyway, I shall steadily think of the Maxwells as <u>cool</u>.

I was—still am—delighted to have your beautiful postcard from Posi-
tano—telling me of the perfect day in Paestum—Tomba del Tuffatore to
show me. I cherish it too for the knowledge that your trip did happen just
as you planned it, such a rare thing somehow—and the rare thing's so of-
ten the right thing—or is that what I was just saying? It's very early in the
morning—I drank my coffee, read in Frank O'Connor's <u>Irish Miles</u>, turned
on the sprinklers, and came upstairs to my typewriter to write to you—every
day I mean to do that. We haven't been quite as hot as Manhattan, but once
you hit the nineties it's all the same thing—we just got there.

You'd know everything Frank O'Connor's ever written—is "Irish Miles"
something you've read in recent years? It goes back to 1945. Chapter I be-
gins, "Exploring the Boyne Valley in the early days of our married life, be-
fore we yet knew what we were looking for and when anything from a high
cross to a keep could lure us off our road, Célimène and I came on the
prehistoric necropolis of Newgrange. Prehistory or high crosses, all were
the same to us." It is marvelous and I had read it a long time ago—it is
James Stern's own copy, which he gave to me I forget whether in New York
or England—a most generous thing to do, because I got the idea it had
already gone out of print?[47] I thought of it again yesterday when a letter
from Daniel Halpern from the Ecco Press came telling me of a travel series
they're planning, which you must know about too, saying if I know of any
travel books I think warrant reprinting, will I let them know. I'm full of an-
swers! ("Eothen"—"The Land of the Great Image"—Pritchett's "The Span-
ish Temper" etc.)[48] So I couldn't stop at coffee time, kept on mile after mile
with Frank O'Connor in Ireland. (Mr. Halpern sent me their new edition of
[Turgenev's] <u>A Sportsman's Notebook</u> in the translation he says you like so
much.[)] Isn't their Chekhov series lovely? (Constance Garnett's the trans-

lation I like so much—not that English newer one which makes the peas-
ants speak Cockney to show their class.)

Bill Erwin has returned to the Beaumont, I saw in the paper.[49] Did you
perchance go back to see him? He was to be on ETV the other night here
and I meant to sit up and watch (10 PM) but I was worn out with watching
the Hearings all day, and one or two clowns appearing on <u>them</u> were plenty.[50]
You are probably listening to Mozart and ocean waves. But I am hypnotized
by these days of testimony—every face, every intonement of voice, every
damning word. (I decided I'd choose Maine to move to if I could pick the
senator and congressman to represent me—Cohen and Mitchell.[51] [)] The
response of the national TV audience is also something we'd better know,
just as unbelievable as what's on the screen. A report from Dallas (for ex-
ample) after the first couple of days of Col. North said that he was the most
wonderful man! who reminded them of So-and-So on the soaps—of no real
people but the heroes of the serials they daily watched—fantasy characters.

If I can't find a big envelope ("plain wrapper") to send it today, Sunday,
I do want to send you a good written-out account of the adventure of the
Dial Archives that was going on while I was in New York last time—I feel
sure I'd have spoken of it to you—I was only a bystander but keeping up
with it, because my friend Laurence Stapleton of Bryn Mawr was wrapped
up in it. She was the actual discoverer of the fact of what was happening
to the papers, that they were about to be taken over by Sotheby's and auc-
tioned off piece by piece. She instantly went to work and with nothing but
the telephone brought about the rescue. I urged her to write it up. I don't
know anybody else who could—she alone knew all the threads, never let
go. I asked her, when she sent me this, if she minded if I showed it to you
for pleasure and for learning if any thought occurred to you about where I
might send it for publication. I think it's a wonderful setting forth of facts,
and nobody but Laurence had them all. She's my old Bryn Mawr friend of
30 years who used to be head of the English Department, retired now and
after an illness more or less confined to her chair, but very much with it, and
alive to all that's going on. She's also the author of books of poems, a book
on Marianne Moore, and a book of literary essays I think you, Emmy, liked
a lot (I sent it to you) called "The Elected Circle." (Donne, de Quincey,
Browne, Eliot etc) Anyway, she went about this Dial thing headlong—from

her chair and not sparing the telephone. She said she grew up on The Dial and was not going to see that priceless collection demolished.

Do you want a William Faulkner stamp? The U.S.P.O. is getting ready to issue one. A ceremony in Oxford, Miss. where Faulkner early on had a job working at the University Post Office on the campus. They invited me (through mysterious reasoning) to pass a few remarks at the scene (and have also asked me to read (so I read in the paper) "Why I Live at the P.O." the night before. It's all madness. The postmaster in Washington wrote to me saying he'd understood I intended to make a few remarks at the ceremony, but he wanted to tell me that <u>he</u> was to make the main address.) It will really be funny, because it's during the Faulkner Conference with scholars from everywhere, and everybody there <u>but</u> the postmaster general, or whoever he is, will know the tale about Faulkner and the job at the post office. He quit, saying he was not going to be at the beck and call of every son-of-a-bitch who had the price of a two-cent stamp. He was trying to get a novel written at the time, while on the job ("As I Lay Dying"?)[52]

Since that happy time when we were together in New York, home is where I've been all summer. Except for a trip to Charleston, West Virginia, where I was presented with the Golden Medallion of Appalachia by the University of W. Va. I went of course because of my mother, and all my first and second cousins for miles around came and clapped for me, and then gave me a party themselves—about 40 of them! My mother's brothers were all prolific. Nearly all the kin I ever knew are gone now, but the young ones are rousing. One of my cousins, at whose home I stayed, has her father's banjo which I heard him play hung up on the wall above the smart-looking bar. It was very stirring for me. The mountains were looking beautiful. The first night I cried from the dinner table "What are those lights shooting up into the sky?" It was just auto lights, on the street outside, going up the hill. (This date was why I couldn't come to the Ceremonial.)

I hope you can read this letter through the typing (like between the lines).[53] It's just my hands being rusty in every way. Remember the old New Yorker cartoon? A doctor is telling his elderly patient, "Mrs. Norris, think of yourself as an old rusty gate." I feel all right, just the same, only tired. But if life these days didn't make me tired, I'd be crazy. There seems to be much I've forgotten to ask you or tell you.—Oh, did you see the TV program on

Rubinstein's 100th birthday?[54] Purest joy. Please give my love to both your girls. And all my love at the same time to you. Eudora

P.S.

Good Lord! I remembered about an earlier letter I started to you, Bill—now I don't see it anywhere, including inside the book. It was written after reading your review of the <u>Berlin Diaries</u>, which you were working on and meeting the deadline for when I was there—And I read the book (for which I thank you) in time for the review, which I think moved your readers as much as the book had moved you. It is a marvelous piece. I don't myself see how a review that had so much to take into account was possible. But you made it possible and necessary—you did fully what you could have hoped. I found the diaries themselves so heartbreaking, with their suspense over so much we know, after the fact, to have been hopeless. Marie Vassiltchikov is so beautiful, brave, touching—The emotional aspects of events as they grow & grow bigger seem on the scale of a Russian novel. And the photographs![55]

I have mislaid a number of things written down somewhere. Maybe I will find everything together. All in one place—like an Easter nest.

Eudora Welty to William Maxwell, July 27, [1987]

July 27, 95° <u>too</u>

Dear Bill,

This is the article I mentioned in yesterday's letter. I feel guilty about sending you <u>anything</u> to look at like this, even though I believe you and Emmy will enjoy it. Scholarship at headlong speed. Any time you get the time & inclination to read it, and advise, I'll be grateful and so will Laurence, who admires you on a long & permanent basis. (She never did anything like this report before. No reason.)

I forgot to say I've been reading the new translation of <u>The Memoirs of Frederic Mistral</u> by George Wickes and feel as if I'm a present inhabitant of Provence—I've ordered a copy for you & Emmy from James Laughlin,[56] and if you already have it, pass it to another Provençal—

Love to both,
Eudora

William Maxwell to Eudora Welty, August 10, 1987

Dearest Eudora:

The [Stapleton] manuscript should be addressed to Hilton Kramer, Editor, <u>The New Criterion</u>, 850 7th Avenue, New York, N.Y. 10019.

It is possible that I have a copy of <u>Irish Miles</u> in New York but I rather doubt it. I will ask Harriet [Sheehy] to keep her eyes open for a copy. And I had a letter from Daniel Halpern asking me to send some paragraphs or pages of my journal. Journal keeping, I had to tell him, is not in me. I am told that John Cheever's diaries have been bought by a publisher who paid $100,000 advance. Considering how pressed he was for money always, I don't know whether this has pleased his ghost or made it furious. The [Charles and Natasha] Hepburn (I think is the way you spell the name) translation of The Sportsman's Notebook is my idea of one of the most beautiful books in the world. If not the. And do you remember the wonderful P.O. report on Mr. Faulkner's performance behind the wicket that somebody sneaked a copy of and that was published in the <u>New Yorker</u>?

It threatens to rain some more, having done so most of the night, and the men are pounding away on the new roof. My study is so small that the only way I can keep any order in it is to overflow periodically onto the dining room table, which is, and for a week has been, on its side. I straighten and straighten and just succeed in rearranging the mess. On the other hand I keep turning up wonderful things (your letter from Bryn Mawr, and another written on both sides of an Algonquin envelope). And then I suddenly turn aside and read something: [Glenway Wescott's] The Pilgrim Hawk, which I didn't care much for the last time I reread it, and this time thought better of. It is full, too full really, of knowledge of life, and is like a spasm, one piece of wisdom cancelling off another. But it did often give me pause.

I have also come upon a letter from somebody who is doing a study of the relationship of you and Diarmuid. If these requests come fairly frequently in my mail, I think what your mail must be like. And hope you don't open it. I have somewhere the interoffice opinion sheet on as I remember "The Whole World Knows." Anyway it was the story in which somebody killed somebody with a croquet mallet and then they both went on playing. This was too much for Ross, and I made the mistake of showing how much

I cared that the story should be accepted, and his reply ended (it was sent to Lobrano) "Maxwell can't make me arty." I don't feel it is proper to the New Yorker to hand over interoffice opinion sheets, and so won't. I think I sent it to you once. The next story that came in they did publish. But what can I say about the relations[hip] between you and Diarmuid except that it was very loving. His opinion of the present commercial/literary scene would be worth hearing.

<div align="right">

Much, much love,

B

</div>

Eudora Welty to William Maxwell, August 18, 1987

Dearest Bill,

Thank you so much for going to that trouble over the Dial Papers piece. Shall get it off to Mr. Kramer right away. (I'd seen him only in the Times, never came by The New Criterion.) I do think the piece deserves to reach the public.

Oh dear, Michael Kreyling will be so mortified to learn he's given you that sort of impression of his coming biography of Diarmuid.[57] It's a serious work and I think it needs doing, D. having been the unique literary agent he was, in his time or any time—indeed, as you say, what would he have had to say about things today? (We know.) Michael is a good critic with two well received books to his credit. He's an academic but not under the curse of their language or distorting—what? Theoretics? He's done a good deal of work on my work ("E.W.'s Achievement of Order," LSU Press. Writing while still in graduate school at Cornell he was the first critic to perceive that Losing Battles was a comedy, and laugh.) I've known him personally for 10 or 15 years. He's a nice, quiet, gentle, independent young man, with a nice young independent wife, whose field is art history. Both are from Cincinnati but have more or less moved South. He's at Vanderbilt at the moment. While reading some of the correspondence and stuff in my papers at the Miss. State Archives (where I put everything over the years) he fell in love with Diarmuid Russell through his letters—quite understandably. At length he came to me fired with the idea of doing a biography of him, and I rejoiced. Mike is good, and there ought to be such a book. I offered to be of what use to him I could.

Before he died, D. told me that when he wound up his affairs at the agency, he brought home all of my letters to him—30 years worth—and wanted me to take them that day into my keeping. So I have had them and one day I'll put them in the Archives with my mss. Etc. but I've never felt able, so far, to go back and read them, or his letters to me, which I've kept. The record of my working life in the two sides of correspondence. I lent it all to Mike to make what use he liked of it—and as I was the first client Russell & Volkening had, it's also a close part of the Agency's story, & D's. Michael has reached the point when he'd like to write to some of the other figures, editors, publishers, writers, old friends here & abroad, of his working life, and alas for how many are gone. I don't remember whether it was he or I who was responsible for his appeal to you, but you can understand his letter now. The "relationship" he brought up to you was a means of introducing himself to you as the biographer. I realize, too late, that giving you this information was something I should have done before Mike reached you. Anyway, here it is now.

I do have that inter-office opinion sheet you sent me—I love it fiercely. You said never to let anyone else see it, so I haven't and won't. It is now somewhere on my dining room table, or I hope it is. My dining room table must look like the kin of yours, more like its grandmother, it hasn't been cleared since perhaps last Christmas. I live in chaos here. What's going to become of me? I might well ask. I straighten and straighten and merely rearrange, just like you on Baptist Church Road, and we may be having the same rain. I've been reading [Jane Austen's] Persuasion under the air conditioner at night in bed, the best part of any day. I had a delighting letter from the Pritchetts. Their health is better—they'd had a fearsome winter. Victor has finished his Chekhov book and returned to writing stories as he's longed to do.

Did you know in time about the Harmonious Convergence?[58] Of all planets on the same side. First time in 2400 (or 24,000) years. I went out to Charlotte Capers'[59] for a drink and we got a few other old friends, enough to converge harmoniously, and drank some bourbon to the day. Thank God I learned about it in time. In case it goes on (a harmonious convergence couldn't get itself over all that fast, could it?) I wish you and Emmy a continuing harmonious converging. In the NY Times I saw the photo of Con-

necticut celebrants on the shore (of Long Island Sound?) attired in drapes and conchshells, greeting the sunrise.

Very much love to both of you. I had the same request from Daniel Halpern, about my journal. I, again like you, have none. What next? They want everything, seems like sometimes—said the old lady.

With all my love,
Eudora

Eudora Welty, New York City, to Emily and William Maxwell,
[Fall 1987]

Dearest Emmy and Bill,

It was such happiness to have one of our long 3-way conversations. What a light heart you always leave me with—while I, on the other hand,—Well, I've remembered something I brought along to show you, a wedding—an account in a Tidewater, Va. paper come by lately. Another clipping is the front page of the Jackson, Miss., paper—you'll recognize the priority of Local Girl Makes Good over Pope Enters Sin City (N.O.). Still lower down on the page is a Baptist story which is also curious except to Baptists. The follow-up of this story is that the church members the expelled preacher shot his pistol at in order to persuade them to take him back, took him back. The French Knighting took place, with the cultural attaché of the embassy in N.O. bringing the champagne as well as the decoration, but no real explanation of it.[60] The Pope didn't stay long enough in N.O. to save it. (A couple of Centuries?) This was in an envelope addressed to you at the time, waiting for a letter I'd been waiting to write. Some Mississippi colleges & libraries had me dated up to help out with various good things, in North Miss. & South Miss. (the Gulf Coast was its old self [partly] if you've ever been there. You know it was a resort of people from Chicago & around there, for years—The Edgewater Gulf Hotel was run by the Edgewater Beach & was glamorous. It's gone now, so many of the ancient live oaks which lined the Gulf are gone too, owing to man (the Interstate went through) and Hurricane Camille. Yet something of its identity was there—the air, maybe, the vast moonlight.[)] Richard Ford was there with me. (We each got hon-

ored—we honor one another all the time in Mississippi—by Miss. Library Assn. for fiction (Richard) and non-fiction (me).) He's a fine man—I like him & his stories very much. Do you? ("Optimists" in the New Yorker.)[61] (Years after I'd been reading him, I met him and learned he'd been born in Jackson, on the same street I was born on, across the street—only a generation later.)

The new Brazilian and/or Japanese management of the Algonquin doesn't think anybody will need more than a single sheet of paper. I'll finish this in the lobby.

Another thing on my mind to ask you—have you seen the new issue of <u>Antaeus</u>? It's all about Literature as Pleasure. I so much liked the essay by James Laughlin "The Pleasures of Reading the Classics in Translation," with passages about Robert Fitzgerald—And his own lines on Catullus:

> ...Catullus could rub words so hard together their friction burned a heat that warms us now 2000 years away.

It's a good issue, I'm still carrying it around to read in (like in lobbies).

It's heartening news about Bill Meredith and his catching-up sleep, and how much better he has come to feel. He himself (I think) inscribed a copy of his book which arrived at home just before I left. It was bad about Howard. Even though the only times I ever saw him were by chance—glimpses —(as in lobbies again) I felt we enjoyed a warm continuum—as if we never really stopped laughing at the same story, if not crying. The wonderful parody biography book, that first one, appeared dedicated to Reynolds and me, and was the direct result (I mean the dedication) of a stalled taxi ride to the Institute with the 3 of us inside, stalled & laughing for hours, until weak. I mean to read <u>The Magic Lantern of Marcel Proust</u> again, remembering him again. But I can always remember him remembering Elizabeth.[62]

Have you seen the Lake Poets exhibition at the NYP Library? I think it's the very same one I saw, and didn't you? at the V & A in London several years ago—Wonderful—Much, much love. Soon to be talking again—Eudora

William Maxwell to Eudora Welty, December 20, 1987, Note card quoting lines from Wallace Stevens's "On the Surface of Things"

Dearest Eudora:

We are in the country. The cat comes in, his fur stiff with the cold, and eats ravenously, and waits at the door. Out, out, he says with the tip of his tail. He is starved for the outdoors, and in town sneaks out into the foyer and stands in front of the elevator by wait of suggesting that we ought to be somewhere where we are not. We have a new roof over the living room, where the thermostat is, and it is insulated, and the furnace can sit down and rest from time to time, which it didn't before. Not to mention the oil bill. I was so delighted to see a review by Sir Victor [Pritchett] in this week's New Yorker. As on top of the subject as ever, even though it was Rebecca West.[63] How I wish they lived up the road. How I wish you lived right in this little house, in the room off the kitchen, or if you liked Brookie's room better, you could have that. I am sure she wouldn't mind.

<div align="right">With oodles of love at Christmas, from us both,

B.</div>

Eudora Welty to Emily and William Maxwell, December 21, 1987

Dearest Emmy and Bill,

Elizabeth Lawrence was a long time friend—It's the easiest thing in the world to me to imagine conversations running between you, among the three of you, no the four of us. She had a garden you would walk into and have a hard time leaving. She came to see me & Mother's garden—once paid a surprise visit and I was by my bad luck away, but she stayed in my room and visited my mother and read all my books, the visit she always said was the best one. Allen Lacy of the NY Times put this book together, a marvelous piece of choosing & editing[64]—I must have sent you her earlier books before, The Little Bulbs in particular?—She could cook, too. And play the flute. This was a long time coming from Duke but you might have a chance to read it in the days waiting for spring.

I hope it's a good spring and that the writing and the painting go well— All else too—

<div align="right">My dearest love to you and the girls,

Eudora</div>

William Maxwell to Eudora Welty, December 31, 1987

New Year's Eve

Dearest Eudora:

We came out to Yorktown after Christmas and are staying until tomorrow morning, when we have to go into town for a party and because Emmy hasn't seen the Wordsworth show at the Public Library. It has been very cold, around six above at night, and five inches of snow on the ground. But very dry, like the winters in Wisconsin that we both remember.

The Partridge-berry wreath is on the dining room table, still fresh, and adorable. I have several times been strongly tempted to put it on my head. Perhaps because it was a dry fall, the holly tree had very few berries on it. The wreath on the front door still smells, when we go in and out. And we were so busy at Christmas that we didn't have time to open all the presents. Kate likes to do this in a leisurely fashion, with plenty of time for admiring, and Brookie wasn't here but in Thailand, so we will have a continuation of Christmas when she has recovered from jet-lag, for she is on her way home from San Francisco right this minute (I think).

Mavis Gallant went to Thailand ten years ago and was enchanted by it.[65] Brookie said, when we talked to her over the phone New York to Hongkong, that it was like California in the fifties, meaning girls on motorcycles. Meaning Bangkok. I believe both of them, since the changes everywhere are taking place so rapidly. Hongkong is much built up since Brookie was there six years ago. Built up where, I said. I thought every inch of ground was built on. Built up, she said. A city of stalagmites (I had to look it up, to be sure I didn't mean stalactites). She has a cousin in Hongkong she is fond of. And went to Thailand because her BF used to work for the Chase Bank and flew so much he got a couple of passes to anywhere he wanted, and chose Thailand. Or they did. They went on a walking tour into the mountains, and across the border into Burma, in the region where the fighting is.[66] More dangerous than Africa, she said, and Africa I thought quite dangerous enough: The guide said "Do you want to cross the river (they were on horseback) where the lions are or where the crocodiles are? Naturally they chose the lions. Do you remember the sleepy creatures at Longleat sitting on their front porch?[67]

About every five years I read my way through the Complete Sherlock Holmes. Last time I was interested in the connubial relationship between Holmes and Watson. This time I find that I sleep like a stone afterward. Better than any sleeping pill. Better even than crackers and milk.

The Wordsworth show is marvelous. Lots of Constables and Turners and [John Sell] Cotmans and [Thomas] Girt[i]ns. The [Thomas] Phillips portrait of Lord Byron dressed like an Albanian soldier. A portrait of Coleridge as a young man, with a blue face, which I hadn't expected. Wordsworth's granny glasses and their worn case. Dorothy's notebooks open to a page describing daffodils. First printings of Tintern Abbey, etc. Blake. Everybody. I wish I had thought to tell you to drop everything and come see it.

On Christmas Eve we went to Robert Mann's to hear Haydn's The Seven Last Words of Christ, which gets more moving every time I hear it. And Christmas Day people dropped in. Or rather, the Steegmullers came for breakfast, and shortly after they left people began dropping in, and this lasted till midnight.[68] Emmy had a goose, which she very sensibly didn't cook. The cat didn't climb up the Christmas tree, which was too small (six feet) to interest him perhaps, though he could have sharpened his claws on it if he had thought of doing that instead of on the slipcovers. For once the outside doesn't attract him. Too cold. The new roof over the living room means that the furnace could rest between times. I have taken to wearing long underwear, as I did when I was a child. When I had a hole in my long black stockings I used ink to conceal it. Washable ink. I was cold all winter, underwear notwithstanding. I don't think children's clothes were anything like as warm then as they are now. It didn't prevent me from making angels in the snow. If a movie called "My Life as a Dog" comes to Jackson, don't miss it.

My wish for you for 1988 is that there will not be a single envelope containing somebody's manuscript he hopes you will read and criticize. My wish for Emmy is that she will feel that she owes it to herself to paint more than she owes anything else to anybody. And for myself that I will wake up every morning full of energy and rush to my dear typewriter. While I am at it, I might as well wish that (SINCE IT DOESN'T COST ANY MORE) for you too.

<div align="right">

With much, much love from us both,
Bill

</div>

William Maxwell to Eudora Welty, January 9, 1988

Dearest Eudora,

The Elizabeth Lawrence book I'm only a little into, but it has made me feel as never before how very different, how deeply human and personal life in the South is. These exchanges of plants and notes that go with them. Everything south of the Mason-Dixon line must be gardens, gardens, gardens. The first time I was aware of Elizabeth Lawrence was in reading about Katharine White's correspondence with her, but the biographer[69] didn't make it very clear who she was. I love the idea of her coming to visit you ("Taffey was a Welshman") and reading your books.[70] Speaking of which, when you were in New York did you go to see the Wordsworth show? And did you get a catalog? Enclosed postcard is to save you time and trouble. Because we ordered a copy of the catalog for you—they ran out of them—but don't want to burden you with a second copy. It was one wonderful thing after another. The poet's glasses and spectacle case, Dorothy Wordsworth's journal opened to a description of daffodils, first editions of <u>Tintern Abbey</u> and <u>The Ancient Mariner</u>. Much corrected pages of "Don Juan" etc., portraits of Byron, Shelley, Keats, Blake and a very strange blue-faced Coleridge that looked as if he had sat for it in Xanadu, though actually I think it was done in Rome by his friend Washington Alston. Lots of Turners, lots of Constables. Cotmans. And a note just meant for you: An art dealer said to Turner, "I have something now that not even you could match." And Turner said, "Then you must have Girt[i]n's 'The White House of Chelsea.'" There on the wall it was. But the strangest and most beautiful painting of all was the Samuel Palmer of a man reaping in the moonlight. It was mostly red or black, but when you stood at the right distance from it everything was shiny with the moon's light.

Devotedly,

B.

Eudora Welty to William Maxwell, [January 1988]. Bill had sent Eudora a self-addressed card with the typed line "I do (not) have the Wordsworth catalog" in the middle of the card. Eudora's message is written around this line.

Dearest Bill, It's lovely to know you thought of me at that exhibition, because having learned it had come to New York I had had visions of seeing it with, of course, you & Emmy. I've seen it—when I visited London several years back, it was at the V. & A.—rooms & rooms, upstairs & downstairs & in my lady's chamber, all hung, filled, <u>strewn</u> with those treasures. The <u>handwriting</u> of everybody, the little pocket sketchbooks & notebooks—all the Constable & Turner eyefuls—I never got the catalogue, because I always intended to go back for another sight of it all, and if you do get yours and one for me, I'll treasure it—all that much more—it will be like seeing it with you after all. Suitable for a dream on my exquisite and marvelously designed & worked pillowcases—about which, letter will follow. It's lovely to have the letters from you. Glad Brookie is safe. Much love to all —Eudora

Emily Maxwell to Eudora Welty, July 19, 1988

Dearest Eudora—

August 16th is Bill's 80th birthday. He doesn't want a party, but I know he'd love to hear from the people closest to his heart. I'm writing to a few friends to say if they want to write, to send it

 c/o Kate Maxwell

 […]

& she will bring it out to Yorktown on his birthday.

He's having a very hard time at the moment. He has Lyme disease, caught from the local deer tick, & it has affected the R side of his face with Bell's palsy, an unpleasant & frightening nerve disease. He's taking antibiotic & cortisone, and we hope & pray that it will go away in time, as it usually but not always does. Meanwhile it's hard for him to see (his glasses don't work) and eat. There's no use calling because it takes time to get over—10 days to six months!

<div align="right">In some haste, and with much much love
Emmy</div>

I like the Glenway Wescott KAP dialogue so well I xeroxed it & am passing it around.

William Maxwell to Eudora Welty, July 17, 1989

Dearest Eudora,

I thought it might interest you to know about the vicarious life you have been leading in New Haven, Connecticut. The writer is in his late thirties, a poet named Michael Collier. He was first brought to our house fifteen years ago by Bill Meredith, whose student he was. And now he is a teacher himself. Until a year ago he was living in Baltimore in a row house with a wife and two small children and we stayed there when I gave a reading at the University of Maryland. When I get to heaven I hope my abode there will turn out to be a row house in Baltimore. You notice I say when and not if. A couple of years ago Yale offered his wife, who was then a librarian at Johns Hopkins, the job of head of all of the science libraries. Which she now is. A whole year Michael commuted between Maryland and New Haven, a thing I would have said was impossible. But he specializes in impossibilities. When the firemen ejected the audience from the auditorium of the Institute, Richard Harteis found a chair in the courtyard and offered it to the two of us and Michael sat on one half and I sat on the other half and it all seemed quite natural, but after a while out of consideration for me he sat on the floor.

Emmy is still not out of the woods.[71]

<div align="right">With much love.

Bill</div>

As for the basket of eggs, it is a story F O [Frank O'Connor] told me. Some writer, which one I have forgotten, was complaining that he would never be able to write another story and somebody else (AE?) said "You are like a hen walking around saying <u>There are no more eggs</u>!"[72]

Attached was a July 10, 1989, letter from Michael Collier to Bill and Emmy:

I think often the most wonderful and powerful aspect of a dream is not the dream itself but the coincidence (if that's what you can call it) that allows us to recall the dream the morning after. We wake blank and forgetful of where our unconscious led us the night before, but if we're patient we are often led to something vivid and memorable. And so this was my experi-

ence this morning when I reread Bill's review of ONE WRITER'S BEGIN-
NINGS and was reminded that I had dreamt of Eudora Welty the night be-
fore. I know that I was led to this dream because of the phone conversation
we had a few days before about Eudora Welty's magical way of reading her
own work. It's interesting that the dream guided me back to Bill's book, in-
evitably I would say. Anyway, the dream was a long one, though certainly
not as long as Coleridge's, and I remember little of it except for a gesture.
I'm not sure why but Eudora Welty reached out and touched me on the
shoulder. The touch calmed and reassured me, so I must've been in need
of some strength she could give. That's all. A visitation of sorts in which all
of us were present. A gathering that could not have been more real had all
four of us shared one chair at the Academy/Institute meeting.

I'm sorry that I've tried to put the logic of a dream on paper with my
rude hand. I always find it difficult writing down any part of a dream. It's
like trying to pick something up from the bottom of an aquarium. We think
we know exactly where it is and then we put our hand into the water to find
the object misjudged. But what do we expect, we are all clumsy enough in
the conscious element.

I enjoyed our conversation the other night very much. Maybe Frank
O'Connor will appear in my dreams tonight. If he does I hope he has a big
basket of eggs.

William Maxwell to Eudora Welty, December 5, 1989

Dearest Eudora:

We were sitting in my study having supper from trays while we watched
MacNeil/Lehrer, when to our delight they announced that there was an in-
terview with you coming up. It wasn't at all like an interview. It was a three-
cornered love affair involving Roger Mudd, you, and the camera man.[73]
He caught you so beautifully, and especially your eyes, that several times I
wanted to reach out and touch you, the way I am sure cats and dogs want
to do when they watch TV. I have a fondness for Roger Mudd, which is not
based on an acquaintance but solely on his appearance and personality. He
reminds me of the men of my childhood. There is an easiness about him
which is not often found any more. You were in splendid form, that is to say,

you were yourself, and when it was over, we rushed to the phone to call you, and the phone rang and rang, but there was no answer. So it seemed clairvoyant of you when a letter turned up in this morning's mail. I am glad you had such a good time in your travels. And as for the tiredness, once when I was bone-tired, I went to my doctor who gave me a shot of vitamin B and said, "You can use all this up today or, if you're more careful and don't rush around very much, it will last you four days, by which time you probably won't be tired anymore." It worked like a charm, and if you have a sympathetic doctor, ask him next time if he thinks it's a good idea.

How I wish I lived in Jackson and could deal with those stairs for you. When I was a little boy my mother frequently sent me upstairs for something she needed and I remember the sense of importance it gave me as I came back with the object she wanted. An extra pair of legs is what it amounted to. And was referred to as.

Did we ever discuss the anti-arthritis diet that Mrs. Wilbur told us about? I mentioned it at the breakfast table this morning and Emmy said "No. It's impossible. It means giving up coffee, tea, meat, and alcohol. Don't bother Eudora with it...." The truth is it does seem to work but at a terrible price in joi[e] de vivre.

You know that wall on the side of a Harlem postoffice that Brookie's hotel children covered with a mural forty feet high and a hundred feet long?[74] Well, in the vacant lot beside it there were a great many dingy objects, scrap metal, bottle caps, pieces of I-don't-know-what and from them the children have constructed a piece of sculpture. Brookie took all thirty-five of them to a museum to show them the possibilities, which they got in an instant and they were off and running, so to speak. We went up this morning to see it. It is a figure twenty feet high that looks like a cross between a football player and Don Quixote. One hand seems to be made of automobile parts and the shield has a heraldic design made of bottle caps. The face stares off into the distance majestically and the feet are solid concrete. People looked to see what we were looking at, but otherwise seemed to have accepted the statue as something always there. It would look stunning in the Museum of Modern Art, but is more needed at Lexington Avenue and a Hundred and Twenty-Fourth Street.

In the interview we were struck by your remark that it wouldn't any

longer be possible for someone with a camera to approach black people in the simple, courteous, interested way that you did back in the thirties. We are looking forward very much to the book.

Don't feel that being eighty means that you are an <u>old</u> person. I am now eighty-one and feeling wonderful. Perhaps too wonderful because if I live forever, I will end up an embarrassment. Of course, I don't <u>do</u> any of the things I mean to do in the course of a given day but I very much enjoy doing the things that I didn't wake up intending to do. We are leading a quiet life because Emmy is still subject to those dreadful attacks that come from a post-operative adhesion. The last one, about a month ago, occurred when we were in the country and had to decide whether to stick it out or at one o'clock in the morning head for New York Hospital. In the end Emmy drifted off to sleep while I was reading Janet Flanner's* Profile of Braque[75] and in the morning she was well. We had been to see the Braque-Picasso show with <u>The New Yorker</u> art critic, on a day when the museum was closed, and emerged from Cubism to find ourselves uninvited guests at the Museum's sixtieth anniversary party. We remembered, of course, the time when dear Monroe Wheeler took all of us through the Turner show.[76] I am glad you remember that occasion also.

There is no end to what I have to say but then you would have to read it.

Much love from us both,

Bill

*The new biography of her is N.G. [no good]

Eudora Welty to Emily and William Maxwell, April 15, 1990, Postcard with photograph of a Hampton Roads private railroad car, 1926

Dearest Emmy and Bill,

I miss you so! but I've been running on the charge of pleasure, comfort, and exhilaration of that wonderful afternoon—Basking in the sheer goodness of the good news. I hope the eye is performing better & better with each day.[77]

If I could just be there to see the exhibition [Emmy's] open at the gallery! I love the announcement card—All my happiest good wishes to it—

Maybe somehow I can see it <u>yet</u>—but I won't say "see it intact," and only hope they (paintings with the red spots attached) are spoken for by the right people.

This is the piece on KAP I was trying to finish in N.Y. I wish I could have done it better but I wanted you to see it all the same.[78] I leave for London on Wednesday, April 17—home May 7—though not on the Hampton Roads bound for Northern Cities—Much much love and thank you again for our fine evening! Love, Eudora

William Maxwell to Eudora Welty, May 1, 1990

Dearest Eudora:

If I didn't already know that needlework gives me insomnia (I tried to help Emmy with the alligator by doing background) I would get a piece of canvas and start in on a sampler of your paragraph on the hard work of writing. "The difficulty that accompanies you is less like the dark than like a trusted lantern to see your way by."[79] That says it. When I catch myself sitting back and having an easy time of it I know that the only thing to do is throw it in the wastebasket and start over.

A fool […] wrote and asked me if he could come and talk to me about your friendship with Katherine Anne Porter. I can't believe that you haven't heard from him also. I wrote him I had no first hand information, yours sincerely. Somebody else sent me KAP's volume of letters. With dread I looked for my name in the index and it was there, but not the thing I was afraid of. Our connection was slight but amiable until she sent in a manuscript, a Miranda story[80] that showed signs of having been around a long long time. Naturally I wanted her for The New Yorker, and made a page of suggestions for making it "work" and sent it on to Mr. Shawn, who was vacationing in Bronxville, and failed to notice that it didn't come back from him in a reasonable time. It had got into his briefcase and was hibernating there. Then I went on my vacation, and when I got back there was an angry letter from KAP demanding her ms back. The only thing that could have made her angrier, I now realize, was my suggestions for improving the story. Anyway it put a crimp on our correspondence. I was afraid there would be, for all time, her angry communication about how she wasn't accustomed to that

kind of neglect. Instead in a letter to somebody else she said that she had lunch with Frank O'Connor and me and that I had got a nursery in Ohio to send her a rosebush (<u>Golden Wings</u>) which she had planted with care.

You have done nicely indeed by that long ago summer, and I was sorry that she didn't go on living in "South Farm" for very long.

Just such an observation car as that was stopped at the crossing by the railway station in Lincoln and I, aged twelve or thirteen, waiting for the train to pull out and the striped gates rise, noticed a woman sitting on the open balcony at the end <u>smoking</u>. I didn't know that women <u>could</u> smoke. She saw me looking at her with my mouth open in surprise and burst out laughing. I think she must have been fast, don't you?

Would you like the ms of the letters from KAP back?

Emmy's opening was a great success. Friends and relations appeared from all over […] The pictures looked wonderful, and she sold five of them.

I hope simultaneously that I will see you at the Ceremonial two weeks from now, and that you will be kind to yourself and not lift a finger about anything.

> Much love from us both,
> Bill

Eudora Welty to Emily and William Maxwell, [Summer 1990], Postcard with photograph of Jane Austen's house at Chawton, Hampshire, England

Dearest Emmy and Bill,

It was so lovely to get your call—hearing your voices and knowing all was well with you—eyes, exhibition, plans—It wasn't good timing for me to set my date with Delta Air Lines to fly the ocean so near the Ceremonial that I couldn't get to NY for the coming home with you for the putting up of feet and the quenching of thirst—that's what I mean by the Ceremonial— But can we hope to have our meeting later on? You're probably already in the country or headed there?

I loved your letter, Bill—Thank you for reading the KAP piece—it had been so hard to do—partly because the academic editor, though kind, was academic—(whose dots…were those in the letters? KAP's or mine? (KAP's

of course......)) When I took something out of the essay, he put it back—
just in a different place—

P.S. I found this picture of Jane's house—It looks big, but is really small.[81]
The opposite of her novels. Small, perfect rooms, closely connected—Let-
ter soon........Much, much love, Eudora

William Maxwell to Eudora Welty,
December 17, 1990

Dearest Eudora:

It's been raining since we got up, at 32 ½ degrees, so it didn't turn into an
ice storm. The cat comes in sopping wet, is dried off while he eats, and goes
out again. This typewriter (which has just been fixed) sticks and I have to
pound it like a horse I was given to ride at a dude ranch in Wyoming some
years ago. I will not change to a word processor. I would write in longhand
which nobody could read before I would do that. My window is full of res-
cued geraniums that are getting leggy but still blooming. Outdoors every-
thing is put away, either in the garden basement or under salt hay. The last
pansy was two weeks ago. If one wanted to risk the elements one could get a
bunch of parsley. I like the look of it out there. You can see we are ready to
sit it out till spring comes.

A little over a month ago I had to have my appendix out. I told the unfor-
tunate MD I was too old for that but he disagreed, and appears to have been
right. It came on on a Sunday night in the country and my regular doctor
was at a meeting in Dallas, and his office was being painted, but his wife/
secretary was uneasy and so was there when I called. It didn't hurt anything
like sixty, but the six hour wait in the hospital while they were waiting to get
me into AN OPERATING ROOM I didn't care for. In four days I was back
in the apartment. I think I brought it on by saying, at my annual check-up "I
feel better than I did ten years ago but I know it's an illusion," and the doc-
tor thumped and listened, took blood tests, and said finally "How you feel is
how you are." It is the sort of remark likely to be overheard Upstairs. Can I
safely say that I now feel <u>almost</u> better than I did ten years ago. Though this
typewriter is very trying.

It is Saturday afternoon and I feel like listening to the opera, but not <u>Salome</u>, which it is. Last night we sat up till eleven thirty watching the Peter Sellars version of <u>The Marriage of Figaro</u>. A kind neighbor taped the last hour and a half for us, to play tonight. We have a VCR but when it comes to taping programs it doesn't speak to our condition. The Mozart was wonderful. I hope you were watching it too. His punk haircut had put me off, but his feeling for the opera is profound, and the singers were better than I have heard at the Met, though unknown, so to speak. The modern dress brought out both the comic and serious elements. It took place in a penthouse of the Trump Tower. A building I have never set foot inside of.

What else? I read [Sir Walter Scott's] <u>Old Mortality</u> and found myself in it. My name, anyway. If you haven't (but then at the right age you read everything) already, I think it is too late. I kept wishing I was having it read to me by Sir Leslie Stephen.[82] The early journals that Edward Perrone brought us have given me a great deal of pleasure. What went on in 22 Hyde Park Gate, before Bloomsbury was even dreamed of. And the trip the four children made to St. Ives after their father died. Mostly I like knowing her when she was very young.[83]

Emmy has a wonderful recipe for Borscht, which she got from The Times. And we are not going to spend the week between Christmas and New Years in the country because Harriet Sheehy is coming over from Ireland and wants to spend three days with us, and the country would not work out well for her. I have ordered Victor's book on Chekhov, and the story I have been working on for the last year, not all that much to be quite honest, is inching toward the final shape. And then I may have a <u>very</u> small book of short fiction.[84] My father used to say, of car after car, this is my last La-Salle, or Cadillac, or whatever, but it never was, at least not for longer than he expected. I feel quite sure this is my last book. Unless I am hit on the head with a falling rock and vast reservoirs of hitherto unperceived material are revealed to me. As it stands I feel pretty much that I have left no stone unturned.

Emmy is very well, thank God. The days rush by. Much love,

Bill

[Enclosed with the letter is a pen-and-ink drawing by Emmy with Christmas greetings.]

Eudora Welty to William Maxwell, December 27, 1990

Dearest Bill,

Your letter is wonderful—but scary—suddenly you were operated on for appendicitis! You are intrepid—Like Elizabeth Bowen I believe in guardian angels—Emmy of course, but she may be augmented. You sound wonderful, thanks be to all. You <u>are</u> leaving no stone unturned—I believe you—Also I can hardly believe you! The expectation of the story now moving into final shape—<u>and</u> the coming book of fiction—Right now I absorb all this as part of Christmas and the New Year. The absolutely lovely ink drawing of pine cone, leaf (needles!) & twig is like good news too. The present of Mary Oliver's poems I open & read in every morning with my coffee when I get up—and she is new to me! I don't know how this happened, but I am getting to know her now, thanks to you and Emmy. I'll be writing you more soon. But the Pritchett book I ordered for you has just come—You may have it already (the Essays, '61–'87) (well here it is!). He's just had that big 90th birthday!

My best wishes to Harriet Sheehy if she is still there—And tell her I have brought out her sheep's wool arthritis mitt and daily put my bad right hand in it, invoking Irish magic.

Much, much love to all of you & tell the girls for me what a Happy New Year I'm wishing them too—

And all take care. We will meet in 1991. I'm looking forward already—

With my love, Eudora

Eudora and the Maxwells did meet in 1991, but not until November, when she traveled to New York for an annual meeting of the American Academy of Arts and Letters. During the previous summer, Eudora was hospitalized with compression fractures in her back. Her recovery had been slow, and the effect of the fractures would linger. The November trip made clear that her travel would henceforth have to be very limited. The arthritis in her hands also posed increasing difficulty for her, affecting her ability to type or even write letters by hand. There are no extant letters from Eudora to the Maxwells after December 1990.

William Maxwell to Eudora Welty, January 5, 1991

Dearest Eudora:

No, we didn't have that new collection of Victor's essays. What a treat! What a treasure. The undiminished energy of his mind expressing itself with every appearance of effortlessness, which no writing ever is, of course. But when I read him I feel him in the room. And Dorothy too.

Somebody else we both love has been in the room. A week or two ago I saw that Channel 13 was doing "The Heat of the Day" and I thought Oh I wish they'd kept their hands off Elizabeth [Bowen]. And didn't watch it, and afterwards a neighbor in the country said it was marvelous and that the dramatization was by Pinter. So I was sorry. But three nights ago, flipping on the dial I came on the beginning of it, on Channel 21, which must have some mirror-image relationship to 13, and we did watch it. As always, where Pinter has a hand in the pie, you forget to breathe. The leading actress [Patricia Hodge] was especially fine. And the next day (since I had a cold and was disconnected from whatever energy my mind ever had) I took the book down and began to read it. For the first time in I suppose twenty years or more. The first time I fought it and never really was able to accept that the man was a spy, or if he was that she would have to be told. This wrestling with preconceived notions must have kept me from reading what was on the page. Anyway, this time I did. And shaking my head in wonder felt over and over that it is a great novel.

Thinking we were coming right back, I left the Pritchett essays beside my chair in the country and then we got stranded here in town by my catching a cold, which I ungenerously gave Emmy. Mine is better, she is still quietly blowing. I always feel that the Management has withdrawn its support and anything can happen. As colds go, this was by no means the worst; just intolerable.

We both send a great deal of love,

B.

William Maxwell to Eudora Welty, January 8, 1991

Dearest Eudora:

It wasn't in the country, it was under a pile of blankets on the couch in

my study and when they were disturbed it plopped on the floor. I was so delighted to read that Gerald Brennan, whose autobiographical books I have read and reread, was Victor's best friend. The thing about V's essays is that they continually make you a present of books you simply have to read. Now I have to run down a copy of [Brenan's] "Thoughts in a Dry Season", which may not be easy, unless the Cambridge University Press also brought it out over here. How I love the thought of the two of them going out for a walk in that mountain village.

Much love,

Bill

William Maxwell to Eudora Welty, [Fall 1991]

Dearest Eudora:

I enjoyed this book so much I wanted you to read it. Which doesn't mean you have to. If you find yourself not responding to it, give it to the library. The author was married to Mike Nichols, and I can't imagine why they are separated but there is always a reason for everything.[85]

Charles Shattuck lost his wife about a month ago. She had had Alzheimer's, and life could hardly have been more difficult for either of them. I would telephone sometimes and we'd have to break off because of an attack of tears. I have known her ever since high school, and him almost that long. Fortunately he has many friends in Urbana. Devoted ones.

Did you happen to hear that program of reading from Shakespeare that John Guilgud [Gielgud] (probably have misspelled his name) went around the country with about twenty years ago? About half through I began to weep and as I kept mopping I kept thinking (of Shakespeare) How did he know? How did he know. The dirge from <u>Cymbeline</u> is the most beautiful expression of parting I would think that was ever written. Thou thy worldly task hast done. Both simple and sublime.[86]

We have just moved in from the country and are still searching around for our winter habits.

Much love,

Bill

William Maxwell to Eudora Welty, November 16, 1992

Dearest Eudora:

Oh the freshness in the air, since Election Day![87]

At the Institute dinner we saw Bill [Smith] and learned he had seen you. That was not as good as seeing you ourselves but it diminished the distance. And I see by today's mail that at long last everybody is a member of the Academy. Louis Auchincloss[88] is said to have said, "Just when I got in they lowered the barrier and let everybody in." I like to think he said it, whether he did or not. At that same dinner somebody read a memorial of James Brooks written by Vonnegut. They were friends. And V said to him one day "Just what is it you do" (I know now what to say to painter friends) and Brooks said "I put a dab of paint on the canvas and it does fifty percent of the rest."

It was lovely of you to send us the Southern Review with the piece about George Yeats.[89] I hadn't imagined her as being like that. I don't, in fact, know what I had imagined her as like. Frank O'Connor was devoted to her. She took pity on him when he was young and shy and they struck up a friendship. I knew WB depended on her for extrarational information, or do I mean supernatural? Superrational? Which made me feel she was capable of being out of her mind but wasn't. And more real than the women he thought he was in love with. It seems to be the fashion among the present day Irish to belittle him. They are out of their minds.

Among the list of contributors I notice Joyce Carol Oates. I haven't ever read her, on the theory that she couldn't pop up everywhere the way she does and think twice about what she puts down on paper.[90]

Years ago I bought the letters of Evelyn Waugh when they were published and was so put off by the editorial notes that I didn't read the letters. But lately I read those last three war novels, and enjoyed the technical virtuosity so much that I regretted that I had thrown the letters away. Only it turned out I hadn't. They were on a high shelf of the bookcase, and I had a cold, and they were ideal reading. I am sure you read them long ago.

We are going to Washington on Thursday to give a reading at the L of C [Library of Congress]. I can't make up my mind what to read. Maybe it will

come to me once I am on the platform, and faced with the sixteen people that I expect to find in the audience. It gives us a chance to see the museums. I particularly want to see the Whistlers in the Freer, which I last saw at the age of seventeen. We are staying with Tony and Helen Hecht, and my admiration for him is such that I wonder if I will be able to think of anything sensible to say.[91] Maybe I won't say anything. Or read anything at the L of C. "It is very pleasant losing one's memory," Waugh says. "One can read old favorites with breathless curiosity."

I am the slave to duty but I wish I were instead wholly given over to reading books I know by heart.

Devotedly,

Bill

William Maxwell to Eudora Welty, December 1, 1992

Dearest Eudora:

If you want a surprise be a surprise.

It was a wrench to leave that lunch party and maddening that we had lingered in the postcard section of the Phillips too long, misjudging the distance to Bethesda and so cut short the time we could have been with you.[92]

I thought you might possibly like this little elegy that I wrote for Charles Shattuck's memorial meeting. I am sure that one or another of his children sent you a programme for the occasion, which has very beautiful pictures of him at various times of his life. The first two times he spoke of you as Miss Welthy I let pass, but the third time I corrected him, stupidly, not realizing that it was an allusion to Ida M'Toy.

Brookie and my son-in-law,[93] I have to get used to the word, came overnight to Yorktown the Saturday after Thanksgiving. Emmy had planned a series of meals, most of which never took place. Chris is mad about golf and there is a course about a mile from our house. He went there at one and arrived home after dark, having fallen into a foursome, one of which he said had very good eyesight. In my childhood I used to caddy for my father and I know for a fact that with the best eyesight in the world you can't follow the flight of a golfball after dark. Emmy and I often have lunch as late as three-

thirty when she is painting, but this time we had lunch at five-thirty, setting a record.

If you even dream of answering this letter I will think you don't love me.

B.

I can't find the copy I made for you. One less piece of paper is a blessing. I have so much enjoyed getting to know Charles's daughters, through their letters. Yesterday, at the Century Club, I opened a volume of the Yeats/Maud Gonne correspondence and read (from her) a short letter beginning Darling (or some such) and thought I have no business reading this letter and stopped.

William Maxwell to Eudora Welty, December 19, 1993

12/19/93 (Kate's 39th birthday!)
Dearest Eudora:

I have just finished putting the lights on the Christmas tree, between the two front windows of the living room (where in generations past there would have been a gilt pier glass). Some animal ate a strategic branch out of the left side, and I hoped to disguise it with decorations, but there has been a mysterious diminishment of those too. I think I will have to cut some little girls out of the New York Times, the way you once did for our children, and see if they will conceal the missing green. Also among things missing are the berries on our holly tree in the country, I went out with Evelyn Jones[94] to get some branches to put on the mantelpiece and there were about six berries on the whole tree. Did a frost last spring nip the flowers of the male tree next to it? Or a flock of birds eat every last one while we were in the city? We bought the Xmas tree in Yorktown, and a very able girl with I am afraid very cold hands tied it on the car so capably that we couldn't get into the trunk or the back seat and I had to hand things from the front seat to the back, which was awkward. We left suddenly because while we were shopping the car radio predicted rain and sleet all night and three inches of snow on top of it. It rained, but that was all, but we were glad to wake up in the city because of all the things that need to be done. Also, if you know what has become of the big red Xmas tree glass balls I wish you would tell me? I should have made a trip to the attic, where there is a supplementary box.

Emmy said "Next year I am going to say to Brookie, "Why don't <u>you</u> have Christmas this year"; but didn't mean it. B and Chris, our since a year ago last October son-in-law[,] are coming Christmas Eve, and Kate hasn't decided whether to come with them or on Christmas morning with the Steegmullers. I mean she thinks she hasn't decided. Committing herself to something isn't one of the things she likes to do, but she will come with Brookie on Christmas Eve, I feel sure. Feeling sure is one of the things I like to do.

My message to Santa Claus was please don't give me anything, I have more than I know what to do with. But he is so busy and may well not get the message.

Lately I have had the feeling that I have my whole life to consider and enjoy, especially the periods that were especially nice and that when I was younger I might have regretted because they didn't go on longer. Now I think, Wasn't that nice, Wasn't I lucky. It could all be a very enjoyable book.

Speaking of which, I went to the Morgan Library because the New Yorker said the ms of [Robert Louis Stevenson's] Weir of Hermiston was on display. It wasn't. I must not have got there soon enough. I know you have read it because you have read everything, but isn't it a glorious piece of writing? And have you read his South Sea Island non-fiction? And The Eldorado Squatters? And An Amateur Immigrant.[95] Much of what he published, the part that was not popular in his life time, would be liked now, if people only knew it was there. I wish I had known him. But then reading him you do. And I know you. Which quite makes up for missing RLS in the flesh, the hardly enough flesh to go around.

Dearest Eudora, what there is to say we have said, in one way or another. You know how much we love you. So it will have to be Merry Christmas and a Happy New Year!

William Maxwell to Eudora Welty, January 15, 1996

Dearest Eudora:

I opened an important-looking envelope and it turned out to be an invitation to your investment, if that is the right word, in the Legion d'Honneur. We are both so pleased. No such honor can be very exciting to you at this

point, since you have been so showered with them, but this one has always seemed very romantic and I hope you enjoy the idea of it. Also the little red ribbon that you can wear on your lapel. I would dearly love to be there for the occasion but any kind of extended travel I draw back from the thought of. Who would also be happy with this is, are Charles and Susan Shattuck.

I have been ordering my papers and sending a lifetime of correspondence off to the University of Illinois library and I could not bear to dispose of their letters without rereading them. Charles's are so witty, so full of feeling, such a complete history of their life. The thread that runs through it is his deep deep love for you. Which I am sure you are aware of. As in all correspondences that are continuous there are forewarnings. In San Francisco Susan was pushed off balance on an escalator and fell and injured herself, and for a week had a memory lapse that anticipated the dreadful Alzheimer's that soon afterward overtook her. And Charles ate something that scratched his throat (but was, of course, the first symptom of throat cancer). Reading the letters has plunged me into such a fit of remembering, not only of them but of almost everything else, that I couldn't sleep because my mind was racing so. It made me realize that remembering can be a kind of illness, and perhaps I have it.

Because of Brookie's visit, I feel I have a fairish idea of how things are with you.[96] Old age has been kind, I should say even fortunate, to both of us. Though Emmy is now seventy-four, she doesn't even have one foot in it, so far as I can see. She sends her love and so do I, and our congratulations.

Bill

Old age did not remain kind. In 1997, Bill's lymphoma returned, though he responded well to chemotherapy. Then in 1998, ovarian cancer struck Emmy, and she began the first of three rounds of chemotherapy. In the midst of these health crises, Bill managed to write a brief essay, one of his last published works, for a 1999 festschrift in honor of Eudora's ninetieth birthday. Appropriately, he cast his essay in the form of a letter.

Eudora dear:

I have been thinking how fortunate we were to have been born toward the end of the first decade of this century. To begin with, the quiet: except on

the Fourth of July. No heavy trucks, no bulldozers, no power lawnmowers, no leaf blowers, no power saws. When there was a sound, just the clop-clop-cloppity-clop of a horse and buggy. You could count the automobiles. The grass was full of wonderful things—spring beauties, dandelions, the one-winged seeds of the maple trees, the shell of a locust that had made itself a new shell, sometimes a piece of tinfoil or a penny. There were shade trees everywhere and their branches met over the street. If there was a red light in the sky, you picked up the telephone receiver and asked Central where the fire was and she knew. Even when nobody's house was on fire, the fire horses had to be exercised and so sometimes on the way to school you got to see the fire engine. For music there was Schumann-Heink and Alma Gluck and Caruso and Scotti and Amelita Galli-Curci and John McCormack. Who could ask for more? The record player was called a Victrola and had to be wound before each record. The blossoms of the trumpet vine made very good orange gloves. In August the rising spirals of the locusts, in January the crunch of packed snow on the sidewalk and ice-landscapes on the windows when you woke up in the morning. Church bells on Sunday morning, wash lines on Monday. No air conditioning. On very hot nights you took your comforter and went from room to room until you found a doorway with a current of air and you lay down there and went to sleep. The streetcars in summer were open on the sides and you could get on or get off anywhere. At the end of the carline the conductor got out himself and re-versed the overhead trolley. Palm leaf fans kept everybody cool. The sound of the ice-cream wagon could have come straight from fairyland. Ice cream made at home tasted of salt but was better than the boughten kind. When the man checked the overhead street lamps, he sometimes left a carbon stick behind where a child could find it and write his name with it. In August the katydids brought home the terrible truth that it was only six weeks more till frost. Sometimes it was, sometimes it wasn't. The same with when the groundhog saw his shadow. I saw William Jennings Bryan plain. On the platform of the Lincoln Chautauqua. You must have seen him too. He was everywhere. There were airplanes but nobody had actually seen one. Punk sticks and pennyroyal kept mosquitoes at a distance. If there was a light in an upstairs window after ten o'clock it meant that somebody was sick. The bobwhite and the whippoorwill were equally tireless. Before anybody was

awake the milkman made his rounds, leaving the milk on the porch steps, in glass bottles, and the cream had already floated to the top of the bottle and was yellow. On Decoration Day old men in uniforms much too large for them who had fought in the Civil War, as some people prefer to say The War Between the States, led the parade. The flag had forty-eight stars and thirteen stripes. There were so many Oz books at the library that you could never come to the end of them (only some were always out). George Washington's birthday was celebrated on the actual day, though the day he cut down the cherry tree nobody has ever announced that I know of. It cost 3¢ to mail a letter, or was it 2¢? Everybody knew the name of everybody else's horse and dog, and there was no extra charge for the rainbow.

Even more fortunate was the fact that we knew each other and were friends.

> With love on your ninetieth from
> Emmy, Kate, Brookie, and Bill Maxwell[97]

A year after writing this letter, Bill learned that his lymphoma was no longer in remission, and Emmy decided to forgo a fourth round of chemotherapy. On July 23, 2000, she died, followed eight days later by Bill. During the year following the Maxwells' deaths, Eudora's own health declined precipitously. Then on July 23, 2001, Eudora's life ended, the result of cardiopulmonary failure.

These losses, however, have not proved absolute. Admiration for Eudora, Bill, and Emmy, like the appreciation of Bill's and Eudora's fiction, remains undiminished. As Eudora wrote in The Optimist's Daughter, *"The memory can be hurt, time and again—but in that may lie its final mercy. As long as it's vulnerable to the living moment, it lives for us, and while it lives, and while we are able, we can give it up its due."[98] The letters exchanged and preserved by Eudora Welty and William Maxwell ensure that the memory of their lives is "vulnerable to the living moment" and that their constant and inviolable friendship, grounded in the love of language and expressed with the art of master storytellers, will endure on the page.*

ACKNOWLEDGMENTS

Timothy Seldes, Eudora Welty's agent and friend, was the first to suggest that a book of the Welty–Maxwell correspondence should be published. Tim encouraged me at every step in the process toward publication, as did his assistant, Joy Azmitia. Elizabeth Welty Thompson, Mary Alice Welty White, Kate Maxwell, and Brookie Maxwell generously supported the project, and Kate assisted with the notes, with selecting photos, and with proofreading. Jenna Johnson, senior editor at Houghton Mifflin Harcourt, offered sage advice as I selected, annotated, and introduced the letters. So, too, did Johnathan Wilber, Patti Carr Black, Harriet Pollack, and Carolyn Brown. The work of Christopher Carduff and Barbara Burkhardt was invaluable to me. The Manuscript and Archives Division staff at the New York Public Library; the special collections staff at the University of Illinois Libraries; Caroline Kiest and Joyce Sutz at the Lincoln, Illinois, Public Library; Kathy Kienholz at the American Academy of Arts and Letters; and the staff at the Mississippi Department of Archives and History were infallibly good-natured and helpful. So were Sara Barrett, Alec Wilkinson, Michael Collier, Greg Smith, Daniel Voll, Louis Lyell, and Susan Haltom. Special thanks to Millsaps College for the sabbatical leave that allowed me time for this project; to the Eudora Welty Foundation for making me its scholar in residence; to Dora Robertson, Katrina Byrd, Bettye Jolly, and my sister, LuAnn Marrs, who assisted with the manuscript preparation; to Katie Hamm, Barbara Jatkola, and Beth Burleigh Fuller for their indispensable work with the copyedited text and page proof; and to Rowan Taylor for his patience and his unflagging support.

NOTES

Introduction

1 Eudora Welty, introduction to *The Norton Book of Friendship*, eds. Eudora Welty and Ronald A. Sharp (New York: Norton, 1991), 37–38.

2 Eudora Welty, review of *The Letters of Virginia Woolf*, ed. Nigel Nicolson and Joanne Trautmann, vol. 2, in *The Eye of the Story* (New York: Random House, 1978), 192, 197.

3 William Maxwell, "Yr. V. W.," review of *The Letters of Virginia Woolf*, ed. Nigel Nicolson and Joanne Trautmann, vols. 1 and 2, in *The New Yorker*, July 18, 1977, 93, 94. The British writer Gerald Brenan (1894–1987) published his first book in 1933. He lived in Spain for many years and is best known for two books about that country, *The Spanish Labyrinth* and *South from Granada*.

4 The estate of William and Emily Maxwell holds the following letters. Eudora Welty to William and/or Emily Maxwell: August 23, [1952]; July 17, 1953; [August 1953]; [Early September 1953]; [September 10, 1953]; October 7, 1953; November 2, [1953]; [Late November 1953]; [Late April 1954]; December 8, [1954]; April 4, [1955]; [March 4, 1956]; [February 1957]; [Spring 1957]; October 14, [1957]; [May 1959]; [March 1961]; April 5, [1961]; [Spring 1965?]; [December 1965]; December 7, [1965]; October 18, [1966]; October 28, 1966; November 16, 1966; [January 1967]; January 24, 1967; [January or February 1967]; March 4, 1967; March 15, 1967; May 2, 1967; June 12, 1967; [Late June 1967]; August 7, 1967; August 28, 1967; January 8, 1968; January 11, [1968]; January 21, 1968; June 9, 1969; July 16, 1969; August 15, [1969]; August 19, 1973; June 24, 1974; [Late September or Early October 1976]; February 21, 1977; April 24, 1978; December 17[–?], 1979. William Maxwell to Eudora Welty: [April 1967].

The following letters are held by the New York Public Library in its *New Yorker* Records. Eudora Welty to the editors of *The New Yorker:* March 15, 1933. Eudora Welty to William Maxwell: December 22, 1942; August 9, 1946; August 21, 1946; September 2, 1946; June 19, 1952; August 11, 1952; August 30, [1952]; October 24, 1952. William Maxwell to Eudora Welty: August 19, 1946; August 30, 1946; September 27, 1946; June 23, 1960; July 5, 1967.

All other letters from William or Emily Maxwell to Eudora Welty are available as scans at the Eudora Welty House, Jackson, Mississippi. All other letters from Eudora Welty to William and/or Emily Maxwell are held by the Rare Book & Manuscript Library at the University of Illinois Urbana-Champaign.

5 "Triumphant vulnerability" is a phrase Welty used to describe the characters in Henry Green's fiction (Eudora Welty, "Henry Green: Novelist of the Imagination," in *The Eye of the Story* [New York: Random House, 1978], 15).

6 Welty, introduction, 40.

7 Howard Gardner, *Creating Minds: An Anatomy of Creativity Seen Through the Lives of Freud, Einstein, Picasso, Stravinsky, Eliot, Graham, and Gandhi* (New York: Basic Books, 1993), 44; Welty, introduction, 40.

8 Virginia Ross and Sally Wolff, "Conversations with Eudora Welty and William Maxwell," *South Atlantic Review* 64, no. 2 (Spring 1999): 136.

9 William Maxwell to Diarmuid Russell, January 3 and April 4, 1947, *The New Yorker* Records, Russell & Volkening files, New York Public Library.

10 William Maxwell to Eudora Welty, October 27, 1953.

11 Maxwell to Welty, January 29, 1968.

12 Welty to Maxwell, [August 1953].

13 Maxwell to Welty, October 4, 1961.

14 Maxwell to Welty, June 12, [1979].

15 Eudora Welty to Frank Lyell, [October 15, 1947], Eudora (Alice) Welty Collection, Mississippi Department of Archives and History, Jackson, Mississippi.

16 See the Library of America Web site, http://www.loa.org.

17 Maxwell to Welty, January [14], 1959.

18 Welty to Maxwell, [Late June 1964].

19 Eudora Welty to Diarmuid Russell, March 29, 1954, as cited in Michael Kreyling, *Author and Agent* (New York: Farrar, Straus & Giroux, 1991), 171.

20 Welty to Maxwell, May 6, 1966.

21 Maxwell to Welty, April 20, 1976; Welty to Maxwell, August 17, 1954.

22 Maxwell to Welty, September 9, 1983.

23 Welty to Maxwell, [Late June 1967].

24 Maxwell to Welty, November 3, 1955; December 29, 1977; January 8, 1955; November 11, 1957.

25 Maxwell to Welty, January 2, 1985; Welty to Maxwell, [September 30, 1956]; Welty to Maxwell, May 8, 1971; Maxwell to Welty, September 13, 1986.

26 William Maxwell, introduction to *The Outermost Dream* (St. Paul: Greywolf Press, 1997), ix; James G. Watson, *William Faulkner: Letters and Fictions* (Austin: University of Texas Press, 1987), xiii.

27 In an August 24, 2008, interview with National Public Radio's Jacki Lyden, Kate Maxwell commented that her father "was more complicated than people usually

describe him as, and perhaps more complicated to family than he was to people who knew his teaching, who were writers. You know, he wasn't always supportive, for example, to his own family. He was totally charming but sometimes could be judgmental. He grew up with a distant, judgmental father himself, and he admitted that, so when I brought certain things to his attention, he said sometimes my father speaks through me, and he was quite embarrassed about it." "Library of America Honors Overshadowed Writer," http://www.npr.org/templates/story/story .php?storyId=93928595.

28 Welty to Maxwell, May 8, 1971; Maxwell to Welty, October 12, 1953; Welty to Maxwell, [Summer 1990]; Maxwell to Welty, January 6, 1954.

29 Introduction of Eudora Welty at the Poetry Center, 92nd Street Y, New York City, April 22, 1985.

30 William Maxwell, "A Note on the Editing," in *The Letters of Sylvia Townsend Warner*, ed. William Maxwell (New York: Viking Press, 1983), xviii.

1. *"Never Lose Letters from an Editor"*

1 Marianne Hauser, "Miss Welty's Fairy Tale," *New York Times Book Review*, November 1, 1942, 7.

2 The content of this lost letter is summarized in a letter Maxwell sent to Welty's agent, Diarmuid Russell, on November 25, 1942: "I've just written a note to Miss Welty reminding her of our front porch gathering in the Rita Grill and also of the fact that we'd like very much to have her in The New Yorker. Anything you can do to persuade her to cast an eye in our direction will be most appreciated." Evidently, Welty missed the Rita Grill gathering, though she had earlier seen Maxwell at a party given by *Harper's Bazaar* fiction editor Mary Louise Aswell. (*The New Yorker* Records, Russell & Volkening files, New York Public Library.)

3 The literary agency Russell & Volkening represented Welty throughout her career.

4 George Price was a cartoonist for *The New Yorker*. The book to which Welty refers is *It's Smart to Be People* (1942).

5 Cézanne was one of e. e. cummings's favorite painters, and cummings himself was a painter as well as a poet. In 1922, according to biographer Christopher Sawyer-Lauçanno, cummings began to use "not only Cézanne's palette but also his vision of light and shape." However, he did so in watercolors, not oils (*E. E. Cummings: A Biography* [Naperville, IL: Sourcebooks, 2004], 216). James Thurber (1894–1961) began writing for *The New Yorker* in 1927 and continued to do so for the rest of his life, publishing both cartoons and witty stories in the magazine. *My Life and Hard Times* and *The Thurber Carnival* are among the most well-known of his nearly forty books.

6 The American poet Vachel Lindsay (1879–1931) published *The Congo and Other Poems* in 1914, complete with stage directions for being read out loud.

2. *"Wonderful to Be a Writer. Wonderful to Grow Roses. Wonderful to Care."*

1 The story, with the new title "Room in Algiers," was written by Mississippian John F. Robinson and published in the October 19, 1946, issue of *The New Yorker*.

2 On March 14, 1951, Eudora sailed for England; her return voyage began July 11, 1951. During her time abroad, Eudora traveled by boat train to Ireland, where she

visited her friend the Anglo-Irish novelist Elizabeth Bowen. Her short story "The Bride of the Innisfallen," based on her trip from London to Cork, became the first Welty story published by *The New Yorker* (December 1, 1951).

3 Welty's short story "Kin" was published in the November 15, 1952, issue of *The New Yorker*.

4 William Shawn was the editor of *The New Yorker*.

5 The story appeared in the September 20, 1952, issue.

6 Henry Volkening was Diarmuid Russell's partner in the literary agency Russell & Volkening.

7 The Perseid meteor showers occur each year sometime between mid-July and mid-August, peaking around August 12.

8 V. S. Pritchett's story "Two Roast Beefs" appeared in the July 12, 1952, issue of *The New Yorker*.

9 Rosa Wells, more familiarly known as Dolly, was a friend of Eudora's from Jackson who was now working in New York.

10 Eudora was reluctant to sign a contract giving *The New Yorker* first right of refusal for her work. Bill believed that it was in her financial interest to do so and on December 21, 1953, wrote to Diarmuid Russell about this: "Here is the remaining payment for *The Ponder Heart*. I can't help thinking what it would be if she had signed the first-reading agreement, but there probably is no point in troubling the harmony of things as they are by mentioning what they might be, and I do understand and respect completely the basis of her reluctance. It is just as important to us as to her that she not feel hemmed in by anything. It is just that as her friend and editor both I want her to have all that she can have; so I say all this to you instead of to her" (*The New Yorker* Records, Russell & Volkening files, New York Public Library).

11 *A Curtain of Green* (1941) was Welty's first book of stories.

12 In 1953, shortly after he became president, Dwight D. Eisenhower signed the Submerged Lands Act, giving states the title to undersea lands extending three miles from their coasts. During the presidential election campaign, Adlai Stevenson had argued that such lands should be under federal control. Emmy, Bill, and Eudora felt that Stevenson's position on this and other issues was so much in line with their own that "they might have invented him." Eudora's own tribute to Stevenson was published in the January 5, 1953, issue of the *New Republic*.

13 William Maxwell to Michael Kreyling, November 16, 1988, as cited in Michael Kreyling, *Author and Agent* (New York: Farrar, Straus & Giroux, 1991), 163–64.

14 Eudora Welty's review of J. D. "Jerry" Salinger's *Nine Stories* was published in the April 5, 1953, *New York Times Book Review*.

15 The Maxwells were leaving for England to visit Sylvia Townsend Warner and then go on to France.

16 *Illuminations Nouvelles*, Léon-Paul Fargue's book about the French artist Raoul Dufy (1877–1953), was published in 1953 with lithographs by Dufy.

17 Howard Moss, a poet himself, was the poetry editor at *The New Yorker*.

18 Maxwell's story "The Pilgrimage" was published in the August 22, 1953, issue of *The New Yorker*.

19 The Maxwells visited novelist Elizabeth Taylor (1912–1975) and her husband at their home in Buckinghamshire, England.

20 Mary Louise Aswell, formerly a fiction editor at *Harper's Bazaar* and at this time working for Ballantine Books, was a good friend of both the Maxwells and Welty.

21 Templeton the Rat is a character in *Charlotte's Web*, E. B. White's children's classic. Eudora had reviewed the book in the October 19, 1952, *New York Times Book Review*.

22 *The Ponder Heart* was under contract to be published first in *The New Yorker* and then in book form by Harcourt, Brace and Company. Welty thought of *The Ponder Heart* as a story rather than a novel and had originally planned to include it in a story collection rather than publishing it separately.

23 Eudora and her niece Elizabeth had seen *Guys and Dolls* in New York and had visited the Maxwells in Yorktown Heights.

24 Louis Forster was assistant to the editor of *The New Yorker* during the editorships of Harold Ross and William Shawn.

25 Bill's good friend Francis Steegmuller, who contributed stories and articles to *The New Yorker*, was a biographer of Gustave Flaubert, Guy de Maupassant, and Jean Cocteau. The new biography of George Sand, titled *Lélia*, was written by André Maurois.

26 "The Ponder Heart" appeared in the December 5, 1953, issue of *The New Yorker* and was published as a book in 1954.

27 Maxwell refers to Welty's recording of "Why I Live at the P.O.," "A Memory," and "A Worn Path" (Caedmon Records, 1952). James Joyce recorded "Anna Livia Plurabelle," which would become part of *Finnegan's Wake*, in 1929. T. S. Eliot recorded his *Four Quartets* in 1947.

28 Eudora's references to Lady Colchester and Biathaganthis Frigidi seem destined to remain mysteries.

29 V. S. Pritchett's story "Passing the Ball" appeared in the September 5, 1953, issue of *The New Yorker*.

30 Perhaps Eudora is referring to the Norse fairy tale "Why the Sea Is Salt."

31 Robert Fitzgerald (1910–1985) was a poet and a noted translator of classical epics and plays. His second wife, Sally (1917–2000), was a friend and editor of Flannery O'Connor.

32 "What Every Boy Should Know" was published in the Spring 1954 issue of *Perspectives*.

33 Thinking themselves unable to have children, the Maxwells had applied to adopt a child from the Cradle, an adoption agency in Chicago.

34 *Old Doc Yak* was a comic strip by Sidney Smith that Eudora had read at the New York 92nd Street YMHA in January 1953.

35 Clement Attlee (1883–1967) replaced Winston Churchill as British prime minister in 1945 and remained in office until 1951. Churchill (1874–1965) then recaptured the position and held it until 1955. During those years, Attlee was leader of the opposition.

36 Bill was working on a novel eventually to be titled *The Château*.

37 Joseph Mitchell, a native of North Carolina, was a writer for *The New Yorker*.

38 The French novel eventually did "round itself off." *The Château* would be published in 1961.

39 Evidently, Eudora's nieces were in some competition for mention in Bill's letters. He had met nine-year-old Elizabeth in New York but had not yet made the acquaintance of six-year-old Mary Alice.

40 The Irish novelist Joyce Cary (1888–1957) published a trilogy of novels between 1952 and 1955. The second novel in the trilogy, *Except the Lord*, was published in the United States by Harper & Brothers in 1953.

41 Bill recalled that Eudora's niece Elizabeth had had a positive effect on revisions to *The Ponder Heart*.

42 R. Hawley Truax was the treasurer of *The New Yorker*, and Raoul Fleischmann was the chairman.

43 Roy Hennessey, a rose grower in Scappoose, Oregon, published a book titled *Hennessey on Roses*.

44 Aswell's story "A Quaker Concern" was published in the December 1, 1956, issue of *The New Yorker*. Nancy Hale (1908–1988) was an American writer best known for her short stories.

45 Kirk Wilkinson, the art director at *Woman's Day* magazine, was a friend of the Maxwells and their neighbor on Baptist Church Road in Yorktown Heights.

46 Margot Morrow was an actress. Her first husband, Dwight, was the brother of Anne Morrow Lindbergh. She would later marry John Wilkie, the president and chairman of Central Hudson Gas and Electric.

47 Bill's antipathy toward V. S. Pritchett was transitory, part of a desire to shield his friends from reviews he deemed unworthy of them. He came to like Pritchett and to admire much, but not all, of his work, and Eudora's fondness for Pritchett's work was matched by her fondness for the man.

48 John Houseman directed a production of *Coriolanus* at New York City's Phoenix Theatre; it opened on January 19, 1954. The Jean Giraudoux play *Ondine* was directed by Alfred Lunt and starred Audrey Hepburn and Mel Ferrer.

49 Maxwell's concern seems to be Senator Joseph McCarthy and the unsubstantiated claims he advanced in hearings he was conducting as chairman of the Senate Permanent Subcommittee on Investigations.

50 Pianists Arthur Rubinstein and Josef Lhévinne. In 1933, Bill and Lhévinne were in residence together at Bonnie Oaks, a summer artists' colony in Wisconsin, and Bill drew on this experience in writing his first novel, *Bright Center of Heaven*. Lhévinne had begun summering at Bonnie Oaks in 1922, and Bill worked there as a farm hand beginning in 1925. In 1933, Bill was invited to Bonnie Oaks as an artist himself. Bill's mysterious comments about the eating habits of Rubinstein and Lhévinne appear to be in response to a missing letter from Eudora.

51 Bowen was planning to visit Eudora in Jackson in March.

52 Bill is referring to the six weeks Eudora spent living in New York in early 1953.

53 The title story of Eudora's collection was "The Bride of the Innisfallen," and Bill was particularly pleased because this was the first Welty story he had acquired for *The New Yorker*.

54 Jack Fischer was editor in chief of *Harper's Magazine*.

55 *The Mabinogion* is a collection of tales from Welsh myths that had been preserved in medieval manuscripts and were first translated into English in 1838–1849 by Lady Charlotte Guest.

3. *"Similar Discoveries"*

1 Eudora eventually had the recipe for the white fruitcake printed as a Christmas gift for friends.

2 Eudora had been selected to receive the William Dean Howells Medal from the American Academy of Arts and Letters for *The Ponder Heart*. The American Academy of Arts and Letters and the National Institute of Arts and Letters are sister organizations. The National Institute was founded in 1898 to honor artists, writers, and composers, and the members decided to honor one-fifth of their number with election to the American Academy. The two organizations merged in 1976. Eudora was elected to membership in the National Institute in 1952 and was elevated to the American Academy in 1972. Bill was elected to the National Institute in 1963 and elevated to the American Academy when its two-tier system of membership was dissolved in 1993.

3 Jerome Chodorov and Joseph Fields were dramatizing *The Ponder Heart* and visited Eudora as they worked on the script.

4 The Maxwells had begun to live full-time in Yorktown Heights, and Bill traveled by train to the *New Yorker* office.

5 Bill is quoting from "Ladies in Spring," one of Eudora's stories in *The Bride of the Innisfallen*.

6 The American Academy of Arts and Letters was interested in displaying *The New Yorker* galleys of "The Ponder Heart" for Eudora's award ceremony.

7 Maxwell is referring to Roy Hennessey. He is probably confusing him with California rose grower Will Tillotson.

8 This story may be "The French Scarecrow."

9 Pearl Kazin was an editor at *Harper's Magazine* and Mary Lou Aswell's friend.

10 This Welty essay was titled "How I Write" and was later revised and published in *The Eye of the Story* (1978) as "Writing and Analyzing a Story."

11 Bill delivered a speech titled "The Writer as Illusionist" at a Smith College symposium on March 4, 1955, and later had the essay privately printed.

12 In her essay "Place in Fiction," Welty wrote, "Some of us grew up with the little china night-light, the little lamp whose lighting showed its secret and with that spread enchantment. The outside is painted with a scene, which is one thing; then, when the lamp is lighted, through the porcelain sides a new picture comes out through the old, and they are seen as one. A lamp I knew of was a view of London till it was lit; but then it was the Great Fire of London, and you could go beautifully to sleep by it. The lamp alight is the combination of internal and external, glowing at the imagination as one; and so is the good novel" (*The Eye of the Story* [New York: Random House, 1978], 119–20). A china night-light also plays a role in Welty's novel *Delta Wedding*.

13 Eudora is referring to the printed version of Bill's speech "The Writer as Illusionist."

14 Maxwell had called a halt to a dramatization he found objectionable. See his letter of January 6, 1954, in chapter 2.

15 Wouk is the author of popular fiction such as *The Caine Mutiny* and *Marjorie Morningstar*.

16 Smith professor Newton Arvin was a noted Melville and Hawthorne scholar.

17 Sassetta was an Italian painter of the early Renaissance.

18 Julia Margaret Cameron (1815–1879) was a British photographer noted for her photographs of famous individuals, such as actress Ellen Terry and Charles Darwin. Cameron was the great-aunt of Virginia Woolf.

19 Gus Lobrano had died on March 1, 1956.

20 E. M. Forster published "a domestic biography" of his great-aunt Marianne Thornton (1797–1887) in 1956.

21 "La Grande Mademoiselle" was Anne Marie Louise d'Orléans, the Duchess of Montpensier (1627–1693), who wrote memoirs about the reign of her cousin Louis XIV.

22 Eudora's review of *Marianne Thornton: A Domestic Biography* was published in the May 27, 1956, *New York Times Book Review*. Eudora had visited Forster in his King's College, Cambridge, rooms in the summer of 1954.

23 Mary Lou Aswell married novelist Fritz Peters in 1949. The marriage was on the rocks within two years and ended in divorce.

24 Walter de la Mare, an English poet, short story writer, and novelist, died on June 22, 1956, at age eighty-three.

25 Eudora may be commenting on Emmy's pregnancy.

26 S. J. Perelman was a humorist who wrote for *The New Yorker*. The piece referred to here may be "Cuckoos Nesting—Do Not Disturb," published in the August 25, 1956, issue.

27 "The French Scarecrow" was published in the October 6, 1956, issue of *The New Yorker*.

28 Hubert Creekmore, a native Mississippian and the brother of Elizabeth and Mary Alice Welty's mother, Mittie, lived in New York. He was a poet, novelist, editor, and literary agent. Lehman Engel, a native of Jackson, Mississippi, was the preeminent musical conductor on Broadway.

29 Katharine White was the *New Yorker* fiction editor who hired William Maxwell.

30 This mysterious communication has evidently gone missing again.

31 In July 1956, a New York taxi dispatcher named Angelo LaMarca kidnapped and later killed a baby named Peter Weinberger. LaMarca was arrested in August, his trial began in November, and he was sentenced to death on December 14.

32 Christopher Carduff, ed., "Chronology," in *Maxwell: Early Novels and Stories* (New York: Library of America, 2008), 957.

33 Bill's review of *Virginia Woolf and Lytton Strachey: Letters*, edited by Leonard Woolf and James Strachey, appeared in the February 9, 1957, issue of *The New Yorker*. Art critic Clive Bell, who was for a time married to Virginia Woolf's sister, Vanessa, had recently published *Old Friends: Personal Recollections*. The "letter from Lytton to Virginia" to which Eudora refers later in this paragraph is actually one he wrote to his brother, James. In it he describes proposing to Woolf in 1909, being accepted, and then being able to make "a fairly honourable retreat." In his

review, Bill asks whether the Woolf-Strachey relationship was "altered, irrevocably, by this incident."

34 This is the work that would eventually become the novel *Losing Battles*, published in 1970.

35 Brigid Brophy (1929–1995) was an English feminist, pacifist, and novelist. Knopf published her novel *The King of a Rainy Country* in 1957.

36 Eudora had sent the poem "A Flock of Guinea Hens Seen from a Car" to *New Yorker* poetry editor Howard Moss as a Christmas card, and he asked permission to publish it. It appeared in the April 20, 1957, issue.

37 Maxwell dedicated his book *The Folded Leaf* (1945) to the American poet Louise Bogan (1897–1970), who had read and commented on drafts of the book and had suggested the title for it.

38 J. D. Salinger's story "Zooey" appeared in the May 4, 1957, issue of *The New Yorker*.

39 A photographer from a local newspaper had photographed Eudora's niece Mary Alice at Jackson's new public library.

40 Margaret McBride, a Scotswoman, was the Maxwells' live-in "mother's helper."

41 In *Old Friends*, Clive Bell includes a long letter from Virginia Woolf to her friend Barbara Bagenal, who had worked at the Hogarth Press.

42 The Thomas Lee House (c. 1660) is located in East Lyme, Connecticut.

43 Lillian Russell (1861–1922) was a popular actress, singer, and newspaper columnist. Julian Eltinge (1881–1941) was an actor who often impersonated women during his vaudeville, stage, and screen career. He was known as "Mr. Lillian Russell."

44 "The sparrows" refers to the story later published as *Losing Battles*. The "new story" is probably one that Eudora would never complete ("Nicotiana"/"The Last of the Figs").

45 E. B. White's "Letter from the East," which criticized the dumping of radioactive waste in the ocean, appeared in the July 27, 1957, issue of *The New Yorker*. E. B. and Katharine White were husband and wife.

46 The infant son of Charles and Anne Morrow Lindbergh was kidnapped on March 1, 1932, and found dead one month later. Bruno Richard Hauptmann was convicted of the murder in 1935 and executed in 1936.

47 Emmy's review of the year's best children's books appeared in the November 23, 1957, issue of *The New Yorker*.

48 Bill is referring to James Agee's posthumously published novel *A Death in the Family* (1957).

49 Eudora's essay "A Sweet Devouring" was published in the December 1957 issue of *Mademoiselle*.

50 Eudora had sent Bill and Emmy a book by Elizabeth Lawrence titled *The Little Bulbs* (New York: Criterion Books, 1957).

51 Bill's story "Two Old Tales About Women" appeared in the March 15, 1958, issue of *The New Yorker*.

52 Eudora's brother Walter was in poor health and had been to New Orleans to consult specialists.

53 Bill received a grant in literature from the National Institute of Arts and Letters in

1958 and would be inducted into the institute in 1963. Eudora had received a similar grant in 1944 and had been inducted into the institute in 1952.

54 Eudora remained at home because Walter was still ill with what doctors now suspected was a rare fungal infection around his heart.

55 Perhaps Eudora is referring to a production of John Osborne's play *Look Back in Anger*, which she saw during her spring 1958 trip to New York. Mary McCarthy discussed this play in the April 1958 issue of *Harper's Bazaar*.

56 Mrs. Green was most likely Mildred Ormsby Green, who, along with her husband, Harrison, ran the Bonnie Oaks artists' colony, where Bill had both worked and been in residence. Jack Huber was a professor of psychology, an author, a close friend of the Maxwells, and Kate Maxwell's godfather. His book *Through an Eastern Window* would be published in 1965. It seems likely that Eudora and the Maxwells had attended Van Cliburn's concert at Carnegie Hall on May 19, 1958.

57 Nine of Bill's fables were published in *The New Yorker* during 1958. They would not be published in book form until 1966, when they appeared along with twenty other tales in *The Old Man at the Railroad Crossing and Other Tales*.

58 Eudora is describing the work that would eventually become *Losing Battles*.

59 *Place in Fiction*, "a condensation of lectures prepared for the Conference on American Studies in Cambridge, England, in 1954," was published by the House of Books in October 1957. Alfred A. Knopf (1892–1984) became Bill's publisher in 1958, and Bill remained at Knopf's publishing house for the rest of his career.

60 Russell Lynes was the managing editor of *Harper's Magazine*.

61 Rather than using the cut-and-paste method of revision with her typescripts, Eudora used the cut-and-pin method, employing straight pins the way a seamstress might.

62 Playwright Arthur Miller brought his famous actress wife to his induction into the National Institute of Arts and Letters, which took place during the same ceremony at which Maxwell received his award.

63 The angry young robins figure in the story young Kate Maxwell had written.

64 Eudora's essay about a Jackson, Mississippi, midwife named Ida M'Toy had been published by the Maxwells' friend Charles Shattuck in the Summer 1942 issue of the journal *Accent*.

65 Eudora was not able to make the trip to Yaddo, an artists' colony in Saratoga Springs, New York, in 1958, but later in the fall she would go to Bryn Mawr, Pennsylvania, and New York.

66 Wolcott Gibbs, the theater critic for *The New Yorker*, died on August 16, 1958. Both Eudora and Bill greatly admired Kenneth Tynan, the British theater critic for the *Observer*. Eudora's review of *The Most of S. J. Perelman* appeared in the October 12, 1958, *New York Times Book Review*.

67 Eudora's review of Virginia Woolf's *Granite and Rainbow* appeared in the September 21, 1958, *New York Times Book Review*.

68 Bill's review of Virginia Woolf's *Granite and Rainbow* appeared in the October 11, 1958, issue of *The New Yorker*.

69 Eric Nyland was the son of Ilonka Karasz and her husband, Willem Nyland. Karasz illustrated Bill's children's book *The Heavenly Tenants* (1946) and 187 *New Yorker* covers.

70 Pellegrina Leoni is the protagonist in Dinesen's story "The Dreamers."

71 Bill seems to have been asking Dinesen to choose between Thomas Mann's *Joseph and His Brothers* (not H. W. Freeman's *Joseph and His Brethren*) and Colette's short novels *My Mother's House* and *Sido*.

72 John Osborne and Anthony Creighton were the authors of *The Epitaph for George Dillon* (1957), a revival of which played in New York at Henry Miller's Theatre from January 12 to February 21, 1959.

73 "The Spahi's Cloak" is a chapter in Colette's novel *My Mother's House*.

74 Gerald and Rhoda Blumberg were the Maxwells' neighbors on Baptist Church Road in Yorktown Heights. Rhoda is a children's book author who has won a Newbery Honor, and the Blumbergs' daughter Leda now writes children's books as well.

75 Bill is responding to the magazine article about Colette that Eudora mentioned in her May 1959 letter.

4. *"Stubborn Enough to Be a Writer"*

1 Eudora is referring to M. R. James's ghost story "The Mezzotint."

2 Mary Lou Aswell and her companion, painter Agnes Sims, were in London, away from their Santa Fe home.

3 Eudora's essay "Henry Green: A Novelist of the Imagination" would appear in the Autumn 1961 issue of *Texas Quarterly*.

4 Sylvia Townsend Warner's story "Youth and the Lady" and Bill's review of Laurie Lee's *The Edge of Day* appeared in the April 16, 1960, issue of *The New Yorker*.

5 Bill included Eudora's story "Kin," which he had edited for *The New Yorker* in 1952, in the anthology *Stories from* The New Yorker, 1950 to 1960.

6 Monroe Wheeler headed the department of exhibitions and publications at the Museum of Modern Art in New York City.

7 Eudora's mother had for some time been afflicted with suspicions and delusions. When it was discovered that a sedative was the source of her mental difficulties, Eudora felt free to leave her mother in the care of others and take a short break from the home front.

8 Bluebell was Maeve Brennan's black Labrador, who spent one or two extended periods with the Maxwells. Brennan (1917–1993) was an Irish writer who moved to the United States in 1934 and later became a member of the *New Yorker* staff. Her sketches, reviews, and essays appeared in the magazine, as did her short stories.

9 Eudora had seen the page proofs of *The Château*.

10 Emmy's lengthy review of the year's children's books appeared in the November 19, 1960, issue of *The New Yorker*.

11 The dinner was for the families of novelist John Cheever, whose work Maxwell edited for *The New Yorker*, and Hawley Truax, the magazine's treasurer.

12 After a short stint at Bryn Mawr and in New York City, Eudora was set to attend a conference at Vassar at which notable women from around the world would discuss "world problems and their implications for education."

13 Barbara Nicholls (as Eudora later spells the name) was Bill's secretary and was helping Eudora with the typing of her novel in progress (*Losing Battles*). "Fax" is short for Thermo-Fax, an early photocopier from 3M.

14 *Zazie dans le métro* is a French novel by Raymond Queneau, published in 1959.

15 Concerns about her mother's health and finding caretakers continued to limit Eudora's ability to travel.

16 Maxwell's comments concern a draft of *Losing Battles*. The character names would be changed before the novel was published in 1970.

17 Harold Brodkey published stories in *The New Yorker* and story collections but experienced difficulty completing a novel. His first novel, *The Runaway Soul*, would be published in 1991.

18 Eudora did take the Maxwells, Elizabeth Bowen, Diarmuid and Rosie Russell, and Howard Moss to dinner on Halloween.

19 Eudora was in residence as a guest lecturer at Smith College during the spring of 1962.

20 Author William Faulkner died on July 6, 1962.

21 As an undergraduate student caught in a romantic triangle, Bill Maxwell had attempted suicide: "I thought I didn't want to live any more and cut my throat and wrists with a straight-edged razor" (as cited in Christopher Carduff, ed., *Maxwell: Early Novels and Stories* [New York: Library of America, 2008], 945). But like his character Lymie Peters in *The Folded Leaf* (1945), he soon realized how much he wanted life to continue. In the following description of Lymie, Maxwell anticipates the advice he offered the young man mentioned in this letter: "He was alive and he knew that he was going to live for a long time. He knew there were things he had not cared enough about, that he had taken for granted, that he would have missed if he had died. He wanted to get well and go back to school and study and walk under the big trees on the campus. He wanted to look into the faces of people that he didn't know and might never see again, hear rain in the night, and sleep, and turn in his sleep and have dreams. Good or bad, it didn't matter. The worst dream imaginable was better than nothing at all, no active mind, no waking up ever." Ibid., 556.

22 In the 1960s and 1970s, Angela Banner published a series of books for children in which the main characters were Ant and Bee.

23 Rachel Carson's book *Silent Spring*, which deals with the effects of pesticides on the environment, was serialized in *The New Yorker* in the summer of 1962.

24 Thea was the Maxwells' live-in mother's helper.

25 Edith Oliver was a drama critic at *The New Yorker*.

26 Perhaps Bill is referring to one of Richard Hughes's children's books. Hughes (1900–1976) was also the author of four novels, including *A High Wind in Jamaica* (1929).

27 Eudora was worried about Emmy's family because the Columbus Day Storm of 1962, which hit Oregon and Washington, was one of the most powerful extratropical cyclones ever to affect the United States.

28 Eudora's gift of a subscription to the British newspaper the *Observer* was particularly welcome because the *New York Times* was mired in a strike that had begun in December 1962 and prevented publication for 114 days.

29 Bill enjoyed reading *Observer* articles by drama critic Kenneth Tynan, diplomat and politician Sir Harold Nicolson, and writer Philip Toynbee.

30 Enclosed were Kate's handwritten programs for two Pollock's Toy Theatre productions.

31 When Eudora was nine years old, her mother bought her a Steinway upright piano. Years later, the piano was in the possession of Elizabeth and Mary Alice Welty, Eudora's nieces. In 1963, her mother requested that it be returned to her home and immediately upon its arrival asked Eudora to play "The West Virginia Hills," a song that recalled her origins in that state.

32 Eleanor Hinkley and Bill met when he was a graduate student at Harvard and her mother invited him to tea. She was the first cousin of T. S. Eliot and was part of a literary circle in Cambridge.

33 This would be Eudora's only children's book, *The Shoe Bird*.

34 Alix Taylor, Kate's godmother, was a mystic and the author of memoirs. Joanna Brodkey was the ex-wife of writer Harold Brodkey.

35 Janet Flanner (1892–1978) was the Paris correspondent for *The New Yorker* from 1925 to 1975 and wrote under the pen name Genêt.

36 Eudora has sent Bill a copy of *Three Papers on Fiction* (1962), published by Smith College and consisting of the three public lectures she gave there: "Place in Fiction," "Words into Fiction," and "The Short Story." The passage about Mammoth Cave appears in "Words into Fiction."

37 Perhaps Bill is referring to Ando Hiroshige, the great nineteenth-century Japanese artist.

38 Fearing is a Texas artist and emeritus faculty member at the University of Texas at Austin, where he was a colleague of Eudora's friend Frank Lyell.

39 Anna Gloria and Roger were the twins in Kate's story about the Middle Ages. The identity of Barbara and the priest remains a mystery.

40 Ivy was the Maxwells' live-in mother's helper.

41 From March to August 1963, Eudora's mother was a resident of the Martha Coker Convalescent Home in Yazoo City, Mississippi, some fifty miles from Jackson. In June 1963, British secretary of state for war John Profumo resigned his post after admitting he had lied in denying an affair with a call girl. The Profumo scandal helped to bring down the government of Prime Minister Harold Macmillan.

42 This is the novel that would eventually be titled *Losing Battles*.

43 Eudora's mother had returned home from Yazoo City.

44 There is no identification of the reading material to which Eudora refers.

45 Eudora spent Halloween 1963 at Yaddo.

46 The novelist and *New Yorker* editor Hamilton Basso died on May 13, 1964.

47 In December 1963, Eudora had taken her mother back to the Yazoo City nursing home where she had been in residence during the spring and summer and where she would remain until her death.

48 Eudora is probably referring to *Losing Battles*.

49 Bill's story "The Value of Money" appeared in the June 6, 1964, issue of *The New Yorker*.

50 Irish-born and one of the founders of the Abbey Theatre in Dublin, poet Padraic Colum (1881–1972) became an American citizen in 1945. He and Eudora both participated in the Suffield (Connecticut) Writer-Reader Conference in the summer of 1964.

51 Brendan Behan (1923–1964) was an Irish playwright, poet, fiction writer, and mem-

oirist who had served as a volunteer in the Irish Republican Army and spent time in jail as a result of that work.

52 This incomplete letter begins in midstream. The word "Later" indicates that Eudora returned to writing a letter she had begun earlier.

53 At the 1964 Republican National Convention, Governor Mark Hatfield of Oregon gave the keynote speech, and Senator Barry Goldwater of Arizona was nominated for president. Eudora was an ardent Democrat, as were the Maxwells. Dr. Kildare was a character in a popular television series at the time. The John Birch Society is a right-wing political advocacy group particularly opposed to communism.

54 The fourth volume of Leonard Woolf's autobiography was published in 1964 under the title *Beginning Again: An Autobiography of the Years 1911 to 1918*. Woolf describes his marriage to Virginia Stephen Woolf and the question raised by her sister, Vanessa Stephen Bell.

55 Alastair Reid's "Letter from Edinburgh" appeared in the October 24, 1964, issue of *The New Yorker*.

56 In 1964 and 1965, Eudora taught at Millsaps College in Jackson.

57 Taylor's *The Soul of Kindness* was published in 1964.

58 *Mrs. Donald's Dog Bun and His Home Away from Home*, a book for young readers with text by William Maxwell and illustrations by James Stevenson, was eventually published by Knopf in 1995. Ursula Nordstrom was the publisher and editor in chief of juvenile books at Harper & Row from 1940 to 1973. The publisher decided against using Emmy's illustrations for the book because her name was not well enough known in the children's book industry.

59 An edition of *The Memoirs of Lady Ottoline Morrell* was published in 1964, and Bill was interested in this woman who had such close ties to the Bloomsbury group. An edited and translated edition of *The Journal of Jules Renard* also was published that year. Renard was a late-nineteenth- and early-twentieth-century French novelist.

60 Eudora Welty to Mary Lou Aswell, January 8, 1965, Eudora (Alice) Welty Collection, Mississippi Department of Archives and History, Jackson, Mississippi.

61 Bowen had sold her family home, Bowen's Court, in Ireland, returned to live in England, and ultimately decided to settle in Hythe, on the south coast.

62 Eudora was returning to the Suffield Writer-Reader Conference.

63 Fiction writer Nancy Hale's mother was artist Lilian Westcott Hale (1880/81–1963).

64 Eudora's speech, given at Millsaps College in December 1964, was published in the October 1965 issue of the *Atlantic Monthly* under the title "Must the Novelist Crusade?" It attempted to distinguish between the role of a fiction writer and that of an editorial writer.

65 Edward Newhouse, a novelist and short story writer, was a member of the *New Yorker* writing staff. Brentano's was a New York City bookstore.

66 *The New Yorker* had accepted Eudora's story "The Demonstrators," which would be published in the November 26, 1966, issue.

67 On November 9, 1965, a major blackout took place in New York, New Jersey, New Hampshire, Massachusetts, Connecticut, Rhode Island, Vermont, and Ontario. The frightening "Fable" to which Eudora refers was published without a title, under the heading "Further Tales About Men and Women," in the November 13,

1965, issue of *The New Yorker*. It was titled "The Poor Orphan Girl" in Bill's collection of "fables," *The Old Man at the Railroad Crossing and Other Tales*, published in 1966.

68 Emmy's review of the year's children's books appeared in the December 4, 1965, issue of *The New Yorker*.

69 Bill means that *The New Yorker* did not typically pay a cost-of-living adjustment to individuals who had not signed an agreement granting the magazine first right of refusal for their work.

5. *"Your Heart Down on Paper"*

1 Eudora was at Bryn Mawr to receive its M. Carey Thomas Award.

2 In 1966, the National Gallery of Art in Washington, D.C., celebrated its twenty-fifth anniversary with an exhibition of French paintings from the collection of Mr. and Mrs. Paul Mellon. Both Eudora and the Maxwells saw the exhibition. In Philadelphia, Eudora visited the Barnes collection, one of the world's largest collections of impressionist, postimpressionist, and early modern paintings. The number of visitors to the collection was restricted and by appointment only. Earlier that spring, Eudora and the Maxwells had visited the J.M.W. Turner exhibit at the Museum of Modern Art in New York.

3 Cerne Abbas is a village in Dorset, in the southwest of England, that dates from the Middle Ages.

4 Finistère is the French region, or administrative division, that is located on the western edge of Brittany.

5 William Keble Martin wrote and illustrated *The Concise British Flora in Colour*. It was published in 1965, when he was eighty-eight years old, and drew on sixty years of research.

6 *Diabolique* is a 1955 French film starring Simone Signoret, Véra Clouzot, and Paul Meurisse. Rosa "Dolly" Wells, Eudora's good friend from Jackson, had lived in New York for many years.

7 Bill is asking Eudora for final revisions to her story "The Demonstrators."

8 *The New Yorker* accepted Eudora's preference for the more dramatic break in the text.

9 The *New Yorker*'s legal department found no problems with an explicit reference to the words of former Mississippi governor Ross Barnett.

10 Harriet O'Connor was the widow of writer Frank O'Connor. Both were good friends of the Maxwells.

11 The Hammond-Harwood House is an architecturally important colonial home in Annapolis, Maryland.

12 Eudora contemplated incorporating material from an old story or play into a story called "Grand Times," which she would join to "Nicotiana"/"The Last of the Figs" and "The Demonstrators," creating a sort of literary triptych following characters and their descendants over time.

13 The quotation is from *Emma*.

14 Kate and Brookie were attending Brearley, the K–12 girls' school in New York City.

15 Virginia Woolf's *Flush* is a biography of Elizabeth Barrett Browning's dog. It first

appeared in four installments in the July, August, September, and October 1933 issues of the *Atlantic Monthly*.

16 The poet Edward Lear was also an artist and illustrator. Eudora had perhaps seen an exhibition of his work in Houston. Emmy herself illustrated this letter.

17 Bill enclosed a letter from civil rights leader Jesse Jackson praising "The Demonstrators" as "true and powerful" (November 27, [1966], Eudora (Alice) Welty Collection, Mississippi Department of Archives and History, Jackson, Mississippi).

18 The toy store FAO Schwarz.

19 The two issues of the *Atlantic Monthly* to which Bill refers are ones containing installments of *Flush*.

20 Eustacia Vye is a central character in Thomas Hardy's *The Return of the Native* (1878).

21 David Scherman was a photographer and editor at *Life*.

22 LeRoy Leatherman had served as Martha Graham's manager and as executive director of the Martha Graham Center of Contemporary Dance. Eudora had been asked to review his book *Martha Graham: Portrait of the Lady as an Artist*.

23 Consuelo Kanaga, a distinguished photographer, was married to artist Wallace Putnam. The Putnams, like the Maxwells, lived on Baptist Church Road in Yorktown Heights.

24 In 1967, Doris Moore published a biography of the English children's writer Edith Nesbit (1858–1924).

25 Edith Iglauer Hamburger, herself a writer of nonfiction books and of articles for major periodicals, had recently been divorced from *New Yorker* writer Philip Hamburger.

26 Bill seems to have given Eudora a subscription to the British newspaper the *Observer*.

27 The Martha Graham Dance Company's season ran from February 21 to March 12, 1967.

28 The Maxwells had given Eudora a poster, perhaps ordered in Paris during their 1966 visit. The poster matched one they had bought for themselves.

29 In 1964, the Metropolitan Opera commissioned Russian-born artist Marc Chagall to design sets and costumes for *The Magic Flute*. Over the next three years, he created large curtains, small curtains, costumes, masks, and murals for the production that opened in 1967.

30 William Meredith (1919–2007) was a Pulitzer Prize–winning poet and a friend of the Maxwells.

31 Eudora took Bill's advice. Her review of LeRoy Leatherman's *Martha Graham: Portrait of the Lady as an Artist* would appear in the Summer 1967 issue of the *Sewanee Review*.

32 In the wake of her mother's death, Eudora had suspended work on her long comic novel and had written a new novella dealing with the experience of loss. It would first be published in *The New Yorker* and then in book form. *The Optimist's Daughter* would win a Pulitzer Prize for Fiction in 1973.

33 Eudora is referring to the Six-Day War (June 5–10, 1967) between Israel and the Arab states of Syria, Egypt, and Jordan.

34 Novelists William Humphrey and Robert Penn Warren.

35 Eudora struggled with the title for this story. Drafts had been titled "An Only Child," "Baltimore," and "Poor Eyes." See also Bill's January 3, 1968, letter and her January 5 and 11, 1968, letters.

36 The Cornstalk is now a quite respectable and much-sought-after New Orleans hotel.

37 Eudora is describing Preservation Hall in New Orleans and the musicians who performed there.

38 Perhaps Eudora is referring to Frank O'Connor's story "An Act of Charity," published posthumously in the May 6, 1967, issue of *The New Yorker*.

39 Diarmuid's essay about his father, the Irish mystic and poet George William Russell, had appeared in the February 1943 issue of the *Atlantic Monthly*. Michael O'Donovan is the given name of the Irish writer Frank O'Connor.

40 Hallie-Óg O'Connor is the daughter of Frank and Harriet O'Connor. In the letters, Hallie-Óg and her mother are sometimes referred to by the name O'Donovan because Frank O'Connor's given name was Michael O'Donovan.

41 Peter Wilkie is the son of John Wilkie and stepson of Margot Wilkie.

42 Bill was working on the *New Yorker* version of "The Optimist's Daughter," which focuses on a character who must have surgery for a detached retina.

43 A 1908 song by Nat Wills, with lyrics about a man who has been away from home for six weeks and returns to ask his servant whether anything has happened. No, the servant replies, only your dog died. How did the dog die? From eating burnt horseflesh. How did he get the meat? He got it when the barn burned down. How did the barn burn down? It burned when the house burned. How did the house burn? It burned when candles caught the curtains afire. Why were candles being used? They lighted the coffin. Who died? Your mother-in-law. What caused her death? Learning that your wife had run off with the chauffeur.

44 Eudora's reference to Miss Bates, a character in Jane Austen's *Emma*, prefigures her 1968 drafting of an essay about Jane Austen. Tom Stoppard's *Rosencrantz and Guildenstern Are Dead* came to Broadway in October 1967 and would remain there for a year. Langston Hughes (1902–1967) wrote the text to accompany photographs by Roy DeCarava (1919–2009) for the book *The Sweet Flypaper of Life* (1955). The Maxwells and Eudora had sent each other copies of this book for Christmas. "Black Saturday," Eudora's first attempt at a photography book, is not extant.

45 Eudora seems to have forgotten that Bill's fortune went to her older niece, Elizabeth.

46 Bill reviewed the fourth volume of Leonard Woolf's autobiography in the December 23, 1967, issue of *The New Yorker*.

47 Eudora had asked her friend Hunter McKelva Cole if she might use the name "McKelva" in "The Optimist's Daughter."

48 Eudora did not choose to follow any of these suggestions.

49 Although Eudora agreed with the suggested cut in this letter, she later reinstated the sentence in question.

50 The postcard to which Eudora refers seems not to be extant.

51 Eudora is alluding to a children's book by Angela Banner.

52 By most accounts, Porter was born in 1890, so this would have been her seventy-eighth birthday.

53 It seems the Katherine Anne Porter Foundation lacked money to fund awards again in 1968. (See Eudora's June 12, 1967, letter.) As a member of that foundation's board, Eudora went to College Park, Maryland, for the 1968 opening of the Katherine Anne Porter Room at the University of Maryland. Novelist Glenway Wescott, one of Porter's longtime friends, was also on the board and also at the library opening.

54 Eudora is recalling her own visits to Ireland in 1950, 1951, and 1954. She met Irish short story writer and novelist Mary Lavin on her first trip to Ireland, and the two became friends.

55 J. M. Synge wrote *In the Shadow of the Glen*, and Sean O'Casey wrote *The Shadow of a Gunman*. Mary Lavin lived on a farm near Bective Abbey.

56 Miss Fitzgerald was the proprietor of the Canon's House, a bed-and-breakfast establishment on Ireland's Dingle Peninsula.

57 Eudora had returned to work on her novel *Losing Battles*.

58 Larry Woiwode published *What I'm Going to Do, I Think* in 1969.

59 Elizabeth Bowen's novel *Eva Trout* was published in 1968.

60 Mary Lavin's *In the Middle of the Fields and Other Stories* was published in 1969 in the United States. Her book *Happiness and Other Stories* was published in 1969 in Britain.

61 Eudora was wondering whether she needed to do more work on the galleys of "The Optimist's Daughter."

62 William Koshland was a vice president at Knopf.

63 Richard Nixon, Hubert Humphrey, and George Wallace were candidates for president of the United States in 1968.

64 Eudora considered Bryn Mawr, a name meaning "big hill" in Welsh, to be the kin of her Welsh books.

65 The Maxwells had given Eudora a 1944 edition of Nigel Heseltine's translation of the medieval Welsh poet Dafydd ap Gwilym with a preface by Frank O'Connor.

66 E.T.A. Hoffmann (1776–1822) wrote stories that included supernatural elements. Two of his stories formed the basis for Tchaikovsky's ballet *The Nutcracker* and Offenbach's opera *The Tales of Hoffmann*.

67 Robert Henderson was a fiction editor at *The New Yorker*.

68 "The Optimist's Daughter" appeared in the March 15, 1969, issue of *The New Yorker*.

69 Bill is quoting from the story "Mon Oncle Jules" by Guy de Maupassant.

70 Bill had asked Eudora to be a member of the Grants Committee at the National Institute of Arts and Letters.

71 Felicia Geffen was assistant to the president of the American Academy of Arts and Letters and assistant secretary-treasurer of the National Institute of Arts and Letters.

72 Eudora is describing the scarf, purchased from an Irish merchant, that she received from the Maxwells as one of her Christmas presents.

73 Eudora loved this lithograph so much that she used a description of it in a draft of *The Optimist's Daughter* when she was expanding the story for publication as a novel. She eventually cut the description from the book manuscript.

74 Eudora had met Alun Jones at Cambridge in 1954 (see her letter of August 17, 1954, in chapter 2) and had served as his guide to New York City in the fall of 1961.

75 Eudora's friend was John Robinson, a fellow Mississippian with whom she had been romantically involved from the late 1930s until the early 1950s (see chapter 2) and who had settled in Italy.

76 In 1967, Bill began working on a book about four generations of his family on both the Maxwell and Blinn sides. This scrapbook helped in his research.

77 At the 1969 ceremonial of the American Academy and National Institute of Arts and Letters, playwright Lillian Hellman presented the Gold Medal for Drama to Tennessee Williams, whose acceptance remarks were off-the-cuff and irrelevant to the award.

78 Bill was hoping to obtain a copy of the *Losing Battles* manuscript from Eudora's agent.

79 Bill is alluding to Edward Barrett's opposition to his daughter Elizabeth's marriage to poet Robert Browning. Barrett did not speak to his daughter after she defied his wishes.

80 "A Sweet Devouring," Eudora's 1957 essay about her childhood reading, was published as a collector's edition by Albondocani Press in 1969. In the essay, Eudora mentions all the titles to which Bill refers.

81 Bill is describing his work on his nonfiction book *Ancestors*.

82 Eudora is playing on Commodore George Dewey's famous command during the Battle of Manila Bay in 1898: "You may fire when you are ready, Gridley."

83 Harcourt, Brace, Jovanovich, Eudora's longtime publisher, had responded to *Losing Battles* by calling for wholesale revisions. As a result, Eudora and her agent were looking for a new publisher. Albert Erskine, vice president and editorial director at Random House, had been Eudora's friend since the 1930s, and Eudora would eventually cast her lot there.

84 In 1966, Eudora told Mary Lou Aswell she was considering "Slack Times," "Ring Around," and "Ignorance" as titles for this novel.

85 Bill's story "The Gardens of Mont-Saint-Michel" was published in the August 9, 1969, issue of *The New Yorker*.

86 During a visit to New York City in late 1969, Eudora had been distressed by the strife between Vietnam War supporters and protesters. She opposed the war but also opposed the lack of civil dialogue about it. She wrote to Mary Lou Aswell, "I felt when I was up last month that I was in a nation of Holy Rollers, all foaming at the mouth and shouting 'Are You Saved?'" (Welty to Aswell, January 8, 1970, Eudora [Alice] Welty Collection, Mississippi Department of Archives and History, Jackson, Mississippi).

87 Maurice Sheehy received a special dispensation from the Vatican allowing him to marry Harriet O'Donovan. He remained a priest but was no longer permitted to say Mass.

88 Granny Vaughn is the elderly matriarch in *Losing Battles*.

89 Kate was a volunteer at the Children's Aid Society, where she worked with foster children.

90 Abstract painter Cleve Gray and his wife, writer Francine du Plessix Gray, friends of the Maxwells.

91 In *Losing Battles*, the students on a ramshackle school bus sing that their school, Banner School, is "beyond compare."

92 Bill had sent Eudora an advance copy of an article titled "The Postmaster," to be published in the November 21, 1970, issue of *The New Yorker*. It includes postal inspector Mark Webster's full report of William Faulkner's tenure as postmaster at the University of Mississippi.

93 The question of whether the National Institute of Arts and Letters should take a stand on the Vietnam War had become an issue during Bill's presidency.

94 Howard Moss reviewed *Losing Battles* in the July 4, 1970, issue of *The New Yorker*.

95 The fifth volume of Leonard Woolf's autobiography, *The Journey Not the Arrival Matters: An Autobiography of the Years 1939 to 1969*, was published in 1969.

96 *The Cabinet of Dr. Caligari* is a German silent film known as a classic of the horror genre.

97 Bill cautions Eudora about protecting her MacDowell Medal because of something that happened in 1955 after she received the Howells Medal. As he later recalled in accepting his own Howells Medal in 1980, "When she got the Howells Medal a stranger came up to her afterwards and asked to see it. Miss Welty obliged, and the stranger dropped the gold medal and, since it really is a gold medal, it cost fifty dollars to have the scratch removed."

98 *One Time, One Place*, Eudora's book of Depression-era photographs, was published in 1971 by Random House.

6. "So Much Honor Coming Down on My Head"

1 Eudora's gift to the Maxwells was *Brewer's Dictionary of Phrase and Fable*.

2 Bill is referring to his book of family history, *Ancestors*.

3 Roger Sessions was a Brooklyn-born composer who taught at the University of California, Berkeley, and Princeton University. "Copeland" is American composer Aaron Copland. Malcolm Cowley is the author of *Exile's Return* and the editor whose book *The Portable Faulkner* revitalized interest in William Faulkner's work. In chairing gatherings at the institute, Bill had trouble being heard and took singing lessons with a breathing specialist, Carl Stough, so as to project his voice more effectively. Howard Moss had just been elected to the institute.

4 The Metropolitan Museum of Art featured works by the Flemish painters Hans Memling and Pieter Bruegel the Elder. Paintings from Picasso's pink period were on exhibition at the Gallery Gertrude Stein, including one owned by William S. Paley, then chairman of the CBS television network.

5 Eudora had negatively reviewed Arthur Mizener's *The Saddest Story: A Biography of Ford Madox Ford* in the May 2, 1971, *New York Times Book Review*.

6 Eudora again mentions the controversy the Vietnam War had aroused at the National Institute of Arts and Letters, and she looks forward to Reynolds Price's American Academy of Arts and Letters Award for Literature.

7 In May 1971, Eudora did travel by bus to Denison University in Ohio and Sewanee in Tennessee, where she received honorary degrees.

8 John Leonard was the editor of the *New York Times Book Review*.

9 In February 1971, Mary Lou Aswell's son Duncan had suffered a nervous breakdown, left his professorial position at Haverford College, and disappeared. Mary Lou did not know if he were alive or dead, and she was overwhelmed with worry. Duncan eventually reestablished contact in early June.

10 Eudora is praising Bill's book *Ancestors*.

11 Eudora and Jackson journalist Frank Hains went together to the play *Follies*. Diarmuid Russell and his family lived in Katonah, New York. Eudora spent the weekend of November 19–21, 1971, in Connecticut at the home of her editor Albert Erskine so that they could work on *The Optimist's Daughter*.

12 Brookie Maxwell was attending Riverdale Country School. Bertie Wooster is a character in P. G. Wodehouse's book *Jeeves and the Tie That Binds*.

13 The picture is one of a young Eudora sitting in her grandmother's lap and reaching up to touch her grandmother's face.

14 Harold Pinter's play *Old Times* ran on Broadway from November 16, 1971, to February 26, 1972.

15 Bill's book *Over by the River and Other Stories* would not be published until 1977.

16 *The Dictionary of Roses in Color* was written by S. Millar Gault and Patrick M. Synge and published in 1971.

17 The book that claimed the admiration of both Sylvia Townsend Warner and Brendan Gill was *One Time, One Place* (1971), a collection of Eudora's photographs taken during the Great Depression. Gill's review of the book appeared in the December 25, 1971, issue of *The New Yorker*.

18 Eudora is referring to her fictional character from *The Ponder Heart*, a book she dedicated to Bill and Emmy Maxwell and Mary Lou Aswell.

19 Eudora donated her photographs, manuscripts, and correspondence to the Mississippi Department of Archives and History, which now houses the large Eudora (Alice) Welty Collection.

20 Walker Percy's novel *Love in the Ruins* was a finalist for the 1972 National Book Award. Painter Agnes Sim's work was to be on display in San Antonio.

21 Eudora had asked Katherine Anne Porter to identify the Shakespearean sonnet that includes the line "Rough winds do shake the darling buds of May." As Eudora noted, it is Sonnet 18, despite Porter's assurances to the contrary.

22 Henry may be Henry Volkening of the Russell & Volkening literary agency. The poem "To a Fat Lady Seen from a Train" was published by Frances Cornford in 1910, although Eudora's quotation from the poem is not exact. Eudora seems in a jocular fashion to be referring to gossip columnist Louella Parsons.

23 Henry Volkening had died on October 18, 1972. Diarmuid Russell died on December 16, 1973, slightly more than a year after this letter was written.

24 Bill had reviewed Pritchett's *Midnight Oil* in the June 17, 1972, issue of *The New Yorker*.

25 Maxwell was working on a review of Quentin Bell's biography of Virginia Woolf, which appeared in the February 3, 1973, issue of *The New Yorker*.

26 Sculptor Richard Lippold had spoken at the dinner meeting of the National Institute of Arts and Letters.

27 Odilon Redon (1840–1916) was a French symbolist painter and printmaker. Shakespeare's *Hamlet* and *The Tempest* inspired three of his paintings.

28 Emmy and Brookie were making a life-size needlework alligator to cover a five-foot-long bench in front of the fireplace in their Yorktown Heights house.

29 In 1972, President Richard Nixon had appointed Eudora to serve on the National Council on the Arts.

30 Editor Joan Russell Noble's *Recollections of Virginia Woolf by her Contemporaries* was published in 1972.

31 The Fortune Society is an organization that helps individuals released from prison to reintegrate into society and promotes alternatives to incarceration.

32 Roger Fry was an artist, art critic, and member of the Bloomsbury group.

33 In 1910, Dr. Hawley Harvey Crippen was executed in England for the murder of his wife. He was apprehended in Canada after he and his mistress fled London. His case attracted a great deal of attention from both the media and historians.

34 Felicia Geffen was retiring after having served as assistant to the president of the academy and assistant secretary-treasurer of the institute for thirty-two years. John Crowe Ransom (1888–1974) received the American Academy's Gold Medal for Poetry in 1973.

35 Eudora was honored at the 1973 Arts Festival in Jackson. Mississippi governor William Waller declared May 2 Eudora Welty Day.

36 Eudora's review of *The Life to Come and Other Stories* by E. M. Forster was published in the May 13, 1973, *New York Times Book Review*.

37 Howard Moss's tribute to Elizabeth Bowen appeared in the April 8, 1973, *New York Times Book Review*.

38 Alan Cameron, Elizabeth Bowen's husband, had died in 1952. He had worked as an educational administrator and later for the BBC. Charles Ritchie was a career Canadian diplomat who had, off and on for thirty-two years, been Bowen's lover. In his book *The Siren Years*, he discusses the beginning of their relationship.

39 The photographer Jill Krementz had taken a photograph of Eudora and Bill together.

40 Nancy Allitt owned a pharmacy in suburban Cork. The Maxwells had met Allitt through Harriet O'Donovan Sheehy, Frank O'Connor's widow. Allitt had been a longtime friend of Frank O'Connor and had become a close friend of Harriet.

41 University of Illinois professor Charles Shattuck and his wife, Susan, were Bill's friends from his undergraduate days at the University of Illinois, which in 1973 conferred an honorary degree on Bill. In 1942, Shattuck had accepted Eudora's essay about Jackson, Mississippi, midwife Ida M'Toy for the journal *Accent*.

42 Larry Barth was Brookie's boyfriend.

43 Jill Krementz and author Kurt Vonnegut were married in 1979.

44 Eudora had just received an honorary degree from Queens College in Charlotte, North Carolina.

45 Eudora and her brother Edward drew dialogue balloons above photographs on magazine pages and folded the pages so that the photographs could not be seen. They exchanged pages, wrote remarks in the balloons, and shared the results.

46 Spencer Curtis Brown (1906–1980) was Bowen's literary agent. Lord David Cecil (1902–1986), a literary scholar, Oxford professor, and biographer, was her friend of long standing.

47 This letter was sent to Eudora in Jackson, but it seems she was in New York at the time it was written. As a young man, Bill met Zona Gale (1874–1938), whose play *Miss Lulu Bett* won a Pulitzer Prize and whose fiction he admired. Over the years, she would provide him with support and advice.

48 The Art Students League, which Emmy attended, is a distinguished art school founded in New York in 1875.

49 Eudora attended the international Willa Cather conference held at the University of Nebraska in honor of the centennial year of Cather's birth. The lecture she gave was published in the conference proceedings and later in *The Eye of the Story* as "The House of Willa Cather."

50 The long-period comet Kohoutek reached its best point for viewing in late December 1973 and early January 1974.

51 Bill lists the distinguished residents of Patchin Place in Greenwich Village: Djuna Barnes (1892–1982), a feminist novelist; e. e. cummings (1894–1962), the well-known poet; and Marion Morehouse Cummings (1906–1969), a fashion model and photographer.

52 The English poet Valentine Ackland was the longtime companion of Sylvia Townsend Warner.

53 Eudora received the Medal of Honor for Literature from the National Arts Club on February 21, 1974, and Bill spoke at the occasion. The National Arts Club was founded in 1898 and is located at 15 Gramercy Park South in New York City.

54 Eudora traveled to Italy and France during June and July 1974. Her friends John and Catherine Prince met her in Italy and drove her through France to Paris. Autun Cathedral in the Burgundy region of France is famous for its Romanesque sculptures done by Gislebertus between 1120 and 1135.

55 Eudora's essay "A Pageant of Birds" had been published in a collector's edition by Albondocani Press (1974) and included photographs of members of the Farish Street Baptist Church who had participated in the pageant.

56 Bill is referring to Eudora's review of the posthumously published *Pictures and Conversations* by Elizabeth Bowen, which appeared in the January 5, 1975, *New York Times Book Review*. In 1936, Eudora spent several months working as a junior publicity agent for the Works Progress Administration (WPA). Her book *One Time, One Place* contains photographs that she took during the 1930s, including some taken on her own time while she was with the WPA.

57 Eudora's essay "Fairy Tale of the Natchez Trace" had been published as a book by the Mississippi Historical Society (1975).

58 Swan Hellenic is a British cruise line.

59 Bill is referring to the Unadilla Sufi Center of the Sufi Order International in upstate New York.

60 WE6-1212 was the telephone number New Yorkers could dial to get the weather forecast.

61 The children's book *The Hollow Tree Snowed-In Book* by Albert Bigelow Paine was published in 1910.

62 Bill's new story was "The Thistles in Sweden."

63 *The Robber Bridegroom*, with Barry Bostwick in the title role, opened on Broadway at the Biltmore Theatre on October 9, 1976. The play's book was written by Alfred Uhry, the libretto by Robert Waldman.

64 It seems likely that Eudora is referring to *The Letters of Virginia Woolf*, volume 2, which she had reviewed in the November 14, 1976, *New York Times Book Review*.

65 Professor James McConkey had invited Eudora to deliver a lecture about Anton Chekhov at Cornell University.

66 Eudora worked for some years on a long story called "The Shadow Club" but was unable to put it into publishable form.

67 In Chekhov's *The Cherry Orchard*, the old footman Firs is boarded up in the house as the play closes, abandoned and left to die.

68 Bill had begun work on the novel *So Long, See You Tomorrow*.

69 Ruth Draper (1884–1956) was an actress who specialized in one-woman shows like the one Lily Tomlin was currently doing.

70 Joan Kahn (1914–1994) was a respected editor of mystery fiction who had her own imprint. Her sister, Olivia (b. 1920), is a painter.

71 James McConkey's book *The Novels of E. M. Forster* was published in 1971. His story "Mythology, Art, and the Farming Life" appeared in the January 3, 1977, issue of *The New Yorker*. It was the third of his ten stories published there.

72 Bill's book *Over by the River and Other Stories* was published by Knopf in 1977, with jacket design by Brookie Maxwell.

73 Eudora's essay about Chekhov would appear in her book *The Eye of the Story*, published by Random House in 1978.

74 Constance Garnett (1861–1946) was one of the first English translators of Chekhov. "Gooseberries" and "About Love" are two of the stories she translated.

75 Perhaps *The Magic Moving Picture Book* by Bliss, Sands & Co. (1975).

76 Bill's book *Over by the River and Other Stories* contained stories written during the past thirty-eight years, including one completed just the year before ("The Thistles in Sweden"). It received very positive reviews.

77 "The Privy Councilor" is the actual title of the story as listed in *The Portable Chekhov*, and this is the title Eudora cited in her Chekhov essay.

78 Novelists Robert Penn Warren and Eleanor Clark were old friends of Eudora's.

79 Bill is referring to the book *Celtic and Anglo-Saxon Painting: Book Illumination in the British Isles, 600–800* by Carl Adam Johan Nordenfalk (1977), which was a Christmas gift from Eudora.

80 Bill is referring to the English poet Thomas Chatterton (1752–1770), who died alone at night in a London garret from arsenic poisoning.

81 Arthritis in Eudora's hands forced her to switch from a manual to an electric typewriter. The switch resulted in numerous typographical errors throughout this letter.

82 Perhaps *La Belle Edmée*, published by Harper & Row in 1978.

83 Eudora seems to be discussing Diane Waldman's book *Joseph Cornell* (1977). Cornell was best known for his shadow boxes.

84 John I. H. Baur was the director of the Whitney Museum of American Art in New York City.

85 In 1929, in Columbus, Mississippi, Charles Henri Ford began a little magazine called *Blues* and brought out nine issues of it. Between 1940 and 1947 in New York City, he edited the surrealist magazine *View*.

86 Eudora eventually found Cornell's letter to her, framed it, and hung it in her breakfast room. The letter was dated February 5, 1945.

87 Nancy Hanks chaired the National Endowment for the Arts and the National Council on the Arts. Eudora had served on the latter since 1972.

88 Eudora's early story "Acrobats in a Park" was at long last published in the November 1977 issue of *Delta*.

89 Bill is referring to *The Eye of the Story*, a collection of Eudora's nonfiction pieces that was published in 1978.

90 In her review of George R. Stewart's *Names on the Land*, Eudora cited Stewart's mention of a town named Bozrah, despite the negative implications of the name in Jeremiah. Stephenson pointed out to her the very positive implications of the name in Isaiah.

91 In preparing her first cover for *New York* magazine, Brookie created a three-dimensional ceramic model of city and hero and then photographed them.

92 Bill and Emmy had sent Eudora an article from the November 20, 1958, issue of the English magazine *Country Life*. In "A Badger About the House," J. N. Hicks describes the three-month sojourn of a badger named Julietta, whom he and his wife had domesticated and welcomed into their home.

93 Eudora and her friend and fellow writer Elizabeth Spencer had driven to the University of Southern Maine for a writers' festival. Louis Rubin of the University of North Carolina was also on the program.

94 The dinner dance was a MacDowell Colony gala. Eudora had previously recorded her stories "A Memory," "Why I Live at the P.O.," and "A Worn Path" for Caedmon Records. Now she was recording "Petrified Man" and "Powerhouse."

95 Part of Eudora's letter is written on a card with an image of "Pheasants at the Fountain," from the second tapestry of the series "The Hunt of the Unicorn."

96 The book is probably Seamus Heaney's *North* (1975).

97 Fitzgerald, Meredith, and Eudora were all at the Modern Language Association meeting in late December 1978. The youngster was Alec Wilkinson, who would join the *New Yorker* staff in 1980. Wilkinson's eight books include *My Mentor*, about William Maxwell. After the meeting, Eudora and her friend Mary Lou Aswell journeyed to Aswell's home in Santa Fe.

98 Bill's "long story" was "So Long, See You Tomorrow," which was published in the October 1 and 8, 1979, issues of *The New Yorker* and would be published separately as a novel in 1980.

99 James and Findlay Muirhead wrote the first of the Blue Guide travel books in 1918. Findlay's son Russell took over as series editor from 1934 to 1963. The Muirhead family connection with the books ended in 1965. Edward Hyde (1609–1674), the 1st Earl of Clarendon and a royalist during the English Civil War, wrote *History of the Rebellion and Civil Wars in England*.

100 Giacometti's sculpture *The Palace at 4 A.M.* suggested a key setting in the novel eventually titled *So Long, See You Tomorrow*.

101 Warner had died in 1978. *Sylvia Townsend Warner: Letters*, edited by William Maxwell, was published in 1983. A native of Colorado, Anne Parrish (1888–1957) was a novelist and writer for children.

102 The Yale editions of Horace Walpole's correspondence run to forty-eight volumes.

103 *The Dick Cavett Show* aired on public television from 1977 to 1982. Eudora appeared on the show in 1979.

104 Bill is speaking of characters in *So Long, See You Tomorrow*. Eudora had been reading the forthcoming novel and had sent her praise of it to him.

105 In 1980, the Franklin Library published a limited signed edition of *The Optimist's Daughter*.

106 The exercises in the Bates method were designed to help individuals improve their vision and avoid the use of glasses.

107 In the summer of 1979, Eudora spent six weeks or so at Oxford University in England as a faculty member for a Millsaps College group.

108 Isabella Bird (1831–1904) was an intrepid traveler and author whose book about the Orient was titled *The Golden Chersonese and the Way Thither* (1883).

109 Turner had just read "So Long, See You Tomorrow" in *The New Yorker*.

110 Tomás O'Crohan, the author of *The Islandman* (1929), was a native of Great Blasket Island off the west coast of Ireland. *Twenty Years A-Growing* (1933) was Maurice O'Sullivan's memoir about growing up on that island.

111 Edward Malins, whom Eudora met in 1954 at Cambridge University in England, wrote the foreword to *A Book of Saints and Wonders Put Down Here by Lady Gregory According to the Old Writings and the Memory of the People of Ireland* (1971).

112 Mount St. Helens, in southwestern Washington State, erupted on May 18, 1980. The eruption was preceded by two months of volcanic activity.

113 Emmy had sent Eudora a homemade Easter card with a drawing of Bee and Ant, the characters from Angela Banner's children's books.

114 Eudora has an arrow pointing to the stationery letterhead: "The Citadel, the Military College of South Carolina, Charleston, S.C."

115 Cleanth Brooks (1906–1994), the noted literary critic, had been Eudora's friend from the time he served as coeditor of the *Southern Review* in the late 1930s. Novelist Andrew Lytle (1902–1995) was also an old friend. Brooks and Lytle had by this time retired from their academic positions at Yale and the University of the South, respectively.

116 The visit to which Bill refers had provided material for his novel *Time Will Darken It* (1948).

117 Eudora had been working on "The Shadow Club" for some years and by 1980 had introduced a character based on Kenneth Millar into that story.

118 David Garnett (1892–1981), the son of Constance Garnett, was a prolific English writer and a founder of the Nonesuch Press.

119 In 1980, Lord John Press published *Acrobats in a Park* in a signed limited edition with a preface by Eudora. Bill clearly felt that such work transcended the commercial concerns of William Jovanovich.

120 Amelita Galli-Curci (1889–1963) was an Italian-born American operatic soprano who was popular from the late 1910s through the 1930s.

121 Virginia Woolf wrote *Freshwater* in 1923. It was performed by a cast of family members in 1935 in her sister's studio. *Bye-Bye Brevoort* was originally part of a revue containing skits written separately by Eudora and by her friend Hildegarde Dolson. It was published for Jackson's New Stage Theatre in December 1980.

122 Jean Giraudoux's play *The Madwoman of Chaillot*, written in 1943, focuses on a "madwoman" who is able to foil the powerful men who would destroy Paris in order to pump oil from beneath its streets. In *Bye-Bye Brevoort*, Fortescue is one of the genteel characters who refuse to accept that the Brevoort Hotel is being demolished around them.

7. *"What There Is to Say We Have Said"*

1 Eudora is referring to Molly Keane's novel *Good Behavior* (1981).

2 Eudora had sent the Maxwells a copy of *Natchez Victorian Children: Photographic Portraits, 1865–1915* by Joan W. Gandy and Thomas H. Gandy (1981).

3 Bill is quoting from Sir Walter Scott's *Marmion*.

4 A British television dramatization of Ford Madox Ford's novel *The Good Soldier* was shown on the PBS series *Masterpiece Theatre*.

5 In 1983, Bernard Malamud did receive the Gold Medal for Fiction from the American Academy of Arts and Letters.

6 George Luks (1867–1933) was a realist painter associated with the Ashcan school. William Rose Benét (1886–1950) won the Pulitzer Prize for Poetry in 1942.

7 William Maxwell, "The Charged Imagination," *The New Yorker*, February 20, 1984, 135.

8 Eudora sent the Maxwells a revised version of the William E. Massey Sr. Lectures in the History of American Civilization she had recently delivered at Harvard. Bill's review of James Matthews's *Voices: A Life of Frank O'Connor* appeared in the June 27, 1983, issue of *The New Yorker*.

9 Bill found that Eudora's Harvard lectures evoked his own childhood and youth, and here he catalogs the ways. Eudora published her revised lectures in 1984 under the title *One Writer's Beginnings*.

10 Opera singer Amelita Galli-Curci made her debut as Gilda in Giuseppe Verdi's *Rigoletto*. American opera star Geraldine Farrar (1882–1967) sang the title role in Jules Massenet's *Manon*.

11 Emmy's father had died on May 28, 1983.

12 *The King of the Golden River* was a fairy tale written by John Ruskin and published in 1851.

13 Bill inaccurately associates this anecdote with the evening he and Eudora became friends, perhaps because in *One Writer's Beginnings* Eudora assigns a World War II date to her mother's "taking the part of the Wolf in a game of 'little Red Riding Hood' with the children." That date surely is in error. Elizabeth Welty was little more than a year old when the war ended; Mary Alice Welty was not born until 1947. The incident instead seems to have taken place during the Korean War, and Eudora seems to have told Bill about it in the summer of 1951, when she spent several days in Mary Lou Aswell's New York City apartment. In a 1999 interview, Bill recalled a time when Eudora "came to New York and stayed in Mary Louise's apartment and invited my wife and me to dinner. What I remember about that evening is the hilarious impersonation she did of her mother reading *Time* and telling the story of Little Red Riding Hood and the wolf to Eudora's niece—both processes going on at the same time." Virginia Ross and Sally Wolff, "Conversations with Eudora Welty and William Maxwell," *South Atlantic Review* 64, no. 2 (Spring 1999): 136. By 1951, Eudora, Bill, and Emmy were already established friends.

14 The distinguished 1982 film *La Nuit de Varennes* revolves around characters who are following Louis XVI and Marie Antoinette as they flee Paris for the small town of Varennes. Marcello Mastroianni, Jean-Louis Barrault, and Harvey Keitel are among its stars.

15 Bill is referring to three poems by William Butler Yeats: "The Song of the Wandering Aengus," "Sailing to Byzantium," and "High Talk." In *One Writer's Beginnings*, Eudora recalls reading "Sailing to Byzantium" and discusses allusions to "The Song of the Wandering Aengus" in her book *The Golden Apples* (1949).

16 Eudora seems to be in error about the date of J.F.H. Claiborne's birth. The Biographical Directory of the United States Congress, http://bioguide.congress.gov/scripts/guidedisplay.pl?index=C000404, lists the date as 1809.

17 This poem by Charles Cotton (1630–1687) is titled "An Epitaph on M. H."

18 Edmund Wilson (1895–1972), often called the twentieth century's most outstanding man of letters, was the chief book critic at *The New Yorker* for twenty-five years.

19 Barbara Ascher's interview with Eudora was published in the Autumn 1984 issue of the *Yale Review*.

20 Eudora's memoir *One Writer's Beginnings* spent forty-three weeks on the *New York Times* bestseller list.

21 Bill's story "The Man in the Moon" appeared in the November 12, 1984, issue of *The New Yorker*.

22 In August 1946, *The New Yorker* devoted an entire issue to John Hersey's article "Hiroshima." Soon afterward, the article was reprinted in book form.

23 Eudora was in New York City to receive a Bobst Award from New York University. She is praising Bill's story "The Man in the Moon."

24 Eudora is referring to her October 1984 return voyage on the *Queen Elizabeth 2* after visiting London and Italy. She was reading Heaney's *Station Island*.

25 Perhaps Bill is referring to Vartan Gregorian of the New York Public Library and to an event at the library. Or perhaps he is referring to Eudora's 1983 appearance at the Morgan Library in Manhattan.

26 Fitzgerald and fellow poet Dudley Fitts would later team up to translate Sophocles' plays *Oedipus Rex*, *Oedipus at Colonus*, and *Antigone*.

27 Brookie had created a fifty-foot-long ceramic sculpture of Forty-second Street, with functional car headlights, streetlights, and neon signs. The sculpture stayed at the Port Authority for six months, then toured the city for six more.

28 Perhaps in writing about an architect, Eudora had been trying to write about Kenneth Millar, who had died in the summer of 1983.

29 Eudora, the Maxwells, and the Pritchetts dined together during this 1985 visit.

30 Eudora's autobiographical essay "The Little Store" was published in a collector's edition by Tamazunchale Press in 1985.

31 This film was based on a story by Emmy's brother Humphrey Noyes.

32 This story is most likely "The Lily-White Boys," published in the Summer/Fall 1986 issue of the *Paris Review*.

33 In January 1986, the Forty-eighth Congress of International PEN, a writers organization, met in New York City. Major writers from around the world attended to discuss the topic "The Writer's Imagination and the Imagination of the State."

34 Price had survived surgery to remove a cancerous tumor wound about his spinal cord and was coping with his resultant paraplegia.

35 "Lincoln City Fire Department Has Protected Life, Property, and Done Humanitarian Work," *Lincoln [IL] Evening Courier*, August 26, 1953, Centennial edition, sec. 8, p. 4.

36 The Beulah Hotel was a setting in Eudora's book *The Ponder Heart*.

37 The BBC biography of Eudora was titled *A Writer's Beginnings* and aired in 1987. It was later redubbed with Charles Kuralt as narrator and shown on PBS.

38 Walker Percy inaugurated the Eudora Welty Chair of Southern Studies at Millsaps College in Jackson with an address titled "Novel-Writing in an Apocalyptic Time." The address, with an afterword by Eudora, was published as a small book in 1986 by Faust Publishing Company in New Orleans. Eudora had sent Bill a copy.

39 Alec Wilkinson's book *Moonshine* was published in 1985.

40 Franco Zeffirelli was the director and set designer for this production.

41 John Lennon had been murdered outside this apartment building in 1980.

42 In 1987, the relatively new owners of *The New Yorker* forced longtime editor William Shawn to retire.

43 *The Dial* was an American magazine published first by the transcendentalists (1840 to 1844), then revived as a political magazine in the 1880s. From 1920 to 1929, it was a literary magazine known for publishing modernist work.

44 *The Dial's* papers from 1920 to 1929 were acquired by Vartan Gregorian for the New York Public Library. Gregorian was president of the library from 1981 to 1989. He later served as president of Brown University and still later as president of the Carnegie Corporation.

45 John Ferrone was the editor of Eudora's *Collected Stories*, published by Harcourt in 1980.

46 Julie Follansbee Pratt Shattuck was an actress and close friend of the Maxwells. In 1988–1989, she would appear in an award-winning off-off-Broadway production of Romulus Linney's *Heathen Valley*. Bill Irwin's *The Regard of Flight and the Clown Bagatelles* ran at the Vivian Beaumont Theatre from April 12 to April 26, 1987.

47 James Stern (1904–1993) was an Anglo-Irish writer of short stories and nonfiction.

48 *Eothen* was an 1844 book by Alexander William Kinglake about travel in the Far East. The Irish writer Maurice Collis published *The Land of the Great Image* in 1943. Eudora reviewed the book, which deals with travel in Portuguese Asia in the seventeenth century, for the *New York Times Book Review*.

49 The play Eudora had enjoyed during its April run, *The Regard of Flight and the Clown Bagatelles*, had returned to the Vivian Beaumont Theatre and would close on August 9.

50 Eudora was watching television coverage of the Iran-contra hearings, which included testimony by Colonel Oliver North.

51 William Cohen, a Republican, and George Mitchell, a Democrat, were the U.S. senators from Maine. In 1974, when Cohen was a member of the House of Representatives, he was one of the first members of his party to support the impeachment of President Richard Nixon.

52 Eudora's account of Faulkner's time as postmaster is not wholly accurate. He was not yet working on *As I Lay Dying* at the time (1924), and he was allowed to resign from his job rather than be fired.

53 The letter includes typed strikeovers and handwritten corrections.

54 Eudora is referring to the Russian composer and pianist Arthur Rubinstein (1887–1982). During World War II, she had been much moved by his playing at an open-air concert in New York's Lewisohn Stadium.

55 Bill's review of Marie Vassiltchikov's *Berlin Diaries* appeared in the May 25, 1987, issue of *The New Yorker*.

56 James Laughlin (1914–1997) was an American poet and the founder of New Directions Publishers.

57 Michael Kreyling's book *Author and Agent* was published by Farrar, Straus & Giroux in 1991.

58 Eudora meant "Harmonic Convergence," a term referring to the alignment of the planets in what is called a "grand trine."

59 Charlotte Capers (1913–1996), a wonderful raconteur, had retired as the longtime director of the Mississippi Department of Archives and History, to which Eudora had donated her manuscripts, correspondence, and photographs. Capers and Eudora had been close friends for decades.

60 Eudora was named a Chevalier de l'Ordre des Arts et Lettres by the French government in a ceremony held in Jackson.

61 Richard Ford's story "Optimists" appeared in the March 30, 1987, issue of *The New Yorker*.

62 William Meredith's *Partial Accounts: New and Selected Poems* was published in 1987. Poet and *New Yorker* poetry editor Howard Moss died on September 16, 1987. He had dedicated his book *Instant Lives* (1974) to Eudora Welty and Reynolds Price. Moss also was the author of *The Magic Lantern of Marcel Proust* (1962), and he wrote a tribute to Elizabeth Bowen for the *New York Times Book Review* after her death in 1973.

63 Pritchett's review of Victoria Glendinning's book *Rebecca West: A Life* appeared in the December 21, 1987, issue of *The New Yorker*.

64 Elizabeth Lawrence died in 1985. Her book *Gardening for Love*, edited by Allen Lacy, was published by Duke University Press in 1987.

65 Mavis Gallant is a Canadian fiction writer who has been published frequently in *The New Yorker*.

66 In 1987, Burma had been racked by protests against military rule, most organized by students and violently suppressed by the government.

67 Longleat is a stately Elizabethan home in Wiltshire, England, with gardens by Capability Brown. It became the site of a safari park in 1966.

68 Robert Mann (1919–2005) was a founding member and first violinist of the Juilliard String Quartet. Francis Steegmuller's first wife, Bea, died in 1961. He married writer Shirley Hazzard in 1963, and it was they who came for Christmas breakfast.

69 Linda H. Davis had published *Onward and Upward: A Biography of Katharine S. White* in 1987.

70 Bill is alluding to the nursery rhyme "Taffy Was a Welshman":

Taffy was a Welshman,
Taffy was a thief;
Taffy came to my house
And stole a piece of beef.

I went to Taffy's house,
Taffy was not home;
Taffy came to my house
And stole a marrow bone.

I went to Taffy's house,
Taffy was not in;
Taffy came to my house
And stole a silver pin.

I went to Taffy's house,
Taffy was in bed;
I took up a poker
And threw it at his head.

71 Emmy had had intestinal surgery.

72 Æ was the pseudonym of the Irish poet and mystic George William Russell, who was the father of Eudora's agent Diarmuid Russell.

73 Eudora first met newsman Jim Lehrer in 1984, and he quickly introduced her to his colleagues Robert MacNeil and Roger Mudd. Late in 1989, as a reporter for *The MacNeil/Lehrer NewsHour* on PBS, Mudd interviewed Eudora about the photographs she had taken during the Great Depression. An extensive collection of these images, titled *Photographs*, had just been published.

74 Brookie had founded the Creative Arts Workshops for Kids, and through this program she worked with children who lived in welfare hotels. One of their projects was painting murals on city buildings.

75 Janet Flanner's profile of the twentieth-century French painter and sculptor Georges Braque, originally published in the October 13, 1956, issue of *The New Yorker*, became part of her book *Men and Monuments* (1957).

76 In 1966, Monroe Wheeler, head of the department of exhibitions and publications at the Museum of Modern Art in New York City, had given Eudora and the Maxwells a private tour of the J.M.W. Turner show there.

77 Eudora is probably referring to the double vision that bothered Bill intermittently in one eye after cataract surgery.

78 Eudora's essay "My Introduction to Katherine Anne Porter" appeared in the Spring/Summer 1990 issue of the *Georgia Review*.

79 This line comes from Eudora's essay "My Introduction to Katherine Anne Porter." Bill is responding to that essay in this letter.

80 Miranda is the central and rather autobiographical character in a number of Porter's stories, including "Old Mortality" and "Pale Horse, Pale Rider."

81 Eudora had visited Jane Austen's house during her 1990 trip to England to see Dorothy and Victor Pritchett.

82 In *To the Lighthouse*, Mr. Ramsey, who is based on Virginia Woolf's father, Sir Leslie Stephen, is reading *Old Mortality*.

83 Bill had been reading *A Passionate Apprentice: The Early Journals of Virginia Woolf* (London: Hogarth Press, 1990).

84 Bill's story "The Front and the Back Parts of the House" was published in the September 23, 1991, issue of *The New Yorker* and would become part of *Billie Dyer and Other Stories* (1992).

85 Bill is referring to *Walled Gardens* by Annabel Davis-Goff (1989). Mike Nichols is the distinguished television, film, and stage director.

86 Enclosed with this letter was the program for Susan Deuel Shattuck's memorial service. It includes an elegy written by Bill and lines from *Cymbeline*, act 4, scene 2.

87 Bill, Emmy, and Eudora had supported Democratic candidate Bill Clinton, who had just been elected president.

88 Louis Auchincloss (1917–2010) was a novelist who wrote about wealthy, upper-class New Yorkers.

89 Eudora had sent the Maxwells the issue of the *Southern Review* that included Donald Pearce's essay "Hours with the Domestic Sibyl: Remembering George Yeats" (*Southern Review* 28, no. 3 [1992]). Evidently, no letter was attached.

90 Joyce Carol Oates's story "Widow" appeared in the same issue of the *Southern Review*.

91 Anthony Hecht (1923–2004) was a distinguished poet who won the 1968 Pulitzer Prize for Poetry for his book *The Hard Hours*.

92 In November and December 1992, Eudora made three trips to Washington, D.C., to receive awards: the Charles Frankel Prize from the National Endowment for the Humanities, the Distinguished Alumni Award from the American Association of State Colleges and Universities, and the PEN/Malamud Award. Happily and unexpectedly, the first of those trips coincided with the Maxwells' visit to the Washington area.

93 Brookie and Christopher Dolan were married on October 11, 1992.

94 Evelyn Jones was a family friend, Yorktown Heights neighbor, and gardening enthusiast.

95 Bill is referring to Stevenson's travel memoirs *The Silverado Squatters* and *The Amateur Emigrant*.

96 Brookie Maxwell and her husband visited Eudora in Jackson late in 1995.

97 William Maxwell, "Eudora Dear," in *Eudora Welty: Writers' Reflections upon First Reading Welty*, ed. Pearl Amelia McHaney (Atlanta: Hill Street Press, 1999), 67–69.

98 Eudora Welty, *The Optimist's Daughter* (New York: Random House, 1972), 179.

PERMISSIONS

reprinted by permission of Kate and Brookie Maxwell, copyright © Kate and Brookie Maxwell.

Maxwell, William, interoffice memorandum concerning "The Whole World Knows," reprinted by permission of *The New Yorker* and of Kate and Brookie Maxwell, copyright © Kate and Brookie Maxwell, 1946.

Maxwell, William, letters (*New Yorker* records), reprinted by permission of the Manuscript and Archives Division, New York Public Library, Astor, Lenox and Tilden Foundations, and of Kate and Brookie Maxwell, copyright © Kate and Brookie Maxwell, 1942–1943, 1946, 1947, 1953, 1960, 1967.

Maxwell, William and Emily, letters to Eudora Welty, reprinted by permission of Kate and Brookie Maxwell, copyright © Kate and Brookie Maxwell, 1949, 1951–1996.

Warner, Sylvia Townsend, excerpts from a letter to William Maxwell, reprinted by permission of the Estate of Sylvia Townsend Warner, copyright © Estate of Sylvia Townsend Warner.

Welty, Eudora, correspondence to William and Emily Maxwell, the William Maxwell Papers, reprinted by permission of the Rare Book & Manuscript Library, The University of Illinois Urbana-Champaign and of Russell & Volkening, Inc., as agents for Eudora Welty, LLC, copyright © Eudora Welty, LLC, 1951–1990.

Welty, Eudora, excerpt from a letter to Mary Louise Aswell, reprinted by permission of the Eudora Welty Collection—Mississippi Department of Archives and History and of Russell & Volkening, Inc., as agents for Eudora Welty, LLC, copyright © Eudora Welty, LLC, 1965.

Welty, Eudora, letters (*New Yorker* records), reprinted by permission of the Manuscript and Archives Division, New York Public Library, Astor, Lenox, and Tilden Foundations, and of Russell & Volkening, Inc., as agents for Eudora Welty, LLC, copyright © Eudora Welty, LLC, 1933, 1942, 1946, 1952.

Welty, Eudora, letters to William and Emily Maxwell, reprinted by permission of Kate and Brookie Maxwell and of Russell & Volkening, Inc., as agents for Eudora Welty, LLC, copyright © Eudora Welty, LLC, 1952–1957, 1959, 1961, 1964–1969, 1973–1974, 1976–1979.